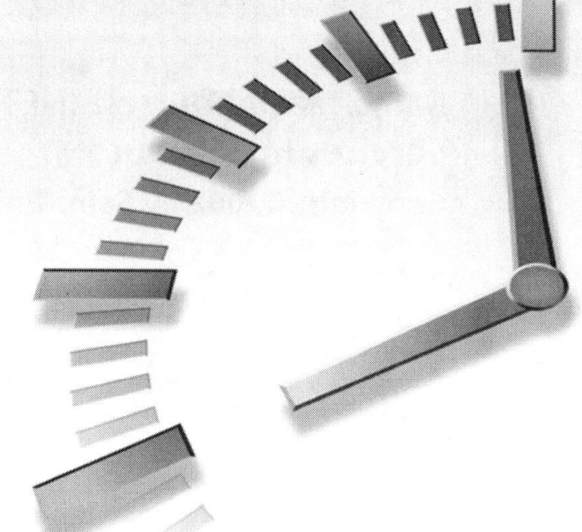

Mark Augustyniak

SAMS

Teach Yourself .NET XML Web Services in 24 Hours

SAMS
201 West 103rd St., Indianapolis, Indiana, 46290 USA

Sams Teach Yourself .NET XML Web Services in 24 Hours

International Standard Book Number: 0-672-32330-3

Library of Congress Catalog Number: 2001094811

Printed in the United States of America

First Printing: December 2001

04 03 02 01 4 3 2 1

Trademarks

All terms mentioned in this book that are known to be trademarks or service marks have been appropriately capitalized. Sams Publishing cannot attest to the accuracy of this information. Use of a term in this book should not be regarded as affecting the validity of any trademark or servicemark.

Warning and Disclaimer

Every effort has been made to make this book as complete and as accurate as possible, but no warranty or fitness is implied. The information provided is on an "as is" basis. The author and the publisher shall have neither liability nor responsibility to any person or entity with respect to any loss or damages arising from the information contained in this book.

Associate Publisher
Jeff Koch

Acquisitions Editor
Neil Rowe

Development Editor
John Gosney

Managing Editor
Matt Purcell

Copy Editor
Michael Kopp,
Publication Services, Inc.

Indexer
Richard Bronson,
Publication Services, Inc.

Proofreader
Publication Services, Inc.

Production Editor
Theodore Young, Jr.,
Publication Services, Inc.

Technical editor
Daniel N. Griffis

Team Coordinator
Denni Bannister

Interior Designer
Gary Adair

Cover Designer
Aren Howell

Page Layout
Michael Tarleton,
Jim Torbit,
Jessica Vonasch,
Publication Services, Inc.

Contents at a Glance

Contents

About the Authors

MARK AUGUSTYNIAK is currently a solutions consultant with SDC Information Services, Inc. in Buffalo, NY where he specializes in Internet applications development. Mark received a degree in Electrical Engineering from the University of Buffalo and has been working in the industry for the past seven years. His clients include Corning, Fisher-Price, and General Motors. Mark can be reached at `Superior_Mark@hotmail.com`

CHRIS PAYNE has had a passion for computers and writing since a young age. He holds a bachelors of science degree in biomedical engineering from Boston University. Chris supported himself through college by working as an independent consultant and by writing technical articles focused on Web development. Currently making his home in Orlando, Florida, with his wife, Eva, Chris is working as a Web developer and continuing his career as an author of both technical and fictional material.

Dedication

For Charlotte and Francis Brown

Acknowledgements

First of all, I would like to thank the following people, in no particular order, who helped me along in the process of writing this book: Neil Rowe, Molly Redenbaugh, Matt Purcell, John Gosney, and the other great people at Sams and Publication Services. This book certainly would never have been finished without you.

I would also like to thank my parents, Richard and Frances Augustyniak, and my sister, Monica Lewandowski, for all of their support.

Thanks also to Rowan, Morrigan, Naya, Melissa, and Lorindol. They know what they did.

I would especially like to thank Danielle for putting up with me while I worked all those long nights. I love you.

Tell Us What You Think!

As the reader of this book, *you* are our most important critic and commentator. We value your opinion and want to know what we're doing right, what we could do better, what areas you'd like to see us publish in, and any other words of wisdom you're willing to pass our way.

As an Associate Publisher for Sams Publishing, I welcome your comments. You can fax, e-mail, or write me directly to let me know what you did or didn't like about this book—as well as what we can do to make our books stronger.

Please note that I cannot help you with technical problems related to the topic of this book, and that due to the high volume of mail I receive, I might not be able to reply to every message.

When you write, please be sure to include this book's title and author name as well as your name and phone or fax number. I will carefully review your comments and share them with the author and editors who worked on the book.

Fax: 317-581-4770

E-mail: `feedback@samspublishing.com`

Mail: Jeff Koch
Sams Publishing
201 West 103rd Street
Indianapolis, IN 46290 USA

Introduction

This book is written for programmers with experience coding in Visual Basic or C# who want to take advantage of a powerful new technology in application development, XML Web Services. Throughout the course of this book, readers will learn both the techniques used to create and work with XML Web Services in Microsoft's Visual Studio.Net as well as the framework of technologies that rests beneath XML Web Services. If you can write a function in Visual Basic or C#, you are ready to tackle XML Web Services.

The book itself is divided into twenty-four one-hour chapters. These chapters can be read one a day or in groups as you have the time. The main goal, though, is to provide you with the maximum amount of information in a relatively small amount of time. You should be more than ready to add XML Web Services to your programming arsenal by the time you are finished reading this book.

Assumptions I've Made

In writing this book, I have made some assumptions about you, the reader. The first assumption that I have made is that you have some experience with Visual Basic or C#. Experience in a language like C++ or Java will probably be more than sufficient, as well. The second assumption that I have made is that you are running Microsoft's Visual Studio.NET Beta 2 or higher on a machine with IIS installed. I would highly recommend Windows 2000, as that was what was used while writing this book.

As XML Web Services make use of a fair amount of Internet protocols and are built on the ASP.NET framework, knowledge of these technologies will help you move much more quickly through this book; however, it is not essential to your success as long as you are willing to pick up these additional skills as you go.

The Sams Teach Yourself in 24 Hours books are marketed as an introductory series of books and, as such, this book is not a tome of all things XML Web Services. What it is is a way to quickly gain an understanding of the XML Web Services architecture and leverage that understanding in your own developments. When you are done with this book, the real learning begins.

I urge you to use the quizzes and exercises at the end of each hour as a yardstick to measure how well you have progressed through a given hour. If you find yourself struggling with a particular section, go back and reread the section. When you can work your way through a sufficient amount of the material at the end of the section, you know that you are ready to move on.

Source Code

I highly urge you to do the examples in the book, as well as the exercises at the end of the chapters, yourself. However, if you should need it, the source code for the programs in this book can be found on the www.samspublishing.com website.

Feel free to use this source code in any way that you see fit. If you manage to further your career, upstage your coworkers, or turn a profit on anything that you found in this book, then it has served its purpose. Feel free to drop me a line and let me know about it.

Getting Started

Congratulations on your decision to learn XML Web Services. The technology can best be described as emerging, and it is always nice to get in on the ground floor of these things. The first section of this book, "Core Concepts," outlines the technologies behind XML Web Services. Those of you wishing to jump right into coding can skip this section and precede to the second section, "Building an XML Web Service," if you promise to go back and read section one before you get too much farther into the book.

Part I
Core Concepts

Hour

Hour 1

What Are XML Web Services and How Do They Fit into the .NET Framework?

Welcome to *Teach Yourself XML Web Services with .NET in 24 Hours*. XML Web services represent an exciting new tool in software creation, and this first hour will introduce you to the technologies and tools behind it. You will become familiar with the protocols used in the XML Web services model, and you will also learn about the .NET framework and how XML Web services fit into it.

In this chapter we will discuss the following:

- What XML Web services really are
- Where to apply XML Web services technology

- The infrastructure behind .NET and XML Web services
- The programming model used in creating Web services

What Are XML Web Services?

An XML Web service is simply a unit of programming functionality that is exposed to client applications via the Internet. At its simplest, an XML Web service is any programming component or object that makes information available via standard Internet protocols such as HTTP.

Distributed Computing

In the past, developers started to move away from the "all in one" style of development, in which all of an application's functionality was contained in one code module. Developers began to move code into objects, called *components,* which existed outside of the initial project. These components could be updated independently of each other and the main program, thus making for smaller and more efficient tasks.

With code now being developed from these component building blocks, it became easier to build a project in teams and to reuse code. Components from one project could be combined with new components to form different applications. It wasn't long before third-party companies began selling components to software developers for use in their own projects.

With the rise of networking and technologies such as DCOM, developers also began to move these components onto different machines across the network. This gave users access to great processing power, via the distribution of tasks to varying machines, and it gave developers the ability to change one component and simultaneously affect all users.

DCOM, or Distributed Component Object Model, is Microsoft's network communication protocol that allows components to be accessed over a network.

Now, with XML Web services, you have the ability to distribute your application across not only a network but also the Internet. Components can be built and hosted anywhere in the world and consumed by other components. Third-party companies no longer just create and sell components; they host them as well.

For a small example, think of a DLL or function library that contains spell-checking software. If you were writing several applications to handle your company's word processing and e-mail capabilities, you would want to add this component into all of your applications.

Now, if someone created this spell-checking component as a Web service, you could simply use that component in all of your applications. If the component were ever to be updated—say an expanded word list were added—none of your applications would be impacted at all. They would all simultaneously have access to the expanded word list.

Achieving Platform Independence with XML Web Services

One of the most important factors in the future of XML Web services technology is its role in creating platform-neutral systems. By "platform-neutral" we mean that XML Web services built and running on one platform, say Unix, can be called on by applications built on and running on a completely unrelated platform—for example, Mac OS 7.0. This is true even for systems that are not running the .NET platform. In Hour 9, you will see some examples of clients that are built on non-.NET platforms. However, XML Web services built on .NET platforms will not be covered in this book.

XML Web services help create platform-neutral systems by using the same set of standards as the Internet. Today, many applications— such as Web browsers, e-mail clients, and FTP programs— are able to utilize Web protocols such as HTML, SMTP, and FTP to trade information seamlessly, without ever being aware of the platform where the information originated.

Using the HTTP protocol, requests are sent from client applications, in an XML standard format, to XML Web services for processing. When the request is processed, another XML document is generated, this one containing any requested data, and sent back to the client application.

Leading up to .NET

The road to XML Web services has been a long one. Probably the first major step in the development of the distributed model seen in XML Web services was the creation of object technologies such as COM and CORBA. The introduction of these object design technologies allowed developers to build programs in smaller components and allowed these components to be reused in other programs.

From COM sprang DCOM and other, similar technologies that allowed these components to be moved off the user's machine and onto servers. This allowed components to be simultaneously used by multiple users and multiple applications.

The rise of the Internet and Internet-enabled applications took the concept of distributing applications one step further by allowing components to be called by Web applications written in ASP or CGI and being used all over the world. Since the rise of the Internet, developers have searched for better ways to expose functionality and services to their user community.

ASP, briefly mentioned above, was another big step in the move toward more distributed applications. ASP allowed developers to write applications using a stripped-down version of the Visual Basic programming language known as VBScript. Previous to ASP, Web programming was done primarily with CGI, or Common Gateway Interface, written in languages such as Perl and C++. ASP provided a much easier method of development, used a commonly known language, and also provided a rich set of built-in objects to help developers quickly put together applications.

The last piece to fall into place in the creation of XML Web services was XML itself. Finally, developers had a standard way in which to describe data and services. From there it was not long before someone, actually several someones, began to write applications that communicated with each other by passing XML documents. These were the first Web services.

XML Messaging Between Systems with SOAP

As you were reading about XML Web services' role in creating platform-independent applications and their use of HTTP protocols to communicate with other applications, you probably noticed the need for a standard format in which clients can actually send requested data, such as method calls with parameters, and receive Web service data, such as strings, arrays, and record sets. Well, that formatting issue was solved with XML.

An XML subset called SOAP, or Simple Object Access Protocol, which you will learn about in Hour 4, is used as the medium by which XML Web services accept and transmit information to the rest of the world. SOAP documents are simply a way of marking up a call to an XML Web service method or function, including all of its required arguments. SOAP is also used to mark up all of the returned results so that the client can understand what is being sent back to it.

A simple SOAP document can be sent to the URL of an XML Web service and, if formatted properly, will cause the service to run a method and send back its results in another SOAP document.

Data is marked up with XML tags denoting the type of data being sent back, such as string or long, and the variable name to which the data was sent, in the case of parameters. This helps XML Web services and their client applications maintain type safety even across differing platforms.

The Basic Components of an XML Web Service

When you develop an XML Web service, you will generate more than just the code that provides the functionality you wish to expose. You will also be creating a host of files, and in the case of UDDI, entries in existing files that will help support your service and describe it to the intended user community. Some of the files that you will create or edit when working with Web services are

- *ASMX.* ASMX files are ASP.NET application files. These are files that are created either by you using a simple text editor or, if you are using Visual Studios .NET, from the code that you develop within the IDE.
- *ASAX.* This is the global file of your XML Web services. This file handles application-level events such as requests and sessions, both of which you will learn more about as you progress through this book.
- *Disco.* XML is also used to help prospective users find a given Web service. Disco files, short for *discovery files,* are created and exposed to the Internet as the primary way of advertising a service. Disco files contain links that point to the service and the service's WSDL files. Hour 5 covers the syntax and usage of Disco files.
- *UDDI.* UDDI, which stands for Universal Description, Discovery, and Integration, is a registry for developers to register their Web services. This repository allows developers looking to consume Web services to search for functionality that matches their needs and to contact the Web service owner about its use. In Hour 5, you will see how to use UDDI for both finding and publishing XML Web services.
- *WSDL.* WSDL documents list the exposed methods of a service and any parameters and return types that those methods expose. The contract is a promise that the listed methods will exist in the format described by the WSDL document. The WSDL can be used either by developers or, as is more likely the case, by tools such as Visual Studios to create consumers (client applications) for the service and guarantee that requested services both exist and function in the manner that the client developer expects them to. You will learn more about WSDL in Hour 3.

Using a Component Model

Another key feature of the XML Web services framework is that they are built as components. What that means is that XML Web services are not built as complete, stand-alone programs, but rather as small building blocks to be used in the creation of other programs. Many such blocks can be used from all over the Internet, an intranet, or both in order to create a single application. In fact, an XML Web service itself may make use of several other Web services in providing its functionality.

Suppose you wished to develop an application that allowed users to track sports scores. You build your application and utilize a Web service that provides updated listings of game scores for several major sports.

Next, you decide that you also wish to provide player statistics for every player in each of the major American sports. You search around and find one that provides such statistics for football and baseball, and you decide to use it in your application. Later, you discover two additional services, one that provides basketball statistics and another that provides statistics for NHL games. You decide to use these as well.

Using this type of component model means that the developer of an application need not worry about every facet of its design. The developer need only worry about what a component does and the data that it returns; he or she does not need to bother with the inner workings of the component. This eliminates the need to duplicate the development efforts of others and greatly reduces the time required to create new applications.

When Are XML Web Services Appropriate?

Building or consuming XML Web services may not be appropriate for every situation. Obviously, if you are building simple desktop applications for computers that have slow Internet connections, or even no connection at all, then XML Web services are not for you. Also, if you are looking to build services that will be exposed and used by the development community at large, you may wish to wait and see if the world adopts the XML Web services development model before you build any large-scale services.

If, however, you are building applications for a committed user base—users who are on board and awaiting the service, not just potential users who may or may not be persuaded to buy in—and your application can benefit from functionality that you cannot provide otherwise due to time or knowledge constraints, then XML Web services might be the perfect solution for you.

Ultimately, only you can really judge if an XML Web service is the correct path for your applications, but there can be no denying that this technology has many uses. XML Web services allow developers to harness the core talents of other programmers, talents that may lie outside their own areas of expertise. They also allow small development teams to make use of the efforts of large development houses, including Microsoft itself, and use services that would take years to be developed in house.

Web classes are appropriate in so many situations that it would be impossible to list all the possible scenarios for creating or consuming them. Some situations lend themselves extremely well to the XML Web services model and, even with Visual Studios .NET and other platforms still in beta, are starting to show up in production as this is being written.

Most of these new XML Web services fall into one of the following rather broad categories: intranet applications development, exposure of current customer services, and preexisting Web applications.

Using Web Services in Your Intranet Applications

Intranet applications offer perhaps the most obvious scenarios for building XML Web services. First of all, your user base is already connected to your Web servers. Second, by virtue of having an intranet, your company has an expressed need to share information and services.

What makes an intranet a perfect venue for XML Web services is that you already have to build the functionality in some programming language. The overhead involved in writing your functionality into an XML Web service is not much greater, and in many cases even less, than what is required to build the functionality in some other format.

Now, once the XML Web service is completed and being used by your intranet applications as was originally intended, it will be easier to reuse the functionality in other intranet applications, desktop applications, and even Internet applications.

Imagine that your company has an intranet application that tracks employee sick days, vacation time, and benefits. Currently, supervisors navigate to files on specific employees, cut and paste information out of the Web application, and use it to generate reports and populate other applications.

Now your company asks you to enhance this intranet site by automating the report processes and exposing your data to other application developers. You could just give these other developers permission to directly hit your database and to place their ASP code on the server with yours, or you could build all of the benefits functionality into an XML Web service and expose it that way.

Now a developer in your company who decides to build a new desktop reporting tool can simply communicate with your Web service to get the needed data. Likewise, when other developers need to build ASP projects that share your functionality but don't have access rights to the server that your application is on, they merely need to be able to browse it and send HTTP requests to it.

Customer Service–Related Web Services

If you are building applications for a company that offers any kind of goods or services, and you need to share information with partners, clients, or potential customers, then XML Web services may be for you.

If you are already building applications to post item quantities and costs, product descriptions, stock evaluations, or even football handicaps to Web sites, then you can leverage your efforts into something much more robust. Simply build the functionality that you are already planning to deliver via standard ASP, CGI, custom DLLs, or whatever into a Web service. Your Web site can still use the service, but now the same development can be used again and again in a host of other applications. These applications need not be Web applications, or even be developed by your company. Depending on the arrangement that you have with your customer, these XML Web services could be used in the customer's own development initiatives as a free service or accompanied by some billing model.

Even if you don't share information via the Internet already, XML Web services could be created that securely expose up-to-the-minute information on your business. Then either your company or a third party can roll out applications that make doing business faster and more efficient.

Porting Preexisting Web Applications to XML Web Services

While I would never suggest that anyone rewrite a program just to take advantage of a new technology when a need does not clearly exist, switching to a new technology when upgrading or building new applications may make sense.

In the case of XML Web services, porting your current Web apps out of standard ASP, CGI, or any other technology may make sense when it comes time to add new features or improve on old ones. If the possibility exists that a Web service built to handle one application could be used in future ones, why not plan ahead and save the additional redesigns down the road? As was previously mentioned, writing XML Web services in Visual Studio .NET is as easy, if not easier, than almost any method you may be using currently to design Internet-based applications.

Using the .NET Framework to Create XML Web Services

Since XML Web services are one of the cornerstones of the .NET platform, no discussion of them is complete without an understanding of what the .NET platform is and what it offers developers.

While XML Web services can and are being built to run on other platforms, no platform seems to offer the developer as much choice and control as .NET. Under .NET, developers are free to create XML Web services using several different languages and have them all communicate seamlessly. Updated versions of technologies such as ASP and ADO make creating XML Web services easier, while tools such as the WSDL.EXE and Visual Studio's Web References Dialog make consuming an XML Web service as easy as using a DLL.

Common Language Runtime Brings Languages Interoperability

One of the most important developments in the .NET framework is the creation of Common Language Runtime, or CLR. CLR is a runtime library used by all Visual Studio languages, with the exception of unmanaged C++. This library ensures that all programming languages work under the same object model when requesting operating system services or even dealing with each other.

CLR also imposes a common data typeset on languages. This mean that programs written in any .NET language can pass parameters to objects written in any other .NET language and be assured that they are type safe.

Another benefit of CLR is that any compiler can be written to make use of it. At present, plans exist to create compilers for .NET versions of Perl, COBOL, Python, and several other programming languages. This means that a large number of developers can leverage their existing skills into the creation of .NET applications and XML Web services without the need to learn a new language.

Compiling to the Intermediate Language (IL)

At the heart of CLR is the intermediate language, or IL. The IL is a low-level language, like assembly language, that is not configured to any one operating system or CPU, unlike assembly language. All languages compiled in Visual Studio, again with the exception of unmanaged C++, compile to IL code.

Any platform that is running the .NET framework can utilize IL code. Windows is currently the only platform that will run .NET, but plans exist for other operating systems. IL code is compiled into native machine code when it is first run. This concept is similar to Java's Just in Time compilation, but differs in one key area: once IL code has been compiled to native machine code, it need never be compiled on that machine again. This gives .NET-generated code the ability, in theory at this point, to be written once and run on multiple platforms. It also avoids the performance hits taken by languages like Java and Visual Basic, which are compiled or interpreted every time they are run.

Another upside of the IL is performance between languages. In the past, vast speed differences existed between languages such as Visual Basic and C++, but now, with all languages compiling to a common low-level language and then ultimately to native code, performance variance between languages should be small and limited to differences in how a language handles individual tasks.

.NET Handles Memory Management and Platform Architecture Specifics

The .NET framework automates many of the lowest-level tasks that programmers currently need to write Windows programs and make use of object-oriented technologies. Currently, developers need to explicitly handle such tasks as object reference counting, application threading, and process management. Under .NET, these tasks are completely automated.

Developers need not worry about memory models, far pointers, or system architecture specifics anymore. As .NET is rolled out on different platforms, the platform-specific implementations such as memory addressing will be handled within the framework and abstracted away from the programmer.

ADO.NET Makes Working with Data Easier

ADO.NET, sometimes referred to as ADO+, is the newest version of Microsoft's Active Data Objects. This set of ActiveX controls provides a consistent set of programmatic controls to a wide array of data sources, not limited to relational databases. Using ADO.NET, programmers need to know very little about the actual data source and how to program to it specifically.

This newest version of ADO.NET has XML functionality built in throughout. Data can now be expressed in terms of XML and transformed and manipulated in much the same way as any other XML documents.

Storing Data in the Dataset

The Dataset is a new feature of ADO.NET. It allows data to be stored in memory in what can best be described as an internal relational database. The Dataset is composed of table objects, called DataTables, maintained by the TablesCollection. The DataTable itself is made up of a RowsCollection and a ColumnsCollection.

Also contained within the Dataset is a RelationsCollection that contains the Dataset's DataRelation objects. DataRelation objects define matches between columns in two tables within the Dataset.

Web Applications with ASP.NET

Perhaps no technology in the new .NET framework is as closely tied to Microsoft's version of XML Web services as ASP.NET, also known as ASP+. In fact, XML Web services in the .NET framework are really just specialized ASP applications.

The biggest difference between ASP+ and previous versions of ASP is compilation. All ASP+ applications compile to native code the first time they are run by an individual client. Each client, be it Internet Explorer 3.2, 4.0, or 6.0, causes a separate compilation to be created, but the compiled code can be cached and reused if so desired.

This compilation works exactly like other applications written in .NET except that ASP+ applications are compiled to IL by IIS. This allows ASP+ developers to work with the same tools they have been using, such as Notepad and Word, and also lets them use Visual Studio .NET to create ASP applications.

With the move toward compiled ASP+ applications and the use of the CLR, ASP+ is now more robust and complete than ever. No longer are ASP applications limited to the functionality built into IIS and its ASP engine; ASP has full access to the same components, error handling, and operating system services as any other programs that you develop.

It should also be noted that with the move to compiled code, ASP+ applications can currently be written in Visual Basic, C#, and JavaScript, but with the advent of more compilers and Visual Studio plug-ins, more languages will be supported in the very near future.

Hailstorm: An XML Web Services Example

To best illustrate where development with XML Web services is heading, it may be good to look at where one of its major players, Microsoft, is heading with it. Microsoft recently announced the Hailstorm project, which is a series of XML Web services built around Microsoft's own passport authentication technology that will allow developers to create applications that truly integrate the user's Web experience.

Table 1.1 provides a listing of the services that Microsoft has currently implemented in the Hailstorm framework. With these services, applications can be built that would allow users to, for example, schedule trips and hotel reservations, keep records of their expenses, and list their itineraries, with access opened up to others in their company to track their whereabouts, keep updated billing information, and notify the users of any additional meetings that the head office may wish to schedule for them.

TABLE 1.1 Current Hailstorm Services

Service	*Description*
myAddress	Provides electronic and geographic address information
myApplication_Settings	Provides application settings
myCalendar	Provides time management functionality
myContacts	Provides an online address book
myDevices	Provides online access to device information
myDocuments	Provides a method for remote document storage
myFavorite_WebSites	Provides a list of favorite URLs, like the option in Internet Explorer
myInbox	Provides access to items such as e-mail and voicemail
myLocation	Another service that provides addressing information
myNotifications	Provides electronic notifications
myProfile	Provides profile information such as name, alias, pictures, etc.
myServices	Provides online access to a list of a user services
myUsage	Provides usage reports on myServices information
myWallet	Provides access to transaction records such as payment information and receipts

Microsoft plans to add more services to the Hailstorm project in the future, creating a very centralized set of services for developers to tap into. Using Hailstorm as a business model, it is not too difficult to imagine companies switching from traditional consulting services to the XML Web services market—either providing XML Web services for third-party software developers to use or creating XML Web services that they themselves integrate into the applications they build for clients.

Summary

In this hour, you learned what XML Web services are. You also examined the core concepts behind the XML Web services platform, such as SOAP and HTTP protocols. In the last half of this hour, you explored the .NET framework of technologies and how they support XML Web services. Finally, you learned about Hailstorm and how it represents Microsoft's vision of the distributed-development paradigm of the future.

Q&A

Q How do Web Services written in languages such as Java or C++ and running on platforms like Unix communicate so seamlessly with .NET applications?

A As you will see throughout this book, XML Web services send and receive information using simple text-based protocols such as SOAP. This way, all data and function requests, regardless of type, are sent across with standardized text markup to denote their actual types. The Web service simply has to read these standardized formats and return data using the same protocol.

Q How do developers use XML Web services in their code without having to write handlers for SOAP messaging?

A Visual Studios provides tools such as WSDL.EXE that create the SOAP handling code, in the form of auto-generated proxy classes, for each XML Web service that a developer uses in his or her projects. You will learn all about these in Hours 8 and 9.

Q If XML Web services are actually ASP+ applications, why am I writing them in Visual Studio using Visual Basic or C#?

A Under the .NET framework, ASP+ applications, whether they are written in Notepad or Visual Studio .NET, compile to native code and use the CLR. Since the CLR is used, ASP+ applications can be written in any language, including C#. Along with this switch to native code, Microsoft also created several new project types in Visual Studio, ASP+, and XML Web services to give ASP+ developers the benefit of a full tool suite.

Workshop

Quiz

1. What is the name of the protocol that XML Web services use to return data?

   A SOAP, or Simple Object Access Protocol

2. What is the name of the description language that Microsoft uses for defining an XML Web service?

   A WSDL, or Service Contract Language

3. Microsoft and several other major companies have joined together in providing an online index or repository of available XML Web services. What is this registry called?

   A UDDI, or Universal Description, Discovery, and Integration

4. What type of file provides information that points developers to an XML Web service and its WSDL files?

   A Disco, or discovery files

5. What feature of .NET allows for the ease of communication between components written in different languages, such as Visual Basic, C#, and even mediated C++?

   A CLR, or Common Language Runtime

Exercises

Now that you know what XML Web services are, try to think up some useful examples for yourself. Include the service's methods and functionality in your examples. By the time you finish this book, you will be able to create these services.

HOUR 2

An XML Primer

In this hour, you will learn the basics of XML. You will learn how XML is used in the XML Web services framework and how a foundation in XML knowledge can help you when creating and consuming XML Web services outside of the classroom.

In this hour we will discuss the following:

- XML's role in XML Web services
- XML document syntax
- XML document content
- XML namespaces

What Is XML?

XML is a syntax for describing data. Working in much the same way as HTML does in describing Web content, XML can be used to describe almost any data, including Web content via XHTML.

XML's power lies in its extensibility. Anyone can add tags to XML to create their own *vocabulary*. A vocabulary is simply a set of XML tags and attributes that are used to describe data. When individuals, groups, or companies decide to adopt a vocabulary for a particular set of data, that data can be shared more easily.

As an example, look at the XML fragment in Listing 2.1. This XML fragment shows data from a video store that contains information on their stock. Do not worry about what the tag actually means; you will learn that later in this hour.

Listing 2.1 XML Document Fragment for a Video Store

```
<?xml version = "1.0"?>
   <Tape>
      <Title>Reservoir Dogs</Title>
      <Status due="3/27/02">Rented</Status>
      <Rating>R</Rating>
      <Title>Reservoir Dogs</Title>
      <Status due="3/27/02">Rented</Status>
      <Rating>R</Rating>
 </Tape>
```

If every video store adopted this as their syntax, Web sites could be built that searched all of the video stores in your area and let you know who had the movie you were seeking in stock.

If the above vocabulary was truly complete, it would probably contain the film's actors, a plot synopsis, the category of the film, the date it was made, and so on, so that you could really search for a film that suits you.

XML Document Structure

An XML document structure is comprised of three major sections: the *Prolog,* the *Document Body,* and the *Epilog*. Of these three sections, only the Document Body is required.

XML Prolog

The Prolog of an XML document is optional, but when one does exist, it may contain the following XML entities: a declaration, processing instructions, and comment lines. The Prolog may also contain, as its last element, the *document type declaration,* known as the DTD.

XML Epilog

Like the Prolog, an XML epilog is an optional structure. When an Epilog is present, it may include comments and processing instructions.

XML Body

The XML Body is the one required portion of an XML document. It may contain any number of elements, comments, processing instructions, and other entities, which are beyond the scope of this book.

Declaration

As described earlier, the optional Prolog section of an XML document may contain an optional declaration. Since Microsoft's SCL contains the declaration and other XML Web service vendors may also include it, we will discuss it here.

The minimum XML declaration, and the one used in SCL, looks like this:

```
<?xml version="1.0"?>
```

Aside from version, the declaration may also contain attributes that describe the document's encoding method, whether or not it is a standalone XML document, or if it relies on other documents for its completion.

If the standalone attribute is included, its values can be either "yes" or "no". Encoding, on the other hand, can support a very large range of encoding schemes. These include "UTF-8" and "UTF-16."

> If a declaration is included in your XML documents, it must be the very first line that appears. No other content, or even blank spaces, may come before it.

Elements

An *element* is the most basic structure in any XML document. Elements consist of case sensitive start and end tags that may surround some type of data. Listing 2.2 shows some examples of XML elements.

LISTING 2.2 Elements in XML

```
 <Car>UGO</Car>
 <Funds></Funds>
<Chair />
```

You will note that line 2 of Listing 2.2 contains an element with a start tag and an end tag but no data. This is called an *empty element,* which is simply an element that contains no data.

The element shown in line 3 is an example of the empty element tag. The space between "`Chair`" and "`/`" is provided to ensure compatability with Netscape Navigator and several other XML parsing programs. Internet Explorer will correctly handle the element even if the space is not present. Since using the space ensures readability in both browser types, as well as every major parser, this syntax is highly recommended. This tag is merely a shortcut to writing out the full start and end tags. It is equivalent to

```
<Chair></Chair>
```

Document Elements

Data in an XML document is represented in a tree structure, with elements nested inside of other elements in order to form a hierarchy. The *document element* is the top element of the document body. It is also the only element that is actually required to be present in an XML document. With that in mind, the following is a legal XML document:

```
<Data/>
```

The above could represent the return of a database query that turned up zero matches for the contents of a container, truck, box, and so on that was represented in another XML document.

Children Elements

Since an XML document is a tree structure with the document element at its root, all other elements are subelements of the root. These elements, known as *children elements,* will make up the bulk of most XML documents. Also, in order to facilitate complex data hierarchies, children elements may have children elements of their own. There is no practical limit to the complexity of the nesting that can be done with elements.

Listing 2.3 shows an example of a complex hierarchy of data in an XML document.

LISTING 2.3 Complex Data in XML

```
<Book>
  <Title>Teach Yourself JavaScript in 24 Hours</Title>
  <Author>Michael Moncur</Author>
  <Contents>
  <Section>
      <Title>Getting Started</Title>
  <Hour1>Understanding JavaScript</Hour1>
```

continues

Listing 2.3 Continued

```
        <Hour2>Creating a Simple Script</Hour2>
        …
      </Section>
    </Contents>
  </Book>
```


As you can see, you can nest elements to achieve complex hierarchies fairly easily. This example barely touched on how complex relationships can get.

Attributes

Attributes are a way of attaching additional data to an element. For example, say we wished to add an ISBN to an element tag containing the title of a book. We could do something similar to Listing 2.4.

Listing 2.4 Adding Attributes to XML Elements

```
<Title ISBN="0-672-31407-x">
  Teach Yourself JavaScript 1.3 in 24 Hours
</Title>
```

The syntax for adding attributes is:

```
<ElementName AttributeName="AttributeText">
```

Attribute data must always be a string type and enclosed in quotation marks. Integer values are not allowed, although they could be enclosed in quotes and represented as string data.

Elements can contain any number of attributes, as long as the same attribute is not repeated for a single element. Listing 2.5 shows our book example with the first printing date and the Library of Congress number included.

Listing 2.5 Multiple Attributes in an XML Element

```
<Title ISBN="0-672-31407-x"
        PrintDate="January 1999"
        LOCN="98-86224">
  Teach Yourself JavaScript 1.3 in 24 Hours
</Title>
```

Comments

Comment lines, like those in programming languages, provide a place to record notes and information that may help people who need to work with the XML document. The syntax for comment lines; a less-than symbol followed by an exclamation point and two dashes, some comment text, and then the closing two dashes and greater-than symbol, is taken directly from the world of Web programming and is as follows:

```
<!-Your Comments Go Here
```

Listing 2.6 shows some XML data that has been commented.

LISTING 2.6 An XML Document Fragment Containing Comments

```
   <!-Names of some cats -->
   <Cat>Rowan</Cat> <!-My First Cat -->
   <Cat>Morrigan</Cat>
   <!-Mother and Daughter -->
   <Cat>Naya
      <Daughter>Missi</Daughter>
   </Cat>
   <Cat>Lorindal</Cat>
<!-No More Cats -->
```

Processing Instructions

Processing Instructions are like comment lines, only they are designed as a way to pass information along to a processing application on how the XML document should be handled.

The syntax for a processing instruction is

```
<?target instruction ?>
```

The `target` is some name that is used to signify an object that should handle the instruction portion of the processing instruction element. `instruction` is merely a string of text that the target application would decipher and use.

The most common use of processing instructions is to signify the association of style sheets with various sections of an XML document.

Namespaces

Namespaces are a topic that comes up a lot in XML Web services, both in developing them in .NET and in describing them, such as in SCL and DISCO documents.

A namespace is a collection of elements grouped together under a reference name. The name was originally a URI, but with the acceptance of namespaces into Visual Studio .NET, the reference can be to any file.

A namespace, once declared in a document, can then be used to resolve name definitions and avoid problems caused by having elements with the same name showing up in a document.

Namespaces help resolve name definitions in Visual Studio .NET whenever you declare them. In order to resolve the huge number of possible libraries that a developer can use in a given program, Visual Studio .NET has the developer use the imports tag in order to declare a name space. After that namespace has been declared, Visual Studio can resolve any function names that the user references by looking at the libraries represented by that namespace.

In XML, this resolution can and will, as you will see in later Hours, occur when the XML document contains references to standard data types. These data types will reference a namespace, in this case an URL, which contains the definitions of these data types. If your application uses the same namespace to define data types, you can exchange data with the XML document without fear of having typing problems.

The other problem that namespaces resolve in XML is that of multiple element types containing the same name. This occurs most often when documents from different sources are combined into one document.

The syntax for declaring a namespace is

```
xlmns="someAddress"
```

This attribute would associate the element that it was declared within, and all of that element's children, with the namespace "`SomeAddress`".

Optionally, a namespace can be given an alias as seen here:

```
xmlns:alias="someAddress"
```

Once a namespace has been declared, its alias can be added to the beginning of element or attribute names in order to create qualified names.

```
<alias:Element> </alias:Element>
```

An example of an XML document containing a namespace declaration can be seen in Listing 2.7.

LISTING 2.7 An XML Document Containing a Namespace Declaration

```
<Catalog xmlns="urn:Music_CD"
     xmlns:music="urn:Music_CD_Info">
   <music:Band>Iron Maiden
 <music:CDs>
        <music:Title>Killers</music:Title>
   <music:Title>Piece of Mind</music:Title>
 </music:CDs>
</music:Band>
</Catalog>
```

If this XML document were to be combined with another document, say the owner's book collection, we would have little to fear as far as processing applications mistaking book titles for music titles.

Validate XML Documents

When XML vocabularies are created, their rules are recorded in documents such as DTDs and XML Schemas. These documents are used to ensure that any XML claiming to be written in a particular vocabulary fits that vocabulary's rules, such as containing any minimum requirements, data order, etc.

> A full discussion of DTDs would take far more space then we have in this book. Suffice it to say, DTDs are used in a manner similar to Schemas, but with a lot less flexibility to create complex structures.

Using Schemas to Validate XML Documents

An important thing to know about schemas, and their biggest advantage over DTDs, is that they use the standard XML syntax. That is correct, Schemas are merely XML used to define and describe other XML. This makes schemas very flexible and easier to learn than DTDs.

The schema is used by parsers, including Internet Explorer and any Visual Studio .NET–generated XML Web service applications, to validate the content of the XML document. This validation includes type information for arguments and return values. You will take a much closer look at the typing system allowed in XML Web services in Hour 3 when you study the WSDL syntax for describing a web service. WSDL is an XML vocabulary, schema included, for describing XML Web services.

The Schema's Root Element

The root element of a schema, know as its *preamble,* contains the `targetNS` and `xmlns`. The `targetNS` defines the namespace for the schema while the `xmlns` points to the namespace of the XML schema specification. An example of the preamble can be seen below:

```
<schema targetNS=http://localhost/schema.xsd
        xmlns="http://schema.xmlsoap.org/wsdl/">
    …
</schema>
```

Declaring Elements

Simple elements are declared within a schema as follows:

```
<xsd:element name="name" type="xsd:string" minOccurs="0" maxOccurs="1"/>
```

`name` is the name of the element being created, `type` is the type of data that the element can contain, and `minOccurs` and `maxOccurs` are optional attributes that describe how many times the element may appear. This will become more important when you examine complex types. Our example above would allow for the following to appear in the XML document:

```
<name>Mark Augustyniak</name>
```

New simple element types can be created by restricting elements via the `restriction` element. This allows for elements to be created that are restricted to certain values or ranges. For example, if you were trying to create an element for a five star movie rating system, you could do the following:

```
<xsd:simpleType name="Stars">
  <xsd:restriction base="xsd:integer">
    <xsd:minInclusive value="1"/>
    <xsd:maxInclusive value="5"/>
  </xsd:restriction>
</xsd:simpleType>
```

This restriction element, along with the enumeration element, is what is used to create enumerations such as the following, which describes a color enumeration limited to values of red, blue, or green:

```
<xsd:simpleType name="Color">
     <xsd:restriction base="s:string">
      <xsd:enumeration value="red"/>
      <xsd:enumeration value="blue"/>
      <xsd:enumeration value="green"/>
     </xsd:restriction>
</xsd:simpleType>
```

Expanding up this idea, more complex elements can be created by adding simple elements together. The following schema declaration defines an element, named `person`, that may contain, in order, elements of type `fname`, `lname`, and `age`.

```
<xsd:complexType name="person" >
  <xsd:sequence>
   <xsd:element name="fname"   type="xsd:string"/>
   <xsd:element name="lname" type="xsd:string"/>
   <xsd:element name="age"   type="xsd:int"/>
  </xsd:sequence>
</xsd:complexType>
```

Using Attributes with Schemas

Attribute declarations are made using the `attribute` element and a `name` attribute that defines the name used by the attribute. Optionally, the `attribute` element can also make use of the `minOccurs` and `maxOccurs` attributes to determine how many times an attribute can be applied to a single instance of the element.

Attributes may also make use of the `fixed` and `default` attributes. The `fixed` attribute is used to set an attribute to a fixed value that it must always posses. `default` sets the value of the attribute when it is not set explicitly.

Finally, attributes can make use of the `type` attribute to determine what type of data must be used to set the attribute in question.

To add an attribute to your earlier example, you could do the following:

```
<xsd:complexType name="person" >
   …
  <xsd:attribute name="DOB" type="xsd:date"/>
 </xsd:complexType>
```

This would create an element that allowed for the following:

```
<person DOB="3/23/73">
```

XML's Role in XML Web Services

XML is used heavily by XML Web services as a communication medium between XML Web services and their clients. XML is also used in describing what methods an XML Web service exposes, what type of data those methods return, and what types of data, if any, they accept as parameters.

For describing the service itself, Microsoft has built a vocabulary called *SCL*, or *Service Contract Language*. When an XML Web service is created, a contract document is also generated. This contract is used by developers and by tools, such as Visual Studio, to create client applications for the service. The use of an easily readable format, such as a standardized XML vocabulary, makes this task much easier than the task would be if every developer created his or her own definition files. You will learn more about SCL in Hour 3.

At the time of this writing, Visual Studio is still using SDL, a subset of WSDL, in order to create its contracts. This is to have changed by the time this book goes to print.

Using SOAP to Communicate with XML Web Services

An XML subset, known as SOAP, is the medium through which most communication is done between XML Web service consumers, either client applications or other XML Web services, and the services themselves. *SOAP*, or *Simple Object Access Protocol*, is an XML vocabulary used to facilitate remote procedure calls across the Internet.

Discovering XML Web Services with DISCO

XML also shows up in the creation of a standard method for publishing an XML Web service. You will learn more about DISCO in Hour 5, but for now, know that it is the document you will most likely encounter first when searching for services. A DISCO document typically contains information to point you to the service and its contract.

Summary

In this hour, you learned the basic syntax of XML documents and how they are used within XML Web services. You learned how to add elements to your XML documents and how to further define these elements through the use of attributes. You also saw how namespaces and DTDs are used to define XML documents and validate their contents.

Q&A

Q Why is it important to learn the basics of XML if Visual Studio .NET does all of the XML work behind the scenes?

A Well, there are two main reasons to learn XML, aside from it being a useful and ever more present technology. Reason one is that not every XML Web service that you encounter will have been created using Microsoft tools. With other vendors getting into the XML Web service market, you may find yourself delving into XML documents in order to bring a new service into your application framework. The second reason is that it is always nice to know what is going on behind the scenes. This is especially true when something goes wrong and you have to find out where and why.

Q Is there a rule for when I should put data in an attribute and when I should place it in an element?

A No, unfortunately there is no rule involving what constitutes an attribute or an element. Any data that you could place in an attribute could conceivably be given an element of its own and vice versa. It is up to you, or whoever develops the vocabulary, to determine what will be placed in attributes.

Q What is the importance of using DTDs and Schemas? Which should I use?

A DTDs and Schemas are important because they help validate XML documents and define what a document can and cannot hold. It is through the use of these documents that we define our vocabularies and, with the use of XML parsers and validators, determine if XML documents that we encounter are valid forms of said vocabulary. That being said, DTDs are slowly losing favor in the development community and Schemas are now the dominant technology. If you have the option, you are probably better off using the Schema.

Workshop

Quiz

1. What is the XML subset used when publishing an XML Web service?

   A DISCO.

2. True or False: Elements are limited to a single attribute.

   A False, elements may contain many attributes.

3. True or False: Attributes contain data types that can not be represented as elements.

   A False, the decision to use attributes instead of elements to describe some data is purely a matter of preference.

4. What are used to differentiate between entities using the same name that originate from different source documents?

   A Namespaces.

5. Write out an attribute declaration for an attribute called `color` that is used on a sky element and defaults to blue.

   A `<!ATTLIST sky color CDATA (blue)>`

Exercises

Try creating some XML structures of your own. Take some of your interests or hobbies and see if you can come up with some simple vocabularies for them. There is no right or wrong answer; as long as you follow the guidelines given in this hour, your XML documents should be fine.

HOUR 3

Defining XML Web Service Operations with WSDL

In this hour, you will learn how WSDL is used to describe XML Web services. You will see how WSDL is used to define how a service exposes itself to various types of HTTP request types. You will also see how the WSDL language is used to inform client applications about argument and return types that are used by the service's methods.

In this hour, we will discuss the following:

- Typing in WSDL
- Messages
- Ports
- Bindings

What Is WSDL?

WSDL, or *Web Services Description Language,* is an XML-based language used to define XML Web services. WSDL describes the service and its methods as well as the manner in which communication between a client and a service should be carried out.

A WSDL Document Example

In order to get a grasp of how WSDL works, one must first look at a WSDL document. The following document describes a service, WSDLTester, that contains one method, `TestMethod1`. This method accepts as its arguments an integer named `iNum1` and a Boolean named `fBool1` and returns a string.

LISTING 3.1 WSDL Document for Service WSDLTester

```
<?xml version="1.0" encoding="utf-8"?>
<definitions xmlns:s="http://www.w3.org/2001/XMLSchema"
xmlns:http="http://schemas.xmlsoap.org/wsdl/http/"
pxmlns:mime="http://schemas.xmlsoap.org/wsdl/mime/"
pxmlns:tm="http://microsoft.com/wsdl/mime/textMatching/"
xmlns:soap="http://schemas.xmlsoap.org/wsdl/soap/"
pxmlns:soapenc="http://schemas.xmlsoap.org/soap/encoding/"
xmlns:s0="http://tempuri.org/" targetNamespace="http://tempuri.org/"
xmlns="http://schemas.xmlsoap.org/wsdl/">
   <types>
     <s:schema attributeFormDefault="qualified"
           elementFormDefault="qualified"
    targetNamespace="http://tempuri.org/">
       <s:element name="TestMethod1">
         <s:complexType>
           <s:sequence>
             <s:element minOccurs="1" maxOccurs="1"
                name="iNum1" type="s:int" />
             <s:element minOccurs="1" maxOccurs="1"
                name="fBool1" type="s:boolean" />
           </s:sequence>
         </s:complexType>
       </s:element>
       <s:element name="TestMethod1Response">
         <s:complexType>
           <s:sequence>
             <s:element minOccurs="1" maxOccurs="1"
               name="TestMethod1Result" nillable="true" type="s:string" />
           </s:sequence>
         </s:complexType>
       </s:element>
       <s:element name="string" nillable="true" type="s:string" />
     </s:schema>
```

continues

LISTING 3.1 Continued

```
</types>
<message name="TestMethod1SoapIn">
  <part name="parameters" element="s0:TestMethod1" />
</message>
<message name="TestMethod1SoapOut">
  <part name="parameters" element="s0:TestMethod1Response" />
</message>
<message name="TestMethod1HttpGetIn">
  <part name="iNum1" type="s:string" />
  <part name="fBool1" type="s:string" />
</message>
<message name="TestMethod1HttpGetOut">
  <part name="Body" element="s0:string" />
</message>
<message name="TestMethod1HttpPostIn">
  <part name="iNum1" type="s:string" />
  <part name="fBool1" type="s:string" />
</message>
<message name="TestMethod1HttpPostOut">
  <part name="Body" element="s0:string" />
</message>
<portType name="WSDLTesterSoap">
  <operation name="TestMethod1">
    <input message="s0:TestMethod1SoapIn" />
    <output message="s0:TestMethod1SoapOut" />
  </operation>
</portType>
<portType name="WSDLTesterHttpGet">
  <operation name="TestMethod1">
    <input message="s0:TestMethod1HttpGetIn" />
    <output message="s0:TestMethod1HttpGetOut" />
  </operation>
</portType>
<portType name="WSDLTesterHttpPost">
  <operation name="TestMethod1">
    <input message="s0:TestMethod1HttpPostIn" />
    <output message="s0:TestMethod1HttpPostOut" />
  </operation>
</portType>
<binding name="WSDLTesterSoap" type="s0:WSDLTesterSoap">
  <soap:binding
   transport="http://schemas.xmlsoap.org/soap/http"
   style="document" />
  <operation name="TestMethod1">
    <soap:operation soapAction="http://tempuri.org/TestMethod1"
          style="document" />
    <input>
      <soap:body use="literal" />
```

continues

LISTING 3.1 Continued

```
      </input>
      <output>
        <soap:body use="literal" />
      </output>
    </operation>
  </binding>
  <binding name="WSDLTesterHttpGet" type="s0:WSDLTesterHttpGet">
    <http:binding verb="GET" />
    <operation name="TestMethod1">
      <http:operation location="/TestMethod1" />
      <input>
     <http:urlEncoded />
      </input>
      <output>
        <mime:mimeXml part="Body" />
      </output>
    </operation>
  </binding>
  <binding name="WSDLTesterHttpPost" type="s0:WSDLTesterHttpPost">
    <http:binding verb="POST" />
    <operation name="TestMethod1">
      <http:operation location="/TestMethod1" />
      <input>
        <mime:content type="application/x-www-form-urlencoded" />
      </input>
      <output>
        <mime:mimeXml part="Body" />
      </output>
    </operation>
  </binding>
  <service name="WSDLTester">
    <port name="WSDLTesterSoap" binding="s0:WSDLTesterSoap">
      <soap:address
        location="http://localhost/WebService3/WSDLTester.asmx" />
    </port>
    <port name="WSDLTesterHttpGet" binding="s0:WSDLTesterHttpGet">
      <http:address
        location="http://localhost/WebService3/WSDLTester.asmx" />
    </port>
    <port name="WSDLTesterHttpPost" binding="s0:WSDLTesterHttpPost">
      <http:address
        location="http://localhost/WebService3/WSDLTester.asmx" />
    </port>
  </service>
</definitions>
```

Analysis of WSDL Document Example

Let's take a moment to analyze the code example above to ensure you understand the various elements that are taking place here.

> WSDL documents are fairly complex and can be extremely confusing to anyone who isn't accustomed to them and, for that reason, Visual Studio/ .NET generates a WSDL document for every XML Web Service that you create. The purpose of this hour is to help you understand what an XML Web Service does based on its WSDL document. Do not worry about memorizing all of the rules and syntax that comprise WSDL as you will probably never be forced to make changes to a WSDL document.

- `Types` (lines 10 through 33)—Provides data type definitions that will be used for communication between the XML Web Service and its clients.
- `Messages` (lines 34 through 53)—Provides a message name, associated with a type, that will be used for communication.
- `PortTypes` (lines 54 through 71)—Associates specific messages with port types, such as HttpPost.
- `Bindings` (lines 72 through 111)—Binds specific ports and XML Web service methods to Internet protocols, such as SOAP.
- `Services` (lines 112 through 125)—Supplies the address information for a service's different ports of communication.

Services Defined in WSDL

In WSDL, a service element is used to group together port elements, the elements that directly address the protocols on which an XML Web service will communicate. The service element contains a `name` attribute, line 1 of Listing 3.2, which is set to the actual name of the XML Web service that the service element represents.

Within each service element may be a `documentation` element and one or more port elements. The `documentation` element, lines 2 and 3, will contain comment information about the XML Web service.

The port elements will contain two attributes of their own, `name` and `binding`. The `name` element provides a unique identifier for each port element within a service. This name is typically created by adding the name of the port's protocol, SOAP in line 4, to the end of the service's name. The binding element points to the actual `portType` element, which you will study in a later section.

Also contained within the port element is the address element. This element points to the actual URL address that client applications will use to contact an XML Web service via the given port. You will notice that the example in Listing 3.2 gives the same address for all three ports. This is typically the case when creating services with Visual Studio .NET, but WSDL allows for developers to create services that utilize different addresses to handle the various port communications.

LISTING 3.2 Services Defined in WSDL

```
<service name="DataTypes">
  <documentation>test of using various data types in
                 XML Web Services</documentation>
  <port name="DataTypesSoap" binding="s0:DataTypesSoap">
    <soap:address location="http://localhost/DataTypes/Service1.asmx" />
  </port>
  <port name="DataTypesHttpGet" binding="s0:DataTypesHttpGet">
    <http:address location="http://localhost/DataTypes/Service1.asmx" />
  </port>
  <port name="DataTypesHttpPost" binding="s0:DataTypesHttpPost">
    <http:address location="http://localhost/DataTypes/Service1.asmx" />
  </port>
</service>
```

Defining Ports

When a method is created for an XML Web service, Visual Studio/ .NET will automatically generate code capable of handling requests from multiple types of HTTP protocols. The WSDL document generated for the service defines the ports on which these various protocols may contact the service. In WSDL, a port is defined as follows:

```
<portType name="nmtoken"> *
<-- extensibility element -->
</portType>
```

In the above definition, `name` represents a unique name among the ports being defined. The `extensibility` element represents a list of operation elements, one for every method exposed by the service. The port defined in Listing 3.3 defines a service, `DataTypes`, exposing its functionality via SOAP. The service contains one operation, or method, called `StringReturn`.

LISTING 3.3 A SOAP `portTypes` in WSDL

```
<portType name="DataTypesSoap">
  <operation name="StringReturn">
    <documentation>This function returns a simple string. I am writing
                 this text as an example of using the description
                 Metadata.</documentation>
    <input message="s0:StringReturnSoapIn" />
    <output message="s0:StringReturnSoapOut" />
  </operation>
</portType>
```

The code in Listing 3.4 shows the same service exposing its functionality via `HttpGet`.

LISTING 3.4 An `HttpGet portType`

```
1:  <portType name="DataTypesHttpGet">
2:    <operation name="StringReturn">
3:      <documentation>This function returns a simple string. I am writing
4:                   this text as an example of using the description
5:                   Metadata.</documentation>
6:      <input message="s0:StringReturnHttpGetIn" />
7:      <output message="s0:StringReturnHttpGetOut" />
8:    </operation>
9:  </portType>
```

Operations

As you have already seen, operations represent the various methods being exposed by the service. A typical operation contains two elements, `input` and `output`, but may also contain `documentation` and `fault`.

The `input` and `output` elements of an operation basically link the services method, `StringReturn` in the case of Listing 3.4, to SOAP messages that will provide the transport for input parameters and output results. Line 6 of Listing 3.4 lets you know that the `StringReturn` method will be called using the message `StringReturnHttpGetIn` and will return its results using `StringReturnHttpGetOut`. A little later in this hour you will see how to define the messages themselves.

Like the `input` and `output` elements, `fault` defines the message that will be used to transport error messages should errors be encountered. In addition, the documentation element, lines 3 through 5 of Listing 3.4, provides a method for attaching comments to a service's methods.

Bindings in WSDL

Bindings provide a method for WSDL to bind operations and ports to protocols. The basic format for this is given below:

```
<wsdl:binding name="nmtoken" type="qname"> *
   <wsdl:operation name="nmtoken"> *
      <wsdl:input name="nmtoken"? > ?
      </wsdl:input>
      <wsdl:output name="nmtoken"? > ?
      </wsdl:output>
      <wsdl:fault name="nmtoken"> *
      </wsdl:fault>
   </wsdl:operation>
</wsdl:binding>
```

In the previous code, `name` is a unique identifier for the particular binding and `type` is the name of the `portType` being bound. Typically, Visual Studio.NET will simply use the `portType` name as the identifier in name.

SOAP Bindings

Listing 3.5 shows a binding for a SOAP port. The port was named `DatTypesSoap`, and thus, the binding is named this as well. As you can see, the binding binds the `portType`, `DataTypesSoap` to the SOAP transport protocol, line 2. Furthermore, each operation—`StringReturn` in this example—has its input, output, and (optionally) its fault messages further defined.

LISTING 3.5 Binding a SOAP `portType` to the SOAP Protocol

```
1:    <binding name="DataTypesSoap" type="s0:DataTypesSoap">
2:      <soap:binding transport="http://schemas.xmlsoap.org/soap/http"
3:                    style="document" />
4:      <operation name="StringReturn">
5:        <soap:operation soapAction="http:\www.myServer.com\
      DataTypes/StringReturn"
6:                        style="document" />
7:        <input>
8:           <soap:body use="literal" />
9:        </input>
10:       <output>
11:          <soap:body use="literal" />
12:       </output>
13:     </operation>
14:   </binding>
```

HttpGet

Since XML Web services must deal with client applications other than those utilizing SOAP protocols, WSDL supports bindings for both `HttpGet` and `HttpPost`. As with SOAP, `HttpGet` bindings bind the `portType`, `DataTypesHttpGet` in Listing 3.6, to the `HttpGet` protocol.

The most important detail here is the specifics of transports for each message. Input communications are set to use the `urlEncoding` method, line 6, whereas outbound information will be presented as the body of an HTML document (line 9).

LISTING 3.6 Binding an `HttpGet` `portType` to the `Get` Protocol

```
1:   <binding name="DataTypesHttpGet" type="s0:DataTypesHttpGet">
2:     <http:binding verb="GET" />
3:     <operation name="StringReturn">
4:       <http:operation location="/StringReturn" />
5:       <input>
6:         <http:urlEncoded />
7:       </input>
8:       <output>
9:         <mime:mimeXml part="Body" />
10:      </output>
11:    </operation>
12:  </binding>
```

HttpPost

Listing 13.7 shows the binding for an `HttpPost` operation. This binding is very similar to that used by `HttpGet`. Of note here is the use of the `HttpPost` method of passing arguments as Form data instead of encoded data in the requesting URL, line 6.

LISTING 3.7 Binding an `HttpPost` `portType` to the `Post` Protocol

```
1:   <binding name="DataTypesHttpPost" type="s0:DataTypesHttpPost">
2:     <http:binding verb="POST" />
3:     <operation name="StringReturn">
4:       <http:operation location="/StringReturn" />
5:       <input>
6:         <mime:content type="application/x-www-form-urlencoded" />
7:       </input>
8:       <output>
9:         <mime:mimeXml part="Body" />
10:       </output>
11:    </operation>
12:  </binding>
```

Messages

Messages define the way information is actually transmitted during communication between the service and its clients. In the case of SOAP clients, the message would help to define the SOAP messages that are being sent. In the case of clients using HTTP protocols, the message would define Form or URI string messages.

The message element itself contains a `name` attribute that is used to uniquely identify the message. When Visual Studio/ .NET creates a WSDL document for you, it typically creates a message whose name is built by combining the method's name, the Port type, and the direction of travel, relative to the service, of the message. For example, `myMethodPostIn`, would be the name of a message calling a method named `myMethod` using the `Post` port.

A message also contains zero or more `part` elements. `part` elements define the actual parts of the message being sent. These `part` elements represent parameters and results being sent back and forth between the client and the service. A `part` consists of two attributes, `name` and `element`. The `name` attribute is either the name of an argument of the method, or as in the case of SOAP port messages, simply the `"parameters"`. The `element` attribute is used to determine the type of the argument or response part.

The following is a message for a SOAP port call to a method named `StringReturnSoapIn`. Note that since the message describes a SOAP communication, the name is `parameters` and the type is a complex type called `StringReturn`.

```
<message name="StringReturnSoapIn">
    <part name="parameters" element="s0:StringReturn" />
</message>
```

The return message for this method looks very similar, with the substitution of `Out` for `In` in the message's name.

```
<message name="StringReturnSoapOut">
   <part name="parameters" element="s0:StringReturnResponse" />
</message>
```

When one of the HTTP protocols is being used, the `part` elements actually contain the parameter's `name` and `type`, as seen below. This message would describe calling a method, `ParamLongReturn`, via `HttpPost` and passing in two strings named `iNum1` and `iNum2`.

```
<message name="ParamLongReturnHttpPostIn">
    <part name="iNum1" type="s:string" />
    <part name="iNum2" type="s:string" />
</message>
```

The return of the method would make use of the message below to return a `long`. The return, or `Out`, messages of HTTP protocol messages are always named `Body`.

```
<message name="ParamLongReturnHttpPostOut">
    <part name="Body" element="s0:long" />
</message>
```

Types

WSDL makes use of XSD, XML Schema Definition, for its type system. Some of the more common types, a few of which you have seen used as the types in message elements, are shown in Table 3.1.

TABLE 3.1 Common Methods of the `Session` Object

Type	*Visual Basic Equivalent*
`anyURI`	String
`base64Binary`	Byte
`boolean`	Boolean
`byte`	Integer
`date`	Date
`dateTime`	Date
`double`	Double
`duration`	String
`ENTITIES`	String
`ENTITY`	String
`float`	Single
`ID`	String
`IDREF`	String
`IDREFS`	String
`int`	Long
`language`	String
`Name`	String
`NCName`	String
`NMTOKEN`	String
`NMTOKENS`	String
`normalizedString`	String

continues

TABLE 3.1 Continued

Type	*Visual Basic Equivalent*
`NOTATION`	String
`QName`	String
`short`	Integer
`string`	String
`time`	Date
`token`	String
`unsignedByte`	Byte
`unsignedShort`	Long

WSDL's type system allows for more complex data types, such as arrays, enumerations, and even objects to be defined by combining the simple types shown in Table 3.1. The following example shows a new type, called `NewType`, which contains an integer named `Var1` and a byte named `Var2`.

```
<s:element name="NewType">
  <s:complextype>
   <s:sequence>
     <s:element minOccurs="1", maxOccurs="1"
      name="Var1" type="s:int">
     <s:element minOccurs="1", maxOccurs="1"
      name="Var2" type="s:byte">
   </s:sequence>
  </s:complextype>
</s:element>
```

Now, apply this to the `StringReturn` method that you have been looking at throughout this hour. The message for the `StringReturn` method defined a message part containing an element named `StringReturn`. `StringReturn` is defined in Listing 3.8 as being an empty element (line 6). This would suggest that the method `StringReturn` accepts no input parameters. The return of the method, on the other hand, does return data. Lines 8 through 15 define a type, `StringReturnResponse`, which contains one, and only one, string type variable.

LISTING 3.8 Typing in WSDL

```
1:   <types>
2:      <s:schema attributeFormDefault="qualified"
3:             elementFormDefault="qualified"
4:             targetNamespace="http:\www.myServer.com\DataTypes">
5:      <s:element name="StringReturn">
6:        <s:complexType />
7:      </s:element>
8:      <s:element name="StringReturnResponse">
```

continues

LISTING 3.8 Continued

```
        <s:complexType>
          <s:sequence>
            <s:element minOccurs="1" maxOccurs="1"
                       name="StringReturnResult"
                      nillable="true" type="s:string" />
          </s:sequence>
        </s:complexType>
      </s:element>
        <s:element name="string" nillable="true" type="s:string" />
  </s:schema>
 </types>
```


If you needed to return an even more complicated type, such as the enumeration shown in Listing 3.9, you would define the enumeration, lines 9 through 15, as a simple type. Yes, a simple type because it will not be made up of other types but will in fact be the building block of more complex types. This enumeration can then be used to create more complex types, such as the `EnumReturnResponse` shown in line 1.

LISTING 3.9 Describing an Enumeration with XSD

```
1:   <s:element name="EnumReturnResponse">
2:     <s:complexType>
3:       <s:sequence>
4:         <s:element minOccurs="1" maxOccurs="1"
5:            name="EnumReturnResult" type="s0:Color" />
6:         </s:sequence>
7:       </s:complexType>
8:     </s:element>
9:     <s:simpleType name="Color">
10:      <s:restriction base="s:string">
11:        <s:enumeration value="Red" />
12:        <s:enumeration value="Blue" />
13:        <s:enumeration value="Green" />
14:      </s:restriction>
15:    </s:simpleType>
16:   </s:element>
```

Summary

In this hour, you saw how to use WSDL to describe a service and point clients to the URL used to contact the service. You also learned how to utilize XSD type schemas to type arguments and returns used by the method of an XML Web service. In addition to this, you examined how WSDL defines the content of messages that can be sent back and forth between client applications and services.

Q&A

Q Why Learn about WSDL?

A WSDL documents tell you the specifics about an XML Web service. If you are building a client application, especially if your client is not using .NET as its platform, it is often invaluable to be able to look into a WSDL document and see how your programs can access the service's functionality. It is also important to have a very good understanding of WSDL if you should ever come across a situation that calls for the WSDL document to have to be hand altered, such as a situation where you wish to force clients to use one specific port and disallow the others.

Q Why is `s` always used as the namespace for simple data types?

A If you look at the definitions element of the Visual Studio .NET–generated WSDL files, you will see that `s` is the name given to the `XMLSchema` namespace. This is the namespace that defines XML's common data types. The use of `s` is, of course, arbitrary and can be replaced with any other valid XML token.

Q WSDL seems very complicated. How do I create a document and not have errors?

A The odds are that you will never have to create WSDL documents by hand. Tools such as Visual Studio/ .NET create them for you. As stated previously, the purpose of learning WSDL is so that you can understand the documents when you encounter them and alter them if you absolutely need to.

Workshop

The Workshop is designed to help you review what you've learned in this hour and to point you ahead to the material that will be covered in future lessons.

Quiz

1. How would you declare an array of integers using XSD?

   A
```
<s:complexType name="ArrayofInt">
        <s:Sequence>
              <s:element minOccurs="0" maxOccurs="unbounded"
                name="int" type="s:int">
            </s:sequence>
        </s:complexType>
```

2. Where would you look to determine the return type of a method?

   A Start by looking at the `portType` for the Service and find output message of the method in question. Then, go to the message and look to see the type.

3. What are the two common attributes of the message element?

   A `name` and `element`

4. What are the three common ports encountered in WSDL documents?

   A SOAP, HttpGet, and HttpPost

5. What element actually contains the `type`, `message`, and `services` elements, that is, the root element?

   A `definitions`

Exercises

Work through the following WSDL file and see if you can figure out the name of the service, the number of its methods, and what each method actually looks like (that is, its name, arguments, and returns).

```
<?xml version="1.0" encoding="utf-8"?>
<definitions xmlns:s="http://www.w3.org/2001/XMLSchema"
xmlns:http="http://schemas.xmlsoap.org/wsdl/http/"
xmlns:mime="http://schemas.xmlsoap.org/wsdl/mime/"
xmlns:tm="http://microsoft.com/wsdl/mime/textMatching/"
xmlns:soap="http://schemas.xmlsoap.org/wsdl/soap/"
xmlns:soapenc="http://schemas.xmlsoap.org/soap/encoding/"
xmlns:s0="http://tempuri.org/" targetNamespace="http://tempuri.org/"
xmlns="http://schemas.xmlsoap.org/wsdl/">
  <types>
    <s:schema attributeFormDefault="qualified" elementFormDefault="qualified"
targetNamespace="http://tempuri.org/">
      <s:element name="Add">
        <s:complexType>
          <s:sequence>
            <s:element minOccurs="1" maxOccurs="1" name="iNum1" type="s:int" />
            <s:element minOccurs="1" maxOccurs="1" name="iNum2" type="s:int" />
          </s:sequence>
        </s:complexType>
      </s:element>
      <s:element name="AddResponse">
        <s:complexType>
          <s:sequence>
            <s:element minOccurs="1" maxOccurs="1" name="AddResult"
               type="s:int" />
          </s:sequence>
        </s:complexType>
      </s:element>
      <s:element name="Subtract">
        <s:complexType>
          <s:sequence>
```

```
            <s:element minOccurs="1" maxOccurs="1" name="iNum1" type="s:int" />
            <s:element minOccurs="1" maxOccurs="1" name="iNum2" type="s:int" />
          </s:sequence>
        </s:complexType>
      </s:element>
      <s:element name="SubtractResponse">
        <s:complexType>
          <s:sequence>
            <s:element minOccurs="1" maxOccurs="1" name="SubtractResult"
type="s:int" />
          </s:sequence>
        </s:complexType>
      </s:element>
      <s:element name="Multipl">
        <s:complexType>
          <s:sequence>
            <s:element minOccurs="1" maxOccurs="1" name="iNum1" type="s:int" />
            <s:element minOccurs="1" maxOccurs="1" name="iNum2" type="s:int" />
          </s:sequence>
        </s:complexType>
      </s:element>
      <s:element name="MultiplResponse">
        <s:complexType>
          <s:sequence>
            <s:element minOccurs="1" maxOccurs="1" name="MultiplResult"
type="s:int" />
          </s:sequence>
        </s:complexType>
      </s:element>
      <s:element name="Divided">
        <s:complexType>
          <s:sequence>
            <s:element minOccurs="1" maxOccurs="1" name="iNum1" type="s:int" />
            <s:element minOccurs="1" maxOccurs="1" name="iNum2" type="s:int" />
          </s:sequence>
        </s:complexType>
      </s:element>
      <s:element name="DividedResponse">
        <s:complexType>
          <s:sequence>
            <s:element minOccurs="1" maxOccurs="1" name="DividedResult"
type="s:int" />
          </s:sequence>
        </s:complexType>
      </s:element>
      <s:element name="int" type="s:int" />
    </s:schema>
  </types>
  <message name="AddSoapIn">
    <part name="parameters" element="s0:Add" />
  </message>
```

```
<message name="AddSoapOut">
  <part name="parameters" element="s0:AddResponse" />
</message>
<message name="SubtractSoapIn">
  <part name="parameters" element="s0:Subtract" />
</message>
<message name="SubtractSoapOut">
  <part name="parameters" element="s0:SubtractResponse" />
</message>
<message name="MultiplSoapIn">
  <part name="parameters" element="s0:Multipl" />
</message>
<message name="MultiplSoapOut">
  <part name="parameters" element="s0:MultiplResponse" />
</message>
<message name="DividedSoapIn">
  <part name="parameters" element="s0:Divided" />
</message>
<message name="DividedSoapOut">
  <part name="parameters" element="s0:DividedResponse" />
</message>
<message name="AddHttpGetIn">
  <part name="iNum1" type="s:string" />
  <part name="iNum2" type="s:string" />
</message>
<message name="AddHttpGetOut">
  <part name="Body" element="s0:int" />
</message>
<message name="SubtractHttpGetIn">
  <part name="iNum1" type="s:string" />
  <part name="iNum2" type="s:string" />
</message>
<message name="SubtractHttpGetOut">
  <part name="Body" element="s0:int" />
</message>
<message name="MultiplHttpGetIn">
  <part name="iNum1" type="s:string" />
  <part name="iNum2" type="s:string" />
</message>
<message name="MultiplHttpGetOut">
  <part name="Body" element="s0:int" />
</message>
<message name="DividedHttpGetIn">
  <part name="iNum1" type="s:string" />
  <part name="iNum2" type="s:string" />
</message>
<message name="DividedHttpGetOut">
  <part name="Body" element="s0:int" />
</message>
<message name="AddHttpPostIn">
  <part name="iNum1" type="s:string" />
```

3

```
    <part name="iNum2" type="s:string" />
  </message>
  <message name="AddHttpPostOut">
    <part name="Body" element="s0:int" />
  </message>
  <message name="SubtractHttpPostIn">
    <part name="iNum1" type="s:string" />
    <part name="iNum2" type="s:string" />
  </message>
  <message name="SubtractHttpPostOut">
    <part name="Body" element="s0:int" />
  </message>
  <message name="MultiplHttpPostIn">
    <part name="iNum1" type="s:string" />
    <part name="iNum2" type="s:string" />
  </message>
  <message name="MultiplHttpPostOut">
    <part name="Body" element="s0:int" />
  </message>
  <message name="DividedHttpPostIn">
    <part name="iNum1" type="s:string" />
    <part name="iNum2" type="s:string" />
  </message>
  <message name="DividedHttpPostOut">
    <part name="Body" element="s0:int" />
  </message>
  <portType name="Calc1Soap">
    <operation name="Add">
      <documentation>This function adds to integers</documentation>
      <input message="s0:AddSoapIn" />
      <output message="s0:AddSoapOut" />
    </operation>
    <operation name="Subtract">
      <input message="s0:SubtractSoapIn" />
      <output message="s0:SubtractSoapOut" />
    </operation>
    <operation name="Multipl">
      <input message="s0:MultiplSoapIn" />
      <output message="s0:MultiplSoapOut" />
    </operation>
    <operation name="Divided">
      <input message="s0:DividedSoapIn" />
      <output message="s0:DividedSoapOut" />
    </operation>
  </portType>
  <portType name="Calc1HttpGet">
    <operation name="Add">
      <documentation>This function adds to integers</documentation>
      <input message="s0:AddHttpGetIn" />
      <output message="s0:AddHttpGetOut" />
    </operation>
```

```
    <operation name="Subtract">
      <input message="s0:SubtractHttpGetIn" />
      <output message="s0:SubtractHttpGetOut" />
    </operation>
    <operation name="Multipl">
      <input message="s0:MultiplHttpGetIn" />
      <output message="s0:MultiplHttpGetOut" />
    </operation>
    <operation name="Divided">
      <input message="s0:DividedHttpGetIn" />
      <output message="s0:DividedHttpGetOut" />
    </operation>
  </portType>
  <portType name="Calc1HttpPost">
    <operation name="Add">
      <documentation>This function adds to integers</documentation>
      <input message="s0:AddHttpPostIn" />
      <output message="s0:AddHttpPostOut" />
    </operation>
    <operation name="Subtract">
      <input message="s0:SubtractHttpPostIn" />
      <output message="s0:SubtractHttpPostOut" />
    </operation>
    <operation name="Multipl">
      <input message="s0:MultiplHttpPostIn" />
      <output message="s0:MultiplHttpPostOut" />
    </operation>
    <operation name="Divided">
      <input message="s0:DividedHttpPostIn" />
      <output message="s0:DividedHttpPostOut" />
    </operation>
  </portType>
  <binding name="Calc1Soap" type="s0:Calc1Soap">
    <soap:binding transport="http://schemas.xmlsoap.org/soap/http"
style="document" />
    <operation name="Add">
      <soap:operation soapAction="http://tempuri.org/Add" style="document" />
      <input>
        <soap:body use="literal" />
      </input>
      <output>
        <soap:body use="literal" />
      </output>
    </operation>
    <operation name="Subtract">
      <soap:operation soapAction="http://tempuri.org/Subtract"
         style="document" />
      <input>
        <soap:body use="literal" />
      </input>
      <output>
```

3

```
      <soap:body use="literal" />
    </output>
  </operation>
  <operation name="Multipl">
    <soap:operation soapAction="http://tempuri.org/Multipl"
       style="document" />
    <input>
      <soap:body use="literal" />
    </input>
    <output>
      <soap:body use="literal" />
    </output>
  </operation>
  <operation name="Divided">
    <soap:operation soapAction="http://tempuri.org/Divided"
       style="document" />
    <input>
      <soap:body use="literal" />
    </input>
    <output>
      <soap:body use="literal" />
    </output>
  </operation>
</binding>
<binding name="Calc1HttpGet" type="s0:Calc1HttpGet">
  <http:binding verb="GET" />
  <operation name="Add">
    <http:operation location="/Add" />
    <input>
      <http:urlEncoded />
    </input>
    <output>
      <mime:mimeXml part="Body" />
    </output>
  </operation>
  <operation name="Subtract">
    <http:operation location="/Subtract" />
    <input>
      <http:urlEncoded />
    </input>
    <output>
      <mime:mimeXml part="Body" />
    </output>
  </operation>
  <operation name="Multipl">
    <http:operation location="/Multipl" />
    <input>
      <http:urlEncoded />
    </input>
    <output>
      <mime:mimeXml part="Body" />
```

```
    </output>
  </operation>
  <operation name="Divided">
    <http:operation location="/Divided" />
    <input>
      <http:urlEncoded />
    </input>
    <output>
      <mime:mimeXml part="Body" />
    </output>
  </operation>
</binding>
<binding name="Calc1HttpPost" type="s0:Calc1HttpPost">
  <http:binding verb="POST" />
  <operation name="Add">
    <http:operation location="/Add" />
    <input>
      <mime:content type="application/x-www-form-urlencoded" />
    </input>
    <output>
      <mime:mimeXml part="Body" />
    </output>
  </operation>
  <operation name="Subtract">
    <http:operation location="/Subtract" />
    <input>
      <mime:content type="application/x-www-form-urlencoded" />
    </input>
    <output>
      <mime:mimeXml part="Body" />
    </output>
  </operation>
  <operation name="Multipl">
    <http:operation location="/Multipl" />
    <input>
      <mime:content type="application/x-www-form-urlencoded" />
    </input>
    <output>
      <mime:mimeXml part="Body" />
    </output>
  </operation>
  <operation name="Divided">
    <http:operation location="/Divided" />
    <input>
      <mime:content type="application/x-www-form-urlencoded" />
    </input>
    <output>
      <mime:mimeXml part="Body" />
    </output>
  </operation>
</binding>
```

```
  <service name="Calc1">
    <port name="Calc1Soap" binding="s0:Calc1Soap">
      <soap:address location="http://localhost/FourFunctionCalc/Calc1.asmx" />
    </port>
    <port name="Calc1HttpGet" binding="s0:Calc1HttpGet">
      <http:address location="http://localhost/FourFunctionCalc/Calc1.asmx" />
    </port>
    <port name="Calc1HttpPost" binding="s0:Calc1HttpPost">
      <http:address location="http://localhost/FourFunctionCalc/Calc1.asmx" />
    </port>
  </service>
</definitions>
```

A: The service, called `Calc1`, exposes four methods:

```
Add(iNum1 as Int, iNum2 as Int) as Int
Subtract(iNum1 as Int, iNum2 as Int) as Int
Multipl(iNum1 as Int, iNum2 as Int) as Int
Divided(iNum1 as Int, iNum2 as Int) as Int
```

HOUR 4

Remote Procedure Calls with SOAP

Now that you've had a primer on XML, you'll learn about a useful implementation for the language—Simple Object Access Protocol, or in other words, SOAP. SOAP is used to relay instructions and data back and forth between an XML Web service and its clients.

In this hour, you will gain a comprehensive understanding of what SOAP is, how it works, and how you're going to use it in your XML Web services. It will be very helpful in later hours to recognize and understand SOAP, so you'll gain a strong background here.

In this hour we will discuss the following:

- What SOAP is and how it works with XML
- What the different parts of SOAP are
- How to encode data in a SOAP message
- What SOAP messages look like in action

What Is SOAP?

Many people hear about SOAP, and a magical technology comes to mind—similar to the images XML conjured up just a few years ago. Most people, however, are still confused about SOAP's (and sometimes XML's) application.

Recall that XML is a way to easily transfer data—almost *any* kind of data—across a network or the Internet. Because XML is plain text, it can be sent anywhere that plain HTML can, which is virtually everywhere—often even through firewalls. This means that you can share your data with anyone, no matter where they are. This is a very important part of SOAP.

The Simple Object Access Protocol, as its name implies, is a way to easily access objects across a network. That object can be anything from an application, such as Microsoft Word, to a stock quotes database. SOAP is a protocol that allows two objects, no matter where they are, to communicate with each other.

So how are XML and SOAP tied together? XML is the language that SOAP speaks in. Because XML can send data virtually anywhere, it makes sense that a protocol that needs to converse between objects that could potentially be located anywhere uses XML. These objects create all types of information that need to be exchanged, such as commands, data, images, and so on. XML is versatile enough that it can handle all of these data types.

Why Do We Need SOAP?

It may seem that XML is capable of just about anything. It can send data across the Internet, so why do we need another protocol, such as SOAP? Isn't SOAP just duplicating XML's functionality?

Imagine the situation in two complementary technologies— HTTP and HTML. You know that HTML is used to build Web pages using a set of tags that provide formatting for plain text. If you wanted your friend to see your HTML pages, you could simply send them via e-mail or on a disk.

However, we all know that the Internet does not work by people exchanging disks with HTML pages. There has to be a method so that a computer can send you an HTML page when you type its name into a browser, such as Internet Explorer. This is the job of the HyperText Transfer Protocol (HTTP). HTTP provides a communication protocol for one computer to send HTML to another computer across the Internet. Without HTTP, you couldn't view HTML pages over the Internet.

Similarly, XML provides a way to "mark up" plain text so that it is more meaningful. One application can generate as much data or XML as it wants, but without a person feeding the results to another application, the two wouldn't be able to communicate with each other unless specifically built to do so (and it's near impossible to build all applications so that they can speak with one another).

SOAP steps in and provides a method for those applications to communicate. It represents all communications as XML. With SOAP, one application can view another across the Internet. Figure 4.1 illustrates this concept.

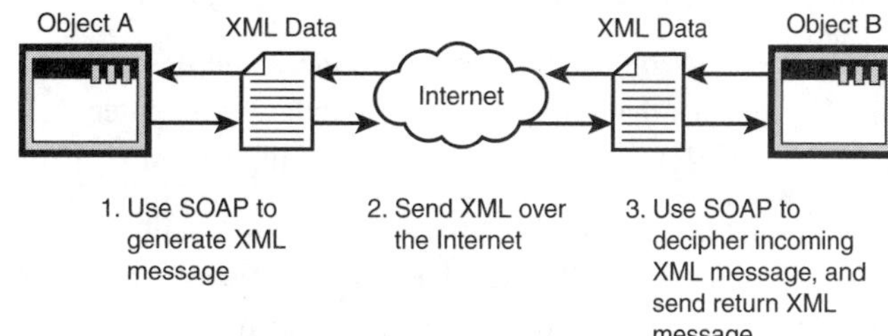

FIGURE 4.1
XML is used to represent the data and messages, but SOAP is used to send/receive them.

XML is great at representing data, just as HTML is great at formatting text to look like a Web page. SOAP and HTTP allow these two languages to be put to use delivering information.

Note that SOAP isn't necessarily the only application of XML. It simply provides the mechanism for two objects to communicate. Someone could potentially come up with another protocol that also uses XML to represent its data, but for the purposes of XML Web services, SOAP is the only protocol of interest.

Also, note that SOAP is actually sent over the HTTP protocol as well. Thus it can be sent anywhere HTML can.

It's difficult to visualize these concepts in one's head. You'll take a look at examples of SOAP using XML later this hour.

What Was There Before SOAP?

The idea of having different objects and applications communicate with one another is certainly not new. People have wanted to do this deceivingly simple task since the early days of computers. It's only been in the past decade, with the rise of the Internet, that the scope of this task has changed to include global applications. The problem has been finding a universally acceptable format that can be used anywhere, without limits on platforms or networks.

The Component Object Model (COM) is a widespread protocol used to enable interoperation between applications. With it, applications can share data and execute each other's functions. Much of the foundations of Microsoft Windows are based on COM interfaces.

ActiveX is another protocol similar to COM. This is how, for example, much of Microsoft Office provides the cross-application data sharing. Microsoft Word can contain an Excel spreadsheet without Microsoft Excel being open.

There are several problems, however, with these and other protocols. First, they are proprietary. This means that only Microsoft Windows computers can use COM and ActiveX, which leaves out Unix, Macs, and other operating systems—hardly a universal solution.

A second limitation is that these protocols were not built with the Internet in mind. This means they inherently don't support accessing objects across a network—your computer's copy of Microsoft Word cannot use your friend's computer's copy of Excel.

The third largest limitation is that the types of communication messages that protocols such as COM and ActiveX generate are very complex and would have trouble being carried over any medium other than what they were specifically built for. It would be difficult if not impossible to send COM messages over the Internet, especially through firewalls.

SOAP addresses all of these issues. It is standard and nonproprietary, meaning it can be used by any computer platform or operating system. It was built specifically for communication across the Internet, and because it uses XML to represent its messages, it can travel across nearly any medium.

Now that you've got a firm background on SOAP, let's take a look at the technical aspects, and how you'll be able to use it.

What's in SOAP?

According to the official SOAP specification (`http://www.w3.org/TR/SOAP`), there are three main parts of SOAP: an envelope; the encoding rules, which govern how data and commands are represented as XML; and a means for SOAP to communicate with its objects, specifically via the request and response model. The third part is usually in the form of HTTP headers (a set of instructions at the beginning of the message). Together, these components make up a SOAP message.

It is helpful to think of a SOAP message as an actual letter (see Figure 4.2). The envelope defines what the message is—when you receive an envelope in the mail, you know it's a letter. Likewise, when an object receives a SOAP envelope, it knows to expect an encoded XML letter.

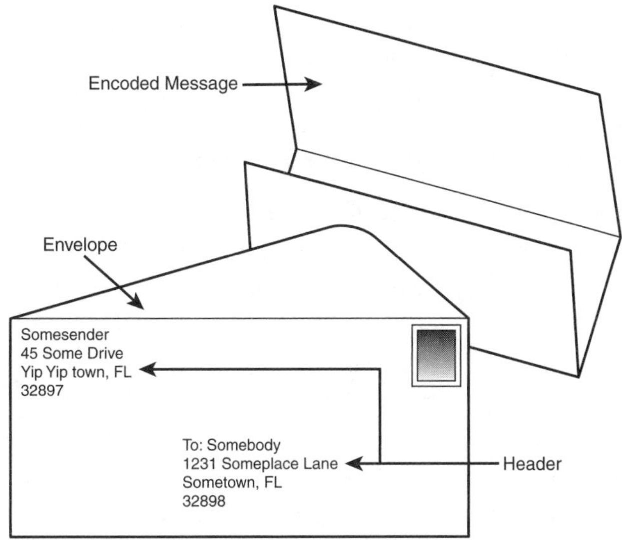

FIGURE 4.2
A SOAP message consists of an envelope, an encoded message, and headers.

The encoded message is the XML data that is to be sent, be it commands to an object or returned data. Finally, the header provides instructions for the sender and receiver objects, just as address labels provide instructions to the Postal Service.

Let's take a look at each of these items in the next few sections.

The Envelope

Let's look at a sample SOAP message, shown in Listing 4.1. On line 1 you can see that the SOAP envelope is simply an XML tag, `<SOAP:Envelope>` (literally, the SOAP envelope is the word "envelope"). This provides the wrapper for the rest of the SOAP message and lets whoever receives this message know what they're dealing with.

LISTING 4.1 A Simple SOAP Message

```
1: <SOAP:Envelope
2:    xmlns:SOAP="http://schemas.xmlsoap.org/soap/envelope/">
3:    <SOAP:Body>
4:       <book>
5:          <name>Sam's Teach Yourself XML Web Services in 24
```

continues

LISTING 4.1 Continued

```
6:                Hours</name>
7:          </book>
8:      </SOAP:Body>
9:  </SOAP:Envelope>
```

Line 2 describes the namespace used for the SOAP envelope. Just as you provided namespaces for XML messages in Hour 2, "An XML Primer," you do so with SOAP messages as well. You should never have a reason to change the namespace from `http://schemas.xmlsoap.org/soap/envelope`.

Additionally, you must specify the `<SOAP:Body>` tag as part of the envelope. Inside this tag is where your encoded message will go (lines 4–7)—but more on that in the section, "The SOAP Body." Finally, on lines 8 and 9 we close the `<SOAP:Envelope>` and `<SOAP:Body>` tags.

As you can see, the SOAP envelope is very simple. You'll create your own later this hour in "A Simple SOAP Application," but for now, let's move on to the headers.

Headers

There are two different types of headers SOAP uses for its messages. The first is a standard HTTP header that's also used for retrieving or sending HTML pages. This is appropriate, as SOAP messages are also relayed via HTTP. An example is shown in Listing 4.2.

LISTING 4.2 HTTP SOAP Headers

```
POST /MyWebService HTTP/1.1
Host: MyHost
Content-Type: text/xml; charset="utf-8"
Content-Length: xxxx

<SOAP:Envelope>
   ...
</SOAP:Envelope>
```

The HTTP header in Listing 4.2 is typical when using an Http-POST to send a SOAP message. The server would respond with a header as follows:

```
HTTP/1.1 200 OK
Content-Type: text/xml; charset="utf-8"
Content-Length: xxxx
```

It would also include any SOAP or XML message it needs to send.

The second type of header, and probably more useful to you as a developer, is known specifically as a SOAP header. This header is used to convey additional information that isn't included in the body of the message or in the HTTP headers. Listing 4.3 shows an example SOAP message with a SOAP header.

LISTING 4.3 Using SOAP Headers

```
1:  <SOAP:Envelope>
2:     <SOAP:Header mustUnderstand>
3:        <authHeader>
4:           password
5:        </authHeader>
6:     </SOAP:Header>
7:     <SOAP:Body>
8:        <executeFunction />
9:     </SOAP:Body>
10: </SOAP:Envelope>
```

The `<SOAP:Header>` tag goes inside the envelope along with the `<SOAP:Body>` tag. In this case, the SOAP header has an element `authHeader`, which supplies a password, as shown on line 4. This password can be used by the receiving object to verify that the sending object has the necessary permissions to do whatever it wants to do.

The optional `mustUnderstand` attribute, shown on line 2, tells the receiving object that is must process the header—it cannot ignore the information contained within. This is useful in this situation where a password must be evaluated before anything else occurs.

You'll examine SOAP headers again in Hour 18, "Security and the Soap Toolkit."

The SOAP Body

Finally, the SOAP body contains the XML message that we wanted to relay from the beginning. You've seen a few examples already, but let's look at another, shown in Listing 4.4.

LISTING 4.4 Examining the SOAP Body

```
<SOAP:Envelope>
   <SOAP:Body>
      <multiply>
         <valueA>8</valueA>
         <valueB>9</valueB>
      </multiply>
   </SOAP:Body>
</SOAP:Envelope>
```

Imagine that you've built an XML Web service that simply multiplies two numbers and returns the results. Listing 3.4 shows the SOAP message that would be generated by your XML Web service client to initiate the calculation (you'll take a look at the service's response to the client in a moment).

On line 3, inside the <SOAP:Body> element, you have another element named multiply. This is presumably the name of the function in your service that calculates the product of two numbers. The multiply element has two subelements, valueA and valueB, which represent the numbers to be multiplied (8 and 9 in this case).

With this simple SOAP body, you've told an XML Web service to execute a function and supplied it with values as well. In this way, you can instruct virtually any XML Web service to perform whatever action you want (provided that the service allows you to do so).

This simple method for accessing remote objects and applications is the beauty of SOAP. Imagine a message, such as that shown in Listing 4.5, that would instruct Microsoft Word to open a document.

LISTING 4.5 Executing a Word Function

```
1:  <SOAP:Envelope>
2:     <SOAP:Body>
3:        <OpenFile>
4:           <filename>/WebService/chapter4.doc</filename>
5:           <readonly>true</readonly>
6:        </OpenFile>
7:     </SOAP:Body>
8:  </SOAP:Envelope>
```

On line 3 you instruct Word to execute the OpenFile function, passing it a filename (line 4) to open as read-only (line 5).

At the time of this writing, there is no Microsoft Word XML Web service, so the SOAP message shown in Listing 4.5 won't actually do anything.

The XML Web service's response to Listing 4.4 would look like Listing 4.6.

LISTING 4.6 The Web Service Response

```
1:  <SOAP:Envelope>
2:     <SOAP:Body>
3:        <multiplyResponse>
4:           72
5:        </multiplyResponse>
6:     </SOAP:Body>
7:  </SOAP:Envelope>
```

The response is very simple, and it always follows a pattern. Note on lines 3 and 5 that the only element in the body that the service returns is the name of the function that was executed (`multiply`, line 3 of Listing 4.4) followed by the word `Response`. Inside the `multiplyResponse` element is simply the value of 8*9, or 72.

In the next section, you'll look at how to return more complex types of data.

Representing Data with SOAP

Using what you've learned of SOAP and the XML so far, you can build useful SOAP messages that any XML Web service could understand. However, what happens when you need to send or return more complex data, such an arrays, or if you simply want to strongly type your data? SOAP supports encoding of data, so that you can more precisely deliver the information as it's meant to be.

Let's take a look at a simple example, using Listing 4.4 and the multiplication XML Web service again. Suppose your client takes the two number inputs from a user. Ideally, everything should be fine as we've already described it. However, what happens if the user mistakenly types in a character instead of a number? The XML Web service obviously cannot multiply a number and a letter. In this case, we should strongly type the values we send in; in other words, you want the XML Web service to make no mistakes interpreting the data you send—it should always be an integer.

To encode data, you'll use a namespace that contains definitions of the most common data types. Let's take a look at a modified version of Listing 4.4.

LISTING 4.7 Using Encoding Rules

```
<SOAP:Envelope
   xmlns:SOAP-ENV="http://schemas.xmlsoap.org/soap/envelope/"
   xmlns:SOAP-ENC="http://schemas.xmlsoap.org/soap/encoding/"
   xmlns:xsd="http://www.w3.org/1999/XMLSchema/"
   xmlns:xsi="http://www.w3.org/1999/XMLSchema/instance/"
```

continues

Listing 4.7 Continued

```
6:      SOAP-ENV:EncodingStyle="http://schemas.xmlsoap.org/soap/encoding/">
7:      <SOAP:Body>
8:         <multiply>
9:            <valueA xsi:type="xsd:integer">8</valueA>
10:            <valueB xsi:type="xsd:integer">9</valueB>
11:         </multiply>
12:      </SOAP:Body>
13:   </SOAP:Envelope>
```

There are a few new lines in this listing, but nothing too complex. First, on lines 2–6, you specify additional namespaces that need to be used so that you can encode your data. Again, these are standard values, and you usually won't have to change them.

The only other change is on lines 9 and 10. We now have the attribute `xsi:type="xsd:integer"` in the `valueA` and `valueB` elements. This simply tells us that these values are integers and should not be interpreted otherwise. When the XML Web service receives this SOAP message, it knows what types of data should be in the `valueA` and `valueB` elements, and if they don't match, the values will be rejected.

The XML namespace provides quite a few data types. For instance, if we wanted to pass characters instead of numbers, we could change line 9 to read:

```
<valueA xsi:type="xsd:string">8</valueA>
```

The response from the XML Web service would look like Listing 4.8.

Listing 4.8 A Response Using Encoding Rules

```
1:  <SOAP:Envelope
2:      xmlns:SOAP-ENV="http://schemas.xmlsoap.org/soap/envelope/"
3:      xmlns:SOAP-ENC="http://schemas.xmlsoap.org/soap/encoding/"
4:      xmlns:xsd="http://www.w3.org/1999/XMLSchema/"
5:      xmlns:xsi="http://www.w3.org/1999/XMLSchema/instance/"
6:      SOAP-ENV:EncodingStyle="http://schemas.xmlsoap.org/soap/encoding/">
7:      <SOAP:Body>
8:         <multiplyResponse xsi:type="xsd:integer">
9:            72
10:         </multiplyResponse>
11:      </SOAP:Body>
12:   </SOAP:Envelope>
```

Again, the only change from the previous response is the addition of the namespaces on lines 2–6 and the `xsi:type="xsd:integer"` attribute on line 8.

What if you need to represent a more complex data type? Let's imagine the multiplication service again, but instead of returning an integer, it returns an array including the product, quotient, sum, and difference of the values. The response would change to Listing 4.9.

LISTING 4.9 Returning an Encoded Array of Values

```
1:  <SOAP:Envelope
2:     xmlns:SOAP-ENV="http://schemas.xmlsoap.org/soap/envelope/"
3:     xmlns:SOAP-ENC="http://schemas.xmlsoap.org/soap/encoding/"
4:     xmlns:xsd="http://www.w3.org/1999/XMLSchema/"
5:     xmlns:xsi="http://www.w3.org/1999/XMLSchema/instance/"
6:     SOAP-ENV:EncodingStyle="http://schemas.xmlsoap.org/soap/encoding/">
7:     <SOAP:Body>
8:        <multiplyResponse xsi:type="SOAP-ENC:Array"
9:           SOAP-ENC:arrayType="Item[]">
9:           <item>
10:             <name xsi:type="xsd:string">product</name>
11:             <value xsi:type="xsd:integer">72</value>
12:          </item>
13:           <item>
14:             <name xsi:type="xsd:string">quotient</name>
15:             <value xsi:type="xsd:integer">1</value>
16:          </item>
17:           <item>
18:             <name xsi:type="xsd:string">sum</name>
19:             <value xsi:type="xsd:integer">17</value>
20:          </item>
21:           <item>
22:             <name xsi:type="xsd:string">difference</name>
23:             <value xsi:type="xsd:integer">-1</value>
24:          </item>
25:       </multiplyResponse>
26:    </SOAP:Body>
27: </SOAP:Envelope>
```


On line 8, the response now has a type of `SOAP-ENC:Array`, and line 9 specifies the names by which the array elements are referred to—`Item`, in this case. Each element of the array is then contained in an `item` element, with `name` and `value` pairs to represent each index. Again, each value is encoded in its proper data type.

On line 15, you might notice something a bit odd. The quotient of 8 and 9 is approximately .8889, yet the response returns 1. This is because you've encoded the value as an integer, and an integer cannot have decimal places. Therefore, the value was rounded to 1.

Thus, you can see that SOAP together with XML can represent quite a large number of data types. You'll see how to use them to return database results in Hours 12, "Passing `DataSets` from XML Web Services," and 13, "Consuming `DataSets` in XML Web Services."

A Simple SOAP Application

Now that you've got the basics of SOAP, let's build a simple application that will send SOAP messages back and forth from a client to a server. And what better way to examine SOAP messages than to look at an actual XML Web service that generates them. Listing 4.10 shows a simple calculator XML Web service. Save it as `calculator.asmx`, and view it in your browser. Figure 4.3 shows the output.

LISTING 4.10 A Calculator XML Web Service

```
<%@ WebService Language="VB" Class="Calculator" %>

Imports System.Web.Services

public Class Calculator : Inherits WebService
   <WebMethod()> Public Function Add(intA As Integer, _
      intB As Integer) As Integer
       Return(intA + intB)
   End Function
 End Class
```

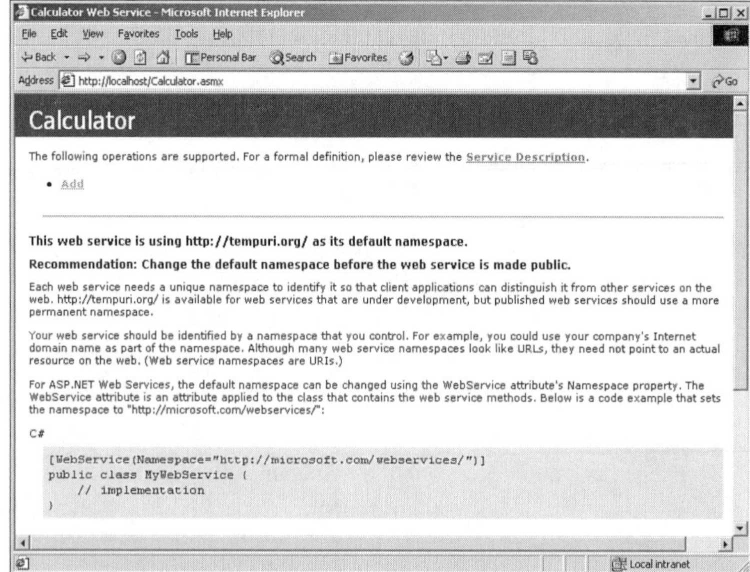

FIGURE 4.3
Viewing an XML Web service in your browser.

We're not going to go over much of the code—we'll save that until Hour 7, "Building the Four Function Calculator." For now, just know that this XML Web service does one thing: add and return two integers.

Figure 4.3 provides a lot of interesting information, especially if you want to build a client for this service. Click the `Add` link near the top of the page (this is the name of the service's only function), and you'll see Figure 4.4.

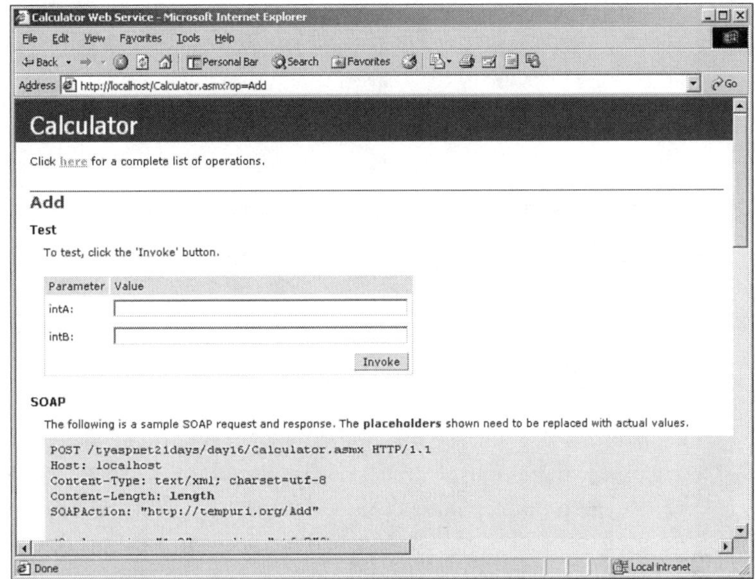

FIGURE 4.4
The XML Web service description.

Here you can actually test out the service. Enter two numbers in the text box provided, and press the `Invoke` button. You'll see the XML response generated by the XML Web service. It amounts to the following code:

```
<?xml version="1.0" encoding="utf-8" ?>
<int xmlns="http://tempuri.org/">17</int>
```

You can see that it returns a very simple XML document with the sum of the two values you entered (8 and 9 in our case).

Scroll down a bit in the window shown in Figure 4.4, and you'll see a sample SOAP message provided by the service. This code is shown in Listing 4.11.

LISTING 4.11 The SOAP Message from the Calculator Service

```
1:  POST /tyaspnet21days/day16/Calculator.asmx HTTP/1.1
2:  Host: localhost
3:  Content-Type: text/xml; charset=utf-8
4:  Content-Length: length
5:  SOAPAction: "http://tempuri.org/Add"
6:
7:  <?xml version="1.0" encoding="utf-8"?>
8:  <soap:Envelope xmlns:xsi="http://www.w3.org/2001/XMLSchema-instance"
9:    xmlns:xsd="http://www.w3.org/2001/XMLSchema"
10:   xmlns:soap="http://schemas.xmlsoap.org/soap/envelope/">
11:   <soap:Body>
12:     <Add xmlns="http://tempuri.org/">
13:       <intA>int</intA>
14:       <intB>int</intB>
15:     </Add>
16:   </soap:Body>
17: </soap:Envelope>
```

Lines 1–5 show the HTTP header. You should be familiar with this by now. The `length` value on line 4 is a placeholder that is substituted with an actual value when the XML Web service is in action.

On lines 8 and 9 you see the familiar `<SOAP:Envelope>` element, along with several namespace definitions. On line 11, you'll notice the `<SOAP:Body>` element, and on lines 12–15 you'll find the body of the message. Line 12 is the name of the XML Web service function that will be called, `Add`, and lines 13 and 14 show the values that will be passed to that function. Again, `intA` and `intB` are placeholders for values that will be inserted when you call the service.

All of the SOAP parts that you've learned about this hour are there. You'll notice that there is an additional namespace used in several places in the message, `http://tempuri.org/`. This namespace doesn't actually exist; rather, the service inserts it so that any undefined element in the message will belong to a namespace. This isn't necessary, but it adheres to strict SOAP guidelines, which is always a good thing to do.

Feel free to modify the service shown in Listing 4.10 to see how the SOAP messages change.

Summary

You've learned quite a bit about SOAP in this hour. SOAP is a protocol that allows remote objects to communicate with each other via XML. It allows commands and data to be exchanged easily, which is a key requirement of XML Web services.

A SOAP message consists of three parts: a header, an envelope, and a body. The envelope is simply an XML wrapper to let the receiving object know what it's looking at. It contains a `<SOAP:Envelope>` and a `<SOAP:Body>` tag.

There are two types of headers: HTTP and SOAP headers. The former is used to instruct HTTP how to send the SOAP message, whereas the latter is used to provide additional information not sent in the SOAP body. SOAP headers are represented in XML with the `<SOAP:Header>` tag.

Finally, the SOAP body is the actual XML message that you want to send. The data can be encoded to bring added versatility to your messages.

Q&A

Q Is SOAP secure?

A Not necessarily. It is sent as plain text, so anyone who intercepts the message can view its contents, just like XML; there is nothing to prevent this unless you build an algorithm to encrypt the contents.

You can, however, implement SOAP headers so that an XML Web service is secure. That is, so that unauthorized users or objects are unable to access its functionality.

Q Do I have to write SOAP messages every time I use an XML Web service?

A Fortunately, no. The XML Web services that you'll likely be using will generate the SOAP commands automatically, saving you a lot of headache. When you start to build your first XML Web service in Hour 7, "Building the Four Function Calculator," you'll see how this is done.

Q Where can I get more technical details on SOAP?

A The first place to look would be the official specification at `http://www.w3.org/TR/SOAP`.

There are quite a few tutorials online that explain SOAP to varying degrees. `http://www.soaprpc.com/tutorials/` lists quite a few good ones.

Workshop

The Workshop is designed to help you review what you've learned in this hour and to point you ahead to the material that will be covered in future hours.

Quiz

1. What does SOAP stand for?

   A Simple Object Access Protocol

2. (True or False) HTTP messages are sent over the SOAP protocol.

   A False. SOAP messages are sent via HTTP.

3. What is the standard namespace for the SOAP envelope?

   A `http://schemas.xmlsoap.org/soap/envelope/`

4. What namespaces are required to encode your data?

   A `SOAP-ENV="http://schemas.xmlsoap.org/soap/envelope/"`

   `SOAP-ENC="http://schemas.xmlsoap.org/soap/encoding/"`

   `xsd="http://www.w3.org/1999/XMLSchema/"`

   `xsi="http://www.w3.org/1999/XMLSchema/instance/"`

   `SOAP-ENV:EncodingStyle="http://schemas.xmlsoap.org/soap/encoding/"`

5. What is the attribute that makes processing of a SOAP header required?

   A `mustUnderstand`

6. (True or False) You can send complex data types over SOAP.

   A True.

Exercises

1. Write an example of a SOAP message, including an HTTP header, that executes the "`SaveDocument`" function, sending a filename as a parameter.

   A

```
POST /MyWebService HTTP/1.1
Host: MyHost
Content-Type: text/xml; charset="utf-8"
Content-Length: xxxx

<SOAP:Envelope>
   <SOAP:Body>
      <SaveDocument>
         <filename>myfile.doc</filename>
      </SaveDocument>
   </SOAP:Body>
</SOAP:Envelope>
```

2. Encode the message from Exercise 1.

A

```
<SOAP:Envelope
   xmlns:SOAP-ENV="http://schemas.xmlsoap.org/soap/envelope/"
   xmlns:SOAP-ENC="http://schemas.xmlsoap.org/soap/encoding/"
   xmlns:xsd="http://www.w3.org/1999/XMLSchema/"
   xmlns:xsi="http://www.w3.org/1999/XMLSchema/instance/"
   SOAP-ENV:EncodingStyle="http://schemas.xmlsoap.org/soap/encoding/">
   <SOAP:Body>
      <SaveDocument>
         <filename xsi:type="xsd:string">mydocument.doc</filename>
      </SaveDocument>
    </SOAP:Body>
 </SOAP:Envelope>
```

3. Write the encoded response for the Exercise 1. It should return true or false depending on if the save was successful.

A

```
<SOAP:Envelope
   xmlns:SOAP-ENV="http://schemas.xmlsoap.org/soap/envelope/"
   xmlns:SOAP-ENC="http://schemas.xmlsoap.org/soap/encoding/"
   xmlns:xsd="http://www.w3.org/1999/XMLSchema/"
   xmlns:xsi="http://www.w3.org/1999/XMLSchema/instance/"
   SOAP-ENV:EncodingStyle="http://schemas.xmlsoap.org/soap/encoding/">
   <SOAP:Body>
      <SaveDocumentResponse xsi:type="xsd:Boolean" >true
      </SaveDocumentResponse>
       </multiplyResponse>
    </SOAP:Body>
 </SOAP:Envelope>
```

HOUR 5

Finding XML Web Services with UDDI and DISCO

Before you can use an XML Web service, you have to find it. There are many different ways to do so, and in this hour we'll take a look at several.

UDDI (or Universal Description, Discovery, and Integration) is a standard method for deploying and finding XML Web services. *DISCO* (or Discovery) is a tool bundled with the .NET Framework that provides a more hands-on method for finding an XML Web service. In this hour, you'll take a look at using the service description directly to find the information you need.

In this hour we will discuss the following:

- What it means to discover an XML Web service
- What UDDI is and how to use it to find services
- How to use the `disco.exe` tool

Finding an XML Web Service

Let's say you've created an XML Web service that performs calculations (similar to the one you saw at the end of Hour 4). You've made the service available for use on the Internet by placing it on a server somewhere—a process known as publishing the XML Web service (more on that in Hour 22, "Publishing an XML Web Service"). Using SOAP, any client, be it another XML Web service, a desktop application, or even a human, can take advantage of the functionality your service provides.

However, we're making a large assumption that the intended client knows about your service in the first place. For example, suppose you were in the mood to dine at a Sicilian restaurant, and there was only one such restaurant in your vicinity. If that restaurant never advertised or was not listed in the Yellow Pages, you might not know about it and would miss out on the experience.

The same principle goes for an XML Web service. Without some form of "advertising," clients would never know one exists.

Fortunately, clients have ways to find services without having to read ads in the Sunday paper. Finding an XML Web service is a process known as *discovery,* and there are several different ways to do so.

Discovery is an optional process; if a client already knows about a specific XML Web service, there is no need to go through discovery. You'll examine this scenario later this hour in "Using the Service Description."

Before we examine the different discovery methods, let's first take a look at what a client needs to know about a service.

What We Need to Know

Recall from Hour 3, "Defining XML Web Service Operations with WSDL," that an XML Web service uses WSDL to provide a description—in XML—of its functionality. Figure 5.1 shows what this service description looks like in the Web browser.

This contains all the information a client needs to know about a service. Discovery, then, is the process by which a client tries to find this service description.

To find this description, you need the URL of the service itself—`http://www.myserver.com/services/calculator.asmx`, for example. Typing this URL into the browser would produce something like Figure 5.1, which is very user-friendly but not very client-application-friendly. By tacking the string `"?WSDL"` on the end of the URL, the client can view the XML description directly, as shown in Figure 5.2.

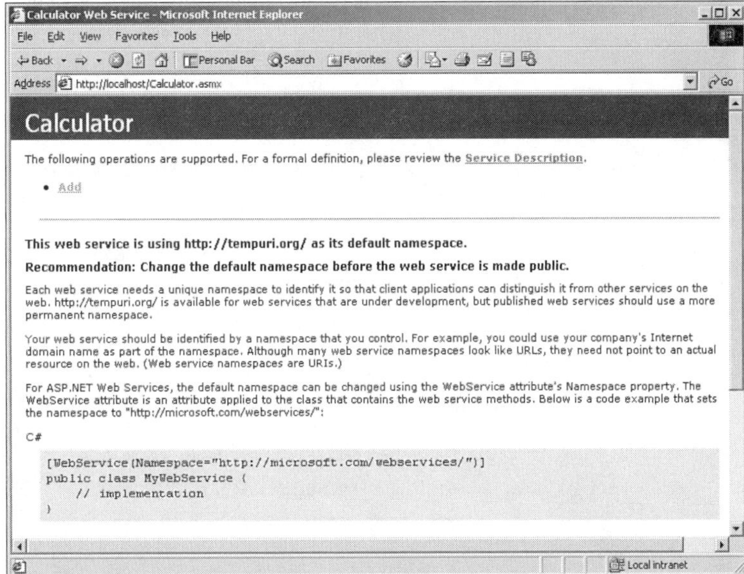

FIGURE 5.1
The service description page.

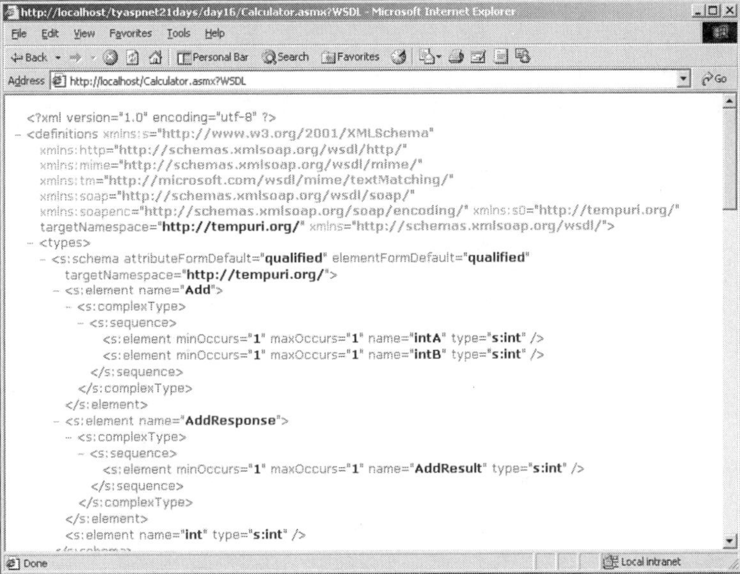

FIGURE 5.2
The XML service description page.

Glancing through this XML description, you'll see elements that describe the data the service expects and returns. You'll also notice several additional elements named `AddSoapIn`, `AddSoapOut`, `AddHttpGetIn`, `AddHttpGetOut`, and so on. These elements describe the different methods of accessing the service, via SOAP, HTTP-GET, and HTTP-POST.

Using this information, the client has everything it needs to know to consume the XML Web service. There are different ways of obtaining the URL of the service, and the next few sections will describe them in detail.

Using UDDI

The UDDI specification is a set of rules that tells XML Web services and their clients how to look for each other—essentially, rules for searching. With all the millions of Web sites and businesses all over the Internet, you can imagine that a good search engine is the only way you'll be able to find what you're looking for easily and accurately.

UDDI provides a standard way for services and clients to interact with this specialized search engine. Many businesses are now using these rules to not only list the XML Web services they provide, but also provide more information about the business itself.

As you may have guessed, the UDDI rules are simply XML schemas that define how discovery messages should be formatted. You can access the XML schema at `http://www.uddi.org/schema/uddi_v2.xsd`. Figure 5.3 shows the schema in Internet Explorer.

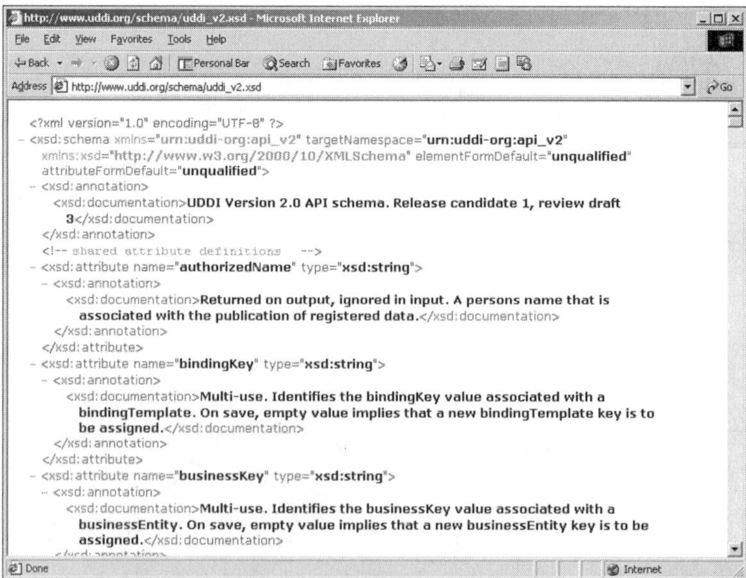

FIGURE 5.3
The UDDI specification schema.

There are elements to describe the business's name, the type of service it offers, and the names and URLs of those services, along with gobs of other information. Thankfully, you don't have to build any of this information—not yet, anyway. For now, let's take a look at how to put UDDI to good use.

The UDDI Business Registry

The UDDI Web site (`www.uddi.org`) provides a registry for businesses that wish to expose their services—an XML Web service search engine of sorts. Figure 5.4 shows the home page of this site.

FIGURE 5.4
The UDDI Web site.

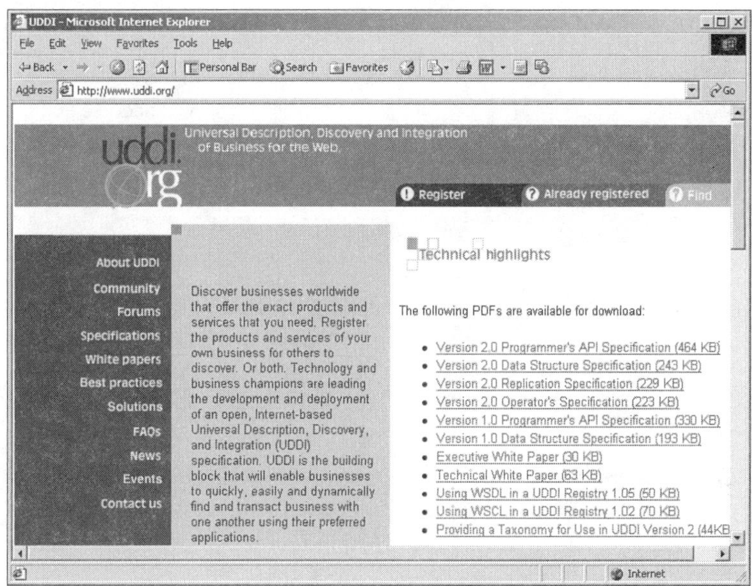

You can register your business and its services to allow other organizations to find you, but we'll skip that step for now. Right now, we're interested in searching for XML Web services, not registering them.

> As you will see in Hour 22, registering your service is simply a matter of visiting `www.uddi.org` and clicking the "Register" link. The entire process doesn't take more than a few minutes.

Currently, only IBM and Microsoft provide searchable directories, or nodes, of services. This doesn't mean that the only services you find will be from Microsoft or IBM, but rather that these two companies provide the actual search engines. Searching Microsoft's node for "calculator" brings up three XML Web services, as shown in Figure 5.5.

FIGURE 5.5
Searching for a calculator XML Web service.

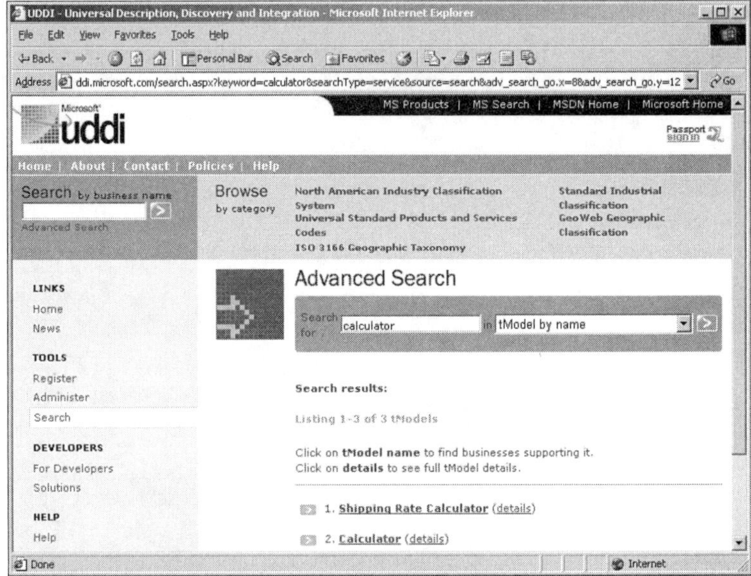

The results are XML Web services available for use. Clicking the `"details"` links will give you more information about each service directly from the UDDI documents. For example, the first result returned in Figure 5.5 is a service that returns shipping rates for various locations around the United States.

Once you've found the service you were looking for, you can get the URL and use it in your XML Web service client, and that's all there is to it! UDDI provides a very easy way to find the services you're looking for. Next, you'll learn about a more hands-on method of finding XML Web services.

The UDDI business directory actually uses SOAP and XML Web services itself to provide the search features for you.

Using DISCO

Aside from UDDI, XML Web services can advertise themselves using discovery documents. We'll examine these documents more in Hour 22, "Publishing an XML Web Service," but for now let's just look at a sample, shown in Listing 5.1.

LISTING 5.1 A Sample Discovery Document

```
1:  <?xml version="1.0" ?>
2:  <disco:discovery xmlns:disco="http://schemas.xmlsoap.org/disco"
3:     xmlns:scl="http://schemas.xmlsoap.org/disco/scl">
4:     <wsdl:contractRef ref="http://localhost/calculator.asmx?WSDL"/>
5:  </disco:discovery>
```

The discovery document is just another XML file with links to an XML Web service description, shown on line 4. Let's save this file as `service.disco` on your Web server's root directory. We'll get back to it in a moment.

Assuming you know the URL of this discovery document, you can use the `disco.exe` tool provided by the Microsoft .NET Framework SDK to retrieve and parse the information. This tool examines the `.disco` file on a Web server and lets the client know what services are available. Let's first take a look at the syntax of this tool, shown in Table 5.1.

TABLE 5.1 The `disco.exe` Tool

Parameter	*Description*
`/out:`*`location`*	The location to save the results of the operation. The default value is the current directory. Optional.
`/username:`*`user`*	The username used to connect to the server. Optional.
`/password:`*`password`*	The password used to connect to the server. Optional.
`/domain:`*`domain`*	The domain to use when connecting to the server. Optional.
`/nosave`	Does not save the resulting output to files.
`url`	The URL of the `.disco` file. Required.

Thus, the command to connect to the `.disco` file shown in Listing 5.1 would look like

```
Disco /out:c:\temp http://localhost/service.disco
```

Type this command at the command prompt. You should see the results shown in Figure 5.6.

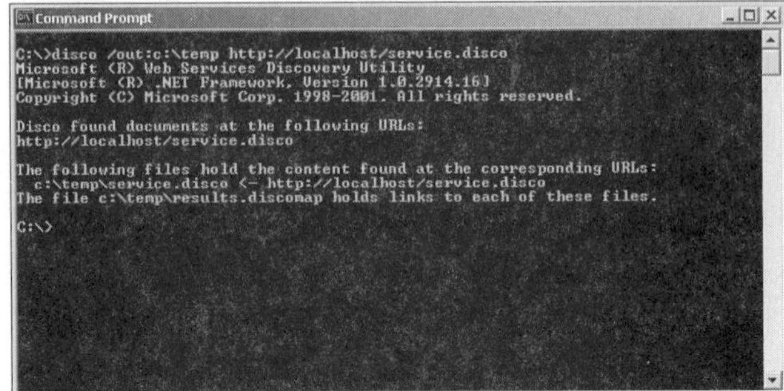

FIGURE 5.6
The results of the `disco.exe` *tool.*

Let's take a look at the files that were output from this tool. The first, `c:\temp\service.disco`, is shown in Listing 5.2.

LISTING 5.2 The Output `service.disco` File

```
<?xml version="1.0" encoding="utf-8"?>
<discovery xmlns:xsi="http://www.w3.org/2001/XMLSchema-instance"
   xmlns:xsd="http://www.w3.org/2001/XMLSchema"
   xmlns="http://schemas.xmlsoap.org/disco/" />
```

This file doesn't tell you much—the output is basically a confirmation that the tool found a service. Let's look at the other file, `results.discomap`, shown in Listing 5.3.

LISTING 5.3 The Output `results.discomap` File

```
1:  <?xml version="1.0" encoding="utf-8"?>
2:    <DiscoveryClientResultsFile
3:        xmlns:xsi="http://www.w3.org/2001/XMLSchema-instance"
4:        xmlns:xsd="http://www.w3.org/2001/XMLSchema">
5:    <Results>
6:      <DiscoveryClientResult
7:        referenceType="System.Web.Services.Discovery.
8:          DiscoveryDocumentReference"
9:        url="http://localhost/service.disco"
10:       filename="service.disco" />
11:   </Results>
12:   </DiscoveryClientResultsFile>
```

This file is much more interesting. Lines 2–4 tell us what we're looking at—that is, a discovery results file. Line 5 provides a wrapper for what the disco tool discovered. Lines 6–10, the actual results, provide a reference to the `.disco` file from Listing 5.1.

Using the Service Description

Finally, if you already know the URL of the XML Web service, you can interrogate it for yourself, without having to use the discovery process. By typing the URL into a browser directly, you can view a description of the service and even test out its functionality. See "A Simple SOAP Application" in Hour 4 for examples on doing so.

Just because you know the URL of the service, though, doesn't mean you're all set to use it with your client. You'll probably have to create a proxy class—an object that acts as an intermediary between your client and the service—before you can take advantage of the service's functionality. You'll examine those issues starting in Hour 8, "Windows Client for the Four Function Calculator."

Summary

As you've learned this hour, discovery is a process by which a client locates and interrogates an XML Web service. This process is used by the client to determine what the service is capable of and what kind of data it expects or returns.

There are a few different ways discovery can be accomplished. The first involves UDDI, a specification that details a standard set of rules for exposing and consuming services. `www.uddi.org` also provides a business registry that you can search to find services that meet your needs.

The second method is to use the `disco.exe` tool, which requires a `.disco` file on the server. This `.disco` file provides links to the XML Web services on a particular server. Unfortunately, this method often requires you to know specific URLs—not a very common situation.

Finally, once you have either the `.disco` file or the service's URL, you can examine in more detail the functionality offered by the service.

After the past few hours, you should have a strong background on XML Web services and the technologies that they use, including SOAP, XML, and WSDL. You can now recognize the difference between a SOAP message and a normal XML file, understand what is contained in a WSDL service description, and know how to find services on the Internet. Beginning in the next hour, you will start to build your own XML Web services in Visual Studio.NET.

Q&A

Q Can I use the `.disco` tool on any XML Web service?

A No. The `.disco` tool can examine only `.disco` files, so if the creators of an XML Web service don't want people to find out about it, they just don't create the `.disco` file. That won't stop you, however, if you know the exact URL of the service.

Q What if I can't find an XML Web service using UDDI or DISCO?

A Unfortunately, XML Web services are a relatively new technology, and chances are that the service with the particular functionality you need doesn't exist. On the other hand, the creator of such a service may have decided not to allow discovery or register with UDDI.

In these situations there is, unfortunately, nothing you can do. It is a perfect opportunity, though, to test your own skills at creating a service, and then you can make it available to others.

Workshop

The Workshop is designed to help you review what you've learned in this hour and to point you ahead to the material that will be covered in future hours.

Quiz

1. (True or False) Discovery is a required step to use an XML Web service.

   A False. Discovery only helps you determine what XML Web services are available. If you already know of a service to use, you don't need discovery.

2. What does UDDI stand for?

   A Universal Description, Discovery, and Integration.

3. Imagine an XML Web service with the discovery document `ShippingCalculator.disco`. What are two files that would be output when using the `disco.exe` tool?

   A `results.discomap` and `ShippingCalculator.disco`.

4. Why is UDDI necessary?

   A It is often very difficult to find what you're looking for on the Internet; sometimes it's impossible to find the service that you need. Therefore, UDDI provides a standard way for any service creator to publish their service for all to see and register it in a convenient search engine, as well.

Exercises

1. Explore more of the UDDI Business Registry. Find XML Web services that are freely available, and try to use discovery on them. Also view their WSDL service descriptions.

5

PART II

Building an XML Web Service

Hour

HOUR 6

Visual Studios Environment or Server Setup

Over the past five hours, you've learned quite a bit about XML Web services, such as the way they work and the types of data they use. Now it's time to get some hands-on training. In this hour, you'll set up the development environment and start to build your very own XML Web services. Then, in Hour 7, you'll build a more complex calculator service.

In this hour, we will discuss the following:

- What Visual Studio.NET is and how to set it up
- How to create an XML Web service using VS.NET
- What code-behind forms are and how to use them
- How the special `\bin` directory works
- What proxy classes are
- How to call an XML Web service from a client application

Visual Studio.NET

Visual Studio.NET is Microsoft's integrated development environment (IDE) that allows you to build .NET applications quickly using visual tools. With it, you can build .NET applications (including ASP.NET pages and XML Web services) from a central location.

If you've used previous versions of Visual Studio (6.0 and below), you'll know that it came with several different environments: VB, C++, Interdev, and so on. VS.NET features a single development environment that you can use to build any type of application in any language you want. Let's get started with this tool.

Obtaining the Visual Studio.NET Beta CD-ROM

First, you'll have to get the beta version of VS.NET if you don't already have it. Unfortunately, Microsoft doesn't offer it as a free download (it spans 3 CD's—too large to download), but you can order it on CD or DVD for just a shipping charge. Check out `http://developerstore.com/devstore/product.asp?productID=7627&store=TOOLBOX_NA` for ordering information.

Installing Visual Studio.NET Beta

Once you have a copy, insert it into your CD (or DVD) drive and you should see the Window shown in Figure 6.1 (some options may be grayed out for you depending on your configuration).

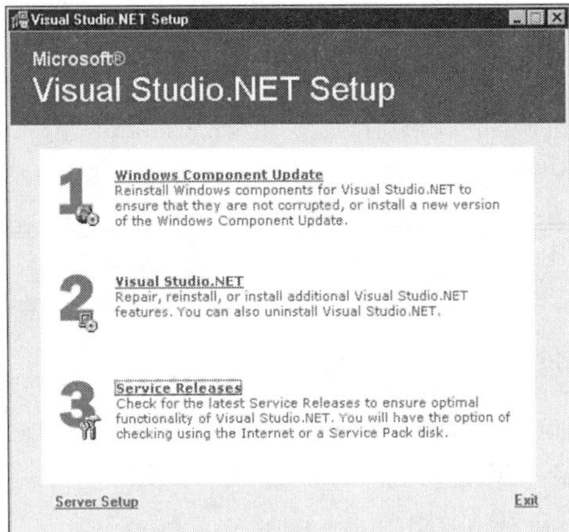

FIGURE 6.1
The VS.NET setup Window.

1. The first step is to update your system so that it is capable of running VS.NET (option 1). This step installs necessary components such as the Windows 2000 Service Pack 2, the .NET Framework SDK, Internet Explorer 6, and various other utilities that are all required by VS.NET. Even if step 2 (Visual Studio.NET) in Figure 6.1 is not grayed out, it may be a good idea to perform step 1 anyway to ensure the utmost compatibility.
2. After you've installed the updated components, step 2 will be available to you. Click it, read the user-agreement that pops up, accept it, and then click next. You should see something similar to Figure 6.2. The left-hand box allows you to select only the components of VS.NET that you want. For this exercise, you'll need at least Visual Basic (under language tools), and you'll probably want to install the MSDN documentation package as well.

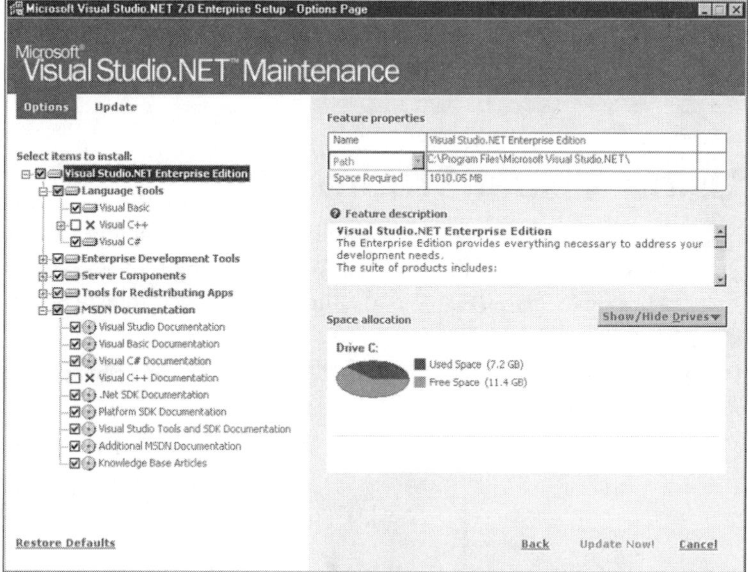

FIGURE 6.2
Select the components you wish to install.

3. Once you've chosen the items to install, click the Install Now! button and sit back—this may take a while. The installer provides you with some reading material while you wait.
4. Finally, once VS.NET is installed, select option 3, Service Releases. This step allows you to check for updates to the Visual Studio environment, which could fix potential bugs or provide additional functionality. Selecting this option will show you Figure 6.3, where you can choose to check for updates via the Internet or with a service pack disk.

At the time of writing, the latest release was Service Pack 2.

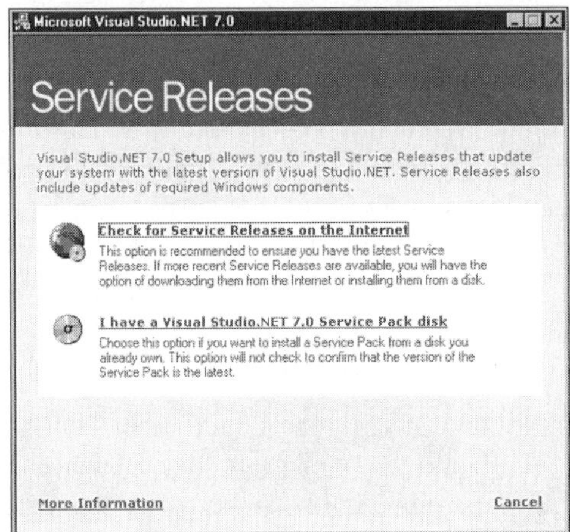

FIGURE 6.3
You can update via service pack disk or the Internet.

Using Visual Studio.NET

Now that you've got VS.NET installed, let's start using it! Open it from Start, Programs, Microsoft Visual Studio.NET 7.0. When you first start VS.NET, you'll be greeted with the "My Profile" page (Figure 6.4), allowing you to customize how the environment is set up.

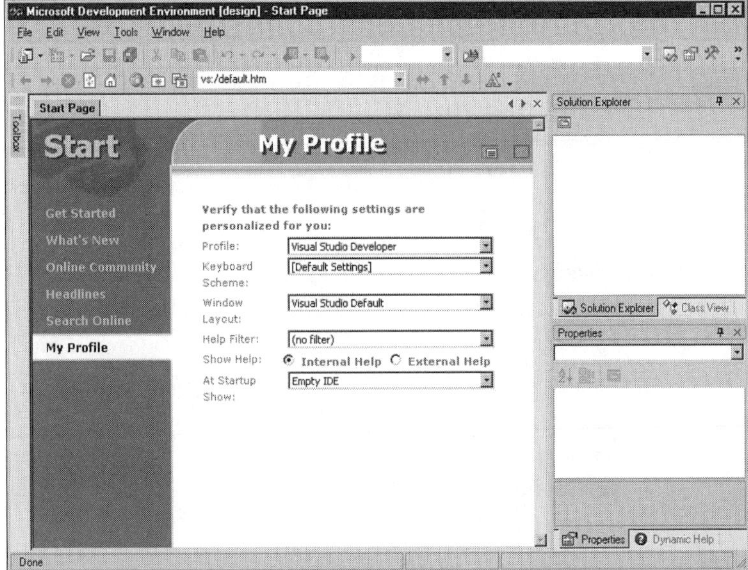

FIGURE 6.4
Running VS.NET for the first time.

Select the options you want and press the "Get Started" link. First you'll want to create a new project, so click on the "Create a New Project" link, or go to File, New, Project. You'll see a dialog similar to Figure 6.5. Depending on the components you installed during setup, you'll see different items to choose from in the list. We want to create an XML Web service, so click on the XML Web service icon in the right-hand pane, enter an appropriate name (we'll use "`MyWebService`"), and click OK.

FIGURE 6.5
VS.NET has many options when creating a new project.

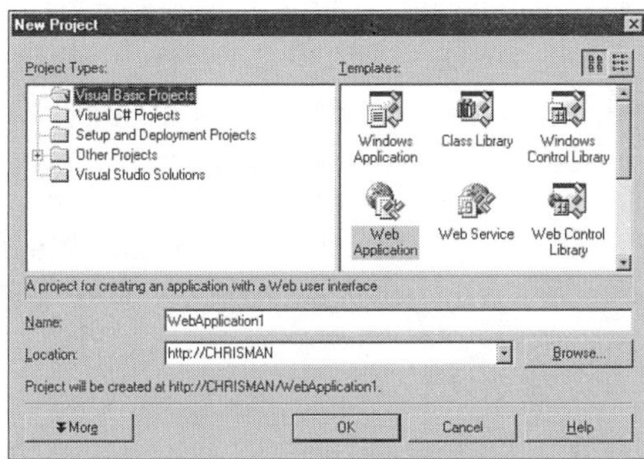

When VS.NET is done churning, the Solution Explorer (upper right of the interface) will show all of the files created for you:

- `AssemblyInfo.vb`—Contains class information that will be used by your service
- `global.asax`—Used for configuration of your service
- `MyWebService.vsdisco`—Visual Studio.NET's version of a `.disco` file
- `Web.config`—Like the `global.asx` file, this will be used for configuration of your service
- `Service1.asmx`—The front end of your XML Web service; often is the main and only page of an XML Web service

Click on the "Show all Files" icon at the top of the Solution Explorer. There will be several additional files displayed, including the `bin` directory, where you'll save any custom components (`.dll` files—more on that later this hour). One file you should pay particular attention to is `Service1.asmx.vb`. This file is known as the *code-behind* `form`. This file is where you'll place any functionality you write—you'll learn why in the "Building an XML Web Service with VS.NET" section later.

Additionally, you'll see a References folder that shows all of the .NET classes your project is referencing, such as `System`, `System.Web`, and so on.

For more information on the `global.asax` and `web.config`, see Hour 22, "Publishing an XML Web Service." For more information on `.disco` files, see Hour 5, "Finding XML Web Services with UDDI and Disco" or Hour 22.

Take some time to explore the interface, as it will be helpful to you later on. Also, try adding and removing files, typing in some code, and using the Toolbox (upper right-hand corner) to add elements to your pages by dragging and dropping.

Let's take a look at the files created by VS.NET. First, in the "My Documents" directory (`c:\Documents and Settings\`*`username`*`\My Documents`), you'll notice a new folder, named Visual Studio Project. Inside this folder will be subfolders—one for each new VS.NET project you create. Inside the `MyWebService` folder is the solution file for your project. This file serves as a collection of the items you add to your project—files, resources, and so on; it acts as a container.

Next, go to the root Web directory (`c:\Inetpub\wwwroot\`), where you'll see a folder named `MyWebService`. This is where all your individual files will be kept. You should see all the files shown in the Solution Explorer, including `global.asax` and `Service1.asmx`. Most of the files in this directory are plain text, so if you ever get tired of the VS.NET interface, you can open these files in your favorite text editor and continue to work on them.

Building a Service with VisualStudio.NET

Now that you're fairly comfortable with working in the VS.NET environment, let's start building some functionality into the XML Web service you just created. Open the `Service1.asmx.vb` code-behind file. XML Web services (and ASP.NET) allow you to separate your code from the user interface (the content). This makes your life easier because you can logically separate your applications in separate tiers, providing for cleaner code and more consistent programming schemes. In a moment, you'll see how this code-behind file works with the XML Web service `.asmx` file.

Listing 6.1 shows the content that is already in this file.

LISTING 6.1 Code Pregenerated by VS.NET

```
Imports System.Web.Services


Public Class Service1
  Inherits System.Web.Services.WebService

```

continues

LISTING 6.1 Continued

```
7:  #Region " Web Services Designer Generated Code "
8:
9:      'Required by the WebServices Designer
10:     Private components As System.ComponentModel.Container
11:
12:     Public Sub New()
13:         MyBase.New()
14:
15:         'CODEGEN: This procedure is required by the WebServices Designer
16:         'Do not modify it using the code editor.
17:         InitializeComponent()
18:
19:         'Add your own initialization code after the InitializeComponent call
20:     End Sub
21:
22:     Private Sub InitializeComponent()
23:         'CODEGEN: This procedure is required by the WebServices Designer
24:         'Do not modify it using the code editor.
25:         components = New System.ComponentModel.Container()
26:     End Sub
27:
28:     Overrides Sub Dispose()
29:         'CODEGEN: This procedure is required by the WebServices Designer
30:         'Do not modify it using the code editor.
31:     End Sub
32:
33: #End Region
34:
35: End Class
```

We won't cover this in depth because you'll be learning it in detail in the next hour. Line 1 is a VB.NET command that tells your application that it will need the objects in the `System.Web.Services` .NET namespace. This namespace has all the objects, methods, and properties you'll need to create your XML Web service. Lines 4 and 5 declare the name of your XML Web service and declare that it inherits from the `System.Web.Services.WebService` object. That is, your XML Web service will automatically contain all the methods and properties from the aforementioned object; thus, they are inherited.

6

Finally, lines 7–33 contain code that is generated by VS.NET. It is used to allow VS.NET to control your service. You shouldn't modify this code, so let's move on.

Adding Functionality to Your XML Web Service

To build the functionality of your XML Web service, you must insert code between the `Public Class` and `End Class` lines. Let's build a simple "Hello World" XML Web service.

This service will send only a string to the clients, who can do with it whatever they wish. Type the code in Listing 6.2 after line 34.

LISTING 6.2 Adding a "Hello World" Function

```
1: <WebMethod()> Public Function HelloWorld() As String
2:    HelloWorld = "Hello World"
3: End Function
```

Again, you'll learn more about the syntax of this function in the next hour. For now, just know that any method you want your XML Web service to expose to clients must have the <WebMethod()> attribute before the declaration of the function.

On line 2, you simply assign the string "Hello World" to the function name, which effectively sends that string to the client when this function is called.

Note that VS.NET is a very smart IDE. If you make simple mistakes while typing, or if you type in the wrong syntax, VS.NET tries to correct it for you. For example, replace line 1 with the following:

```
Public Function <WebMethod()> HelloWorld() As String
```

VS.NET will automatically reformat the line so it looks like line 1 from Listing 6.2. Talk about a smart IDE! Don't forget to save the changes you made.

Building a .NET Assembly

Service1.asmx.vb will be compiled into an *assembly* and placed in the \bin directory. An assembly is simply a compiled collection of classes and functions. When it is compiled, the computer can understand it with much greater ease than if it were not, and therefore the performance of your application is boosted. Assemblies in .NET have the .dll file extension, similar to the dynamic linked libraries of the pre-.NET era.

When placed in the special \bin directory, .NET knows that it must load this file whenever your application is requested by a client. That way, any files in your application can access the functions that are compiled in this file. The Service1.asmx file, when requested by a client, will then access the compiled Service1.asmx.vb file and use it to process the commands sent by the client.

So the next step is to compile Service1.asmx.vb. Under the Build menu in VS.NET, select Build. This will compile your files and make your service ready for action. Before you do that, though, let's take a look at the \bin directory (c:\inetpub\wwwroot\MyWebService\bin) again.

You should now see two files: `MyWebService.dll` (the compiled `Service1.asmx.vb` file) and `MyWebService.pdb`. The former, as discussed, is the assembly for your XML Web service. The latter is known as a symbols file. It allows VS.NET to help you debug your service—we'll ignore it for now.

Previewing Your XML Web Service

Finally, right click `Service1.asmx` from the Solution Explorer and select View In Browser. This function provides a preview for what your service will look like to clients. Figure 6.6 shows the output.

> The beta version of VS.NET has a few inconsistencies with the latest versions of the .NET Framework. When you try to execute your service, you may receive an error in the `web.config` file regarding the value "`inproc.`" VS.NET inserts this word into your `web.config` file as all lowercase, when in fact it should be "`InProc.`" After this simple change your service should run fine.

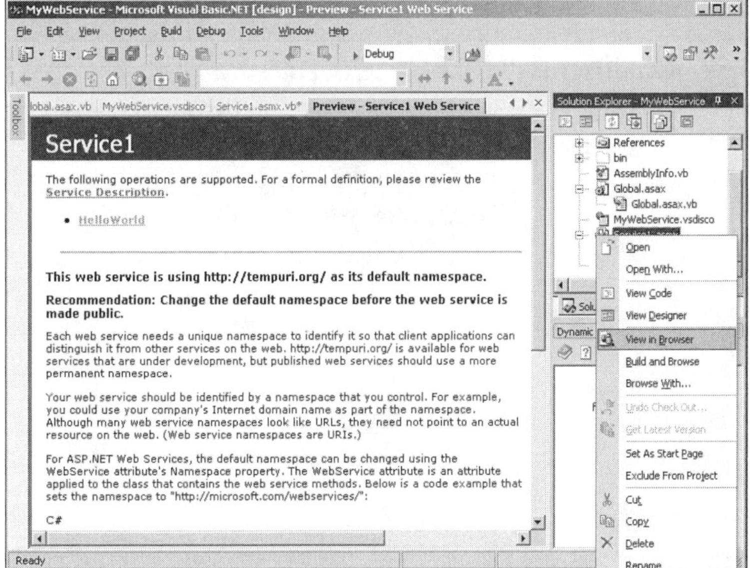

FIGURE 6.6
VS.NET's preview mode.

The page displayed is known as the service description. It is created by ASP.NET to provide additional information about your service, including links to the WSDL XML description and links to any functions you've built. Click on the `HelloWorld` link, and press the `Invoke` button that appears on the next page. The response that would be sent from your service to a client is shown in XML:

```
<?xml version="1.0" encoding="utf-8" ?>
<string xmlns="http://tempuri.org/">Hello World</string>
```

That's all there is to it! You've successfully built an XML Web service using Visual Studio.NET. In the rest of the book you can now use this IDE to develop your applications.

Building a Client with VisualStudio.NET

Before you move on, let's try building a client to your XML Web service as well. In doing so, you'll learn about clients and proxy classes.

To start, save and close the `MyWebService` project and open a new one. This time, select Web Application in the New Project dialog box and name it `MyWebClient`. When VS.NET is through creating your files, you should see many similar files in the Solution Explorer as with the `MyWebService` project, with a few changes. Specifically, instead of `Service1.asmx`, you see `WebForm1.aspx`. This is an ASP.NET page that will be used as the client for your service.

Adding a Web Reference

Next you need to add a reference to your XML Web service. This is done by clicking on the Project menu and selecting Add Web Reference. You'll see this in Figure 6.7.

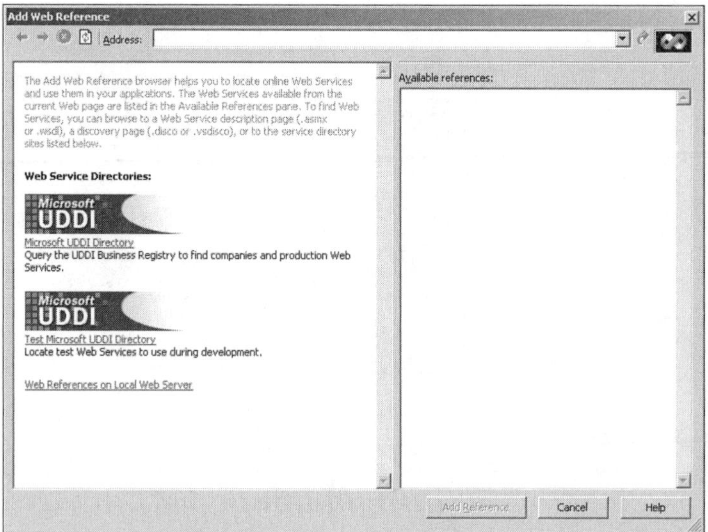

FIGURE 6.7
Adding a reference to your XML Web service.

Three links are provided: one for Microsoft's UDDI server (see Hour 5), one for a test server, and one to view to services on your local computer, which is what you want. Click the third link, "Web References on Local Server." This will bring up the dialog shown in Figure 6.8.

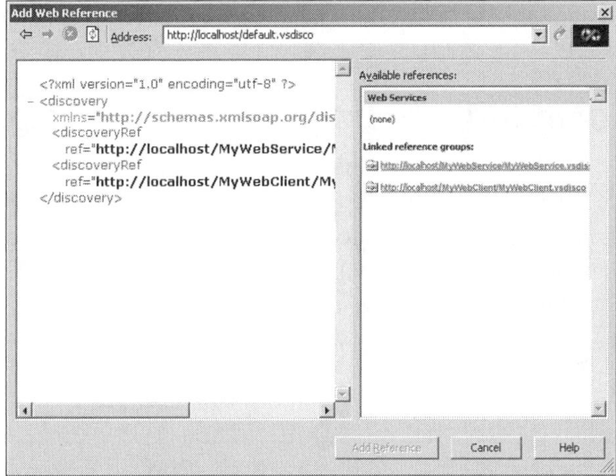

FIGURE 6.8
The projects on your local computer.

The left-hand pane shows a `.disco` file for your server. In the right-hand pane, you'll see references to your projects. Click on the first link, `http://localhost/MyWebService/MyWebService.vsdisco`. The right-hand pane will be replaced with links to the service's WSDL service description. Click on the Add Reference link in the bottom of the window to finish this step.

In the Solution Explorer, you should now see a new folder called `Web References`. Under this you'll see `localhost` (your server) and under that a few files: `Reference.map`, `Service1.wsdl`, `Service1.vb`, and `MyWebService.disco`. `Service1.wsdl` is the service description of the XML Web service, and `MyWebService.disco` is simply a copy of the `.vsdisco` file that VS.NET created for your service. `Reference.map` simply tells you where these files were created on your computer. To figure out what `Service1.vb` is, let's examine what VS.NET did when you added the Web reference.

> `Service1.vb` may not be visible to you when you first open the Solutions Explorer. If it is not, click the "show all files" button at the top of the Solutions Explorer. After you have done that, `Service1.WSDL` should have a plus sign next to it. Clicking this will expand the entry and allow you to have access to the previously hidden `Service1.vb` file.

VS.NET invisibly accessed the `MyWebService` XML Web service and examined the WSDL service description. Using this, it created a *proxy class*. This proxy class is responsible for one thing—encapsulating the mechanism for you to send and receive calls to the XML Web service, so you don't have to worry about it. In other words, sending and receiving messages involves a few steps that are rather complicated and that we'd rather not have to deal with. Thus, the proxy class was generated to make our lives easier.

Calling an XML Web Service with a Proxy Class

In your ASP.NET page, when you call the service, you're actually calling the proxy class, which is stored locally. The proxy class is then, in turn, calling the XML Web service and sending the returning data to your calling ASP.NET page. To anyone who didn't know about the proxy class, it looks exactly as if you're making calls to the service directly—without the hassle of sending and receiving SOAP messages. Listing 6.3 shows the first few lines of this proxy class.

LISTING 6.3 The Auto-Generated Proxy Class

```
'------------------------------------------------------
' <autogenerated>
'     This code was generated by a tool.
'     Runtime Version: 1.0.2914.16
'
'     Changes to this file may cause incorrect behavior and
      will be lost if the code is regenerated.
' </autogenerated>
'------------------------------------------------------

Option Strict Off
Option Explicit On

Imports System
Imports System.Diagnostics
Imports System.Web.Services
Imports System.Web.Services.Protocols
Imports System.Xml.Serialization

Namespace localhost

<System.Web.Services.WebServiceBindingAttribute(
   Name:="Service1Soap", [Namespace]:="http://tempuri.org/")>
Public Class MyWebService
Inherits System.Web.Services.Protocols.SoapHttpClientProtocol

```

continues

LISTING 6.3 Continued

```
            <System.Diagnostics.DebuggerStepThroughAttribute()> _
            Public Sub New()
                MyBase.New
                Me.Url = "http://localhost/MyWebService/MyWebService.asmx"
            End Sub
    ...
    ...
```

This file can get pretty complex, but as long as you know what it is for, you don't need to know the details. In fact, that's what this class is for—hiding the details of accessing an XML Web service. When you compile this file, it will also be placed in your project's `\bin` directory for use with the rest of your application.

Calling the Service

We're almost ready to access the service. Double click the `WebForm1.aspx` file in Solution Explorer. This brings up the `WebForm1.aspx` designer. Note the two tabs at the bottom of the page that allow you to switch from design view to HTML view. For now, you will be working strictly in the design view.

From the Toolbox, if the View menu if the Toolbox is not currently available, select the Web Forms, select Label, and draw it onto the designer form. Now, go to the Properties Window, also available from the View menu, and change the Label's ID field to **`lblMessage`**.

Return to the Solutions Explorer and click on `WebForm1.aspx` again. This time, click on the View Code button at the top of the Solutions Explorer; this option is also available for the View Menu. This brings up the `WebForm.aspx.vb` form, which, as mentioned earlier, is the code that runs behind the actual ASP page. Go to the `Page_Load` event and type in the code in Listing 6.4. Don't worry too much about what it does; you will see that in future chapters.

LISTING 6.4 The Code to Access Your Service

```
Private Sub Page_Load(ByVal sender As System.Object, _
    ByVal e As System.EventArgs) Handles MyBase.Load
    'Put user code to initialize the page here
    Dim objService As New localhost.Service1()

    lblmessage.text = objService.HelloWorld
End Sub
```

Select Build from the Build menu, and then right-click `WebForm1.aspx` and click View in Browser. You should see Figure 6.9.

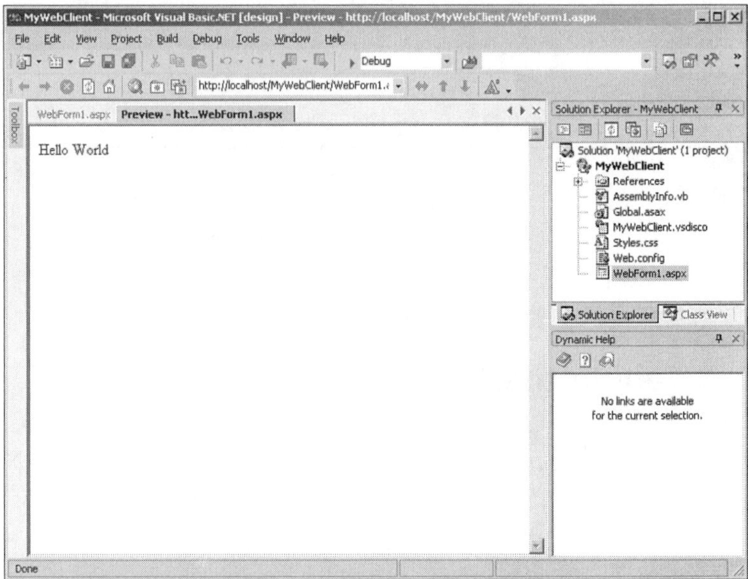

FIGURE 6.9
The output from your XML Web service client.

The output "Hello World" is now displayed. Let's examine the process of calling your XML Web service in more detail:

1. Line 4 in Listing 6.4 created a new instance of your *proxy class,* not the XML Web service.
2. Line 6 makes a call to the `HelloWorld` function of the proxy.
3. The proxy creates a SOAP message based on the function you called and any parameters you passed in and sends the message to the service.
4. The service received the SOAP message, executed the function instructed (`HelloWorld`, in this case), and sent the output as XML back to the proxy.
5. The proxy received the XML message, parsed it, and returned only the return value from the `HelloWorld` function.
6. Your ASP.NET page then displayed this output in the label control that you place in the designer.

It's a relatively lengthy process, but recall that you wrote very few lines of code! VS.NET handled steps 2–5, and all you were left to do was call the function and display the results. This process can be repeated for any XML Web service you find, no matter where on the Internet it is.

Summary

The Visual Studio.NET environment is integrated to allow you to develop any .NET application from a central location. In this hour, you used it to create two projects: an XML Web service and an XML Web service client.

To create the XML Web service, you needed only to create a new XML Web service project from VS.NET's list of choices. All the necessary files were created for you, and all you had to do was add a 3-line function to the service to make it functional. Don't forget to select Build from the Build menu so that your application will be compiled and the appropriate assemblies created. The View in Browser option allows you to preview the service as if you were a potential client.

To build a client, you created a new Web application project and added a Web reference to your XML Web service. VS.NET created some additional files for you, including the proxy class that acts on your behalf to call the XML Web service. This class encapsulates all the complexity of making Internet calls so you don't have to deal with it. Then you simply added some code to an ASP.NET file and called your XML Web service, displaying the results in a label.

VS.NET is a very powerful tool, as you learned today, hiding much of the complexity of creating applications. In the next few hours, you'll put this knowledge to use to create a useful calculator XML Web service.

Q&A

Q I hate this VS.NET auto-complete mechanism. Can I turn it off or customize VS.NET?

A You bet. To turn off the auto-complete, go into the Options under the Tools menu. In the Environment folder, select General, and then uncheck "Enable Command Window autocompletion."

Additionally, you can customize the IDE to look however you want. Drag each window's title bar around to find the look and feel you prefer. You can close any window by clicking on the little 'x' icon or by highlighting the window and selecting Hide from the Window menu.

Q Do I have to put my service code in the `.asmx.vb` code-behind file?

A No, you can place your code directly into your `.aspx` pages via the HTML view, but this does violate the basic reason for having the `asmx.vb` code behind in the first place. The `.aspx.vb` files allow developers to separate form and function, allowing for greater ease of maintenance and design. If, at some stage, you find yourself working with teams of Web Developers, it is much easier to allow the Web designer to make their changes without fear of breaking the ASP.NET code, as well as allow the actual ASP developers to work without fear of breaking HTML content.

Workshop

The Workshop is designed to help you review what you've learned in this hour and to point you ahead to the material that will be covered in future hours.

Quiz

1. What is a proxy class, and what does it do?

A A proxy class is auto-generated by VS.NET and contains methods that receive and send XML and SOAP messages, so you don't have to build them yourself. You can interact with the proxy class just as if you were interacting with the XML Web service directly.

2. What is the <WebMethod()> attribute?

A Any functions that you wish to expose in your Web client (that is, make available to clients) must have this attribute. It is placed immediately before the declaration of the function.

3. What is the `web.config` file used for?

A It contains configuration settings for your application.

4. What is the file extension for assemblies?

A `.dll`

5. True or false: The `\bin` directory is required for your applications.

A False. You need only the `\bin` directory if you're going to create assemblies.

6. What must you do in VS.NET to create a client for an XML Web service?

A You must add a Web Reference (the Project menu) and build your project. This creates a proxy class and then compiles it into an assembly.

7. Let's assume you have built an XML Web service named `Calculator` and have already created your proxy class for your client. Is there anything wrong with the following client-side ASP.NET code?

```
Private Sub Page_Load(ByVal sender As System.Object, _
    ByVal e As System.EventArgs) Handles MyBase.Load
    'Put user code to initialize the page here
     lblMessage.Text = Calculator.Add(8,9)

End Sub
```

A Yes. You didn't create an instance of the proxy class. Add the following code after line 4:

```
dim objService as New Calculator.Calculator
```

Then change line 5 to read

```
lblMessage.Text = objService.Add(8,9)
```

Exercises

1. It's time to create an XML Web service and client on your own. Create an XML Web service, in VS.NET, that returns the current time. Don't forget to build and test it!

   A Create a new XML Web service project in VS.NET and name it `TimeService`. Open the `Service1.asmx` file and change its filename (in the Properties box) to `TimeService.asmx`. The code (not including VS.NET auto-generated code) for this file is as follows:

   ```
   <WebMethod()> Public Function CurrentTime() As DateTime
      CurrentTime = System.Date.Now
   End Function
   ```

   Build the project (Build menu, Build), right-click `TimeService.asmx`, and select View in Browser. You should now be able to test the output of your function.

2. Build the client for your `TimeService` service.

   A Create a new Web application project in VS.NET and name it `TimeServiceClient`. Add a Web reference to your `TimeService` service by going to Project, Add Web Reference, Web References on Local Web Server, and select the `TimeService` service. Click Add Reference. Insert the following code into `WebForm1.aspx.vb` and place a Label on the designer

   ```
    Private Sub Page_Load(ByVal sender As System.Object, _
        ByVal e As System.EventArgs) Handles MyBase.Load
        'Put user code to initialize the page here
         dim objService as new localhost.Service1

        lblmessage.text = objService.CurrentTime
      end sub
   ```

   Build and run the project.

HOUR 7

Building the Four Function Calculator

So far, you have learned the principles and architecture behind XML Web services. In this hour, you are going to develop your first service, a four-function calculator. Through this simple example, you will learn enough to immediately begin building a host of more complicated services with real-world applications.

In this hour, we will discuss the following tasks:

- Creating XML Web services
- Adding methods in XML Web services
- Testing your output
- Generating the contract file

Designing the Service

The first step in the creation of an XML Web service, or any other program actually, is to decide what it will do and to create a design that will give the service the needed functionality. For this demonstration, we will create a very simple design.

My suggestion for designing an XML Web service is to list all the functions that you plan to expose in this manner:

```
Public Function Add(ByVal iNum1 as Integer, ByVal iNum2 as Integer) as Double
```

The preceding function declaration uses standard VB notation to describe input parameters, their variable types, and the return type.

The actual function declarations in an XML Web service are slightly different. This declaration is just to be used for the conceptual design of your service.

We want client applications to be able to use our service to add, subtract, multiply, and divide two integers. We will return a double in each instance. All the function declarations look identical to the one for Add, so I won't repeat them here.

Creating the Service

To create this service, open Visual Studio .NET and select New Project from the Start window. This will bring up the New Project dialog box shown in Figure 7.1.

Select Visual Basic Projects and choose Web Service. Name the service **`FourFunctionCalc`** and set its location to the server that will host the service. In my example, this is simply **`http://Localhost`**.

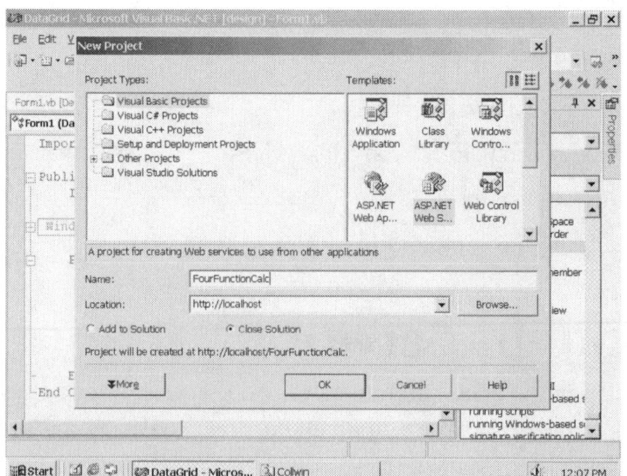

FIGURE 7.1
Creating the new XML Web service project.

Adding Classes to an XML Web Service

Once you have created your project template, Visual Studio .NET adds two classes to your project. These are the `Global` *Class,* which we will look at extensively in later hours, and the `Service1` *class,* which we will focus on in this hour.

`Service1`, as the name implies, is a service. If you think of an XML Web service as a COM DLL, then a service is simply an object that is exposed by that DLL. An XML Web service project can contain many services, and we will see examples of that in Hour 23. The Global Class is a class that handles events throughout an XML Web service application, regardless of the number of services that we add to it. You will learn to use the global file in Hour 17.

When you examine a new service, you will notice that the template includes a few methods and some commented example code. The commented example code, seen in Listing 7.1 for Visual Basic and in Listing 7.2 for C#, will act as a model for every other method that you add to an XML Web service. Notice the addition of the `<WebMethod>` tag to the standard function declaration. This tag instructs .NET to expose this function to XML Web service consumers.

Listing 7.1 `HelloWorld` Method in Visual Basic

```
<WebMethod> Public Function HelloWorld() as String
      HelloWorld = "Hello World"
End Function
```

Listing 7.2 `HelloWorld` Method in C#

```
[WebMethod]
Public String HelloWorld()
   {
    Return "Hello World"
   }
```

Obviously, your calculator doesn't use the Hello World function, so you will leave the example code commented out, but it nicely reminds you what our calls should look like.

If you create an XML Web service and find that some of your methods cannot be called from your client application, go back and check that you have included the `<WebMethod>` tag in your calls. Failure to include this tag will create methods that are exposed only to code within your XML Web service project.

Inheriting the `WebService` Class

When you create an XML Web service, what you are really doing is inheriting the `WebService` class and altering some of its methods. Two important things in your XML Web service code make this happen. The first is the inclusion of the `System.Web.Services` namespace, which occurs in the general declarations section of your code as follows:

```
Imports System.Web.Services
```

The second is the declaration of your service class, which has the following form:

```
Public Class ServiceName Inherits System.Web.Services.WebService
```

These two lines of code will exist in every XML Web service that you create, and they give you access to the framework of the XML Web services architecture. By building your class upon the `WebService` class, you can override the `WebService` constructors and destructors as well as add new methods.

> The Web Service Template Project in Visual Studio .NET will include `WebService` namespace and class declarations for you. Removing or altering these lines is a surefire way to ensure that your service doesn't function.

Calling the Constructor

By now, you have probably noticed a line in the pregenerated code that reads, "Web Services Designer Generated Code." Click on the plus sign next to that text to view the constructor function, `New()`. If you are in C#, you will not find the `New()` method but will instead find a public method with same name as your service. This method is known as the constructor in the traditional object-oriented programming model and is called whenever an object is created from your class.

This method is where you will add any initialization code that your object needs, such as setting the values of variables, connecting to a database, and so on. If you need initialization code to instantiate a custom object, place it here, after the `InitializeComponent()` call that .NET added for you. Listing 7.3 shows an example of initializing a custom object.

Listing 7.3 Using the `New()` Method to Initialize Objects

```
Public Sub New()
    MyBase.New()

    'CODEGEN: This procedure is required by the Web Services Designer
```

continues

Listing 7.3 Continued

```
        'Do not modify it using the code editor.
        InitializeComponent()

        Dim objConn as ADODB.Connection
        Set objConn = New Connection
    End Sub
```

Our four-function calculator doesn't require any initialization code, so we will leave the constructor as it is at this point. In Hours 11 and 17, we will see several examples of using the `New()` method in XML Web services.

Do not add code to the `New()` method before the `InitializeComponent()` call. Code written before this line may cause serious errors at runtime.

The `Dispose` and `Finalize` Methods

Notice in our service that .NET has created a `Dispose` method for both Visual Basic and C# classes. This method is called when the service goes out of scope or is explicitly destroyed. This is the place in your service where you would perform garbage-collection activities, such as releasing database connections and destroying object references. This method is made public so that client code can call it before setting its reference equal to nothing.

```
ServiceName.Dispose()
```

For those of you who haven't done much object-oriented programming, *garbage collection* is the term commonly used to refer to the act of reclaiming memory used by objects created in your code. It is important to destroy these objects when they are no longer needed in order to keep them from taking up valuable space in memory and causing your program to perform poorly.

.NET also allows you to add a method called `Finalize`. `Finalize` is the actual destructor of the service. In traditional object-oriented programming, this is where you would do your cleanup. Under the .NET model, however, both `Dispose` and `Finalize` can be called by the garbage collector. This is done with no guarantee as to the order in which those calls will be made or even as to when they will occur during execution. In fact,

Microsoft goes so far as to caution that you cannot guarantee that the `Finalize` method will ever get called. Indeed, if you create a service and test for this method, you will see it occur infrequently.

Because of this, I recommend using `Dispose` for all your cleanup code and explicitly calling it in all your client applications. `Finalize` should then be used as a backup to ensure that references are dropped in the event that `Dispose` is not called explicitly by client code.

You will use the `Dispose` and `Finalize` methods heavily in Hours 14 and 17. Until then, just know that these methods are how you can exit your service gracefully.

Adding the Four-Function Calculator Code

Now that you know a bit more about what is going on in your newly created XML Web service, let's add some code and see how XML Web services actually work.

For the calculator, you should add four methods. Listing 7.4 shows the Visual Basic code that we will add. Listing 7.5 shows what one of the methods looks like in C#.

LISTING 7.4 Calculator Methods in Visual Basic

```
#Region "Calc Functions"
<WebMethod()> Public Function Add(ByVal iNum1 As Integer, _
                                  ByVal iNum2 As Integer) As Double
    Return iNum1 + iNum2
End Function

<WebMethod()> Public Function Subtract(ByVal iNum1 As Integer, _
                                  ByVal iNum2 As Integer) As Double
    Return iNum1 - iNum2
End Function

<WebMethod()> Public Function Mulitply(ByVal iNum1 As Integer, _
                                  ByVal iNum2 As Integer) As Double
    Return iNum1 * iNum2
End Function

<WebMethod()> Public Function Divide(ByVal iNum1 As Integer, _
                                  ByVal iNum2 As Integer) As Double
    Return iNum1 / iNum2
End Function
#End Region
```

LISTING 7.5 C# Add Method for the Four Function Calculator

```
        [WebMethod]
        public int Add(int iNum1, int iNum2)
        {
            return iNum1 + iNum2;
        }
```

C# programmers should have no trouble at all creating the other three methods after looking at the example. Simply copy the `Add()` method three more times, being very careful to include the `[WebMethod]` tag above every method that you intend your XML Web service to expose. Then, rename each method to correspond to the three additional methods in Listing 7.4, and change the plus sign to the corresponding mathematical symbol.

Adding Descriptions to Methods

You can add an optional description to each of the methods in your service. This is accomplished by setting an optional parameter of the `<WebMethod>` declaration. This is its syntax in Visual Basic:

```
<WebMethod(Description:="Some Text")>
```

In C#, it looks like this:

```
[WebMethod (Description="Some Text")]
```

To add a description to your `Add()` method, for example, change the `<WebMethod>` declaration as follows:

```
<WebMethod(Description:="This is a function to add two integers")>
```

The description will show up in the services WSDL file, which we described in Hour 3, and when you run the service. Figure 7.4 shows the `Add()` method with the new description.

Using Regions

You may have noticed that the first line of code in Listing 7.4 contained a `#Region` compiler directive. For those of you who haven't discovered regions in your use of .NET, they are an extremely useful new element.

A region is a related group of code, possibly a group of functions, such as our four mathematical functions, that can be minimized by the developer. This allows you to "close down" code that you aren't currently working on and view only that which is important at the moment. This makes the code window much easier to navigate.

A region is created simply by adding the following line to your code:

```
#Region "Region Name"
```

In C#, use the following:

```
#region "Region Name"
```

"Region Name" represents any meaningful description of the region that you care to enter. After this line is added, navigate to the end of the area of code that you want to include in this region and add this line:

```
#End Region
```

In C#, use the following:

```
#endregion
```

Figure 7.2 shows the region in our four-function calculator. Notice the minus sign next to our new region. This allows us to minimize the region. The plus sign next to the line "Web Services Designer Generated Code" can be used to open up the group of functions included in our code when we first created the service.

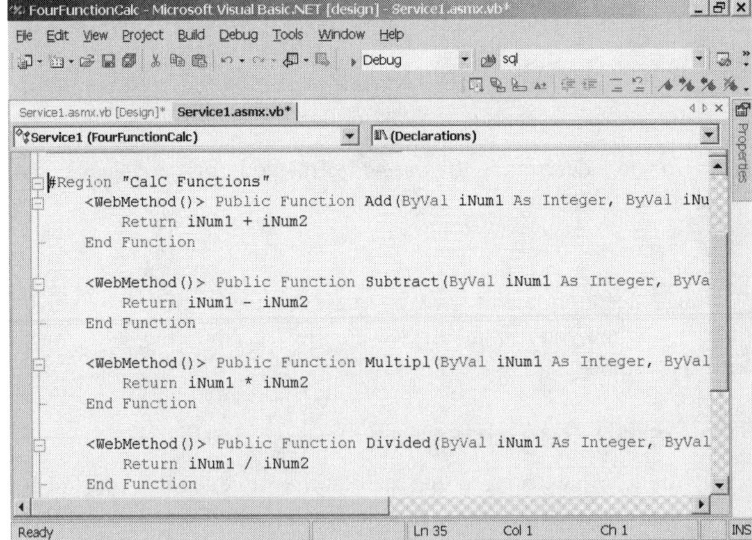

FIGURE 7.2
Regions in action.

Building the Service

Now that you have entered all of the code for your service, you need to build the executable version of your code. Visual Studio will compile your code into a series of `asmx` files, one for each service in your project, and a `Global.asax` file for the Global Class in your service.

To build the project, type `Ctrl+Shift+B` or select Build under Build on the menu bar. If you typed everything correctly, the build should run smoothly and you should not receive any error messages. If you do receive error messages, carefully compare your code with that in Listing 7.4 and make sure that they match exactly. We will cover debugging XML Web services in Hour 20.

Build Versus Rebuild

You may have noticed that the Build menu contains Build and Rebuild, and you may wonder what the difference is. For the purposes of an XML Web service, Build is used to compile only services and classes that have changed since the last time that you built the project. This is useful in keeping the compile time down on large projects that contain many services.

Rebuild is used when you want to force the entire project to be rebuilt. Rebuild forces the building of services and classes that have not been modified since the previous build.

Running the Service

Now that you have successfully built the service, it is time to make sure that it actually runs. Visual Studio includes a very helpful method for running your services without the need to write any code at all.

To run your service, type F5 or choose Start from the Debug menu. When you have done this, Visual Studio will open your `asmx` file in Internet Explorer, as shown in Figure 7.3.

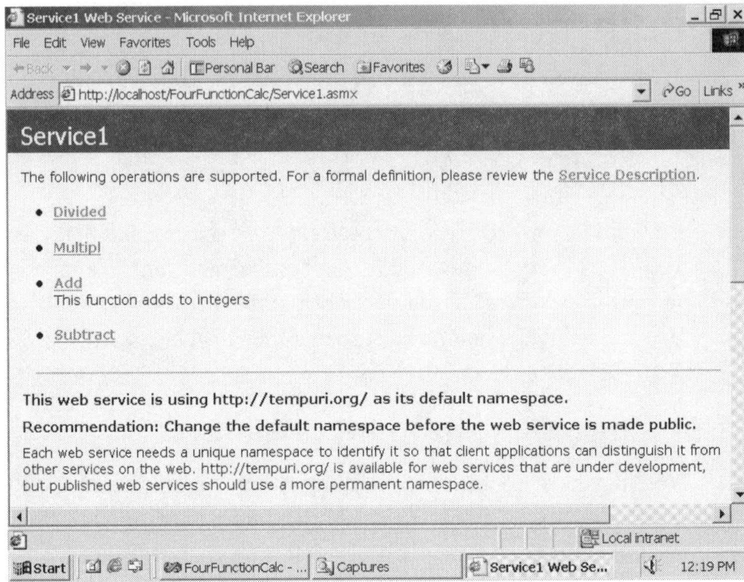

FIGURE 7.3
Our four-function calculator in Internet Explorer.

The Internet Explorer interface to your service is very slick and can be used to expose a lot of information to potential users. Notice in Figure 7.3 that the names of all of your methods are listed. Also note that you are provided with a link to the WSDL contract. This is a very important feature; you will make use of this link in just a few moments.

By clicking on any of the method names, you will be taken to a page that Internet Explorer includes for each of your methods. In these pages, you are shown the names of input parameters and the variable type to be returned by the method, as well as SOAP, HttpPost, and HttpGet return and response information.

You are also given a Web form with which to use each method. Figure 7.4 shows your `Add` Method in Internet Explorer. Type a few values for the `Add` method and click on the button labeled "Invoke."

Internet Explorer now opens a new window containing the XML that will be returned to clients that use your service (see Figure 7.5). Notice that you receive your value wrapped in XML tags that contain the data type being returned. This allows your client application to type check data in much the same way that COM applications do.

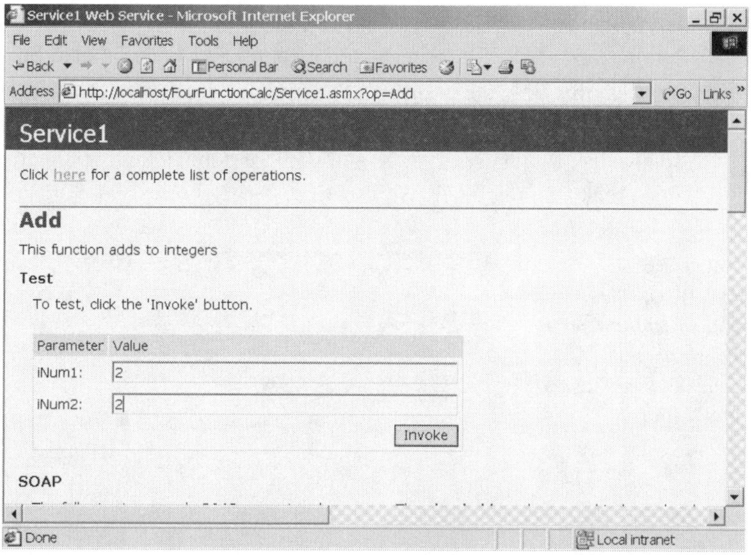

FIGURE 7.4
Using the Add method of your XML Web service.

FIGURE 7.5
The answer returned by your XML Web service.

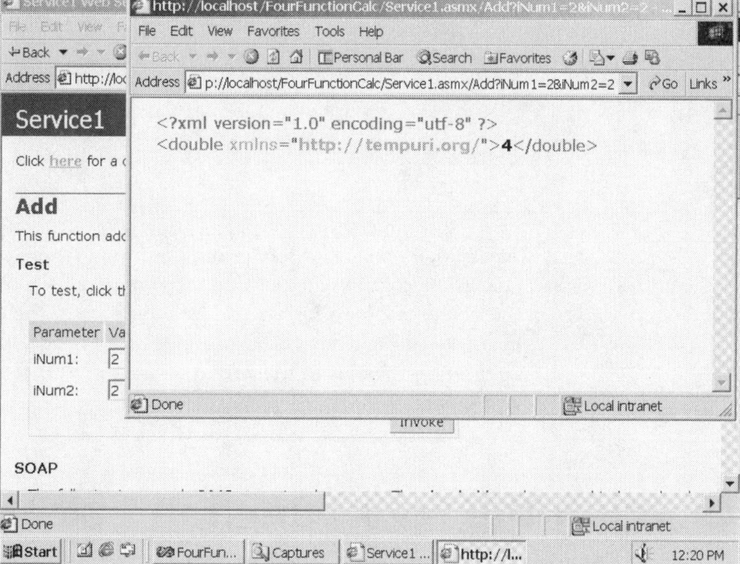

Creating an XML Web Service Contract

As we discussed in Hour 3, an XML Web service is defined using a WSDL contract. This WSDL contract file is then used by .NET to create proxy classes that allow client applications to interface with the XML Web service. You will build your first proxy class in Hour 8 when you create a client-side interface for the Four-Function Calculator.

Creating the WSDL file is extremely easy. If you look back at Figure 7.3, you will see a link to the WSDL file near the top of our ASMX file labeled Service Description. If you click on this link, the entire WSDL file will be opened in Internet Explorer. Figure 7.6 shows a portion of the WSDL file used to define the calculator service. Simply save this file to disk as `Service1.WSDL` and you are done. Client applications can now be developed that use your XML Web service.

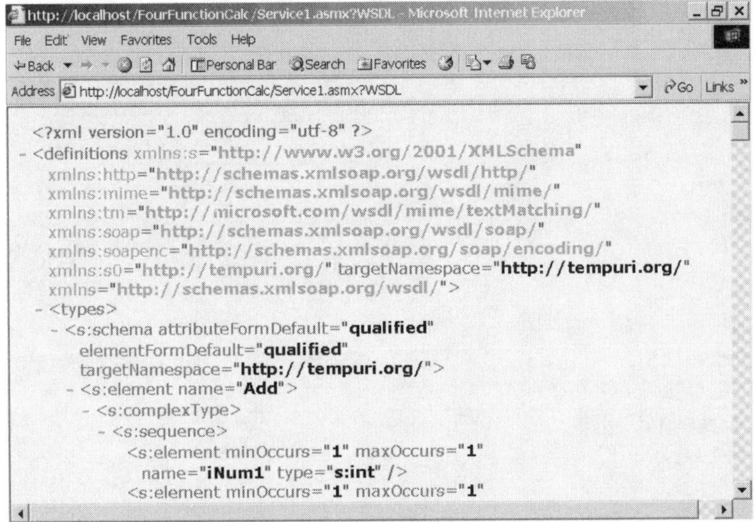

FIGURE 7.6
This WSDL file acts as a contract between the Four-Function Calculator and client applications.

When you deploy your service on a different server, you will have to create a new WSDL contract file because the complete path of your service is listed in the WSDL. In Figure 7.6, you can see the path to the `FourFunctionCalc` listed in SOAP `<address>` space. Failure to create a new SDL file may cause a client application to point to the wrong server and thus cause your XML Web service to fail.

Creating the Four Function Calculator in ASP

Those of you who are building ASP applications in the .NET framework but who are not always using the Visual Studio.NET tools can still create XML Web services. Type the code in Listing 7.6 into Notepad and save it as `SmallCalc.asmx`. This file must be saved to a directory that IIS can run code from. Now, run it in Internet Explorer to see the results. You should get a service with an `Add` method that is identical to the service created earlier with Visual Studio.NET.

Listing 7.6 ASP Code for Creating the `SmallCalc` XML Web Service

```
1:   <%@ Web Service Language="VB" Class="SmallCalc" %>
2:
3:   Imports System
4:   Imports System.Web.Services
5:
6:   Public Class SmallCalc:
7:
8:          <WebMethod()> Public Function Add(iNum1 as Integer, _
9:                             iNum2 as Integer) As Double
10:                            Return (iNum1 + iNum2)
11:         End Function
12:
13:   End Class
```

The first item that you should notice is the header of the ASP file (line 1 in Listing 7.6). The addition of the `Web Service` tag lets the ASP compiler know that you are building a service.

Line 4 of the code is where you import the `System.Web.Services` namespace. This namespace contains the `Web Service` class that our class, `SmallCalc`, is built upon. This is done when `SmallCalc` is declared, in line 6, as inheriting from `Web Service`.

Last, note that the function declaration for `Add()`, line 8 of Listing 7.6, is identical to the declaration used in your Visual Basic code, line 2 of Listing 7.4.

You should be able to add the other three functions to this code and create the WSDL contract file for this service. Doing so should help get you used to working with XML Web services.

> In ASP.NET, `asax` and `asmx` files are compiled on their initial use. This means that, even if you use Notepad to create your files, you create robust applications built on native code.

Summary

In this hour, you learned the steps of creating simple XML Web services and running them in .NET. You also learned about some of the important methods that take place inside a service, and you looked at the SDL contract and the steps used to create one. You ended with a brief lesson in how to create XML Web services with simple ASP tools, including Notepad.

Q&A

Q Why use Visual Studio if the .NET Framework allows you to create XML Web services in Notepad?

A Although Notepad is sufficient for the small examples that you worked on in this hour, your code will quickly become more difficult to manage without the help of Visual Studio. The ability to create code regions, place code in modules, access help files, and use a myriad of other features provided by Visual Studio will prove invaluable when you begin creating real-world services.

Q Can a single XML Web service project provide multiple services?

A Yes, you can add multiple services to your XML Web service project. These services are all compiled as different `asmx` files and share the same `Global.asax` file. For example, we could have added a second set of functions to our calculator to support working with hexadecimal numbers. We could have placed these functions in a second service and allowed clients to access them separately. In future hours, we will see examples of XML Web service projects that expose multiple services.

Q Is adding the optional description to methods worth the extra effort?

A Yes, it certainly is. If your methods are exposed to external clients, life is much simpler if they can see a small description of each method when they write code to use your service. Even if your methods are exposed only internally and used only by the people who wrote them, you will eventually forget what some functions do; having these little reminders can save you the trouble of having to look up reference material or seeking out the source code to read the comment lines.

Workshop

The workshop is designed to help you review what you've learned in this hour and to prepare you for the material that will be covered in future hours. The answers to the quiz are in Appendix A.

Quiz

1. You have created an XML Web service that compiles correctly but when run exposes no methods. Why?

   A You forgot to include the `<WebMethod()>` declaration in your code.

2. Why is it important to create a new WSDL file after deploying your XML Web service?

   A The original WSDL file points to your development server, not the location where the service has been deployed.

3. You need to close down a connection to a database and drop some object references. Where should this be done?

   A The `Dispose()` method is where XML Web services do their cleanup.

Exercises

Experiment with the four-function calculator. Try creating other simple mathematical functions, such as squaring an integer, returning the sine and cosine of a number, or returning the value of pi to some user-requested number of decimal places. You can cheat on that last function by simply storing pi as a constant of some arbitrary length and rounding it to fit the user's request.

A. The following code could be added to your `FourFunctionCalc` code to create a squaring function:

```
        <WebMethod()> Public Function Squared(iNum1 as Integer) _
                                  As Long

                          Return (iNum1 * iNum1)
End Function
```

It must be noted that the `FourFunctionCalc` is now grossly misnamed.

HOUR 8

Windows Client for the Four Function Calculator

In this hour, you will learn to create client applications that consume XML Web services. You will also learn how to create proxy classes that enable your application code and XML Web services to easily communicate via SOAP messages. Also in this hour, you will see how to use the `WebServiceUtil.exe` file to accomplish many important XML Web service–related tasks.

In this hour, we will discuss the following items:

- Consuming XML Web services
- Using dialogs to create proxy classes
- Adding Web references
- Using the WSDL.exe

Creating a Client Application

Since an XML Web service lacks any real interface of its own, it requires that client applications be built to use its functionality. Client applications can range from ASP applications and Windows-native applications to simple Web pages that use `get` and `post` form methods to communicate with a service.

In Hour 9, you will learn to create applications that make use of XML Web services via scripting code and form methods; for now, we will focus on creating Windows-native clients and ASP applications that use XML Web services.

Building the Four Function Calculator Client Application

Create a Windows application and call it `CalcClient`. Create a form in the `CalcClient` application that contains three text boxes and four buttons. Set up the form to look like Figure 8.1. For convenience, leave the name property of all the controls to the default settings (that is, `Button1`, `Button2`, and so on).

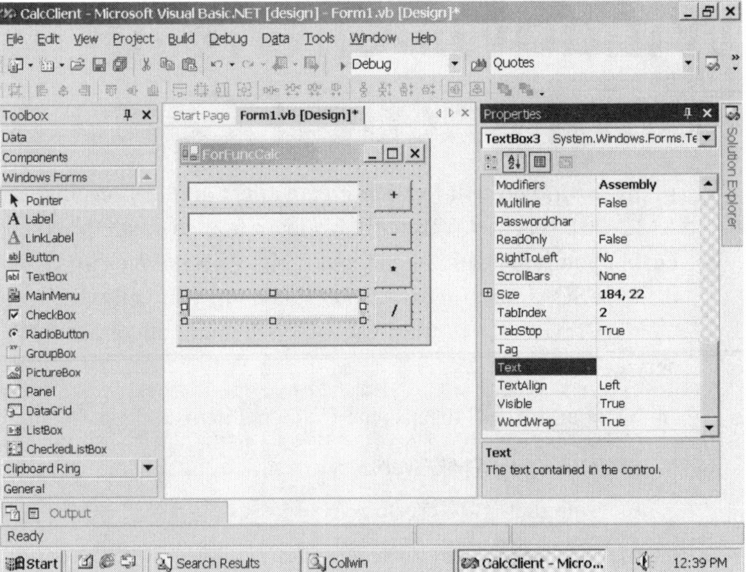

FIGURE 8.1
The client for the four function calculator.

Proxy Classes

To use your four function calculator XML Web service, you need to create a proxy class to handle the calls to your service. What the proxy class does is expose methods to your application that are identical to the methods used by the XML Web service. For example, if you have an XML Web service method named `Chance` that accepts an integer and a string and returns a long, your proxy class will also have a method named `Chance` that accepts and integer and a string and returns a long.

Behind the scenes, the proxy class wraps your parameters (an integer and a string in this example) into a SOAP call to the Web class method (`Chance` in this case). The Web class then returns a SOAP package containing the long return value to the proxy class, which unwraps it and passes the long value to your application.

Creating the Proxy Class

To create the proxy class to your XML Web service, choose Add Web Reference from the Project menu of Visual Studio .NET. When you use this wizard, Visual Studio creates and compiles the proxy class into a DLL and includes a reference to it in your project automatically.

After you choose Add Web Reference, the screen in Figure 8.2 is displayed. From this screen, you are able to choose known local XML Web services by clicking the link `Web References on Local Web Server`, or you can seek other services via the link `Microsoft UDDI`. For this example, we will use the local link.

If you wish to review how to use UDDI in searching for XML Web services, reread Hour 5.

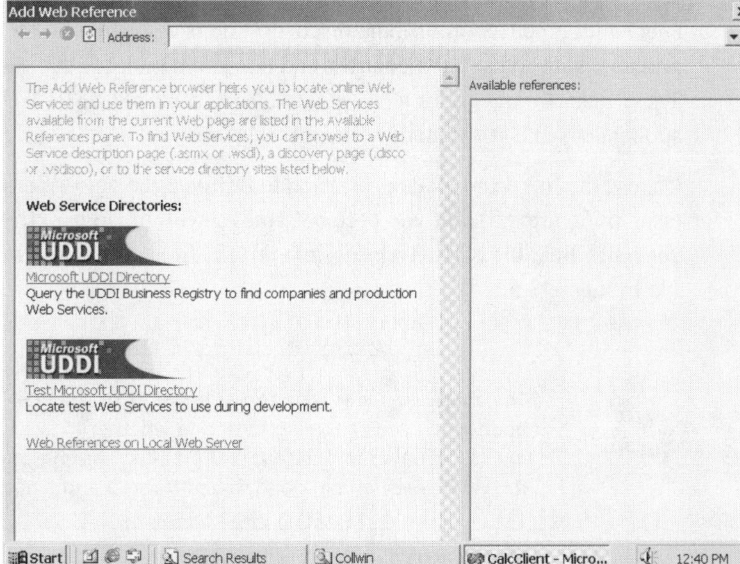

FIGURE 8.2
Using the Web Reference dialog.

Now Visual Studio brings up a list of all the discovery (DISCO) files as Linked Reference Groups, related services that are usually members of the same project, on your local server (see Figure 8.3). Search through this listing and find the URL to `FourFunctionCalc.disco`.

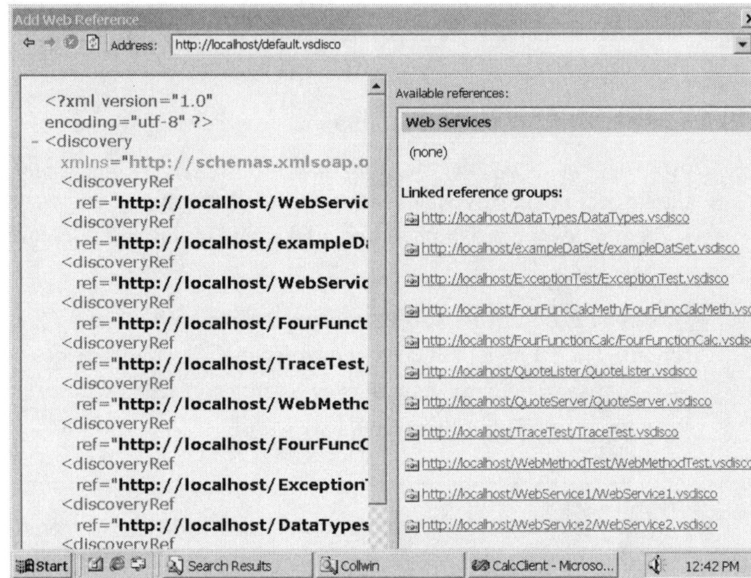

FIGURE 8.3
Finding the XML Web service on the server.

After you select the link to an XML Web service (in this case, `Service1` of your `FourFunctionCalc` Group), the discovery file is displayed on the screen, and you are provided with links to the contract and documentation for this service (see Figure 8.4). These links are important when you are using multiple XML Web services to develop applications and you cannot remember what they all do.

Choose the link `View Documentation` to bring up the auto-generated documentation files (seen in Figure 8.5) that you became familiar with in Hour 7. If you choose the `View Contract` link, the XML Web services WSDL file is displayed in place of documentation file in Figure 8.5.

> The ability to understand the XML syntax of the WSDL document is a major boon when you are trying to decide whether a given XML Web service meets the needs of your application. If you are having trouble deciphering the WSDL files, go back and reread Hours 2 and 3 again.

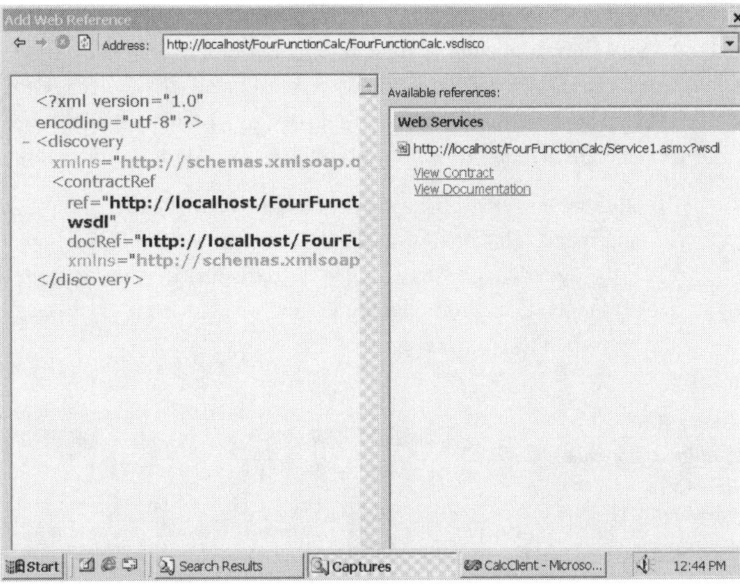

FIGURE 8.4
Viewing the DISCO file of the XML Web service.

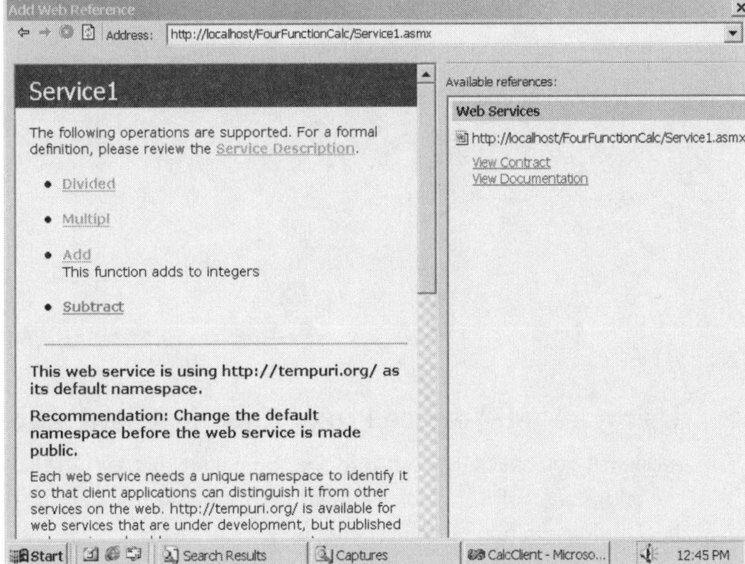

FIGURE 8.5
Viewing the documentation of the XML Web service.

After you have navigated to the service that you wish to reference in your project, click the Add Reference button and Visual Studio.Net will add the appropriate reference to your project and create a proxy class for the service.

Now that Visual Studio.NET has created the proxy class for you and included it in your `CalcClient` application, you can add any other references that you need for your project. In this case, you will need to add a reference to the `System.Web.Services.dll`. This DLL exposes some extra functionality that comes in handy when developing XML Web service clients, and it is good practice to include it in your client applications.

To add the `System.Web.Services.dll` to your project, choose Add Reference from the Project menu. This brings up the Add Reference window, shown in Figure 8.6. Double-click the `System.Web.Services.dll` to display it in the bottom window, Selected Components. Once you have done this, you can click Okay to close the window and add the reference to your project.

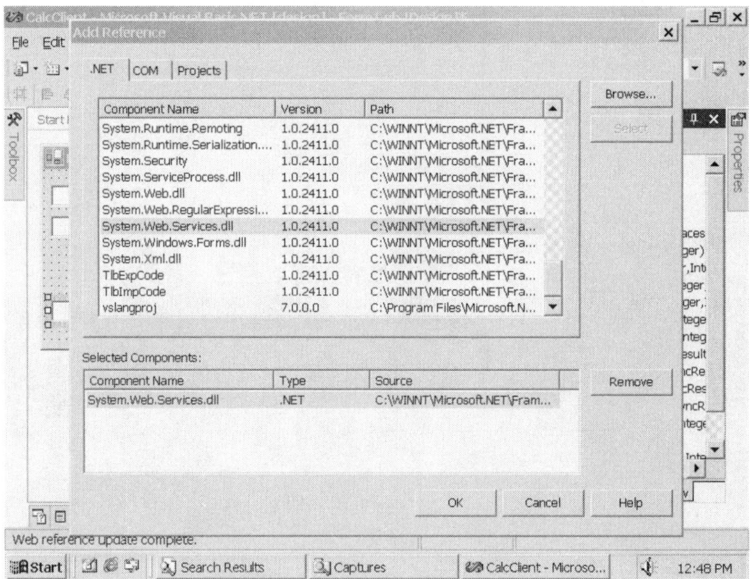

FIGURE 8.6
Adding a reference to the `System.Web.Services.dll`.

Using a Web Service Proxy Class in Client Applications

Now that you have a reference to the `FourFunctionCalc` XML Web service, you can create an instance of it in your application. Add the following line of code to the general declarations section of your client application's `Form1`.

```
Dim oCalc As New localhost.Service1()
```

If you are using C#, your object declaration should be the following:

```
localHost.Service1 oCalc = New localhost.Service1;
```

With the new `oCalc` object created in your application, you can begin using the methods of the XML Web service, via the proxy, in your application. The general syntax for calling a XML Web service's method is

```
proxyObject.MethodName(args)
```

where `proxyObject` is the name of your object, `oCalc` is the case of your `CalcClient` application, and `MethodName` is the name of the method that you are trying to access. Any arguments that the XML Web service's method expects are represented by `args`.

> One tremendous benefit of the proxy class is that, because it contains local methods for all the methods exposed by the service, it allows you to take advantage of Visual Studio .NET's autocompletion features. This saves you from having to memorize all of the function calls and their methods when you try to implement a service in your applications.

Listing 8.1 shows the Visual Basic code to add the `FourFunctionCalc` methods to the button-click events of your form. Each of the calls uses the `CInt` function to convert the contents of the text boxes into the integer variables that the method requires. You then use the `ToString` method to convert the type long answer returned by the service's method into a string that can be displayed in the output text box.

LISTING 8.1 The Four Function Calculator's Button Events

```
Protected Sub Button1_Click(ByVal sender As Object, _
                        ByVal e As System.EventArgs)

     TextBox3.Text = oCalc.Add(CInt(TextBox1.Text), _
                        CInt(TextBox2.Text)).ToString

End Sub

Protected Sub Button2_Click(ByVal sender As Object, _
                        ByVal e As System.EventArgs)

       TextBox3.Text = oCalc.Subtract( _
       CInt(TextBox1.Text), CInt(TextBox2.Text)).ToString

 End Sub

 Public Sub Button3_Click(ByVal sender As Object, _
                      ByVal e As System.EventArgs)

```

continues

LISTING 8.1 Continued

```
        TextBox3.Text = oCalc.Mulitply(CInt(TextBox1.Text), _
                              CInt(TextBox2.Text)).ToString

    End Sub
    Public Sub Button4_Click(ByVal sender As Object, _
                          ByVal e As System.EventArgs)

        TextBox3.Text = oCalc.Divide(CInt(TextBox1.Text), _
                              CInt(TextBox2.Text)).ToString

     End Sub
```

Once you have finished coding the button-click events, save your project. Now, choose Start from the Build menu, or simply press F5. This will start the `CalcClient` application, shown in Figure 8.7.

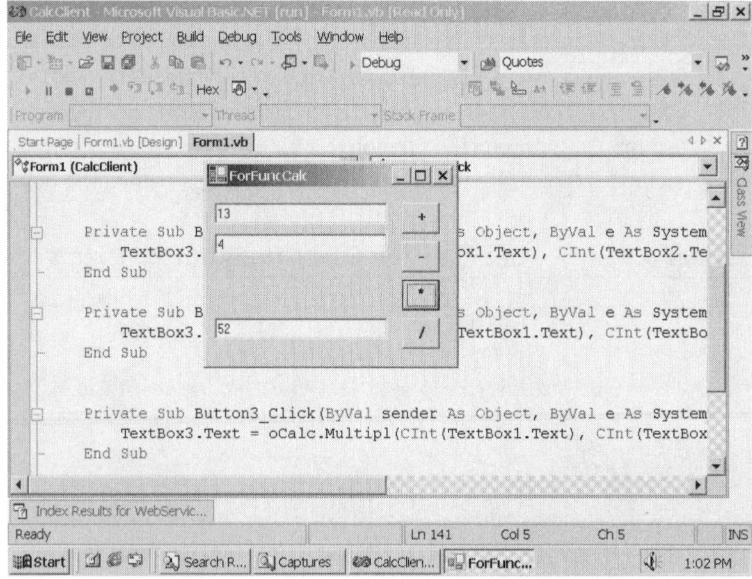

FIGURE 8.7
The four-function calculator at work.

Try typing some variables and testing that the code works. Remember that we have not added any code to ensure that only integers are typed into the text boxes. If you wish to add code to ensure that the data entered into TextBox1 and TextBox2 is of type integer, you are free to do so.

Building a Proxy Class with WSDL.exe

An alternative to using the Visual Studio.NET Web Reference wizard to create your proxy classes is a DOS utility called WSDL.exe. WSDL.exe, although much more complicated to use than the Visual Studio tool, provides far greater control over the DLL that is created.

Another great benefit of the WSDL.exe is that it is built into the .NET framework. This means that developers creating ASP applications without the benefit of the Visual Studio.NET tool set can create proxy classes, compile them using a set of DOS compilers, and consume Web services in their applications.

Listing 8.2 shows the syntax for using the WSDL.exe. The switches, any of the commands proceeded by a /, are used to set various parameters of the utility. Switches in brackets, [], are optional, and if left off will either revert to some default or not be used at all.

LISTING 8.2 The Syntax for the WSDL.exe

```
WSDL.exe [/language:] [/protocol:] [/namespace:]
         [/username] [/password] [/domain]
         [/out:] <url or path>
```

Table 8.1 shows the various switches used by the WSDL.exe application. The switches pertaining to working with a proxy server and to switching base URLs have been left out. If you need to accomplish one of these tasks, you can get help by simply typing

```
Wsdl /?
```

TABLE 8.1 WSDL.exe's Switches

Command	*Short*	*Description*
url or path		The URL, or path name if the file has been stored locally, to an SDL, XSD, or discomap file.
/nologo		Turns off the banner.
/language	/l	Chooses the language that the proxy will be generated in. VB, JS, and CS are all valid.
/server		Triggers the generation of an abstract class for the XML Web service.
/namespace	/n	Determines the namespace of the generated proxy class.
/out	/o	The path and file name of the generated proxy class.
/protocol		Can set the proxy to work with SOAP, httpGet, or httpPost protocols.
/username	/u	Username for authenticating to a server.
/password	/p	Password for authenticating to a server.
/domain	/	Domain for authenticating to a server.
/proxy		Url of the proxy server being used for http requests.

The out switch and path or url are the two settings that you will need to concern yourself with the most when creating proxies. In order to create a proxy, the out switch needs to be set to a valid file name—for example, SomeName.VB, in the case of a Visual Basic proxy. The path needs to be set to the URL or local file path of the Web Service's WSDL file.

It is a good idea to use a tool such as Internet Explorer to confirm the path to a Web Service's WSDL file before you enter it into the WSDL.exe's path switch. Errors will result if the path switch has the utility pointing to an incorrect URL.

Creating the Four Function Calculator's Proxy with WSDL.exe

Open a DOS Window and, at the C prompt, type in the command in Listing 8.3. This will create a proxy class called FourFunctionCalc.cs and place it in a directory called book on your C drive. Feel free to modify the directory that you save the proxy class to. The command also gives the proxy a namespace of FourCalc.

LISTING 8.3 Using WSDL.exe to Create a Proxy Class for the Four-Function Calculator

```
C:\>WSDL.exe /language:CS /namespace:FourCalc /out:c:\Captures\FourCalc.cs
http:\\localhost/FourFunctionCalc/Service1.asmx?sdl
```

You can use the optional language tag to create the proxy class in Visual Basic if you wish to examine the code and are more comfortable with Visual Basic. There is almost never a reason to alter this class yourself. For the purposes of this example, you can let the proxy be created using the default language, C#.

Figure 8.8 shows how the DOS window should appear if you have successfully created your proxy class.

Now, you can compile the class into a usable dll. This can be done by either opening the class in Visual Studios, or by using one of the command line compilers that ships with the .NET framework. Those compilers, reachable through a DOS prompt, are csc, to

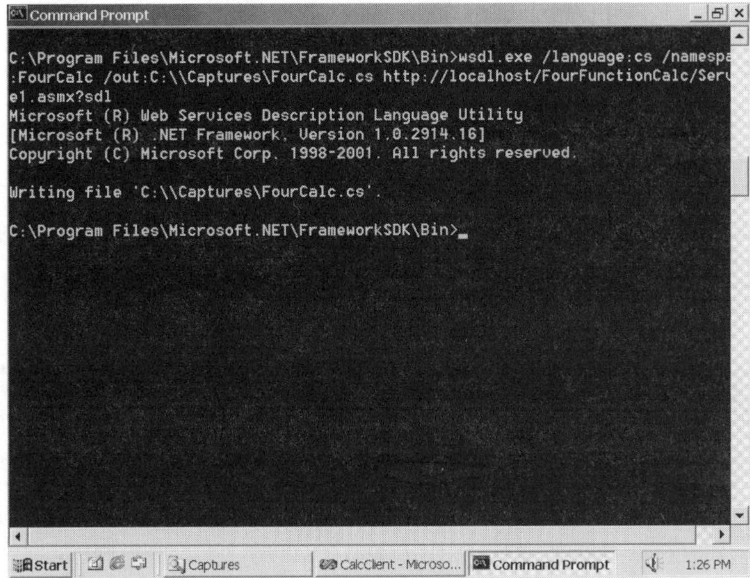

FIGURE 8.8
Creating the Four Function Calculators Proxy Code

compile C# code, and vbc, for compiling Visual Basic code. With these compilers, it is possible, though not at all advisable, to write complete programs in a Word Processor, even one as simple as Notepad, and compile them.

Listing 8.4 shows the command syntax for compiling your C# class.

LISTING 8.4 Compiling the Proxy Class

```
C:\>csc /t:library /r:System.Web.Services.dll
/out:c:\Book\FourCalc.dll c:\Captures\FourCalc.CS
```

> The command in Listing 8.4 should be entered in as one continuous line with space appearing before each / switch.

The `/t` or `target` switch is set to `library`, which lets the compiler know that you are trying to create a DLL. The `/r` or `reference` switch tells the compiler to include a reference to `System.Web.Services.dll`.

The final switch of the command is the /out switch, which sets the name and path of the DLL you wish to create. In this case, you are creating a DLL called `FourCalc` to be placed in the directory `c:\Book`. You may feel free to change the directory to whatever you like.

The last portion of the command is the path to the proxy class that was created by the WSDL.exe, c:\Captures\FourCalc.cs or whatever path you saved the file to.

To obtain help on the csc, C# compiler, type in the following command at a DOS prompt:

```
csc /?
```

In order to obtain help on the Visual Basic command line compiler, vbc, type the following in at a DOS prompt:

```
vbc /?
```

These compilers include the ability to generate bug reports, link additional resources, set precompiler directives, and much more.

Adding a Reference to a Proxy DLL

Once you have created and compiled the FourCalc.dll, you can begin using it in your client applications. Create a new Windows application called FourCalcClient to act as the client to your new proxy.

Inside your new project, create a form identical to the one you created in the CalcClient application (see Figure 8.1 for the form's layout).

You can now add a reference to your FourCalc proxy. This time, because the proxy is already created and local, you will add the reference the way you would any other DLL. Choose Add Reference from the Project menu to bring up the Add Reference dialog. From there, choose Browse and navigate to your FourFunc.dll. Figure 8.9 shows the Select Component dialog for finding components.

Now that you have found and selected your component, add a reference to the System.Web.Services.dll. You should see both DLLs at the bottom of the Add Reference screen, in the Selected Components window (see Figure 8.10).

Using the WSDL.exe-Generated Proxy Class

After you have added your references, using the XML Web service proxy is just like using the proxy generated by Visual Studio .NET, except that you have control over the location of the DLL and can reuse the DLL in additional projects without having to go through the trouble of using the Add Web Reference dialog again.

To create an instance of the FourCalc.dll's Service1 object, add the following line to the general declarations section of your FourCalcClient's Form1:

```
Dim oCalc As New FourCalc.Service1()
```

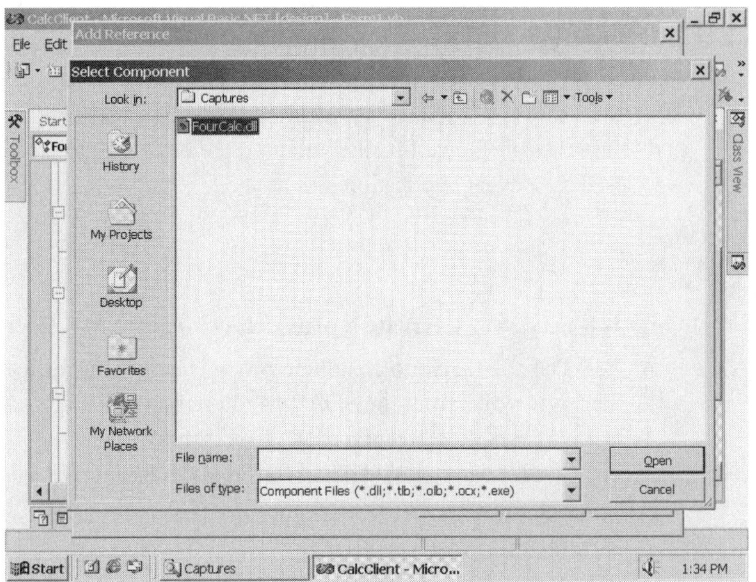

FIGURE 8.9
Adding a reference to the four function calculator's proxy.

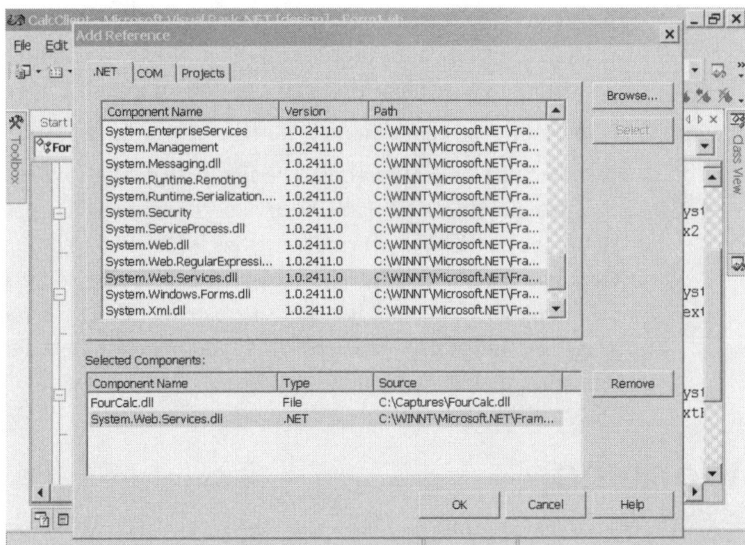

FIGURE 8.10
Adding all the references to the four function calculator.

After creating the `oCalc` object, you can add code to the button events of `Form1`. The code for these events is identical to that of the `CalcClient` application, shown in Listing 8.1.

You can now run the application and verify that both versions of the four-function calculator's clients behave in exactly the same manner.

Summary

In this hour, you learned how to create proxy classes that help your applications use XML Web services. You also learned how to declare XML Web services in your code and to use their methods. Finally, you used the `WSDL.exe` to create proxy classes that were used by a client application.

Q&A

Q Is it necessary to create a proxy class for my XML Web service clients?

A Yes. The alternative to creating a proxy class via one of the tools described in this hour is to write all of the SOAP-handling functionality yourself and, for all intents and purposes, to recreate a proxy from scratch. This may be interesting as a learning exercise but is not practical for most development scenarios.

Q Is there a way to create a single class that can broker selected references from several XML Web services?

A It is possible to create a single class that handles the methods of multiple XML Web services. This is done using `WSDL.exe`. To selectively eliminate unwanted methods from the resultant class, you have to directly remove them from the generated source code before compiling. This is beyond the scope of this book; attempting to alter these files can cause them to fail.

Q Is there ever a reason to use `WSDL.exe` if you have Visual Studio .NET?

A Yes, there are several reasons. The first is that `WSDL.exe` allows you to create a class from multiple XML Web services at one time. This allows one class to serve all of your XML Web service functions, or at least to group together related services into several classes. The second reason is that you can control the location of the output DLL, making it easier to create one DLL and reuse it in multiple projects. You should expect Microsoft to add many of these features to the Web Reference dialogues in future releases.

Workshop

The workshop is designed to help you review what you've learned in this hour and to prepare you for the material that will be covered in future hours. The answers to the quiz are in Appendix A.

Quiz

1. Where is `WSDL.exe` found?

   A At the DOS prompt of any machine with the .NET framework installed.

2. How do you add a Web reference to a project in Visual Studio .NET?

   A By using the dialog displayed by Add Web Reference under the Project menu.

3. How do you create a new object, called `oService`, based on the `Accounting` class of a XML Web service DLL called `AccountSoft`

   A In Visual Basic:

   ```
   Dim oService as new AccountSoft.Accounting
   ```

   In C#:

   ```
   AccountSoft.Accounting oService = new_ AccountSoft.Accounting
   ```

4. What does the `/language` setting of `WSDL.exe` do?

   A It controls the language in which the resulting proxy class is created.

5. What is the name of the DLL that is commonly added to XML Web service clients to obtain functionality specific to XML Web service clients?

   A `System.Web.Services.dll`.

Exercises

Create code for any new method that you added to the four-function calculator in the last hour. Also, if you have created any new XML Web services, try creating clients for them as well.

Here is the code for the squaring function that was added at the end of Hour 7.

```
Public Sub Button5_Click(ByVal sender As Object, _
                   ByVal e As System.EventArgs)

   TextBox3.Text = oCalc.Squared(CInt(TextBox1.Text)).ToString

 End Sub
```

Hour 9

Web Clients for the Four Function Calculator

In this hour, you will look at the standard HTTP protocols httpGet and httpPost, and you will learn how to use them to make requests of XML Web services. You will make further use of these protocols in building client applications that work on operating systems that are not running the .NET platform. Finally, you will learn about the XML Web service method and how it can be used to create Web-embedded scripts that make calls to XML Web services.

Throughout this hour, we will discuss the following:

- Accessing XML Web services via httpGet
- Using httpPost to access XML Web services
- Building clients using `Get` and `Post`
- The XML Web service method

Accessing XML Web Services via httpGet and httpPost

As you learned earlier, XML Web services communicate with client applications via standard Internet HTTP protocols. These protocols, httpGet and httpPost, can be used to communicate with XML Web services without the need to use the .NET-created proxy classes that you learned about in Hour 8. This is important if you are building simple Web pages that will run on non-ASP enabled servers or if you are writing Windows client applications for platforms that will not run the .NET platform.

For those of you who are unfamiliar with httpGet and httpPost from their use in HTML Forms, they are both methods for sending information back to a Web server and requesting that a particular program or script be run. Where httpGet and httpPost differ is in the method that they use to send information back to the server.

httpGet, or the `Get` method as it is often called, is the default method for sending requests. httpGet appends any parameters as name value pairs at the end of the requesting URL string. This takes the following form:

```
http://SomeAdress\appname.ext?var1=val1&var2=val2
```

Where `appname.ext` represents some application or script, such as `counter.cgi` or `newpage.asp`, `SomeAddress` represents a valid URL such as `www.Microsoft.com` or `Localhost`. Name values pairs are added to the end of the URL, one after the other, such as `var1 = val1`, and are separated by the ampersand symbol.

httpPost, on the other hand, does not append values to a URL, but instead packages the exact same name value pair into the return document itself. The httpPost method is often preferred because it allows larger amounts of data to be transferred and keeps secret information, such as passwords, from being displayed to the screen.

Using httpGet to Access an XML Web Service

You have already seen the httpGet method of contacting XML Web services in action, even if you didn't realize it. Whenever you utilize the Internet Explorer form that is automatically generated for an XML Web service, you are using an httpGet client.

Listing 9.1 shows the HTML to create a form that utilizes the `Get` method, or httpGet protocol, to contact an XML Web service and request that a method be run. Type this code in Notepad or your favorite Web editing software and then open it in Explorer.

Listing 9.1 HTML Form Using httpGet to Access the Four Function Calculator

```
1:  <html>
2:  <head>
3:  <title>Four Function Adder httpGet Client</title>
4:  </head>
5:
6:  <body>
7:  Add Method
8:  <form METHOD="GET" target="_blank"
9:   action='http://localhost/FourFunctionCalc/Service1.asmx/Add'>
10:  <input type="text" size="50" name='iNum1'\">
11:  <input type="text" size="50" name='iNum2'\">
12:  <BR>
13:  <input type=submit value="Invoke">
14:  </form>
15:  </body>
16:  </html>
```

The important thing to notice here is the action method of the form in line 8. Notice that you call the XML Web service directly from its URL and not via some reference to a proxy application. When you run this in a browser and click the Invoke button—see Figure 9.1—the answer will be brought up in a new window.

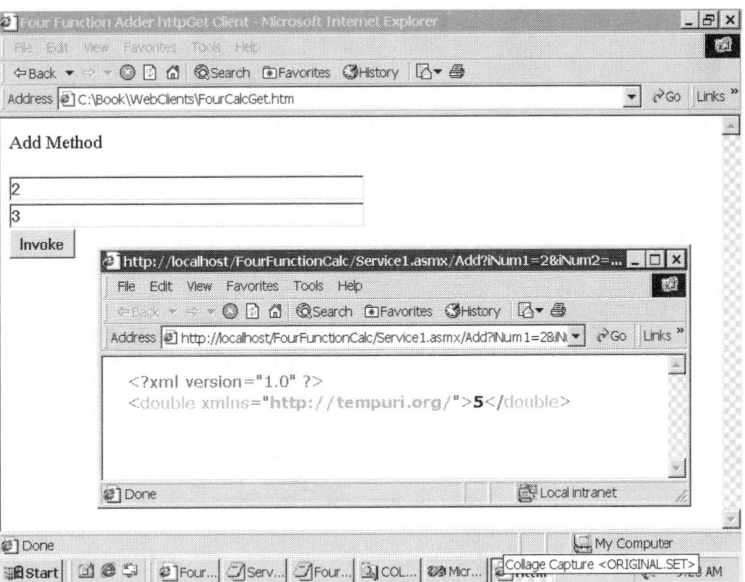

Figure 9.1
The `Add` *method of the* `FourFunctionCalc` *XML Web service via httpGet.*

Note the URL inside of the new window. This address can be used to directly contact the XML Web service and request a method. Try typing the following URL directly into Internet Explorer:

```
http://localhost/FourFunctionCalc/Service1.asmx/Add?iNum1=4&iNum2=4
```

If you change the values of `iNum1` and `iNum2` and refresh the screen, the `FourFunctionCalc`'s `Add` method will be called with those values. This will be useful to you when you create an httpGet client application later in this hour.

Using httpPost to Access an XML Web Service

Similar to the httpGet file above, the HTML in Listing 9.2 creates a form that can be used to communicate with an XML Web service. The only real difference between the two listings is the use of the POST method in line 8 of Listing 9.2.

LISTING 9.2 HTML Form Using httpPost to Access the `FourFunctionCalc`

```
1:   <html>
2:   <head>
3:   <title>Four Function Adder httpPost Client</title>
4:   </head>
5:
6:   <body>
7:   Add Method
8:   <form METHOD="POST" target=_Blank
9:      action='http://localhost/FourFunctionCalc/Service1.asmx/Add'>
10:  <input type="text" size="50" name='iNum1'\">
11:  <input type="text" size="50" name='iNum2'\">
12:  <BR>
13:  <input type=submit value="Invoke">
14:  </form>
15:  </body>
16:  </html>
```

When you run this example, see Figure 9.2, you will note that the `parameters` string is not appended to the end of the requesting URL. This means that you will need to package variables into the packet sent back to the Web server.

It should be noted that httpPost and httpGet could have been used interchangeably in the example above. Keeping that in mind, httpPost is generally the preferred method, next to the SOAP method demonstrated in Hour 8, for communicating with Web services. This is due to the manner in which each sends arguments across the Intenet. HttpGet, the older protocol, simply appends the arguments to the end of the URL and is therefore a much less secure method of transmitting data.

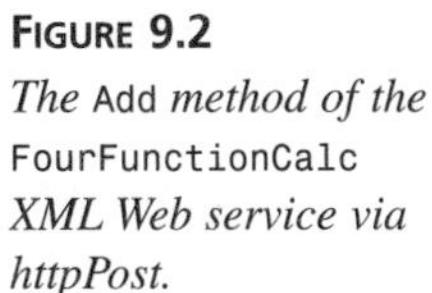

FIGURE 9.2
The `Add` *method of the* `FourFunctionCalc` *XML Web service via httpPost.*

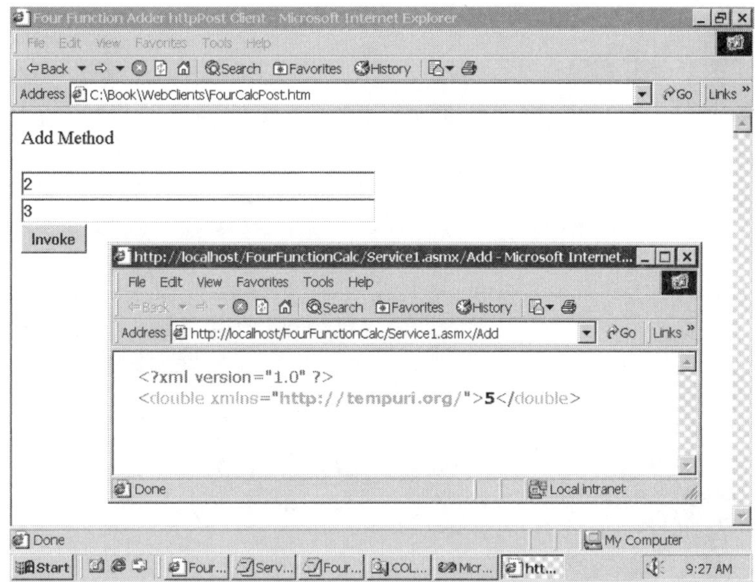

Creating an XML Web Service Consumer Using httpGet

Now that you have seen how the httpGet and httpPost methods work in calling XML Web services, you can put this knowledge to use in building client applications with them.

> Much of the code in this section is written in Visual Basic 6.0. If you do not have Visual Basic 6.0 available to you for these projects, you could adapt the code to work in other languages, including any language found in Visual Studio .NET. Although Visual Studio would normally provide a proxy, you can still write your code this way as a learning exercise.

Open a new Standard EXE project in Visual Basic 6.0 and call it `GetCalc`. To this project we will add the Microsoft Internet Transfer Control to handle all of our HTTP communications with the Web server. To add this component, choose Components from the Project menu. This will bring up the Components Dialog seen in Figure 9.3. Find the Microsoft Internet Transfer Control and check it, and then select Okay.

Now add three text boxes and four buttons to the form, as shown in Figure 9.4. The four buttons should be in a control array, but the three text boxes should not. Set the `TextBox3`, the large text box at the bottom of the form, `MultiLine` property to `True`. Then add an Internet Transfer Control to the form. Don't worry about where you place it, as it is invisible at run time.

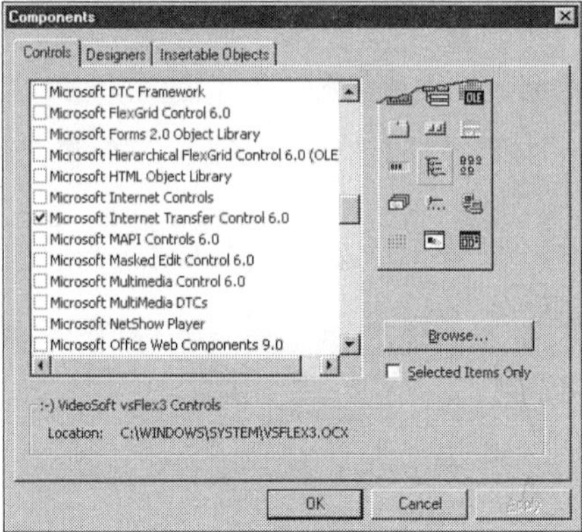

FIGURE 9.3
Adding the Microsoft Internet Transfer Control.

FIGURE 9.4
The Visual Basic 6.0 form for `GetCalc`.

A control array is a group of controls of the same type, that is, Textboxes, Listboxes, and so on, each having the same value for their name property. These controls are then distinguished by an integer-valued index in the same manner as other arrays that you have worked with. The easiest way to create a control array is to place a control upon a form and set its properties. Then, when this is done, use copy and paste to create additional copies of the control. Visual Studios will prompt you to ask if you wish to create a control array.

Use the code in Listing 9.3 to initialize the Internet Transfer Control, named `Inet1`, to work with HTTP.

LISTING 9.3 Initializing the Internet Transfer Control

```
Private Sub Form_Load()
   Inet1.Protocol = icHTTP
End Sub
```

Now add the code in Listing 9.4 to the Click event of the button array.

LISTING 9.4 Using httpGet to Communicate with an XML Web Service in Visual Basic 6.0

```
1:    Private Sub Command1_Click(Index As Integer)
2:    Dim sType As String
3:
4:     Select Case Index
5:      Case 0
6:         sType = "Add"
7:      Case 1
8:         sType = "Subtract"
9:      Case 2
10:        sType = "Multiply"
11:     Case 3
12:         sType = "Divide"
13:    End Select
14:
15:    Text3.Text = Inet1.OpenURL("http://localhost/FourFunctionCalc/
          Service1.asmx/" _
16:    & sType & "?iNum1=" & CInt(Text1) & " &iNum2=" & CInt(Text2), icString)
17:
18:   End Sub
```

The first portion of the code, the `Select` statement, merely determines which calculator function button you choose and stores the name of the corresponding XML Web service's method to a string variable called `sType`.

In line 15, you set the `OpenURL` property of the Internet Transfer Control to the URL of the service. The `OpenURL` method of the Internet Transfer Control sends a URL request to a server and returns a string containing the returned HTML or XML document. Notice that, after the URL, name-value pairs are appended to the URL.

When you run the `GetCalc` program, as shown in Figure 9.5, the return value is currently the entire SOAP return message from the `FourFunctionCalc` XML Web service.

There are several ways that you could deal with this return-value SOAP document. The first would be to use an XML handling Library, such as MSXML 3.0. This works fine, and in fact, you will use it in the next example. Another method is simply to parse the

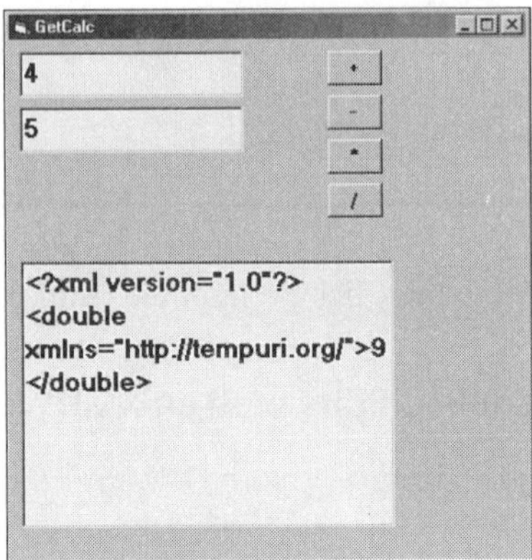

FIGURE 9.5
Running the `GetCalc` *client application.*

returned string. Since you know that the resulting SOAP message will always be of the same format, you can just drop the XML tags and keep the number value. Listing 9.5 shows an example of some code that may be added to your button click event in order to reduce the return value to just the expected numeric result.

LISTING 9.5 Parsing the String Returned from the `FourFunctionCalc` XML Web Service

```
sReturn = Inet1.OpenURL("http://localhost/FourFunctionCalc/Service1.asmx/" _
  & sType & "?iNum1=" & CInt(Text1) & " &iNum2=" & CInt(Text2), icString)
sReturn = Right(sReturn, Len(sReturn) - 59)
sReturn = Left(sReturn, InStr(sReturn, "<") - 1)
Text3.Text = sReturn
```

If you replace line 15 in Listing 9.4 with the code in Listing 9.5, remember to declare the variable `sReturn` as type `String` before using it, and then run the program. You now have a calculator that returns a more conventional result (see Figure 9.6).

Creating an XML Web Service Consumer Using httpPost

Now that you have seen how to contact an XML Web service by using simple Web protocols in your applications, you are ready for a more complicated example. In this example, you will use the httpPost method and the Microsoft XML Parsing library to contact a Web server and handle the retrieved data.

Create a new Standard EXE project in Visual Basic 6.0 and call it `PostCalc`. Within `PostCalc`, create a form that looks just like the one you created in Figure 9.4. Again, the four buttons will be part of a control array, but the text boxes will not be.

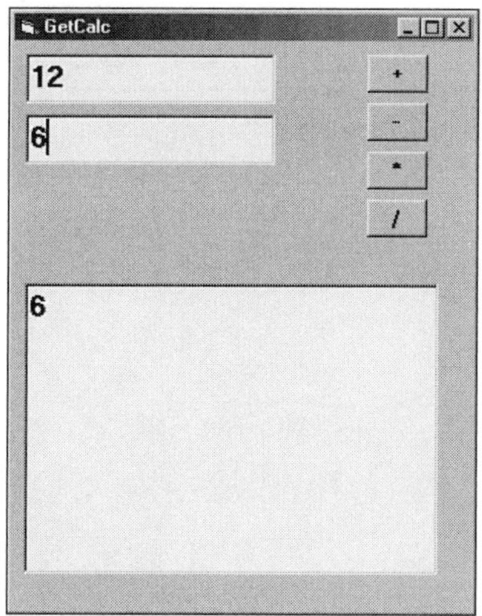

FIGURE 9.6
Returning the parsed value from the `FourFunctionCalc` *XML Web service.*

You will not need the Internet Transfer Control for this example. Instead, you will be using Microsoft's XML (MSXML) library, which is available for download at

`http://msdn.microsoft.com/downloads`

Bring up the References Dialog, shown in Figure 9.7, by selecting References from the Project menu. Search through the listing until you see a listing for "Microsoft XML, v3.0"; check it and then select Okay.

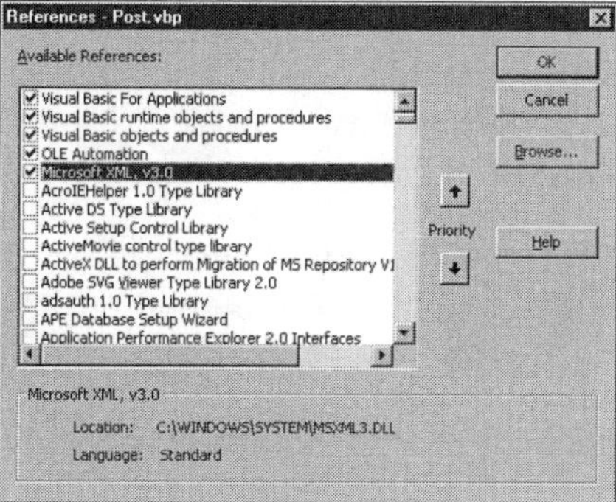

FIGURE 9.7
Adding a reference to Microsoft XML v3.0.

With the form set up, you can add the code in Listing 9.6 to the Click event of your button array.

LISTING 9.6 Using httpPost to Communicate with XML Web Services in Visual Basic 6.0

```
1:   Private Sub Command1_Click(Index As Integer)
2:    Dim oHTTP As New XMLHTTP
3:    Dim oReturn As DOMDocument
4:    Dim sType As String
5:    Dim sReturn As String
6:
7:   Select Case Index
8:    Case 0
9:        sType = "Add"
10:    Case 1
11:        sType = "Subtract"
12:    Case 2
13:        sType = "Mulitply"
14:    Case 3
15:        sType = "Divide"
16:  End Select
17:
18:  oHTTP.open "POST" _
19:   "http://localhost/FourFunctionCalc/Service1.asmx/" & sType, False
20:  oHTTP.setRequestHeader "Content-Type" _
21:   "application/x-www-form-urlencoded"
22:  oHTTP.send "iNum1=" & CInt(Text1) & "&iNum2=" & CInt(Text2)
23:
24:  Set oReturn = oHTTP.responseXML
25:
26:  Text3 = oReturn.Text
27:  End Sub
```

The first section of the code, determining your method name via the `Select Case`, is already familiar to you. Lines 18–22 use the XMLHTTP library to send an HTTP request to the XML Web service.

Line 18 uses the `Open` method to create the request and set its type to POST. It is here that we set the URL of the service, as well. Notice that the parameter data is not appended to the string.

After you open the request, you set the request header to use URL encoding. This ensures that MSXML sends the data over as an HTML form. This is important if your methods parameters are to be correctly interpreted by the XML Web service being summoned.

Finally, you use the `send` method to append the parameters, in name-value pairs, to the request and send it to the server.

Next, we create a `DOMDocument` object to hold the returning SOAP document (see line 24 of Listing 9.6), and we use the object's `Text` property to return only the value of the returned value to `Text3`. Figure 9.8 shows `PostCalc` after a successful XML Web service call.

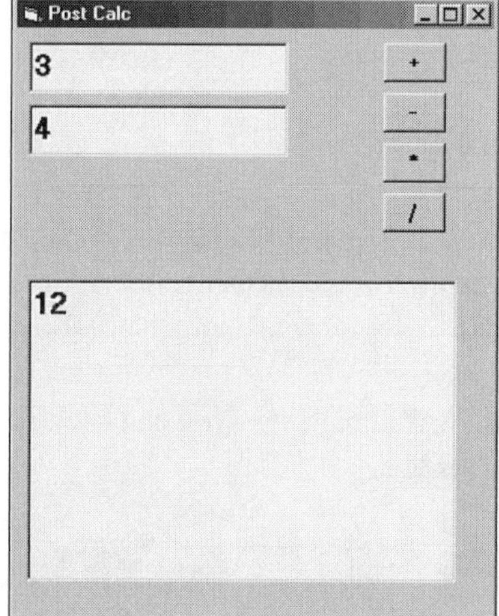

FIGURE 9.8
Running the `PostCalc` *Client.*

In more complex situations, such as methods returning arrays or objects, you could use MSXML object to parse through the document and pull out each individual value, or you could use XML Transforms to change the document into a different return structure altogether. These methods are beyond the scope of this book, though.

XML Web Service Behavior

The XML Web service behavior is a DHTML component that can be used by Internet Explorer 5.0 or higher to directly communicate with XML Web services via scripting. This allows you to design fully functioning Web pages that consume XML Web services without the use of a proxy and can easily manipulate any returned data, unlike the httpGet and httpPost form examples that you saw earlier in this hour.

At the time of this writing, the Web service behavior only works of the Web age being called is running in the same domain as the XML Web service being called. If you are having trouble getting your page to call a service and you think that you have done all of your coding correctly, try moving the HTML page into the directory that the service is in. If it doesn't function there, then the odds are that you still have a coding error to work out.

The XML Web service behavior works through the use of an HTML component call `webservice.htc`. This component is placed on the XML Web server along with any pages that make use of it.

If you are unfamiliar with DHTML and Web scripting, you may wish to come back to this section after you have gained some experience in those areas.

Figure 9.9 shows an example of a Web page that you can use to consume the `FourFunctionCalc` XML Web service.

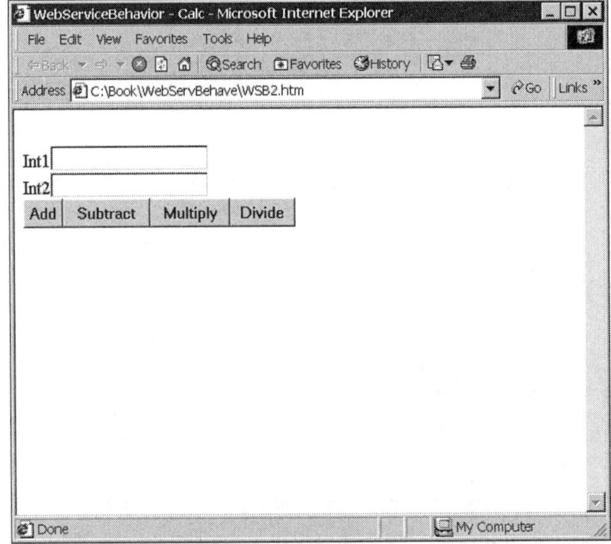

FIGURE 9.9
The form for the XML Web service behavior `FourFunctionCalc` *client.*

The first step in using an XML Web service behavior is to bind it to a DHTML element. In the example in Figure 9.7, line 47 shows the XML Web service behavior being bound to a DIV tag. The syntax for binding the XML Web service behavior is as follows:

```
<tag id="name" style="behavior:url(webservice.htc)">
```

With the XML Web service behavior bound to a control, you can begin to make references to XML Web services. This is accomplished by using the `useService` method of the XML Web service behavior to create a service reference as follows:

```
Tag.useService("URL", "name")
```

Tag is the name of the tag that the XML Web service behavior is bound to, URL is the URL of the XML Web service being called, and name is the name that you will use to refer to the service in code.

Line 10 of Listing 9.7 shows the useService method being used to refer to the FourFunctionCalc XML Web service. It has been given the name calc for use in further scripting. Additionally, you could have referenced additional XML Web services from within this project.

When you need to call the service, you use the callService method of the XML Web service behavior. Lines 35 through 45 show the callService method being used in the onClick events of the form's buttons in order to call specific methods of the service. This is done in the following format:

```
IRet = Tag.name.callService(["Handler"],"method", "param1", "param2",…"paramn")
```

Again, Tag is the name of the DHTML element that the XML Web service behavior is bound to, name is the name that you gave the service, method is a string containing the name of the XML Web service method being called, and param1 through paramn are a comma-separated list of any parameters that need to be sent to the XML Web service. IRet is the return value of the callService method. This result is an identifier and not the XML Web service method return. Handler is an optional function name that will handle the results. The default value for Handler is the onresult property of Tag.

LISTING 9.7 Using the XML Web Service Behavior

```
1:  <html>
2:  <head>
3:  <title>WebServiceBehavior - Calc</title>
4:  <script language="JavaScript">5
5:
6:  var iRetID;
7:
8:  function init()
9:  {
10:  ReturnSpace.useService(
11:     "http://localhost/FourFunctionCalc/Service1.asmx?WSDL","calc");
12:   }
13: function onResultRet()
14:   {
15:    if((event.result.error)&&(iRetID==event.result.id))
16:     {
17:      var sMessage = event.result.errorDetail.string;
18:      var sReturn = event.result.errorDetail.raw;
19:
20:      ReturnSpace.innerHTML= sMessage + "<BR>" +  sReturn;
```

continues

LISTING 9.7 Continued

```
    }
   else
    {
     ReturnSpace.innerHTML= event.result.value;
    }
  }
 </script>
 </head>
 <body onload="init();">
 <BR>
 Int1<input type='text' id='iVal1'>
 <BR>
  Int2<input type='text' id='iVal2'>
 <BR>
 <button onclick='iRetID =
  ReturnSpace.calc.callService("Add",iVal1.value,iVal2.value);'>Add</button>
 <button onclick='iRetID =
   ReturnSpace.calc.callService("Subtract",iVal1.value,iVal2.value);'>
   Subtract</button>
<button onclick='iRetID =
  ReturnSpace.calc.callService("Multiply",iVal1.value,iVal2.value);'>
  Multiply</button>
 <button onclick='iRetID =
  ReturnSpace.calc.callService("Divide",iVal1.value,iVal2.value);'>
  Divide</button>

 <div id="ReturnSpace" style="behavior:url(webservice.htc)"
   onresult="onResultRet();">
 </div>

 </body>
 </html>
```

Summary

In this hour, you learned to utilize httpPost and httpGet in order to create standard Web forms that request XML Web service methods. You also learned how to create XML Web service–consuming applications that run on non-.NET platforms. You ended this hour by examining the XML Web service method and building a Web page that communicates with an XML Web service via scripting.

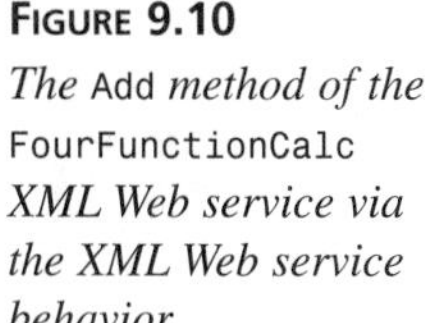

FIGURE 9.10
The `Add` *method of the* `FourFunctionCalc` *XML Web service via the XML Web service behavior.*

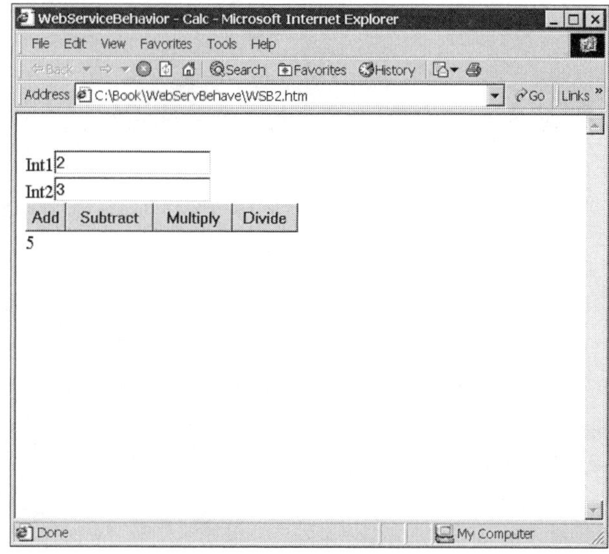

Figure 9.10 shows the return values for your `WebserviceBehavior` Web page.

Q&A

Q Can an HTML form using simple httpPost or httpGet protocols be set up to call different methods of a service by clicking different buttons?

A Yes, you would have to use scripting. Set the `Action` method of the form equal to a function in your script and then redirect the form from there.

Q Do I have to use the Internet Transfer Control to communicate with XML Web services via httpGet?

A No, you can use any library or component that facilitates Internet communications in order to send your httpGet requests.

Q Is there a way to create Web applications that consume XML Web services without using the XML Web service behavior and DHTML scripting?

A Yes, you could use ASP in conjunction with any of the other methods that we have learned. If ASP is not available to your Web page, and you need to fully utilize XML Web service calls within your document, the XML Web service behavior is your best bet.

Workshop

The Workshop is designed to help you review what you've learned in this hour and to point you ahead to the material that will be covered in future hours.

Quiz

1. What is the default method for sending Form requests via HTTP?

   A httpGet

2. Where is parameter data stored when requests are sent via httpPost?

   A Any data sent via httpPost requests are packaged, as name-value pairs, into the document that is sent to the contacted service.

3. What method, httpPost or httpGet, can be used to access XML Web services directly from Internet Explorer's address bar?

   A httpGet is the default method and, thus, the one that can be used by directly typing URLs into the address bar.

4. Can you consume multiple XML Web services in a Web page making use of the XML Web service behavior?

   A Yes, as long as you give them all unique names, you can consume multiple services.

5. Using an XML Web service behavior, how would you call a method named `Counter` for an XML Web service that you have already declared using the name `Bean`? The XML Web service behavior is bound to an element called `Navy` and there are no parameters to the method.

   A `iRet = Navy.Bean.callService("Counter")`

Exercises

Try experimenting with the different methods of requesting XML Web services. Try writing some Web pages using httpPost and httpGet. Write some new DHTML code to utilize the XML Web service behavior, such as calling any additional functions that you created at the end of Hour 7.

A. An httpGet HTML page for the `Multiply` method.

```
<html>
<head>
<title>Four Function Adder httpGet Client</title>
</head>
```

```

 <body>
 Add Method
 <form METHOD="GET" target="_blank"
  action='http://localhost/FourFunctionCalc/Service1.asmx/Multiply'>
  <input type="text" size="50" name='iNum1'\">
  <input type="text" size="50" name='iNum2'\">
  <BR>
  <input type=submit value="Invoke">
  </form>
  </body>
  </html>
```

Following is the code to add `Squared` (from the Hour 7 exercises) to your XML Web service behavior project. Add this code in after the Divide button.

```
<button onclick='iRetID =
 ReturnSpace.calc.callService("Squared",iVal1.value);'>
 Square</button>
```

PART III
Data in XML Web Services

Hour

HOUR 10

Data Types in XML Web Services

In this hour, you are going to learn about many of the data types that can be used in XML Web services. By the end of this hour you will be able to create services that accept and return primitive data types, arrays, and even classes.

In this hour we will discuss the following:

- Primitive data types
- Enumerations
- Arrays
- Handling classes
- Passing arguments `ByVal` and `ByRef`

Data Types in .NET

XML Web services offer a wide variety of options when it comes to how you represent and store data, from simple types for storing numbers, such as decimals and integers, to more complex types, such as arrays and classes. Table 10.1 shows some of the common data types in the .NET framework and their Visual Basic (VB) and C# equivalent names.

TABLE 10.1 Data Types in .NET

Data Type	*Visual Basic Name*	*C# Name*
Boolean	Boolean	bool
Byte	Byte	byte
Char	Char	char
Date	Date	date
Decimal	Decimal	decimal
Double	Double	double
_Int32	Integer	int
_Int64	Long	long
_Int16	Short	short
Single	Single	float
String	String	String

The data types that you choose in your XML Web service applications will play a crucial part in their performance. Remember, you are building an application that may be handling hundreds or thousands of requests at any given time; the larger the size of the variables that you use, the more memory your application will require and the slower it will run. Also, remember that in the operation of your service the IIS server and the client applications will be sending data back and forth between each other, and by using the smallest data types possible, you reduce network traffic and increase the efficiency of your apps.

Table 10.2 shows the size of some of the more common data types available to you. From looking at this table, and the data ranges given, you can quickly determine what data best suits your needs. If, for example, you were building a function that returned the number of tickets available at a particular venue and seating in the theater was around three thousand people, you would know to avoid data types such as Decimal and Long.

TABLE 10.2 Data Type's Sizes and Range

Data Type	*Bytes*	*Range*
Boolean	4	True or False
Byte	1	0 to 255
Char	2	0 to 65535
Date	8	Jan 1, 1 CE to Dec 31, 9999
Decimal	12	79,288,162,154,264,337,593,543,950, 335 with no decimal +/–E87.9,288,162,154,264,337,593, 543,950,335 with decimal
Double	8	–1.79769313486231E308 to –4.94065645841247E-324 AND 4.94065645841247E-324 to –1.79769313486232E308
_Int32	4	–2,147,483,648 to –2,147,483,647
_Int64	8	–9,223,372,036,854,775,808 to 9,223,372,036,854,775, 807
_Int16	2	–32,768 to 32,767
Single	4	–3.402823E38 to –1.401298E-45 OR 1.401298E-45 to –3.402823E38
String	10 + 2/Char	0 to 2 Billion Characters

10

Handling Primitive Data Types

Create a new XML Web services project and call it `DataTypes`. You can use this project to test all of the different data type handling methods that you will learn in this hour.

In the examples that you have seen so far in this book, only primitive data types have been returned. By this point, you should be fairly familiar with their use. Any of the primitive data types, such as Integer, String, or Long, can be returned in exactly the same manner.

Listing 10.1 shows an example of a method that returns a string. To return any other type, you would simply alter line 1 of the function declaration to return any of the other data types in Table 10.1.

LISTING 10.1 Returning a Simple Data Type in VB

```
<WebMethod()> Public Function StringReturn() As String
     Return "This is a string"
End Function
```

Listing 10.2 shows the equivalent function in C#. Again, you can use this method as a template to return any of the data types shown in Table 6.1.

LISTING 10.2 Returning a Simple Data Type in C#

```
[WebMethod]
public string StringReturn()
{
   return "This is a string";
}
```

Passing Arrays of Primitive Data Types

If you have never written code that returned an array of some data type before, there are a few things to keep in mind. Look at the code in Listing 10.3. In line 1, you will notice that the data type is listed as `Integer()`. The `()` indicate that our method will be returning an array of some unknown size. For those of you following along in C#, line 2 of Listing 10.4 shows the equivalent declaration using `int[]` to return an array of integers.

> As shown in Table 10.1, `int` is the C# version of a Visual Basic Integer.

LISTING 10.3 Returning an Array in VB

```
1:    <WebMethod()> Public Function ArrayReturn() As Integer()
2:         Dim a(5) As Integer
3:         Dim i As Integer
4:
5:         For i = 0 To 5
6:             a(i) = i + 1
7:         Next
8:
9:         Return a
10:   End Function
```

LISTING 10.4 Returning an Array in C#

```
1:   [WebMethod]
2:   public int[] ArrayReturn()
3:   {
4:      int[] a = new int[6];
5:     for (int i=0; i <6; i++ )
6:     {
7:       a[i] = i + 1;
8:     }
9:      return  a;
10:  }
```

When returning an array, simply return the array name without any brackets, as shown in line 9 of both Listing 10.3 and 10.4. This will return the entire array. Client code can check for the upper bounds of the array in order to retrieve the number of elements that the array contains.

When an array is returned from an XML Web service, the SOAP document contains the type declaration and value for every value in the array (see Figure 10.1) that is contained inside an XML tag proclaiming the contents to be type `ArrayofInt`.

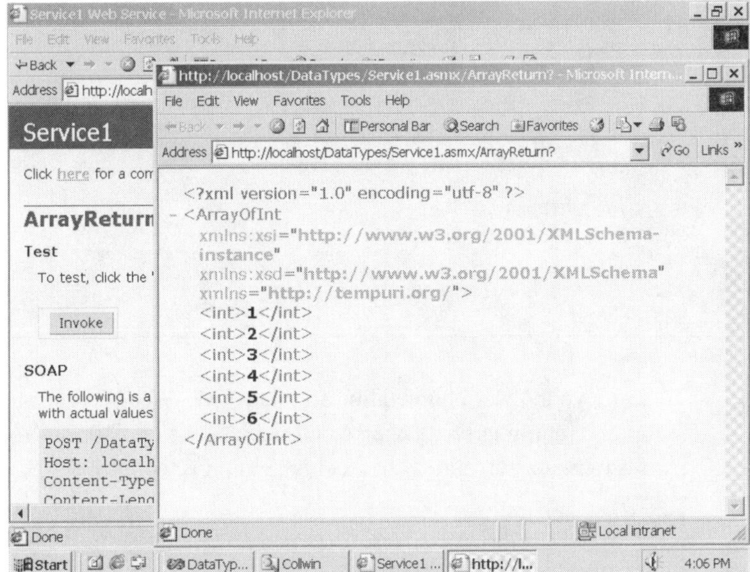

FIGURE 10.1
Returning an array from your XML Web service.

Working with Enumerations

An enumeration is a special data type that the user defines. At its core, an enumeration is a list of constants, but it is the ability to group these constants that makes an enumeration so powerful. Say, for example, that you were creating a service that tracked travel tickets, and each ticket sold could belong to a train, plane, or car. You could create an enumeration called `vehicle` and have it contain constants for each of the vehicle types.

To create an enumeration, you declare a variable of type `enum`, as shown in line 1 of Listing 10.5 (10.6 for C#). You then type your constant names—in this case the colors red, blue, and green—before you end the `enum`. You can now create variables of type `Color` in your service.

LISTING 10.5 Returning an Enumeration in VB

```
1:   Public Enum Color
2:      Red = 1
3:      Blue = 2
4:      Green = 3
5:   End Enum
6:
7:   <WebMethod()> Public Function EnumReturn() As Color
8:     Return Color.Red
9:   End Function
```

LISTING 10.6 Returning an Enumeration in C#

```
1:    public enum Color
2:      {
3:      Red = 1,
4:      Blue = 2,
5:      Green = 3
6:      }
7:
8:   [WebMethod]
9:   public Color EnumReturn()
10:    {
11:     return Color.Red;
12:    }
```

To return your Color enumeration from an XML Web service, simply declare your method as returning type `Color` (see Listings 10.5 and 10.6) and return a color. The syntax for retrieving a value from an enumeration is as follows:

```
EnumName.EnumValue
```

In the examples above, you return:

```
Color.Red
```

When an XML Web service returns an enumeration, it actually returns the value's name, not its value. In the example above, the service returns a data type `Color` with a value of `Red` (see Figure 10.2).

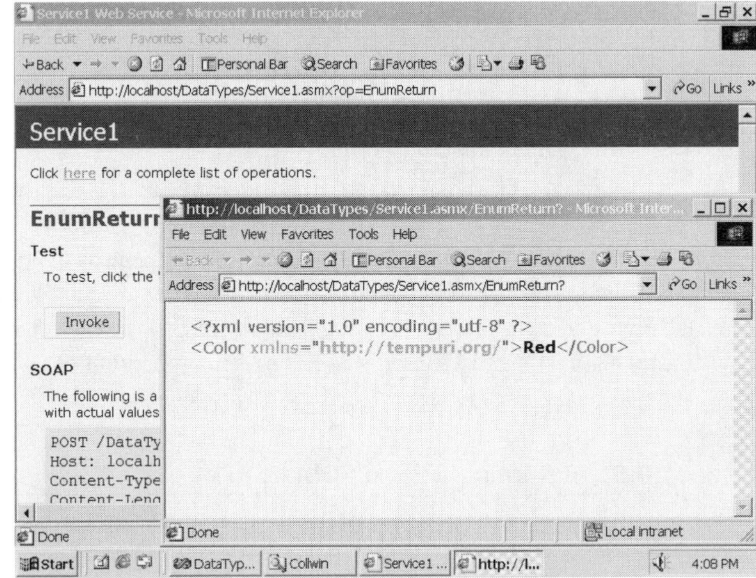

FIGURE 10.2
Returning an enumeration from an XML Web service.

Returning Classes

A class is a compound data type completely defined by you, the programmer. Much like the enumerations shown in Listings 10.5 and 10.6, a class is defined in your code, and the variables can be declared as the type of your class.

Listing 10.7 shows a simple class declared in Visual Basic. This class includes two variables, a string type called `Name` and an Integer type called `ID`. Listing 10.8 shows the same class declared in C#. Applications using your service would be unable to tell the two of them apart.

> Although classes can contain any data type, even enumerations and other classes, a complete discussion of classes is beyond the scope of this book. The examples used in this hour are very basic.

LISTING 10.7 A Class Declaration in VB

```
Public Class Person
   Public Name As String
   Public ID As Integer
End Class
```

Listing 10.8 A Class Declaration in C#

```
public class Person
  {
     public string Name;
     public int ID;
  }
```

When you wish to use your class, you declare a variable as the type of your class—in this example, `Person`. You then use the `New` keyword to actually create the object. With the object created, you can now begin setting its properties. In Listing 10.9 (Visual Basic) and Listing 10.10 (C#), we set the `Name` property of our new `Person` object, `oPerson`, equal to `"Jim Smith"` and the `ID` property to `5`.

Listing 10.9 Returning a Person Object in VB

```
1: <WebMethod()> Public Function ClassReturn() As Person
2:
3:    Dim oPerson As New Person()
4:
5:    oPerson.Name = "Jim Smith"
6:    oPerson.ID = 5
7:
8:    Return oPerson
9: End Function
```

Listing 10.10 Returning a Person Object in C#

```
[WebMethod]
public Person ClassReturn()
 {
   Person oPerson = new Person();

   oPerson.Name =  "Jim Smith";
   oPerson.ID = 5;
   return oPerson;
  }
```

To return your `oPerson` object to client applications, you declare your method to return type `Person`, as seen in line 1 of Listing 10.9, and then you simply return your `oPerson` object, as in Line 8 of the same listing.

When your object is returned, individual type information is not included. Instead, as shown in Figure 10.3, the objects are typed to their variable names. In this example, the return type is `Person` and contains types `Name` and `ID`.

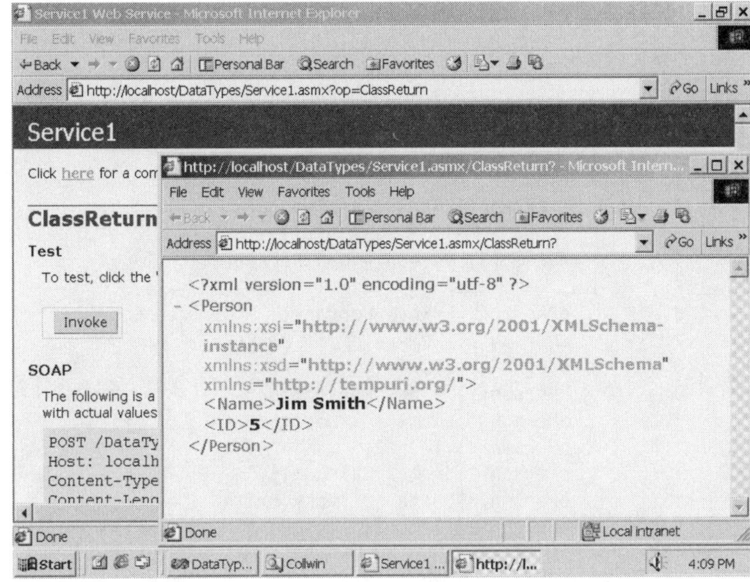

FIGURE 10.3
Returning an object of type `Person`.

Returning an Array of Classes

Returning an array of classes is very similar to returning a single class. First, you declare your method to return an array of some object type. Listing 10.11, for example, shows a method returning type `Person`.

Next, you create your array of objects, in our case three of them, and set their properties. When you are done setting their properties and running any other code that your method may require, you return your array, as shown in line 15.

LISTING 10.11 Returning an Array of `Person` Objects in VB

```
1:   <WebMethod()> Public Function ClassesReturn() As Person()
2:
3:      Dim oPerson(2) As Person
4:
5:      oPerson(0) = New Person()
6:      oPerson(0).Name = "Jim Smith"
7:      oPerson(0).ID = 1
8:      oPerson(1) = New Person()
9:      oPerson(1).Name = "Edgar Smith"
10:     oPerson(1).ID = 2
11:     oPerson(2) = New Person()
12:     oPerson(2).Name = "Mary Smith"
13:     oPerson(2).ID = 3
14:
15:     Return oPerson
16:    End Function
```

Listing 10.12 shows how C# returns an array of `Person` objects in the same manner as the previous Visual Basic example.

LISTING 10.12 Returning an Array of `Person` Objects in C#

```
[WebMethod]
public Person[] ArrayClassReturn()
   {
     Person[] oPerson = new Person[3];

     oPerson[0] = new Person();
     oPerson[0].Name =  "Jim Smith";
     oPerson[0].ID = 1;
     oPerson[1] = new Person();
     oPerson[1].Name =  "Edgar Smith";
     oPerson[1].ID = 2;
     oPerson[2] = new Person();
     oPerson[2].Name =  "Mary Smith";
     oPerson[2].ID = 3;

     return oPerson;
   }
```

The returned SOAP document for the array of `Person` objects is very similar to that shown in the previous example, only now, as shown in Figure 10.4, all three of your `Person` objects are wrapped in an XML tag showing a type `ArrayofPerson`.

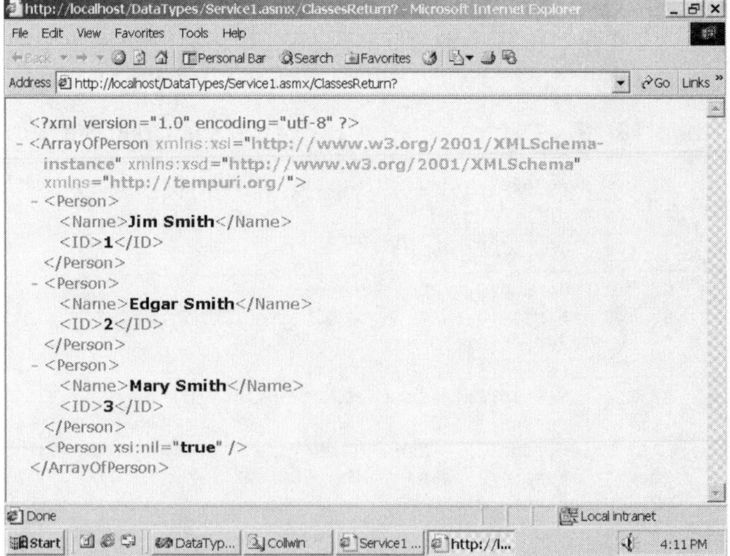

FIGURE 10.4
Returning an array of objects of type `Person`.

Passing Arguments

Often, it is necessary to do more than simply have your methods return data to a user request. Oftentimes, you will require some information from them in order to perform your tasks. This is where parameters come in. Parameters define the types of information that you are requesting from a client.

XML Web services accept all primitive data types as parameters. The syntax for declaring your parameters is exactly the same as it is in function calls in non XML Web service programming. That is to say, it takes the following form:

```
<Webmethod()> Public Function FuntionName (ByVal/byRef paramName as Type) as
type
```

Or in C#

```
Public type FunctionName(type paramName)
```

> `byVal` and `byRef` denote the way in which incoming variables are treated. For now, we will be using only `byVal`, which accepts a copy of the data and leaves the original unchanged. In later examples, we will want to change the original variables, and `byRef` will be used.

If you need to use multiple parameters, they must be separated by a comma.

Listing 10.13 shows an XML Web service method that accepts two strings as its parameters, concatenates them with the word "and" in between them, and returns the resulting string.

LISTING 10.13 Primitive Data Type Parameters in VB

```
<WebMethod()> Public Function ParamStringReturn( _
    ByVal sWord1 As String, ByVal sWord2 As String) As String

     Return sWord1 & " and " & sWord2

End Function
```

The C# declaration for that same example is as follows:

```
public string ParamStringReturn(string sWord1, string sWord2)
```

To call the above function, a client application could now use the following syntax:

```
SVar = Service.ParamStringReturn("HITHER", "THITHER")
```

In the above, `sVar` is a string variable for the return value and `Service` is the object reference to your XML Web service.

You can also accept more complicated types, such as enumerations, as parameters in your code. Listing 10.14 shows a new enumeration in Visual Basic.

LISTING 10.14 Enumeration Called `Champion` in VB

```
Public Enum Champion
     Corum = 1
     Renark = 2
     Urlich = 3
     Hawkmoon = 4
End Enum
```

Now we can accept this enumeration in code in exactly the same way as we did the previous primitive types. Listing 10.15 shows a method that will accept a variable of type `Champion`.

LISTING 10.15 Passing Enumerations into VB

```
<WebMethod()> Public Function ParamEnumReturn( _
         ByVal enumName As Champion) As champion

      Return enumName

End Function
```

The C# code for declaring the function would be

```
public Champion ParamEnumReturn(Champion enumName )
```

XML Web services allow us to accept variable sized arrays as parameters in our code. To do so, you would simply declare parameters as such:

```
ByVal/byRef paramName() as Type
```

Listing 10.16 demonstrates the Visual Basic method of accepting an array of integers, `iName`, as a parameter. This method then returns an integer—in this case the number of elements in the array.

LISTING 10.16 Accepting Arrays as Parameters in VB

```
<WebMethod()> Public Function ParamArrayReturn( _
       ByVal iName() As Integer) As Integer

     Return UBound(iName)

End Function
```

Listing 10.17 shows the C# method for accepting an array as a parameter. It also returns the number of elements in the array by using the `GetUpperBound` method. The ability to retrieve the number of elements in an array is crucial to working with them.

LISTING 10.17 Accepting Arrays as Parameters in C#

```
[WebMethod]
public int ParamArrayReturn( int[] iName )
  {
   return iName.GetUpperBound(0);
  }
```


Passing Arguments by Reference

Up until now, all the examples that you have seen have passed values in `byVal`. Using `byVal`, a copy of the variable is sent to the method and the original data is left unchanged. In this section, we will look at `byRef`. Using `byRef`, or `ref` in C#, a reference to the original variable is used and any alterations that the method does to its parameters are also done to the original variable in the calling program.

If you have been adding the previous methods into your `DataTypes` XML Web service, continue doing so with the following examples. If you haven't, you may wish to start, as you will soon be building a small client application to demonstrate how the following methods change the value of variables on the client.

Add Listing 10.18 to your service. This method accepts an integer as its parameter and then decrements it by one. It also saves a copy of the original value to pass back as its return value.

LISTING 10.18 Passing a Primitive Data Type `byRef` Parameters in VB

```
<WebMethod()> Public Function RefReturn ( _
      ByRef iVal As Integer) As Integer

   Dim iOld As Integer

   iOld = iVal
   iVal = iVal - 1

   Return iOld
End Function
```

If you are using C#, you will have to build your method using the following declaration:

```
public int RefReturn(ref int iVal)
```

After you have added the `refReturn` method, go back and make sure that you have the declaration for the `Person` class, Listing 10.7 (Listing 10.8 for C#), in your code. You will be using this class shortly.

Now, add listing 10.19 to your service. This new method will accept a `Person` object as a parameter and change its values.

LISTING 10.19 Accepting an Object as a Parameter in VB

```
<WebMethod()> Public Sub refClassReturn(ByRef oPers As Person)

  oPers.ID = oPers.ID - 1
  oPers.Name = "Hi " & oPers.Name

End Sub
```

For those following along in C#, declare your refClassReturn with the following line:

```
public void refClassReturn(ref Person oPers)
```

Now, save and build the project. At this point, you will begin work on a simple client application that will call your XML Web service and display the return values.

Create a new Windows application and add a Web reference to your DataType XML Web service. See Hour 8 if you need a reminder on how this is done.

Next, create a form that looks like the one shown in Figure 10.5. For simplicity's sake, leave the default names for all of the controls.

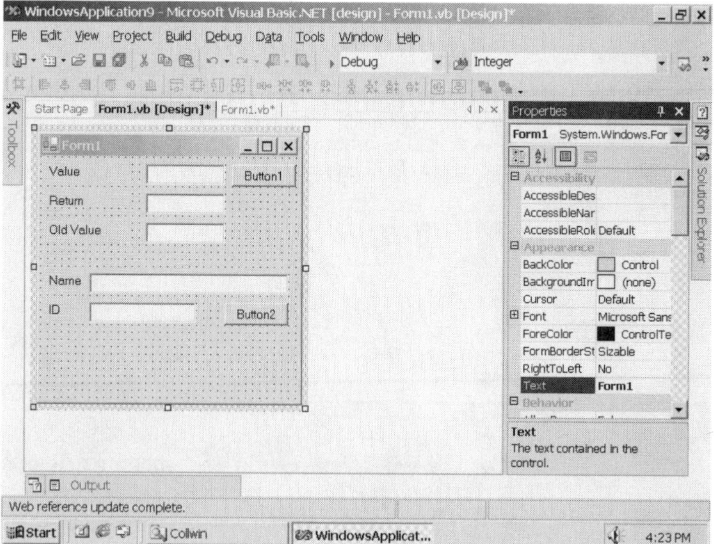

FIGURE 10.5
The form for your `byRef` *client application.*

Now, add the following line to your general declarations:

```
Dim oData As New localhost.Service1()
```

This will create the object reference to your DataType XML Web service.

Now, add listing 10.20 to the button click event of `Button1`. This code will take the integer value typed into TextBox1 and store it to a variable called `iVal`. `iVal` is then passed to the `RefReturn` method and the return value is displayed in `TextBox2`. The new value of `iVal` is displayed in `TextBox3`.

LISTING 10.20 Passing a Primitive Data Type by Reference

```
Protected Sub Button1_Click(ByVal sender As System.Object,_
        ByVal e As System.EventArgs) Handles Button1.Click

   Dim iVal As Integer

   iVal = CInt(TextBox1.Text)

   textbox3.text = CStr(oData.RefReturn (iVal))

    Textbox2.Text = CStr(iVal)

 End Sub
```

Figure 10.6 shows the end result of clicking `Button1`. Notice that the value of `iVal`, labeled "`Old Value`," is now decremented by one.

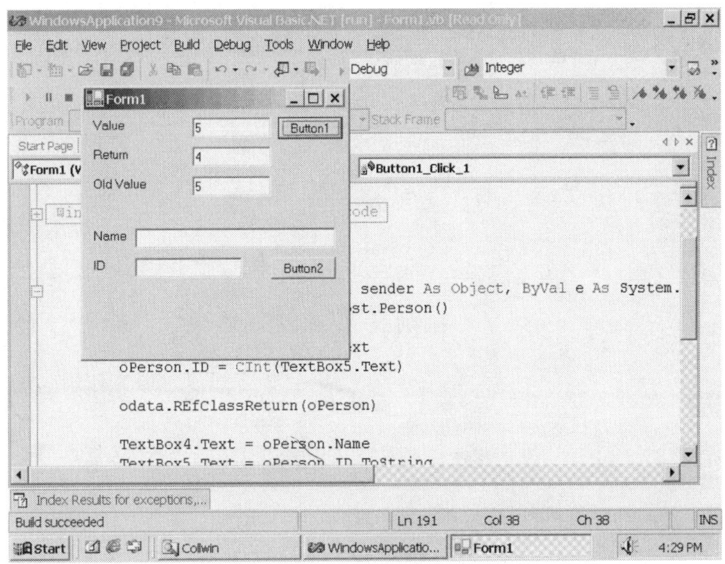

FIGURE 10.6
Returning values from your `refReturn` *method.*

Listing 10.21 shows the code that you should now add to the Click event of `Button2`. This code will take the values in `TextBox4` and `TextBox5` and store them into the `Name` and `Id` properties of our `oPerson` object. `oPerson` is then passed, `byRef`, to the `refClassReturn` method and the value refreshed to its respective textboxes.

LISTING 10.21 Passing an Object as a Parameter

```
Public Sub Button2_Click(ByVal sender As Object,_
     ByVal e As System.EventArgs) Handles Button2.Click

    Dim oPerson As New localhost.Person()

    oPerson.Name = textbox4.Text
    oPerson.ID = Cint(Textbox5.Text)

    odata.refClassReturn(oPerson)

     Textbox4.Text = oPerson.Name
     Textbox5.Text = CStr(operson.ID)
  End Sub
```

Figure 10.7 shows the results of passing the `Name` `"Danielle"` and `ID` `"6"` to the `refClassReturn` method.

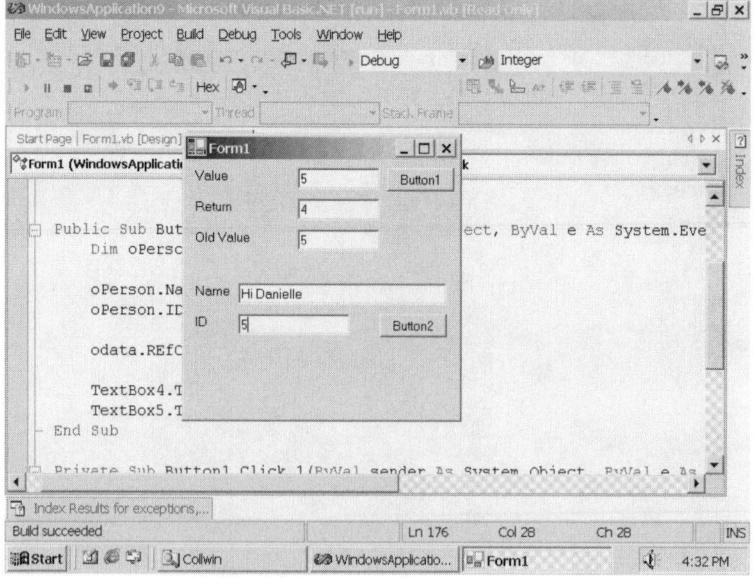

FIGURE 10.7
Returning an array of objects of type `Person`.

Summary

In this hour, you learned about some of the data types in .NET and what value ranges they can each hold. You also saw how to return variables of different types from XML Web service applications, as well as how to accept parameters both by value and by reference. Now, with these building blocks, you can move on to creating larger and more meaningful services.

Q&A

Q What is the purpose of having so many similar variable types, for example integers and longs?

A The purpose to having so many variable types is to help developers, such as you, better manage resources. You should always pick the smallest number possible of variable types that can handle the needs of your application.

Q What do I do if I want to create a function that alters the parameters passed to it, but doesn't return a value?

A The first part of the answer is to declare your parameters as either `ByRef` in Visual Basic or `ref` in C#. The second part of the answer, creating a function that returns nothing, can be done in Visual Basic by using a subroutine instead of a function. In C#, you would still use a function, but you would declare it as returning type `VOID`.

Q I need to create an XML Web service that will alter information about an appliance being serviced. The information will include the owner name, the date, and a status. I would like to return all of this information to the client application in one method. How can I do this?

A Create a class based on your application and give it all the attributes that you need to pass back to the client. Then, simply create your method and have it return the class you created.

Workshop

The Workshop is designed to help you review what you've learned in this hour and to point you ahead to the material that will be covered in future hours.

Quiz

1. You need to return a value between 0 and 20. What data type should return?

   A Byte

2. You need to alter the variables being passed to your method. How do you declare them?

   A `ByRef` in Visual Basic. `Ref` in C#

3. What return type would you use when declaring a method that lets a client application know if a given pH is Acid, Base, or Neutral?

   A You would use an Enumeration (possibly called `pH`) and give it Acid, Base, and Neutral as possible values.

4. What do you place after the return statement if you are trying to return the following array of integers: `myArray(3)`?

   A You would return `myArray`.

5. You have a class called `myClient` of type `Client` and it contains two public attributes. What do you declare as your return type?

   A `Client`

6. In Question 5, what do you place after the return statement?

   A `myClient`

Exercises

Try experimenting with the different data types that you learned about in this hour. Write methods that accept different methods as parameters as well as those that return them. Do as many as it takes to make you feel comfortable with passing data back and forth between your XML Web service and client applications.

```
#Region "Simple Data Types"

    'Returning a String
    <WebMethod()> Public Function StringReturn() As String
        Return "This is a string"
    End Function

    'Return a Byte (0 to 255)
    <WebMethod()> Public Function ByteReturn() As Byte
        Return 222
    End Function

    'Return Boolean (true or false)
    <WebMethod()> Public Function BoolReturn() As Boolean
        Return True
    End Function

    'Return Short or Int16
```

```
    <WebMethod()> Public Function ShortReturn() As Short
        Return 23344
    End Function

    'Return Integer or Int32
    <WebMethod()> Public Function IntReturn() As Integer
        Return -23343444
    End Function

    'Return Long or Int64
    <WebMethod()> Public Function LongReturn() As Long
        Return 23344444444444444
    End Function

    'Return Single
    <WebMethod()> Public Function SingleReturn() As Single
        Return 233400000000000
    End Function

    'Return Single
    <WebMethod()> Public Function DoubleReturn() As Double
        Return 3443344400000000000
    End Function

#End Region

#Region "Returning Enums"

    'Declaring an Enum
    Public Enum Color
        Red = 1
        Blue = 2
        Green = 3
    End Enum

    'Returning an Enum
    <WebMethod()> Public Function EnumReturn() As Color
        Return Color.Red
    End Function

#End Region

#Region "Returning Arrays"

    'Returning an Array
    <WebMethod()> Public Function ArrayReturn() As Integer()
        Dim a(4) As Integer
        Dim i As Integer

        For i = 0 To 4
```

```
            a(i) = i + 1
        Next

        Return a
    End Function

#End Region

#Region "Returning Classes"

    'Declaring a Class
    Public Class Person
        Public Name As String
        Public ID As Integer
    End Class

    'Returning a Class
    <WebMethod()> Public Function ClassReturn() As Person

        Dim oPerson As New Person()

        oPerson.Name = "Jim Smith"
        oPerson.ID = 5

        Return oPerson
    End Function

    'Returning an Array of Classes
    <WebMethod()> Public Function ClassesReturn() As Person()

        Dim oPerson(2) As Person

        oPerson(0) = New Person()
        oPerson(0).Name = "Jim Smith"
        oPerson(0).ID = 1
        oPerson(1) = New Person()
        oPerson(1).Name = "Edgar Smith"
        oPerson(1).ID = 2
        oPerson(2) = New Person()
        oPerson(2).Name = "Mary Smith"
        oPerson(2).ID = 3

        Return oPerson
    End Function

#End Region

#Region "Params"

    'Accepting a String as a param
```

```
    <WebMethod()> Public Function ParamStringReturn( _
                  ByVal sWord1 As String, _
                  ByVal sWord2 As String) As String

        Return sWord1 & " and " & sWord2
    End Function

    'Accepting a Long as a param
    <WebMethod()> Public Function ParamLongReturn( _
                     ByVal iNum1 As Long, _
                     ByVal iNum2 As Long) As Long

        Return iNum2 - iNum1
    End Function

    'New Enum
    Public Enum Champion
        Corum = 1
        Renark = 2
        Urlich = 3
        Hawkmoon = 4
    End Enum

    'Accepting a Enum as a Parameter
    <WebMethod()> Public Function ParamEnumReturn( _
                     ByVal enumName As Champion) As champion

        Return enumName
    End Function

    'Accepting an Array as a Param
    <WebMethod()> Public Function ParamArrayReturn( _
                     ByVal iName() As Integer) As Integer

        Return UBound(iName)
    End Function
#End Region

#Region "ByRefParams"

     'Accepting Integer by Reference
    <WebMethod()> Public Function RefReturnReturn( _
                     ByRef iVal As Integer) As Integer

        Dim iOld As Integer

        iOld = iVal
        iVal = iVal - 1
        Return iOld
```

```
    End Function

     'Accepting Classes by Reference
    <WebMethod()> Public Sub RefClassReturn( _
                    ByRef oPers As Person)

        oPers.ID = oPers.ID - 1
        oPers.Name = "Hi " & oPers.Name
    End Sub
#End Region
```

HOUR 11

Working with Data in XML Web Services

In this hour, you will see how relational data sources, such as SQL Server and MS Access, are accessed using ADO.NET. You will also learn about the different objects that comprise ADO.NET, such as the connection and command objects. You will also learn to use data readers to deal with connected data sources and `DataSet` objects to deal with data that is disconnected from its original source.

Throughout this hour we will discuss the following:

- Using ADO.NET to access data stores
- ADO.NET's common objects
- Data readers for viewing data and running queries
- `DataSet` objects for handling disconnected data

Using ADO in .NET

ADO.NET, or Active Data objects .NET, is Microsoft's top-level data access technology. ADO.NET allows you to access relational databases, formatted text files, and even XML data sources.

The power of ADO.NET is that it provides a common programming interface to almost any data source. ADO.NET abstracts the particulars of any data source away from the developers and provides them with a common set of methods and properties to manipulate data with. Developers no longer need to worry about using proprietary objects and libraries when dealing with data; they simply let ADO.NET work with data sources drivers and APIs.

Changes to ADO

Several years ago, Microsoft introduced *ADO* (*ActiveX Data Objects*) as a way to provide a standard method for developers to access data regardless of its type. This meant that a developer who knew how to write code utilizing an Oracle database did not have to learn a totally new method of data access if the next project utilized SQL Server.

In previous versions of ADO, data was modeled and transported using `recordset` objects. `recordset` objects were a proprietary object model that allowed only a single table structure to be created and passed between components of an application that utilized ADO.

With .NET, Microsoft overhauled ADO from the ground up with an eye toward flexibility of data modeling and the ability to share data, using technologies such as XML Web services, with applications on a variety of platforms. The single greatest change to ADO, and the one that provided for these objectives, is the `DataSet` object. The `DataSet` object replaces the proprietary `recordset` object model with an architecture that models and transports its data in XML.

The change from the `recordset` object to the `Dataset` allows for data to be modeled in a much more meaningful manner. Now, multiple tables can be included in a single `Dataset`, and relationships between them can also be included. Modeling data in XML also means that applications written in .NET languages can share their data with non .NET applications by simply sending them the data's XML representation. This is extremely important to XML Web services and will be the focus of the next few hours.

ADO.NET Namespaces

The objects that ADO.NET is comprised of are split up over several namespaces, including several used only for XML-based data sources. These namespaces, utilized via the *Imports* keyword, allow developers to make use of ADO.NET objects in their code. The main namespaces for dealing with relational data sources are shown in Table 11.1.

TABLE 11.1 The Main Namespaces in ADO.NET

NameSpace	*Description*
`System.Data`	The main namespace used by ADO.NET. Contains all of the generalized classes for dealing with data. Among the objects found in this namespace are the `ADOConnection`, `ADOCommand`, `DataSet`, and `DataTable` objects.
`System.Data.OLEDB`	Contains the objects used when dealing with OLE-DB data sources. Among its main objects are `OleDbConnection` and `OleDbCommand` objects.
`System.Data.SqlClient`	Contains the objects specifically used when dealing with calls to SQL Server. Its objects include `SQLConnection` and `SQLCommand`.

These namespaces represent only a small portion of what is available to .NET developers. Other namespaces exist to allow developers to work with less common data objects and non .NET data types that may exist for specific databases.

In order to use the code in this hour, which makes use of a Microsoft Access Database, you will need to add the following namespaces to your code:

```
Imports System,Data.oleDB
Imports System.Data
```


Building the Access Database

For the examples in this hour, a database named `Book` was created using MS Access 2000. If you are using an older version, you should still be okay, but the following directions may need to be altered to fit you particular program.

In order to create this database for yourself, open Access from the start menu. You should immediately be confronted with an MS Access Dialogue that gives you the option to open an existing database or create a new database. Since you are intending to create a new database, select Blank Access Database and click Okay.

This will take you to the File New Database window. You can use this dialogue to navigate to the folder that you wish to save this database to. Note that you can't create a database and then save it like you can with other applications. Type the name you wish to give the database—in this case **`Book.mdb`**—into the combo box labeled File Name and then click the Create button.

Your database has now been created, but it lacks any tables. To add a new table to your database, click the Tables button, located at the left of the database window (shown in Figure 11.1), and then double click "Create table in Design view" in the center pane.

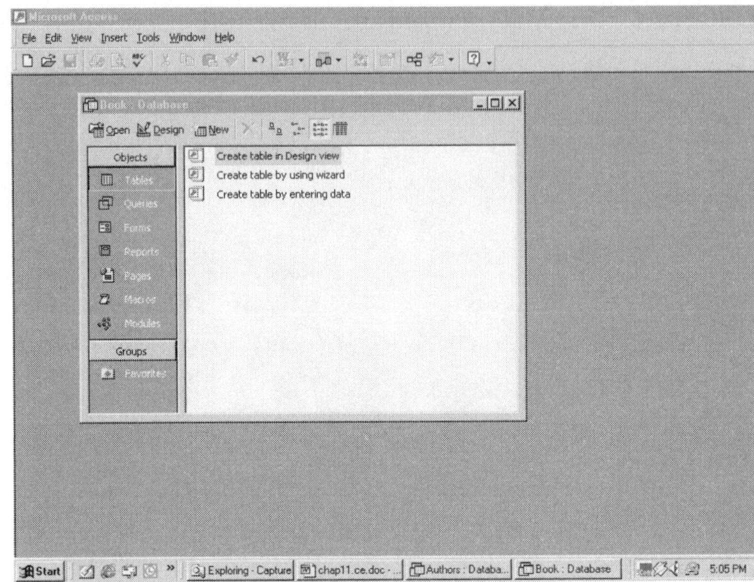

FIGURE 11.1
Creating a New Table in Access 2000.

Once you are in design view (shown in Figure 11.2), creating the table is relatively simple. Type a name—in this case **`ID`**—into the column marked Field Name. Now, under Data Type, select a variable type for the field. For `ID`, choose AutoNumber. This will

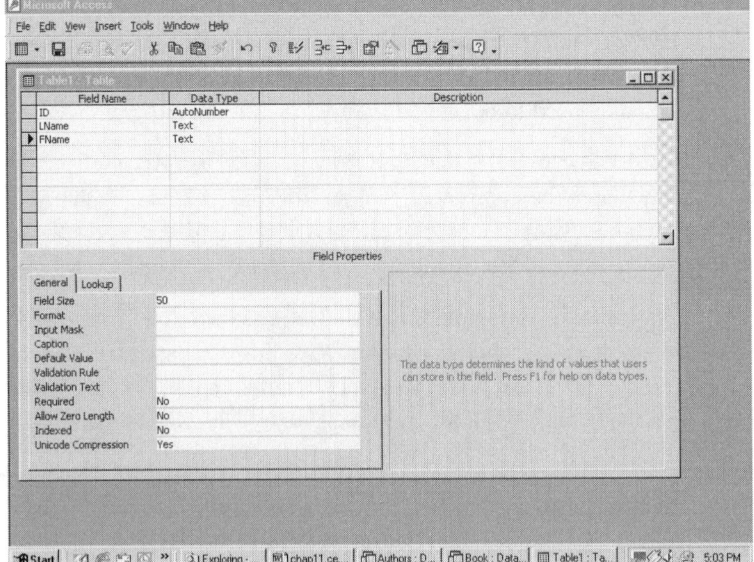

FIGURE 11.2
Adding Fields to a Table in Access 2000.

assign a new and unique identifier to every new entry added to the database. If you wish, you can also add some descriptive comment text to the column labeled Description.

For this table, which will store the names of authors, you will need to add two more fields—one for the first name and another for the last. Call these fields `LName` and `Fname`, respectively, and assign them text as their data types.

To save this table click on the save icon, the one in Figure 11.2 that looks like a diskette. This will bring up the Save As Input box. Give this table the name `tblAuthors` and click OK.

You will need to add a second table to this database before you are done. Follow the steps that you used to create the `tblAuthors` table to create `tblTitles`. Give `tblTitles` an `ID` field of data type `AutoNumber`, a `Titles` field of type text, and an `AuthorID` of type `Number`. This last field will be used to point to the author of each book.

Lastly, you need to enter some data. Start with `tblAuthors` table as you will need the ID field from this table to enter into the `AuthorID` field of `tblTitles`. To enter data into `tblAuthor`, double click on `tblAuthor` in the main window of Book database window; this will open the table for entry. Now, simply type a few names, first and last, into the table. Notice that the ID field as `autoincremented`. If you type only a few entries in, make a note of the ID field for each.

Now, open `tblTitles` and add some titles in. For the `AuthorID` field of each title that you enter, type in the ID of the author from `tblAuthors`. You now have a simple database to use for these examples.

If you wish to learn more about database programming, I highly recommend Sams' upcoming title, *Teach Yourself Database Programming with Visual Basic.Net in 21 Days*.

Connecting to Data Stores with the Connection Object

In order to work with data, an application must first open a connection to a data source. In ADO.NET, this is done through the use of a connection object.

As you saw in Table 11.1, there are several types of connection objects available to developers, depending on the type of data source that you are trying to connect to.

The basic syntax, in Visual Basic, for using a connection object and its main methods, `open` and `close`, is shown in Listing 11.1.

LISTING 11.1 Connecting to Data Stores with the Connection Object

```
Dim conn as New OleDBConnection(sSource)
conn.Open()
conn.Close()
```

In the code in Listing 11.1, `sSource` is a string variable containing the connection string to the database. Connection strings contain information for connection to a data source, such as server path names, database names, DSN names, and password information. A typical connection string might look like this:

```
"server=(local)\\myBook;uid=sAccount;pwd=sPassword;database=Book"
```

Using this connection string in a connection object would open the Book database on the local server using the account name `sAccount` and password `sPassword`.

You will see more examples of connection strings throughout this hour, so don't worry if you are unsure of how to write one yourself at this point in time.

Executing Commands with the ADO Command Object

Command objects are used by ADO to allow you to execute various database commands, such as SQL statements, stored procedures, or Table retrievals. The basic syntax for creating a command object is

```
Dim cmd as New SQLCommand(sCommand, conn)
```

A command object contains a command string, `sCommand`, that is an SQL statement; the name of a stored procedure; or the name of a table to be retrieved. The active connection, `conn`, represents the connection object that you saw earlier.

You can change the command object's command string at any time in your code using the following syntax:

```
cmd.CommandText = sCommand
```

Likewise, it is possible to change from one connection object to another via the `Connection` property:

```
cmd.Connection = conn
```

The command object also features a `CommandType` property that allows you to set the type of command being utilized. The default is `Text`, but the type can also be set to `StoredProcedure` or `TableDirect`. Listing 11.2 shows an example of setting the `CommandType` to `TableDirect`.

LISTING 11.2 Using `TableDirect` to Retrieve Tables

```
dim cmd as new OleDBCommand("Authors", conn)
cmd.CommandType = CommandType.TableDirect
```

Passing Parameters

If you are using stored procedures with `CommandType` set to `StoredProcedure`, it is possible to pass in parameters to your command object. This is accomplished using the parameters collection.

To add parameters to a command object, you invoke the `Add` method of the parameters collection:

```
cmd.Parameters.Add(New SQLParameter("@Name", sqlDbType.VarChar, "value of some
parameter"))
```

The previous code adds a new parameter called `@Name` to the command. `SQLDataType.dataType` is the syntax for declaring the parameter's data type. `SQLDataType` is an enumeration that allows you to declare any of a large variety of variable types including `SmallDateTime`, `Text`, `VarChar`, and dozens more.

Optionally, you can also include the size, as an integer, of the data that may be accepted; `isNullable`, as a Boolean, to allow null value to be passed; and `Direction`, as type `ParameterDirection`, to determine if the parameter represents input or return values.

After a parameter has been added, its value may be set, or changed if it was set when the parameter was created, as in our previous example, by calling the parameters index number or name and setting its value property as follows:

```
cmd.Parameters("@Name").Value = sVal
```

Using Command Objects Execution Methods

Once you have set the command object's text and connection properties, you can use the command objects execute method to do the actual work.

The command objects expose several methods for executing commands. The most common are shown in Table 11.2.

TABLE 11.2 Common Execute Methods of the Command Objects

Method	*Description*
`ExecuteNonQuery`	Returns only the number of records affected
`ExecuteReader`	Connects a `DataReader` object to a `recordset`
`ExecuteScalar`	Returns a single value or row

ExecuteNonQuery

This method of the command object is used to run SQL statements that do not return results, such as `Delete` and `Insert` queries. It can also be used to run stored procedures. These stored procedures may or may not return data.

```
cmd.ExecuteNonQuery
```

The previous line would execute the command currently stored in the command object, `cmd`. Optionally, some variable of type `integer` could be used to accept the return value that contains the number of records that were affected by the command's execution.

ExecuteReader

This object returns a `DataReader` object. The `DataReader`, which you will see more of later in this hour, provides a connected method through which to manipulate data on a data source.

In order to use the `ExecuteReader` method of the command object, you must have a `DataReader` object declared to receive the return. This can be done as follows:

```
Dim oRead as SQLDataReader()
```

You may then set the `DataReader`, `oRead`, equal to the return value of the `ExecuteReader` method:

```
ORead = cmd.ExecuteReader
```

Working with the Data Reader

The `DataReader`, which comes in both `SQLDataReader` and `OleDbDataReader` varieties, provides the means by which to receive connected data access.

Because the data reader uses an active, "live" set of data, the connection object that it uses is locked until the data reader releases it. The only action that can be performed on a connection object being used by a data reader is the `Close` method.

To create a `DataReader` object, you simply use the `ExecuteReader` method of the command object. Listing 11.3 shows an `SQLDataReader` object that contains the content of the `tblBooks` table.

LISTING 11.3 Using the `DataReader` Object

```
Dim myReader As OleDbDataReader
Dim sSource As String

sSource = "Provider=Microsoft.Jet.OLEDB.4.0; " & _
    "Data Source=C:\Book\Books.mdb;Persist Security Info=False"

Dim conn As New OleDbConnection(sSource)
conn.Open()

Dim cmd As New OleDbCommand("SELECT * FROM tblTitles", conn)
myReader = cmd.ExecuteReader
```

Table 11.3 shows some of the more common properties of the data reader object.

TABLE 11.3 Common Properties of the Data Reader

Property	*Description*
`FieldCount`	Read-only property that indicates the number of fields the record contains
`HasMoreResults`	Read-only property that indicates whether there are more results left to retrieve (Used in SQL batch processing)
`HasMoreRows`	Read-only property that indicates whether there are more rows left to retrieve (Used in SQL batch processing)
`IsClosed`	Read-only property that indicates whether the data reader is closed
`Item`	Returns the value from a column

The data reader also exposes a number of important methods, which are shown in Table 11.4.

TABLE 11.4 Common Methods of the Data Reader

Property	*Description*
`Close`	Closes the data reader
`NextResult`	Advances to the next record (Used in SQL Batch Processing)
`Read`	Advances to the next record
`IsNull`	Returns true if the field contains a null value

Now that you have seen the data reader's properties and methods, take a look at an example of a data reader in action. Listing 11.4 shows the data reader working its way through a set of records returned from an Access Database.

Listing 11.4 Advancing through Records with the `DataReader` Object

```
Dim myReader As OleDbDataReader
Dim sSource As String

sSource = "Provider=Microsoft.Jet.OLEDB.4.0; " & _
    "Data Source=C:\Book\Books.mdb;Persist Security Info=False"

Dim conn As New OleDbConnection(sSource)
conn.Open()

Dim cmd As New OleDbCommand("SELECT * FROM tblTitles", conn)

myReader = cmd.ExecuteReader()

While myReader.Read()
   TextBox1.Text = TextBox1.Text & "||" & myReader.GetString(1)
End While
```

In Listing 11.4, you can see that the data reader `myReader` will keep advancing through the records and returning true, via its `Read` method, until it reaches the end of the data. At this point, the `Read` method will return false and the `While` loop will end.

Disconnected Data with the `DataSet` Object

A `DataSet` provides a simple container for disconnected data. The container keeps data in tables via the `DataTable` object and keeps track of data relationships via the `DataRelations` collection. A `DataSet` is best thought of as a simple, relational database contained within your applications.

Data in a `DataSet` can be imported from almost any source, be it a relational database, a simple text file, or even just data points you enter via code. The data itself is contained completely within the dataset object, hence the disconnected label, along with any constraints, information on data type, and so on.

Table 11.5 shows the most common methods of the `DataSet` object.

Table 11.5 Common Methods of the `DataSet`

Method	*Description*
`AcceptChanges`	Commits all changes made to `DataSet`
Clear	Clears the `DataSet`
`Clone`	Clones the `Dataset`'s structure
`Copy`	Copies the `Dataset`

continues

TABLE 11.5 Continued

Method	*Description*
`GetChanges`	Returns a copy of the `DataSet` with all current changes
`HasChanges`	Returns `True` if the `DataSet` has changes
`Merge`	Merges `DataSet` with a second `DataSet`
`RejectChanges`	Rolls back changes to the `Dataset`, returning it to the state it was in when loaded or when changes were last committed

Connecting Data to the `DataSet` with `DataAdapter` Objects

Before you look at the objects that make up the `DataSet`, you need to look at the object that actually gets data into the `Dataset`. `DataAdapters` do exactly what their name implies; they adapt data to fit into the dataset format.

The basic methods of the `DataAdapter` are fill and update. These methods are shown in Table 11.6.

TABLE 11.6 Common Methods of the `DataAdapter`

Method	*Description*
`Fill`	Fills the `DataSet` with data.
`Update`	Used to update the data source of all changes made to the `Dataset`. This includes inserts and deletions.

Now, take a look at a few examples that show how to use the `DataAdapter` to fill a Dataset. The first example, Listing 11.5, shows how to create a `DataAdapter` using an SQL query string, whereas the second example, Listing 11.6, makes use of the `DataAdapter`'s `SelectCommand` property.

LISTING 11.5 Using Query Strings in the `DataAdapter`

```
Dim sSource As String

sSource = "Provider=Microsoft.Jet.OLEDB.4.0; " & _
    "Data Source=C:\Book\Books.mdb;Persist Security Info=False"

Dim conn As New OleDbConnection(sSource)
conn.Open()

Dim sSQL As String = "SELECT * FROM tblAuthors"
Dim myAdapter As New OleDbDataAdapter(sSQL, conn)
Dim myDataSet As New DataSet()
myAdapter.Fill(myDataSet, "Authors")
```

The `Fill` method in line 4 of Listing 11.5 creates a `DataTable` named `Authors` within the `DataSet` and populates it with the return of the SQL Query string, `sSQL`.

LISTING 11.6 Using the `SelectCommand` Method of the `DataAdapter`

```
1:  Dim sSource As String
2:
3:  sSource = "Provider=Microsoft.Jet.OLEDB.4.0; " & _
4:      "Data Source=C:\Book\Books.mdb;Persist Security Info=False"
5:
6:  Dim conn As New OleDbConnection(sSource)
7:  conn.Open()
8:
9:  Dim myAdapter As New OleDbDataAdapter()
10: Dim myDataSet As New DataSet()
11: Dim cmd As New OleDbCommand()
12:
13: cmd.CommandText = "SELECT * FROM tblTitles"
14: cmd.Connection = conn
15: myAdapter.SelectCommand = cmd
16: myAdapter.Fill(myDataSet, "Books")
```

The `Fill` method in line 3 of Listing 11.6 populates the Dataset with a `DataTable` called `Books` that contains the contents of a database table named `tblBooks`.

Storing Data in the `DataTable`

`DataTables` are the `DataSet` equivalent of database tables. A `DataTable` object contains a collection of `DataColumn` and `DataRow` objects, which you will see later in this hour, that contain the properties and values for information stored in the table.

Table 11.7 shows the methods that are commonly used with the `DataTable` object.

TABLE 11.7 Common Methods of the `DataTable`

Method	*Description*
`Clear`	Clears all data from the table
`NewRow`	Creates a new row for data to inserted into the table
`Select`	Allows for the creation of filtered sets of rows from the table

The `DataTable` also contains all of the `DataSet` object methods for dealing with changes (see Table 11.5). These methods allow you to roll back or accept changes at the table level in addition to the `Dataset` level.

Using DataRow Objects to Work with Data

DataRows represent the actual records in a DataSet. DataRow objects contain a field for every DataColumn object in the Columns collection. The methods you are most likely to encounter when working with the DataRow object are shown in Table 11.8.

TABLE 11.8 Common Methods of the DataRow Object

Method	*Description*
BeginEdit	Used to begin editing on a DataRow.
CancelEdit	Cancels the Edit operation on a DataRow.
Delete	Deletes a DataRow.
EndEdit	Ends the Edit operation on a DataRow.
GetChildRows	Returns the Child Rows of a DataRow.
GetParentRows	Returns the Parent Rows of a DataRow.

The code in Listing 11.7 shows an example of DataRow objects being used to access data in a DataSet.

LISTING 11.7 Using a DataRow Object to Access Data

```
Dim sSource As String

sSource = "Provider=Microsoft.Jet.OLEDB.4.0; " & _
    "Data Source=C:\Book\Books.mdb;Persist Security Info=False"

Dim conn As New OleDbConnection(sSource)
conn.Open()

Dim myAdapter As New OleDbDataAdapter()
Dim myDataSet As New DataSet()
Dim cmd As New OleDbCommand()

cmd.CommandText = "SELECT * FROM tblTitles"
cmd.Connection = conn
myAdapter.SelectCommand = cmd
myAdapter.Fill(myDataSet, "Books")

Dim myRow As DataRow
For Each myRow In myDataSet.Tables("Books").Rows
   Debug.WriteLine(myRow(0))
Next
```

Using Data Columns to Define Data

Similar to the DataRow object, the DataColumn represents an actual column in a database table. A DataColumn holds information about a single column in a DataSet's DataTable. It is through the DataColumn object that we can retrieve or set a column's name, data type, or other important information. Table 11.9 shows the methods that are most often encountered when working with DataColumn objects. Most of these properties are set for you if the DataSet is created from a DataSource. If you create your own DataTable, then you will set these properties programmatically.

TABLE 11.9 Common Properties of the DataColumn

Property	*Description*
AllowNull	Determines whether the column accepts null values
AutoIncrement	Determines whether the column automatically increments when new rows are added
AutoIncrementSeed	Sets the starting value for Autoincrementing
AutoIncrementStep	Sets the step for AutoIncrementing
Caption	Sets the column's caption
ColumnName	Sets the column name in the column collection
DataType	Determines the type of data contained in the column
DefaultValue	Sets a default value for new rows
Expression	Sets an expression used to calculate values or filter rows
Ordinal	Returns the position in the Columns Collection
ReadOnly	Used to disallow changes to a column once a row has been added
Unique	Determines whether each row must contain a unique value

The code in Listing 11.8 iterates through the columns collection and prints the caption of each individual column and its data type.

LISTING 11.8 Using the Columns Collection

```
Dim sSource As String

sSource = "Provider=Microsoft.Jet.OLEDB.4.0; " & _
    "Data Source=C:\Book\Books.mdb;Persist Security Info=False"

Dim conn As New OleDbConnection(sSource)
conn.Open()

Dim myAdapter As New OleDbDataAdapter()
```

continues

LISTING 11.8 Continued

```
Dim myDataSet As New DataSet()
Dim cmd As New OleDbCommand()

cmd.CommandText = "SELECT * FROM tblTitles"
cmd.Connection = conn
myAdapter.SelectCommand = cmd
myAdapter.Fill(myDataSet, "Books")

Dim myCol As DataColumn
For Each myCol In myDataSet.Tables("Books").Columns
    Debug.WriteLine(myCol.Caption & " - " & CStr(myCol.DataType.FullName))
Next
```

Defining Relational Data with the `DataRelation` Object

The `DataRelation` object is used to store information, specifically the primary key of one table and the foreign key of another, in order to establish and enforce relationships between tables in a data set. This is a vast improvement over previous versions of ADO that relied on code or the data source itself to enforce referential integrity (relationships between tables). With a `DataRelation` in place, errors will be generated when data that violates the relationship is first entered into a row.

> When a `DataRelation` is added after data is already populating the rows of a `DataSet`, errors may be generated immediately if any existing data violates the relationship.

The syntax to create a `DataRelation` is

```
ORelation = New DataRelation(Name, Column1, Column2)
```

where `Name` is a string representing the name you wish to call the relationship, and `Column1` and `Column2` are existing columns in `DataTables` in the `DataSet`.

`DataRelations` are held in the relations collection of the `DataSet` object. Listing 11.9 shows how we create a new relationship in our `DataSet` using the `Add` method of the relations collection.

LISTING 11.9 Using the Columns Collection

```
Dim sSource As String

sSource = "Provider=Microsoft.Jet.OLEDB.4.0; " & _
```

continues

LISTING 11.9 Continued

```
    "Data Source=C:\Book\Books.mdb;Persist Security Info=False"

Dim conn As New OleDbConnection(sSource)
conn.Open()

Dim sSQL As String = "SELECT * FROM tblAuthors"
Dim myAdapter As New OleDbDataAdapter(sSQL, conn)
Dim myDataSet As New DataSet()
myAdapter.Fill(myDataSet, "Authors")

Dim cmd As New OleDbCommand()
cmd.CommandText = "SELECT * FROM tblTitles"
cmd.Connection = conn
myAdapter.SelectCommand = cmd
myAdapter.Fill(myDataSet, "Books")

Dim relAuthorToBook As DataRelation
relAuthorToBook = New DataRelation("AuthorToBook", _
myDataSet.Tables("Authors").Columns("ID"), _
myDataSet.Tables("Books").Columns("AuthorID"))

myDataSet.Relations.Add(relAuthorToBook)
```

Summary

In this hour, you learned how to access data stores utilizing ADO.NET. You also saw how to populate and view data with both data readers and `DataSets`. Finally, you learned how to update data sources from within ADO.NET.

Q&A

Q Why take such a long look at ADO.NET in a book on XML Web services?

A Most XML Web services that you will create will need to work with a data source, be it uploading information to share with a client application, such as stock prices or football scores, or tracking information, such as product orders or survey information. Since ADO.net is the principle matter for dealing with data sources in the .NET platform and is totally revised from older versions of ADO, it is important to get a firm understanding of it in order to develop successful XML Web services.

Q How do I determine when to use a `DataSet` or a data reader in my applications?

A The data reader is a smaller, less memory-intensive object and is perfect for viewing data connected directly to your application. For this reason, a data reader is a great option for opening data stores that initialize data in your XML Web Service. You can then use SQL inserts and updates to update the data store at appropriate times in the application, such as the `Application_End` event.

The `DataSet`, on the other hand, is perfect for when you need to send data to other applications, such as the data returned from an XML Web service. Also, because the data set allows you to work with multiple tables, it is sometimes the most appropriate method to handle more complex situations, such as ones that would require multiple data readers and connection objects.

Q What is the purpose of the command object? Why not just use strings to hold SQL statements?

A Like most programming tasks, there usually exist multiple methods to perform the same task. Although it is possible to perform most operations without the use of command objects, they are often the best method. The command object's parameters collection makes it perfect for dealing with stored procedures, and it also represents a method with fairly low overhead for running `Update`, `Insert`, and `Delete` queries. Also, the ability to perform many different types of executions from one object adds to the power of the command object.

Q What will my XML Web services pass to client applications?

A Your applications, as you will see in the next hour, will pass back Datasets under most conditions. Because `DataSet` objects are heavily XML based, a property that you will make more use of in Hour 16, they are the perfect data type to send over http protocols.

Workshop

The Workshop is designed to help you review what you've learned in this hour and to point you ahead to the material that will be covered in future hours.

Quiz

1. If your program received a `DataSet` from an XML Web service and you need to programmatically extract the names of each field, what object and property would you use?

   A You would use the `ColumnName` property of the `DataColumn` object.

2. What object's `Fill` method is used to populate `DataSet` objects?

   A The `DataAdapter` is used to populate `Dataset` objects.

3. What namespace contains the `SqlCommand` object?

   A `System.Data.SqlClient`

4. What method commits changes to a table or `Dataset`?

   A `AcceptChanges` commits data changes.

5. What property of the `DataColumn` object would you set to `true` if you were creating a column in `DataSet` and you planned to use it as the Primary Key (that is, no duplicate values in any rows)?

   A You would use the `Unique` property.

6. What method of the `Command` object is used to return data to a data reader?

   A `ExecuteReader` provides a live connection to the data source and its data.

Exercises

Try using the data reader and `DataSet` object to manipulate a database of your choosing. If you wish, simply use `Debug.Write` or `Debug.WriteLine` to output the data.

A. The following code opens `tblAuthors` from a database named `book`, using a DSN, and writes all of the information in the table to the debug screen.

```
Dim sSource As String

sSource = "Provider=Microsoft.Jet.OLEDB.4.0; " & _
    "Data Source=C:\Book\Books.mdb;Persist Security Info=False"

Dim sSQL As String = "SELECT * FROM tblAuthors"

Dim myDataSet As New DataSet()
Dim conn As New OleDbConnection(sSource)

conn.Open()

Dim cmd = New OleDbCommand(sSQL, conn)
Dim myAdapter As New OleDbDataAdapter()
myAdapter.SelectCommand = cmd
myAdapter.Fill(myDataSet, "Authors")

conn.close()

Dim oDataRow As DataRow
Dim oDataCol As DataColumn

For Each oDataRow In myDataSet.Tables("Authors").Rows
    For Each oDataCol In myDataSet.Tables("Authors").Columns
        Debug.WriteLine(oDataRow(oDataCol.Ordinal))
    Next
    Debug.WriteLine("======================")
Next
```

HOUR 12

Passing DataSets from XML Web Services

In the last hour, you saw the basic functionality of ADO.NET and how it can be used to provide data access to a divergent array of data sources. Now, in this hour you will learn how to create XML Web services that both expose and consume XML-based DataSets. You will learn how to use ADO.NET to manipulate data sources from within your services and present filtered, meaningful results to your clients.

Throughout this hour we will discuss the following:

- Passing ADO.NET DataSources from an XML Web service
- Updating data sources from within an XML Web service
- Using the DataSource as a method argument
- Consuming DataSources in client applications
- The XML behind DataSources

ADO.NET in XML Web Services

Those of you who have programmed with previous versions of ADO will have noticed that ADO.NET is a radical departure from previous incarnations. In fact, aside from a few object and method names, ADO.NET is completely different from any ADO variation that came before it.

One of the main reasons for the rewrite is Microsoft's vision of XML Web services. In XML Web services, a program, the service itself, sends data to other programs, the client applications, for them to consume. As Microsoft envisioned it, these client applications can be running on any platform and can be written in any language. In Hour 9, for example, you saw client applications that were not built in or running on the .NET platform. If an XML Web service was to pass complex data to these clients, it could not rely on them possessing ADO recordsets or other proprietary data handlers.

The answer to this was ADO.NET and the DataSet. The DataSet is built upon the Java document as a means to hold and manipulate data pulled from data sources. Placing the data in an XML format had several major benefits, not the least being that XML is the native format for data transmission in XML Web services.

Once the data has been transmitted from the XML Web service, client applications written in .NET have the benefit of consuming the DataSet and using it in its ADO.NET DataSet form. Clients written in a non-.Net platform, such as the Visual Basic 6 example we spoke of earlier, could also consume the DataSet by manipulating it as they would any other XML document. Later in this hour, when you study the format that the DataSet is sent over in, you will see how much information has been provided, via the XML document, to allow non-.NET developers to handle the XML document and provide their applications with all of the power and control provided in .NET itself.

Returning a DataSet from an XML Web Service

Sometimes, when building an XML Web service, you may find it advantageous to return large, complex groups of data, such as a list of products and their prices and stock levels at various locations in an area. This can easily be accomplished using the DataSet object.

If you wish to work along with this hour's examples, create a new XML Web service and call it `exampleDataSet`.

The database used in the examples in this book contains the tables shown as Table 12.1 and Table 12.2.

TABLE 12.1 Table `tblBands`

Column Name	*Data Type*	*Constraints*
ID	Long Integer	AutoIncrement
`BandName`	Text	Size 50

TABLE 12.2 Table `tblCD`

Column Name	*Data Type*	*Constraints*
ID	Long Integer	AutoIncrement
Title	Text	Size 50
Band_ID	Long Integer	

With the Database in place, you now need to import your namespaces. Since you are using an Access Database, you will need to place the following two declarations at the top of your XML Web service:

```
Imports System.Data
Imports System.Data.OleDb
```

Returning a DataSet is fairly straightforward. First, declare a new function and set its return type to `DataSet`. Then, add a new `DataSet` object and its supporting `Connection` and `DataAdapter` objects, as shown in Listing 12.1. Next, build a query string and populate your DataSet. Finally, all you need to do is return the DataSet as shown in line 12.

LISTING 12.1 Returning a DataSet from an XML Web Service

```
1:   <WebMethod()> Public Function ReturnBands() As DataSet
2:     Dim myDataSet As New DataSet()
3:     Dim conn As New OleDbConnection()
4:
5:     Conn.ConnectionString = "Provider=Microsoft.Jet.OLEDB.4.0; " & _
6:         "Data Source=C:\Book\CD.mdb;Persist Security Info=False"
7:     Conn.Open()
8:
9:     Dim sSQL As String = "SELECT * FROM tblBands"
10    Dim myAdapter As New OleDbDataAdapter(sSQL, Conn)
11:
12:    myAdapter.Fill(myDataSet, "Bands")
```

continues

LISTING 12.1 Continued

```
    Conn.close()

    Return myDataSet

  End Function
```

The net result of Listing 12.1 is the creation and transmission of a data set containing the entire contents of a table, in this case `tblBands`, from the Music database.

Returning the DataSet as an XML Document

The true power in returning a DataSet from your XML Web service comes from the XML document representation of the data that is returned to the client. By using the DataSet, which itself represents data as XML, it is possible to quickly send an entire table, or multiple tables as you will see later in this hour, of data over to a client application, while preserving the data's structure.

Listing 12.2 shows a schema portion of the document that is created when your service sends a DataSet to client applications. Notice that this schema defines an element, called `Bands`, which in turn contains two elements, `ID` and `BandName`. The schema further defines `BandName` as a string and `ID` as an integer.

LISTING 12.2 XSD Declaration for DataTable Bands

```
<xsd:element name="Bands">
 <xsd:complexType>
  <xsd:sequence>
   <xsd:element name="ID" type="xsd:int" minOccurs="0" />
   <xsd:element name="BandName" type="xsd:string" minOccurs="0" />
  </xsd:sequence>
 </xsd:complexType>
</xsd:element>
```

Listing 12.3 shows the actual DataSet for the `Bands` table. This XML representation is what ADO.NET enabled client applications will consume as native DataSets. As you can see from Listings 12.2 and 12.3, client applications that are built on platforms not supporting ADO.NET will have an easy time working with the DataSet through the use of XML parsers.

Listing 12.3 The DataSet Containing Table Bands.

```
<NewDataSet xmlns="">
 <Bands diffgr:id="Bands1" msdata:rowOrder="0">
  <ID>1</ID>
  <BandName>Digital Ruin</BandName>
 </Bands>
 <Bands diffgr:id="Bands2" msdata:rowOrder="1">
  <ID>2</ID>
  <BandName>Manilla Road</BandName>
 </Bands>
 <Bands diffgr:id="Bands3" msdata:rowOrder="2">
  <ID>3</ID>
  <BandName>Faithful Breath</BandName>
 </Bands>
 <Bands diffgr:id="Bands4" msdata:rowOrder="3">
  <ID>4</ID>
  <BandName>Rhapsody</BandName>
 </Bands>
</NewDataSet>
```

Returning Multi-Table DataSets from an XML Web Service

As you saw in Hour 14, it is possible to create multiple tables within a single DataSet. Listing 12.4 shows an XML Web service method, titled `ReturnCatalog`, that returns both the table `Bands` and the table `CDs`. The return statement for this is identical to that of the previous example in listing 12.1. As you see, the difference really lies in the return document and what you can do with it.

Listing 12.4 Returning a DataSet with Multiple DataTables

```
<WebMethod()> Public Function ReturnCatalog() As DataSet
  Dim myDataSet As New DataSet()
  Dim conn As New OleDbConnection()

  Conn.ConnectionString = "Provider=Microsoft.Jet.OLEDB.4.0; " & _
        "Data Source=C:\Book\CD.mdb;Persist Security Info=False"
  Conn.Open()

  Dim sSQL As String = "SELECT * FROM tblBands"

  Dim myAdapter As New OleDbDataAdapter(sSQL, Conn)
  myAdapter.Fill(myDataSet, "Bands")

  sSQL = "SELECT * FROM tblCD"
```

continues

LISTING 12.4 Continued

```

    Dim myAdapter2 As New OleDbDataAdapter(sSQL, Conn)
    MyAdapter2.Fill(myDataSet, "CDS")

    Conn.close()

    Return myDataSet

End Function
```

Returning Multiple DataTables as an XML Document

In Listing 12.5, you can see the XSD schema information that is returned as part of the DataSet when you invoke `ReturnCatalog`. Notice that this time the schema includes a second table, the `CDS` table, and its columns and their types. Shortly, you will see how this schema may be used to define relationships and enforce referential integrity.

LISTING 12.5 XSD Declaration for Multiple DataTables

```
<xsd:element name="Bands">
 <xsd:complexType>
  <xsd:sequence>
    <xsd:element name="ID" type="xsd:int" minOccurs="0" />
    <xsd:element name="BandName" type="xsd:string" minOccurs="0" />
  </xsd:sequence>
 </xsd:complexType>
</xsd:element>
<xsd:element name="CDS">
 <xsd:complexType>
  <xsd:sequence>
   <xsd:element name="ID" type="xsd:int" minOccurs="0" />
   <xsd:element name="Title" type="xsd:string" minOccurs="0" />
   <xsd:element name="Band_ID" type="xsd:int" minOccurs="0" />
  </xsd:sequence>
 </xsd:complexType>
</xsd:element>
```

Listing 12.6 shows a segment of the DataSet from `ReturnCatalog`. Notice in the document structure how each data grouping, `ID` and `BandName` in the case of the `Bands` table, is contained in a separate `Bands` element. Also notice that the individual `Bands` elements are not further grouped together to separate them from `CDS` elements. This is acceptable because of the way XML is parsed. A parser would create a tree with `Bands` and `CDS` on it at the same level and then drop individual elements onto the tree under each.

LISTING 12.6 Partial DataSet for Multiple DataTables

```
<Bands diffgr:id="Bands3" msdata:rowOrder="2">
  <ID>3</ID>
  <BandName>Faithful Breath</BandName>
</Bands>
<Bands diffgr:id="Bands4" msdata:rowOrder="3">
  <ID>4</ID>
  <BandName>Rhapsody</BandName>
</Bands>
<CDS diffgr:id="CDS1" msdata:rowOrder="0">
  <ID>1</ID>
  <Title>Dawn of Victory</Title>
  <Band_ID>4</Band_ID>
</CDS>
<CDS diffgr:id="CDS2" msdata:rowOrder="1">
  <ID>2</ID>
  <Title>Legendary Tales</Title>
  <Band_ID>4</Band_ID>
</CDS>
<CDS diffgr:id="CDS3" msdata:rowOrder="2">
  <ID>3</ID>
  <Title>Symphony of Enchanted Lands</Title>
  <Band_ID>4</Band_ID>
</CDS>
```

Adding and Returning Relationships to an XML Web Service

Now that you have created a DataSet that returns more than one table, you can begin exploring how to create and enforce relationships between these tables. These relationships will be included in the DataSet XML that is consumed by client applications and, if the client application is using ADO.NET, enforced in the client's code automatically.

The code in Listing 12.7 adds a relationship, between the `ID` field of the `Bands` table and the `Band_Id` field of the `CDs` table, to the `ReturnCatalog` XML Web service method from Listing 12.4. Place the code just before the `Return` statement in line 20 of Listing 12.4 and the relationship will be in place just prior to returning the DataSet.

LISTING 12.7 Adding a Relationship to the DataSet

```
Dim myCol1 As DataColumn
Dim myCol2 As DataColumn

myCol1 = myDataSet.Tables("Bands").Columns("ID")
myCol2 = myDataSet.Tables("CDS").Columns("Band_ID")
```

continues

Listing 12.7 Continued

```

Dim myRelation As DataRelation
myRelation = New DataRelation("BandsToCds", myCol1, myCol2)

myDataSet.Relations.Add(myRelation)
```

You have now created a `DataRelation` entitled `BandsToCds` and have set the `Bands` table as the parent field. This means that you are setting rows in the `CDS` table as children rows of the corresponding rows in the `Bands` table.

DataRelations in XML

Now look at the XSD schema fragment shown in Listing 12.8. This fragment, which is now part of the definition of `Bands`, defines a unique construction entitled `Constraint1` and defines it as the ID field using `XPath`.

Listing 12.8 XSD Declaration for a Constraint in a DataTable

```
1:   <xsd:unique name="Constraint1">
2:    <xsd:selector xpath=".//Bands" />
3:    <xsd:field xpath="ID" />
4:   </xsd:unique>
```

In the schema definition for table `CDS`, the `DataRelation`, `BandsToCds`, is defined by declaring a reference to `Constraint1`, defined in Listing 12.8. This is shown in Listing 12.9.

Listing 12.9 XSD Declaration for the DataRelation

```
1:   <xsd:keyref name="BandsToCds" refer="Constraint1">
2:    <xsd:selector xpath=".//CDS" />
3:    <xsd:field xpath="Band_ID" />
4:   </xsd:keyref>
```

Note line 1 of Listings 12.8 and 12.9. The `ID` field of `Bands` is listed as unique whereas the `Band_ID` field of table `CDs` is listed as a `keyref`. This is how one-to-many relations are defined.

Using DataSets as Function Arguments

In some cases, it may be necessary to allow client applications to pass DataSets to your XML Web service for processing. Some examples of this may include a service that runs accounting calculations and needs to update daily, weekly, or monthly data; a service that updates pricing information on collectables and antiques; or a service that updates a central database with user profiles from multiple locations.

Listing 12.10 contains an XML Web service method that accepts a DataSet containing a table titled `Bands`. The Function uses the `NewRow` method to create a new entry in the DataTable and then returns the record count of the DataSet. Notice that the DataSet is declared as an argument in exactly the same way as any other data type.

LISTING 12.10 Web Method to Receive a DataSet

```
<WebMethod()> Public Function AcceptBands(ByVal dsBands As DataSet) As Integer
    Dim myTable As DataTable = New DataTable()
    Dim myRow As DataRow
    myTable = dsBands.Tables("Bands")
    myRow = myTable.NewRow()
    myRow(1) = "Tribe After Tribe"
    myTable.Rows.Add(myRow)
    Return myTable.Rows.Count
End Function
```

It may not be the most useful method ever created, but it does demonstrate a few key points. First, this method expects the DataSet to arrive containing a `Bands` table. It also expects that the `Bands` table can be successfully added to by simply adding text to the table's second column. This is the biggest problem with handling DataSets as arguments. Client applications have to know in advance exactly what the DataSet needs to be formatted as.

Adding Additional Functions to Your Data Enabled XML Web Service

In this section, you will create a few extra support functions that demonstrate some of the functionality that you may need to add to an XML Web service when dealing with data sources. All of this code is built upon concepts that you have already learned, but it serves as an example of where you can go from here.

If you wanted to create an XML Web service that allowed users to store information in a database, you could use code similar to that shown in Listing 12.11. This code accepts a band name as a string parameter, creates a `Connection` object to connect to the data source, and then uses an SQL statement and a `Command` object to insert the new band name into the database.

LISTING 12.11 Method to Add A New Band

```
<WebMethod()> Public Function AddBand(ByVal sBand As String) As DataSet
  Dim myDataSet As New DataSet()
  Dim conn As New OleDbConnection()

  Conn.ConnectionString = "Provider=Microsoft.Jet.OLEDB.4.0; " & _
         "Data Source=C:\Book\CD.mdb;Persist Security Info=False"
  Conn.Open()

  Dim sSQL As String = "INSERT INTO tblBands(BandName) Values('" & sBand & "')"

  Dim cmd as New OleDbCommand(sSQL, conn)
  cmd.ExecuteNonQuery()

  sSQL = "SELECT * FROM tblBands"
  Dim myAdapter As New OleDbDataAdapter(sSQL, Conn)

  myAdapter.Fill(myDataSet, "Bands")
  Conn.close()

  Return myDataSet

End Function
```

When this code has finished inserting the band name into the table `tblBands`, it creates a new DataSet object and imports the entire contents of `tblBands` into it. This new DataSet is then used as the functions return as seen in Figure 12.1. This last step is done so that in the next Hour you can build a client application that actually tests to see that the insertion takes place.

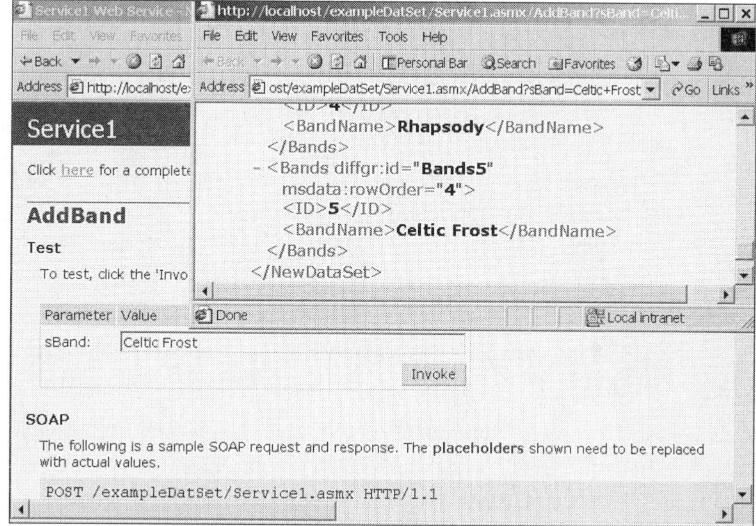

FIGURE 12.1
Returning the updated DataSet with DataTable Bands.

Next, you will create the code to enter a new CD title in the database. This is different from entering a band name in that it requires a `Band_Id` value to associate the CD with a particular band. There are several methods that you could employ to retrieve this `Band_ID` value, including looking it up based on a supplied band name. In this example however, you will simply have the client pass in the `Band_ID` as a parameter. This is demonstrated in Listing 12.12.

LISTING 12.12 Method to Add a New CD

```
<WebMethod()> Public Function AddTitle(ByVal iBand As Integer, _
                                ByVal sTitle as String)

  Dim myDataSet As New DataSet()
  Dim conn As New OleDbConnection()
  Dim sSQL as string

  Conn.ConnectionString = "Provider=Microsoft.Jet.OLEDB.4.0; " & _
      "Data Source=C:\Book\CD.mdb;Persist Security Info=False"
   Conn.Open()

  sSQL = "INSERT INTO tblCD(Band_ID, Title) Values("
  sSQL = sSQL & iBand & ", '" & sTitle &  "')"

  Dim cmd as New OleDbCommand(sSQL, conn)
  cmd.ExecuteNonQuery()

End Function
```

Summary

In this hour, you learned how to create XML Web services that expose entire DataSets. You also looked at the various portions of the outputted DataSets XML document and how they were structured to include elements, relationships, and constraints. At the end of the hour, you learned how to update data sources with values passed to the XML Web service from client applications.

Q&A

Q Why return DataSets when we could move the data into objects as we saw in Hour 11?

A There are several answers to that question. The first reason is that the tools for working with DataSets are already in place, so why would we want to write a bunch of custom code that we don't have to? Another reason is that the XML nature of DataSets makes them very easy to work with on the client side even if ADO.NET is not present.

Q What happens if I create a DataSet with DataRelations and my XML Web service is consumed by clients that do not use ADO.NET?

A When a DataSet is exposed by an XML Web service, it is exposed as an XML document, complete with markup to define relationships. When these XML documents are parsed on the client side, this relationship information may be ignored; there is no guarantee that the parser being used can read XSD schemas or that the developer who writes the client code even cares about your relationships. Even a .NET client is free to remove the DataRelations from the DataSet once it is within the client's control. Ultimately, the best you can do is to include DataRelations in your services for those who choose not to ignore them.

Q Is there a limit to the amount of Data that I should send over in a DataSet?

A There is no hard rule on how much information is too much, but you should always try to limit what you send across networks, especially the Internet, to only what is absolutely necessary. Most times, you can filter down your datasets to just a few records before sending them to clients, but there are other times when a large, multi-table recordset is the only way to go.

Q Is it possible to organize extremely complex data into multiple DataSets and then return them?

A Yes, it is actually possible to return an array of DataSets. This is not something that you would normally do, as the overhead could get to be a bit large, and working with an array of data types can be somewhat cumbersome and difficult for the client developers. Still, it can be done.

Workshop

The Workshop is designed to help you review what you've learned in this hour and to point you ahead to the material that will be covered in future lessons.

Quiz

1. What XML subset does XML Web services use to define DataRelations?

   A `XPath`.

2. (True or False) The sequence of columns is not preserved when DataSets are transmitted.

   A False, the sequence is preserved and enforced in the XSD schema.

3. What type of DataAdapter is used to connect to an MS Access database?

   A `OleDbDataAdapter`.

4. If you need to add a row to a table, prior to returning it, what method would you use?

   A `NewRow`.

5. What is the return type of the `Command` object's `ExecuteNonQuery` method?

   A The number of records affected by the operation as an integer.

Exercises

Try creating and returning a DataSet built completely within the method, that is, no data connections. Now, make the return an array of two DataSets, with at least one containing two or more tables. Also, include at least one DataRelation.

12

The following code creates an XML Web service method that returns a DataSet array. The array contains two DataSets, one with a DataTable containing the names of five cats and the other containing a DataTable of fish tanks and another of fish type. The second DataSet contains a DataRelation between the fish and the tanks.

```
<WebMethod()> Public Function ReturnPets() As DataSet()
     Dim myDataSet(2) As DataSet
     Dim myColumn As DataColumn
     Dim myRow As DataRow

     myDataSet(0) = New DataSet()

     'Create Tanks Table
     Dim myDataTable As DataTable = New DataTable()
     myDataTable.TableName = "Tanks"
     myDataSet(0).Tables.Add(myDataTable)
```

```
myColumn = New DataColumn()
myColumn.DataType = System.Type.GetType("System.Int32")
myColumn.ColumnName = "ID"
myDataTable.Columns.Add(myColumn)

' Create second column.
myColumn = New DataColumn()
myColumn.DataType = Type.GetType("System.String")
myColumn.ColumnName = "Tank"
myDataTable.Columns.Add(myColumn)

'Add Tanks
myRow = myDataTable.NewRow()
myRow("ID") = 1
myRow("Tank") = "3 Gallon"
myDataTable.Rows.Add(myRow)

myRow = myDataTable.NewRow()
myRow("ID") = 2
myRow("Tank") = "10 Gallon"
myDataTable.Rows.Add(myRow)

myRow = myDataTable.NewRow()
myRow("ID") = 3
myRow("Tank") = "20 Gallon"
myDataTable.Rows.Add(myRow)

'Create Fish Table
myDataTable = New DataTable()
myDataTable.TableName = "Fish"
myDataSet(0).Tables.Add(myDataTable)

myColumn = New DataColumn()
myColumn.DataType = System.Type.GetType("System.Int32")
myColumn.ColumnName = "ID"
myDataTable.Columns.Add(myColumn)

' Create second column.
myColumn = New DataColumn()
myColumn.DataType = Type.GetType("System.String")
myColumn.ColumnName = "Fish"
myDataTable.Columns.Add(myColumn)

' Create third column.
myColumn = New DataColumn()
myColumn.DataType = Type.GetType("System.Int32")
myColumn.ColumnName = "Number"
myDataTable.Columns.Add(myColumn)

' Create fourth column.
myColumn = New DataColumn()
```

```
myColumn.DataType = Type.GetType("System.Int32")
myColumn.ColumnName = "Tank_ID"
myDataTable.Columns.Add(myColumn)

'Add Fish
myRow = myDataTable.NewRow()
myRow("ID") = 1
myRow("Fish") = "Beta"
myRow("Number") = 1
myRow("Tank_ID") = 1
myDataTable.Rows.Add(myRow)

myRow = myDataTable.NewRow()
myRow("ID") = 1
myRow("Fish") = "Feather Fin Catfish"
myRow("Number") = 4
myRow("Tank_ID") = 3
myDataTable.Rows.Add(myRow)

myDataSet(1) = New DataSet()
myDataTable = New DataTable()
myDataTable.TableName = "Cats"
myDataSet(1).Tables.Add(myDataTable)

myColumn = New DataColumn()
myColumn.DataType = System.Type.GetType("System.Int32")
myColumn.ColumnName = "ID"
myDataTable.Columns.Add(myColumn)

' Create second column.
myColumn = New DataColumn()
myColumn.DataType = Type.GetType("System.String")
myColumn.ColumnName = "Name"
myDataTable.Columns.Add(myColumn)

'Add Cats
myRow = myDataTable.NewRow()
myRow("ID") = 1
myRow("Name") = "Rowan"
myDataTable.Rows.Add(myRow)

myRow = myDataTable.NewRow()
myRow("ID") = 2
myRow("Name") = "Morrigan"
myDataTable.Rows.Add(myRow)

myRow = myDataTable.NewRow()
myRow("ID") = 3
myRow("Name") = "Nayarlathotep"
myDataTable.Rows.Add(myRow)
```

```
    myRow = myDataTable.NewRow()
    myRow("ID") = 1
    myRow("Name") = "Melissa"
    myDataTable.Rows.Add(myRow)

    myRow = myDataTable.NewRow()
    myRow("ID") = 1
    myRow("Name") = "Lorindal"
    myDataTable.Rows.Add(myRow)

    Dim myCol1 As DataColumn
    Dim myCol2 As DataColumn

    myCol1 = myDataSet(0).Tables("Tanks").Columns("ID")
    myCol2 = myDataSet(0).Tables("Fish").Columns("Tank_ID")

    Dim myRelation As DataRelation
    myRelation = New DataRelation("TanksToFish", myCol1, myCol2)

    myDataSet(0).Relations.Add(myRelation)

    Return myDataSet

End Function
```

HOUR 13

Consuming DataSets in XML Web Services

In this hour you will learn how to consume a DataSet that has been passed to your application from an XML Web service. You will see how to read through DataSet records and even how to work through the hierarchies created through the use of DataRelations. Finally, you will take a brief look at the `DataGrid` control and how it can be used to quickly display DataSets.

Throughout this hour we will discuss the following:

- Receiving DataSets from XML Web services
- Working with DataSet Collections
- Navigating DataRelations
- DataGrid control

Building Clients for XML Web Service Returned DataSets

Many of the XML Web services that you will work with in the future will return DataSets, so it is important that you know how to handle these DataSets. In this hour, you will create an application that consumes the `exampleDataSet` XML Web service that you created in Hour 12.

Create a new Windows Application and call it `DataSetClient`. Now, add a Web reference to the `exampleDataSet` XML Web service using the methods that you first encountered back in Hour 8.

Now, add a couple of command buttons and textboxes to the default form in `DataSetClient`. Also, add a ComboBox and a TreeView control to the form. The ComboBox will contain the list of band names that we will use when adding new CDs to our catalog, and the TreeView will be used to display the entire catalog. Figure 13.1 shows the layout of the form.

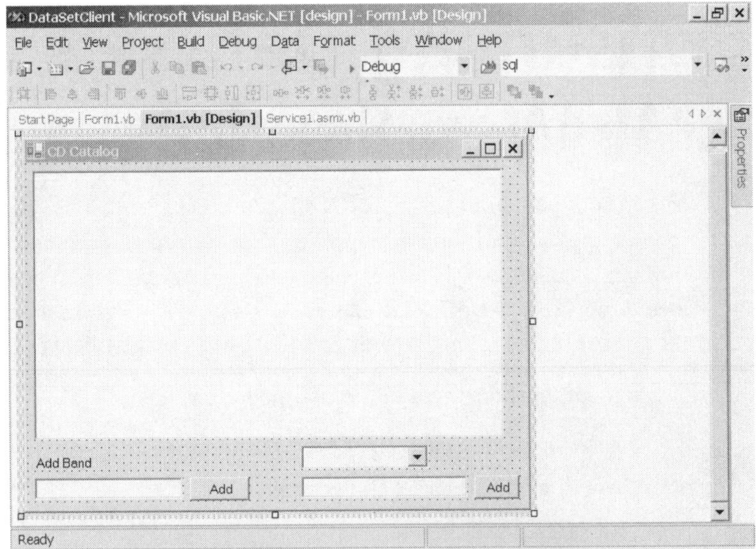

FIGURE 13.1
Form for the DataSetClient application.

Use Table 13.1 to set the properties of the various controls on your form. Don't worry too much about making the form user friendly as it exists only to demonstrate that the returns from the `exampleDataSet` XML Web service are actually working.

TABLE 13.1 Properties for the `DataSetClient`'s Controls

Control	*Property*	*Value*
Command Button	Name	cmdAddBand
	Text	Add
Command Button	Name	cmdAddTitle
	Text	Add
TextBox	Name	txtBand
	Text	
TextBox	Name	txtTitle
	Text	
Label	Text	Add Bands
ComboBox	Name	cbBands
	Text	
	Sort	True
TreeView	Name	tvCatalog
Form	Text	CD Catalog

The next thing that you need to do is prepare your application for using DataSets. In the code view for `Form1`, add the following statement to import the `System.Data` Namespace. This should go in the namespace section of your code, up at the very top of the code window.

```
Imports System.Data
```

Now, create a DataSet that can be used to populate the various display controls in the application. Let's call this DataSet `myDataSet` and declare it in the general declarations section of the `Form1` class, just below the class declaration but outside of any functions. Your declaration should look like the following:

```
Private myBands As New DataSet()
```

Now that you have your form set up and your project ready to use the `exampleDataSet` XML Web service, it is time to add some code and start consuming DataSets. The first code you should add displays the actual catalog and will be used to display results from all of the other operations. This code is shown in Listing 13.1. Do not worry too much about the specifics of it at this point in time; you won't actually learn the details behind this code until slightly later in the hour, but it is necessary to use it now in order to see the results of the various operations that you will be performing.

LISTING 13.1 Function to Load the DataTree with Data

```
Private Sub LoadDataTree()
  Dim myCatalog As New DataSet()
  Dim oMusic As New localhost.Service1()
  Dim myRow As DataRow
  Dim myChildren() As DataRow
  Dim myChildRow As DataRow
  Dim newNode As TreeNode
  Dim iChild As Integer

  myCatalog = oMusic.ReturnCatalog()
  tvCatalog.Nodes.Clear()

  For Each myRow In myCatalog.Tables("Bands").Rows
    newNode = New TreeNode(myRow(1))
    iChild = tvCatalog.Nodes.Add(newNode)

    myChildren = myRow.GetChildRows("BandsToCds")
    For Each myChildrow In myChildren
      newNode = New TreeNode(myChildRow("Title"))
      tvCatalog.Nodes(iChild).Nodes.Add(newNode)
    Next
  Next

End Sub
```

The code in Listing 13.1 calls the `ReturnCatalog` method of the `exampleDataSet` XML Web service and displays the entire catalog in the TreeView control. Again, you will learn the particulars behind this shortly. In order for the TreeView to be filled when the application starts, you need to call the `LoadDataTree` method when the form loads. Place the following function call inside the `Form1_Load` event handler:

```
LoadDataTree()
```

At this point, save the program and run it. If you typed everything correctly, you should see something resembling Figure 13.2. If not, go back and make sure that everything was typed correctly and that all of the declarations are in the correct area.

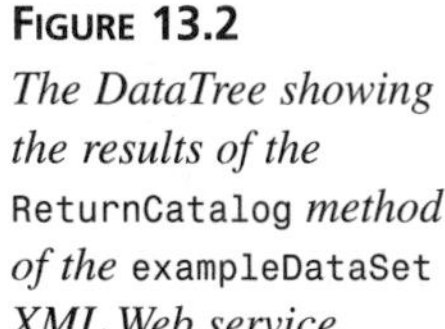

FIGURE 13.2
The DataTree showing the results of the `ReturnCatalog` *method of the* `exampleDataSet` *XML Web service.*

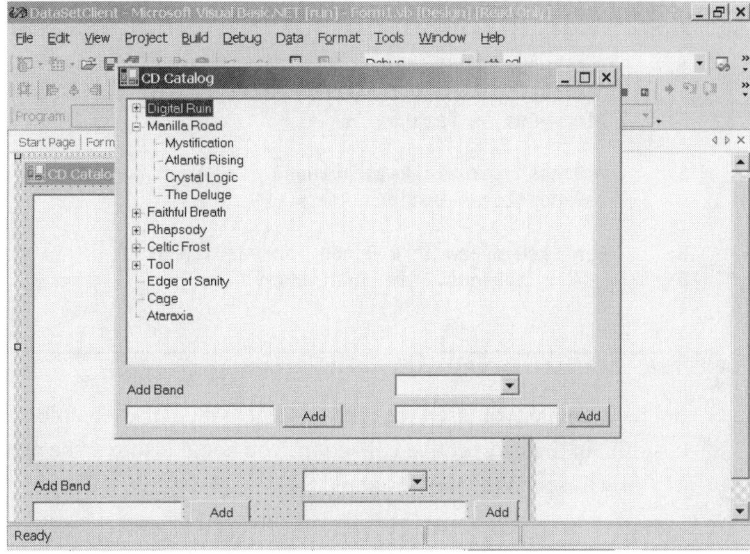

Populating a Drop-Down List with a DataSet

With the results of your DataSet returns now visible, it is time to start looking at how a DataSet is actually navigated through code. To accomplish this, you will call the `ReturnBands` method of the `exampleDataSet` service and read through the resulting DataSet, adding each band's name to the `cbBands` ComboBox.

> In a real life situation, you would use the same Dataset that was returned for populating the Treeview, see Listing 13.1. This additional call to the XML Web Service, done here to reinforce the methods of consuming service, would require the additional overhead and performance hits that developers should strive to avoid. Remember, plan you client applications carefully to ensure that you only call a service when you have to.

Look at the code in Listing 13.2. In line 2, you create an object of type `Service1`, the actual service used in `exampleDataSet`, and a DataRow object called `myRow`. You will use `myRow` to cycle through the rows of the DataTable.

In line 5 of the code, you call the `ReturnBands` method and store its returned DataSet in the `myBands` DataSet that you created at the beginning of this project. You can now use the `myRow` DataRow object to cycle through the Rows collection of `myBands.Tables(0)` and add the value of `myRow(1)`, the second column of the row, to your ComboBox.

LISTING 13.2 Using `ReturnBands` to Load a Drop-Down List

```
Private Sub LoadCombo()
  Dim oMusic As New localhost.Service1()
  Dim myRow As DataRow

  myBands = oMusic.ReturnBands
  cbBands.Items.Clear()

  For Each myRow In myBands.Tables(0).Rows
        cbBands.Items.Add(myRow(1))
  Next
End Sub
```

In this example, you used the actual integer value of each column and table's index, or position, in their respective collection. You could also use the actual name of each object, as you will see in the next example.

Add the call to the `LoadCombo` function to the `Form1_Load` event handler like you did with the `LoadDataTree` method above. The syntax should look like this:

```
LoadCombo()
```

Save and run the project. Figure 13.3 shows ComboBox `cbBands` loaded with the band names returned from `ReturnBands` method of the Web Service.

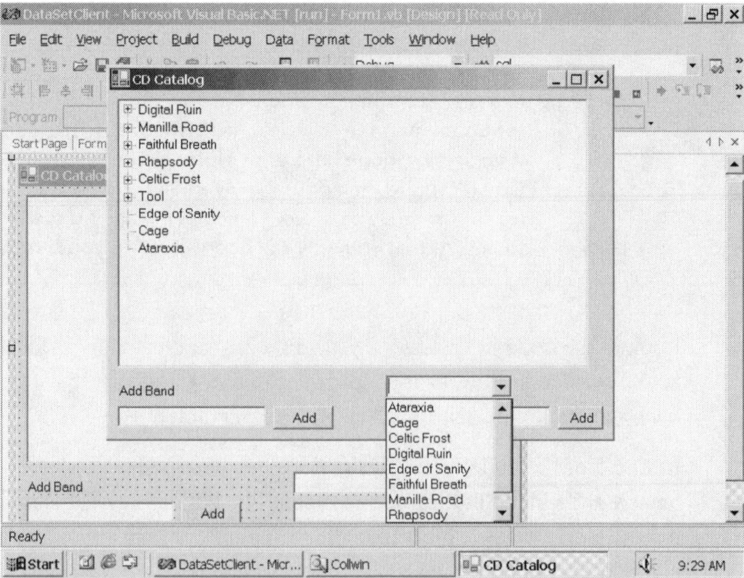

FIGURE 13.3
The drop-down list populated with the results of ReturnBands.

Adding Values to a Database through an XML Web Service Method

Now it is time for you to interact with the original data source, the Access database named `CD.mdb` that the `exampleDataSet` XML Web services uses. The code in Listing 13.3 uses the `AddBand` method of `exampleDataSet` to add a band name to the `tblBands` table of the database. See hour 12 for details on `CD.mdb`.

LISTING 13.3 Adding Bands to the Bands Table Using the `AddBand` Method of `exampleDataSet`

```
Private Sub cmdAddBand_Click(ByVal sender As System.Object, _
      ByVal e As System.EventArgs) Handles cmdAddBand.Click

  If Len(txtBand.Text) > 0 Then

    Dim oMusic As New localhost.Service1()

    oMusic.AddBand(txtBand.Text)

     LoadCombo()
     LoadDataTree()
   End If

End Sub
```

The code in Listing 13.3 is pretty straightforward. It simply checks to see if a value is present in `txtBand`, the TextBox used to enter a new band name and, if there is, passes it to the `AddBand` method of the service. After the service has been called, calls are made to `LoadCombo` and `LoadDataTree` in order to update the form.

It would save a great deal of overhead if the calls to `AddBand` were eliminated and the function was written to call `ReturnCatalog` in order to refresh the `myBands` DataSet and use that throughout the application. The separate calls exist here so that you can clearly see what is going on and get a little more exposure to calling services.

At this point, it would be a good idea to save your work and run the program. Try typing a value in the `AddBand` TextBox, `txtBand`, and click Add. Your new Band name should show up in the ComboBox, `cbBands`, and the TreeView control, `tvCatalog`. Figure 13.4 shows the band Nightwish being added.

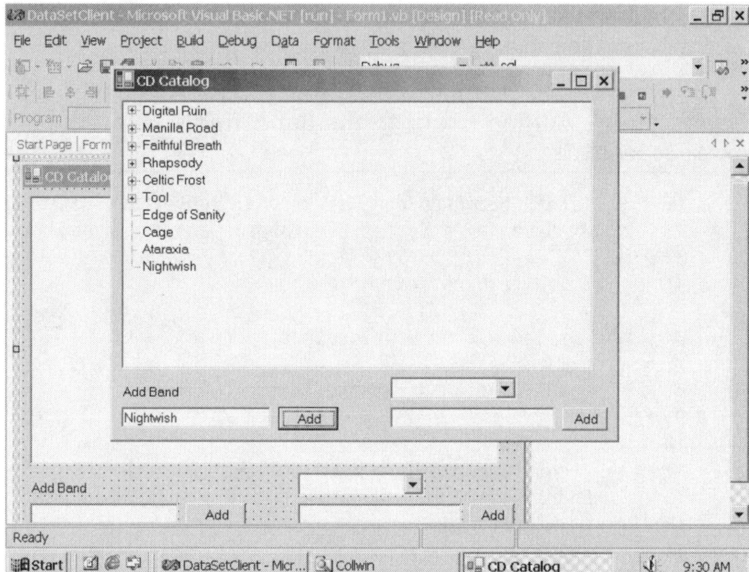

FIGURE 13.4
Adding a band to table Bands.

Maintaining Referential Integrity When Adding Data to a Database through an XML Web Service Method

To add a new CD title to the `CD.mdb` database is a bit more complicated than adding a band was. Because the database requires that any CD title be associated with a band, via the `Band_ID` field of `tblCD`, you need to have a valid ID from table bands.

Use the `cmdAddTitle_Click` event, shown in Listing 13.4, to call the `AddTitle` method of `exampleDataSet.Begin`, in lines 4 and 5, by checking to see if the necessary information is present. Next, you need to determine the `ID` of the band chosen in the ComboBox. You will need this value to call `AddTitle`.

LISTING 13.4 Using the `AddTitle` Method of `exampleDataSet` to Add CDs to a Specific Band

```
Private Sub cmdAddTitle_Click(ByVal sender As Object,_
        ByVal e As System.EventArgs) Handles cmdAddTitle.Click

  If Len(txtTitle.Text) > 0 Then
    If Len(cbBands.Text) > 0 Then
      Dim oMusic As New localhost.Service1()
      Dim iID As Integer
      Dim myRow As DataRow()

      Dim sSeek as String
      sSeek = "BandName = '" & cbBands.Text & "'"

      myRow = myBands.Tables("Bands").Select(sSeek)

      iID = myRow(0)("ID")

      oMusic.AddTitle(iID, txtTitle.Text)

      LoadDataTree()

    End If
  End If
End Sub
```

In order to find the `ID`, use the `Select` method of the DataTable `Bands`. The `Select` method returns an array of sub rows that match the string criteria passed into it. In this case, you know that only one row can be returned, so you don't need to do any other processing on the returned row.

At this point, you can retrieve the array by accessing the ID field of the first, and only, row element returned. Use this `ID` and the band name in `txtTitle` as arguments for the `AddTitle` Method. The final step is to simply call `LoadDataTree` to update the display.

When you run the application, choose a band from the drop-down list, `cbBands`, and type a CD title into the TextBox beneath it, `txtTitle`. When you click the Add button, the TreeView should be updated so that the band that you selected now has a new title listed as a child node. Figure 13.5 shows the addition of the *Oceanborn* CD to the band Nightwish.

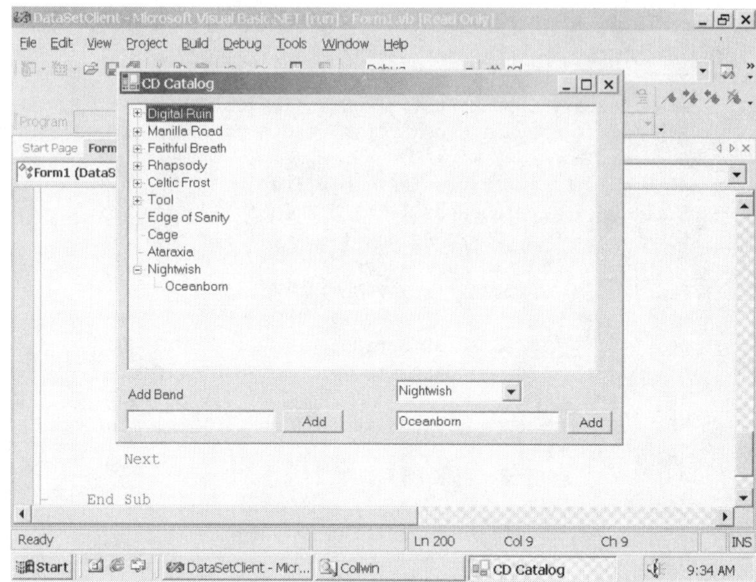

FIGURE 13.5
The OceanBorn CD Added to the CD Catalog.

Navigating DataRelation Hierarchies

Earlier in this hour, you created the `LoadDataTree` object, which utilized a DataRelation to connect the `Bands` table and the `CDs` table. Now, you will learn how the navigation of the DataRelational hierarchy actually took place.

You begin navigating the hierarchy by iterating through the parent table, `Bands`, as you have done in the previous examples. Now, as each `Row` object is read, you create a new TreeView node object containing the name of the band, from `myrow(1)`, and then we add it to the Nodes collections of `tvCatalog`—see line 14 of Listing 13.1. Store the returned index of the new node in the variable `iChild`. You will use this index to add any CD titles that the band may have as child nodes to that band.

Now, you will use an array of DataRows, line 18 of Listing 13.1, `myChildren`, to hold any children, or CD titles, that the band may possess. You retrieve the child elements by calling the `GetChildRows` method of your DataRow, `myRow`. The syntax for that method is as follows:

```
ArrayDataRows = oDataRow.GetChildRows(sDataRelation)
```

`sDataRelation` is a string containing the name of the DataRelation contained in the DataSet being navigated. `GetChildRows` will return an array of rows from the related table, in this case CDs, that adheres to the relation defined in `sDataRelation`. In this case the BandsToCds relation that defines that `ID` in table `Bands` equals the `Bands_ID` in table `CD`.

You can now iterate through this array of rows in almost exactly the same manner as you were navigating through the parent DataTable, Line 18 of Listing 13.1. The syntax for doing this is:

```
For Each oDataRow in ArrayDataRows
```

To finish out your function, you simply add the child rows to the TreeView as children of the appropriate `Band` node. You do this using the `Add` method of the `Nodes` object in conjunction with the `Index` property of the nodes collection, as shown in line 20 of Listing 13.1. The syntax for that is the following:

```
oTreeView.Nodes(index).Nodes.Add(newNode)
```

Binding DataSets to the DataGrid Control

The DataGrid is a fairly simple yet very powerful way to display data from Arrays, DataSets, DataTables, and more.

Create a new Windows application and call it DataGrid. As you did with the previous project, add a Web reference to the `exampleDataSet. Then,` add a DataGrid contol to the default so that it looks like Figure 13.6. You will not need to add any other controls to the form because you are concerned only with how the DataGrid displays information from your XML Web service returned DataSets.

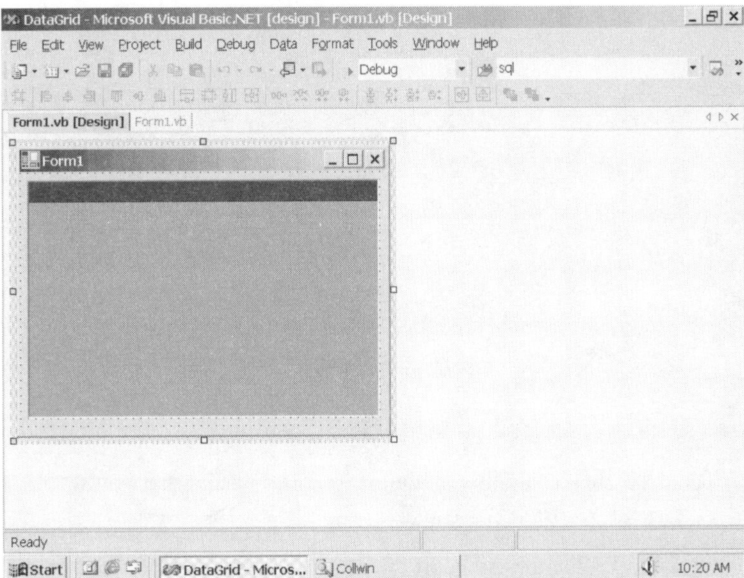

FIGURE 13.6
The form for the DataGrid test application.

Add the code shown in Listing 13.5 to the `Form_Load` event and run the application. The `SetDataBinding` method of the DataGrid control does all the work in pulling your Datasets' DataTable, in this case `Bands`, to the grid and displaying it.

LISTING 13.5 `Form1_Load` Event Code to Initialize the DataGrid

```
Dim oMusic As New localhost.Service1()
Dim myDataSet As New DataSet()

myDataSet = oMusic.ReturnBands()
DataGrid1.SetDataBinding(myDataSet, "Bands")
```

The syntax for using `SetDataBinding` on a DataSet is as follows:

```
ODataGrid.SetDataBinding(myDataSet, sTableName)
```

`sTableName` is a string representing a valid table in the DataSet.

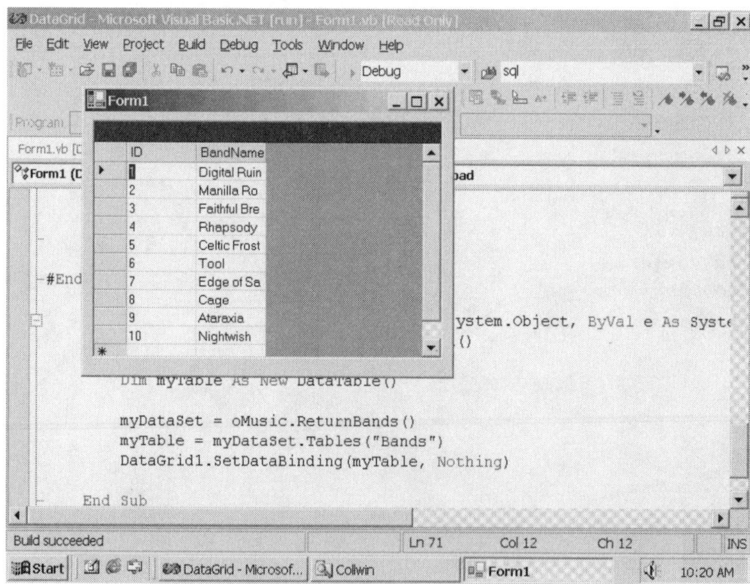

FIGURE 13.7
The DataGrid displays the results of the `ReturnBands` *method.*

```
DataGrid.SetDataBinding(myTable, Nothing)
```

In C#, the declaration is almost identical except that you would use the `Null` keyword instead of Visual Basic's `Nothing`.

Table 13.2 shows some of the commonly used properties of the DataGrid object.

TABLE 13.2 Common Properties for the DataGrid Control

Property	*Description*
`AllowzSorting`	Determines if columns can be sorted by clicking their headers
`Captiontext`	Text of the DataGrid's caption
`CaptionVisible`	Determines if caption is visible
`ColumnHeadersVisible`	Determines if headers are visible
`CurrentCell`	Curently selected cell
`CurrentRowIndex`	The Index value of the currently Selected row
`DataMemeber`	The data member, such as a table in a DataSet, that the DataGrid is bound to
`DataSource`	The source of value used to populate the DataGrid
`GridLineColor`	The color of the grid lines
`GridLineStyle`	The style of the grid lines
`Item`	Value of a specific cell
`PreferredRowWidth`	The default width of the grid rows
`PreferredColumnWidth`	The default width of grid columns
`Visible`	Boolean that determines if DataGrid is displayed
`VisibleColumnCount`	Number of visible columns
`VisibleRowCount`	Number of visible rows

Table 13.3 shows the common methods of the DataGrid control.

TABLE 13.3 Common Events for the DataGrid Control

Event	*Description*
`BeginEdit`	Begins an edit operation
`Collapse`	Collapses all child relations
`EndEdit`	Ends an edit
`Expand`	Displays any child relations for all rows
`GetCurrentCellBounds`	Gets a rectangle that specifies the four corners of selected cells
`IsExpanded`	Indicates if a specified row's node is expanded
`IsSelected`	Indicates if a specified row is selected
`Select`	Selects a specified row
`UnSelect`	Unselects a specified row

Summary

In this hour, you saw how to retrieve DataSets from XML Web services and use them within your applications. You learned how to use the `getChildRows` property of a DataRow to maneuver through DataRelation created table hierarchies. At the end of the hour, you saw how to harness some of the power of the DataGrid control.

Q&A

Q Is it possible to navigate hierarchies that are more complicated than a single relationship?

A Yes, it is quite possible to navigate down many layers of child rows, for example, by using the `GetChildRow` methods on each child row.

Q Can I send and receive smaller sections of a DataSet via XML Web services?

A Actually, no. As of this writing, any attempts to use DataTables or DataRows have met with errors. Even if you were allowed to do such a thing, however, it would not be good form. By keeping your tables and rows together in a DataSet, you help to ensure that all clients, even those not using .Net, know how to parse your XML DataSet return.

Q Why do we need to create a new DataRow object just to read the rows in our DataTable?

A In ADO.NET DataSets, a row, or DataRow to be precise, is part of a collection. Using the `for each` method of iterating through a collection, although admittedly not the only method to of doing so, is one of the more elegant ways of navigating a collection and the one I recommend. So to answer the question, you don't have to create a new DataRow to navigate the collection, but it makes your code much more readable and maintainable than if you used the collections index, for example, to navigate.

Q Is it possible to receive DataSets from two separate XML Web services and set up DataRelations between them?

A Yes, this can be done by merging the two DataSets, using the merge method of the DataSet object, and then creating the DataRelations as you saw in Hour 12.

Workshop

The Workshop is designed to help you review what you've learned in this hour and to point you ahead to the material that will be covered in future hours.

Quiz

1. What Row object method returns any child objects of the current row?

   A `GetChildRows`

2. What is the syntax to get the value of the third column of a DataRow called `drRows`?

   A `drRows(2)`

3. How would you bind a table, Cheeses, from a Dataset call `dsSnacks` to a DataGrid named `dgData`?

   A `DgData.SetDataBinding(dsSnacks, "Cheese")`

4. What is the syntax to retrieve the `ID` field from the third row of an array of DataRows called `drCalendars`?

   A `drCalendars(2)("ID")`

5. What property of the DataGrid determines what table in a datasource it is bound to?

   A `DataMember.`

Exercises

Try altering the DataGrid project to utilize the `ReturnCatalog` method of `exampleDataSet` to see how the grid can be used to output related tables. Also, experiment with some of the methods of the DataGrid Control.

A. Here is the code to open the DataSet returned from ReturnCatalog.

```
Dim oMusic As New localhost.Service1()
Dim myDataSet As New DataSet()

myDataSet = oMusic.ReturnCatalog()
DataGrid1.SetDataBinding(myDataSet, Nothing)
```

Hour 14

XML in Web Services

In this hour, you will look at some of the ways that Visual Studio.NET allows you to manipulate XML Data. You will also look at how XML Web services can retrieve data from XML sources and pass that information on to client applications. Finally, you will examine how to change, or transform, the entire hierarchy of an XML document and thereby provide even greater flexibility in the manner that your services handle data.

In this hour, we will discuss the following:

- The `DataSet` object's XML handling capabilities
- `XmlReader` Objects
- `XmlDocument` Objects
- `XslTransform` Objects

Using DataSet Objects to Handle XML Data

In the previous hours, you learned how to use ADO.NET within your XML Web services in order to handle complex data and return order information to your client applications. Now you will take a look at the XML handling capabilities that are built into the ADO.NET DataSet object. Table 14.1 shows the DataSet methods that are used to handle XML data. In particular, note the ReadXML and ReadXMLSchema methods. These methods allow you to open XML documents and read in their structure and data, or just the structure in the case of the GetXMLSchema method. You can then manipulate and return this XML data as you would any DataSet object.

TABLE 14.1 XML Methods of the DataSet Object

Method	*Description*
GetXML	Returns the XML form of the DataSet
GetXMLSchema	Returns the XSD schema for the Dataset
InferXMLSchema	Infers the XML schema for a file or textreader object and imports it into the Dataset
ReadXML	Reads XML data into the DataSet
ReadXMLSchema	Reads an XML schema into the DataSet
WriteXML	Writes XML document from the DataSet
WriteXMLSchema	Writes the XML schema for the DataSet

Return XML from DataSet Objects as Simple Strings

The DataSet object contains a method called GetXML that allows you to return the entire XML contents of your DataSet as one long string. Although, in most cases, it is a much better idea to send the DataSet object itself to clients, you may encounter situations where it is advantageous to send the string object instead. This would include a situation where you knew you that most of your client applications would not be written in .NET and would not utilize the DataSet object model and where you wished to trim some of the extra DataSet specific markup from your return.

Listing 14.1 shows the GetXml method being used to return the XML string representation of a database table. Notice that the DataSet is loaded from a relational data source using the normal methods.

LISTING 14.1 Using the DataSet's GetXml Method

```
<WebMethod()> Public Function XML_String() As String
  Dim myDataSet As New DataSet()
```

continues

LISTING 14.1 Continued

```
    Dim conn As New OleDbConnection()

    conn.ConnectionString = "Provider=Microsoft.Jet.OLEDB.4.0; _
    Data Source=C:\Book\CD.mdb;Persist Security Info=False"
    conn.Open()

    Dim sSQL As String = "SELECT * FROM tblBands"
    Dim myAdapter As New OleDbDataAdapter(sSQL, conn)

    myAdapter.Fill(myDataSet, "Bands")
    conn.Close()

    Return myDataSet.GetXml

  End Function
```

The returned XML string is shown in Figure 14.1. If you compare this to the `DataSet` returned by the example in Listing 12.1, you will notice that the new example is much more compact because it lacks the `DataSet` object's structure and the extra XSD markup.

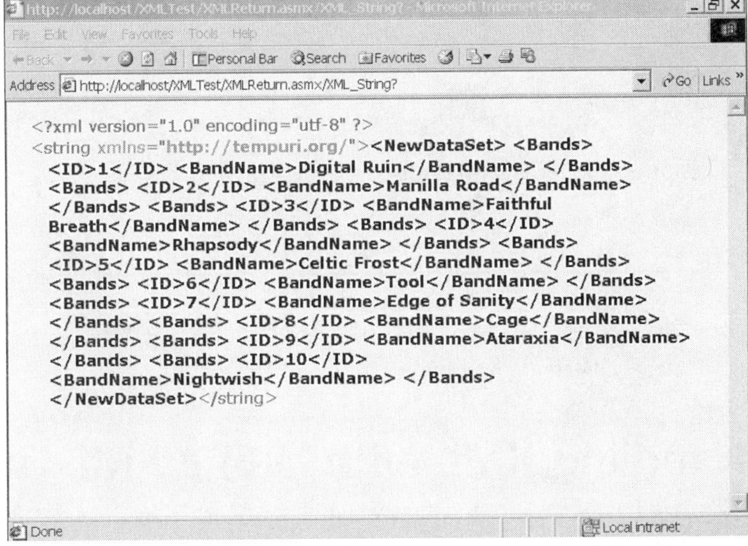

FIGURE 14.1
The `DataSet` *object's* `GetXml` *return.*

In Listing 14.2, the `GetXMLSchema` is used to return only the schema of the XML data. A practical application of this may be the sending of the schema to a client application so that it can validate an XML document before sending the document back to the service. Again, this would primarily be done in situations where the client application is not using `DataSet` objects.

LISTING 14.2 Returning the Schema from a `DataSet`

```
<WebMethod()> Public Function Schema_String() As String
   Dim myDataSet As New DataSet()
   Dim conn As New OleDbConnection()

   conn.ConnectionString = "Provider=Microsoft.Jet.OLEDB.4.0; " _
        & "Data Source=C:\Book\CD.mdb;Persist Security Info=False"
   conn.Open()

   Dim sSQL As String = "SELECT * FROM tblBands"

   Dim myAdapter As New OleDbDataAdapter(sSQL, conn)
   myAdapter.Fill(myDataSet, "Bands")

   sSQL = "SELECT * FROM tblCD"

   Dim myAdapter2 As New OleDbDataAdapter(sSQL, conn)
   myAdapter2.Fill(myDataSet, "CDS")

   conn.Close()

    Dim myCol1 As DataColumn
    Dim myCol2 As DataColumn

   myCol1 = myDataSet.Tables("Bands").Columns("ID")
   myCol2 = myDataSet.Tables("CDS").Columns("Band_ID")

   Dim myRelation As DataRelation
   myRelation = New DataRelation("BandsToCds", myCol1, myCol2)

   myDataSet.Relations.Add(myRelation)

   Return myDataSet.GetXmlSchema
End Function
```

The returned schema, shown in Figure 14.2, can now be used to create valid XML documents containing information about a CD catalog.

Handling XML with .NET's XML Object Set

.NET provides a very extensive number of objects to allow developers to read, write, and manipulate XML data. These objects, primarily contained within the *System.XML* namespace, include a series of master classes that act as templates for the classes that you will use in your code. Because of these classes, learning how to use one class, say the `XmlTextWriter` Class, will also give you familiarity with other classes, such as the `XmlNodeReader`.

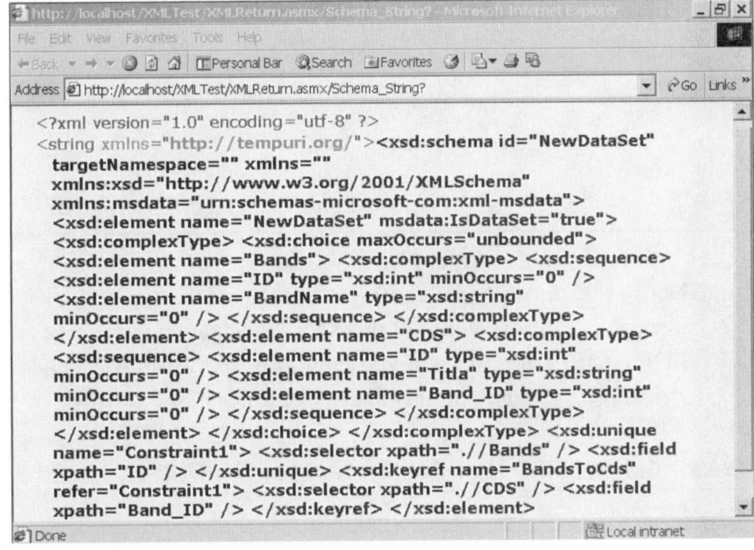

FIGURE 14.2
The schema returned using a `DataSet` *object's* `GetXMLSchema` *method.*

Reading XML Data with the XmlReader Class

The XmlReader class is an abstract class, which means that it acts as a template for other classes to be built from and is not really used on its own. From the XmlReader class, you will find several derived classes that can be used to read in XML from XML sources.

- `XmlTextReader`—Provides forward-only access to the XML data stream
- `XmlNodeReader`—Utilizes `XmlNode` objects to contain the structure of the XML data
- `XmlValidatingReader`—Adds validation to the XML via schemas or DTDs

The basic properties and methods of an XmlReader object may vary some among each of the various classes that implement it, but by learning how to use the `XmlTextReader` object, shown in Tables 14.2 and 14.3, you will be very prepared to use the other two classes when the need arises.

TABLE 14.2 Properties of the `XmlTextReader` Object

Property	*Description*
`AttributeCount`	Gets the number of attributes for the current node
`EOF`	Gets `True` if the reader is at the end of the XML stream
`HasAttributes`	Indicates whether the current node has any attributes
`Item`	Gets the value of an attribute

continues

14

TABLE 14.2 Continued

Property	*Description*
`LocalName`	Gets the name of the current node
`Name`	Gets the fully qualified name of the the current node
`NodeType`	Gets the current node's type
`Value`	Gets the current node's text

Notice that the `XmlTextReader` provides an EOF property. This allows you to move through the various nodes of the XML data one by one, using the `Read` method, until EOF returns `True`. Those of you familiar with the old ADO `Recordset` objects will already be familiar with this manner of navigation.

TABLE 14.3 Methods of the `XmlTextReader` Object

Method	*Description*
`Close`	Closes the XMLTextReader
`GetAttribute`	Returns an Attribute's value
`MoveToElement`	Moves reader to element that contains the current attribute node
`ReadElementString`	Returns the text contents of the current element node
`ReadEndElement`	Advances the reader to the next node if current node is an end tag
`ReadInnerXML`	Reads all content of the node
`ReadOuterXML`	Reads all content, including markup, of the current node
`Skip`	Skips the current element

Many of the methods in Table 14.3, particularly those beginning with "`Read`" or "`MoveTo`," are just a representative sampling of all of the methods that the class exposes. Many other methods exist to read in or move to various other XML document element types.

Now it is time to look at the XML reader in action. The XML document in Listing 14.3 will be used for all of the examples that follow. Notice the simple structure by which each team gets `ID`, `City`, and `TeamName` elements. Feel free to add more NFL teams if you wish or use a completely different XML document altogether.

LISTING 14.3 The `NFL.Xml` XML Document

```
<?xml version="1.0" standalone="yes"?>
<NFL>
 <Teams>
   <ID>1</ID>
```

continues

Listing 14.3 Continued

```
      <City>Baltimore</City>
      <TeamName>Ravens</TeamName>
    </Teams>
    <Teams>
      <ID>2</ID>
      <City>Buffalo</City>
      <TeamName>Bills</TeamName>
    </Teams>
    <Teams>
      <ID>3</ID>
      <City>Cinncinnati</City>
      <TeamName>Bengals</TeamName>
    </Teams>
    <Teams>
      <ID>4</ID>
      <City>Cleveland</City>
      <TeamName>Browns</TeamName>
    </Teams>
    <Teams>
   <ID>5</ID>
      <City>Denver</City>
      <TeamName>Broncos</TeamName>
    </Teams>
    <Teams>
      <ID>6</ID>
      <City>Indianapolis</City>
      <TeamName>Colts</TeamName>
    </Teams>
    <Teams>
      <ID>7</ID>
      <City>Jacksonville</City>
      <TeamName>Jaguars</TeamName>
    </Teams>
  </NFL>
```

Create a new XML Web service project and give it the name `XMLReturn`. Remember to import the `System.XML` namespace into your project:

```
Imports System.Xml
```

You will also need to import the `System.IO`, `System.Data`, and `System.Data.OleDB` namespaces into your project.

The first example that you will look at shows the `XmlTextReader` object being used to open an XML data source, your file from Listing 14.3, and to pass it into a `DataSet` object. Line 5 shows the creation of the `XmlTextReader`, `myXmlReader`. A `FileStream` object is passed into the `XmlTextReader` and the data is read in from there. Finally, the `ReadXml` method of the `DataSet` object, `myDataSet`, is used to read the XML document from the `XmlTextReader` into the `DataSet`, as shown in Listing 14.4.

LISTING 14.4 Reading the XML Document into a `DataSet`

```
<WebMethod()> Public Function XML_to_DataSet() As DataSet
  Dim myDataSet As New DataSet()
  Dim myfStream As New FileStream( _
        "C:\Book\NFL.xml", System.IO.FileMode.Open)
  Dim myXmlReader As New XmlTextReader(myfStream)

  myDataSet.ReadXml(myXmlReader)
  myXmlReader.Close()

  Return myDataSet
End Function
```

The returned `DataSet` for the `NFL.Xml` document can be seen in Figure 14.3. The structure of the original XML document has been preserved completely.

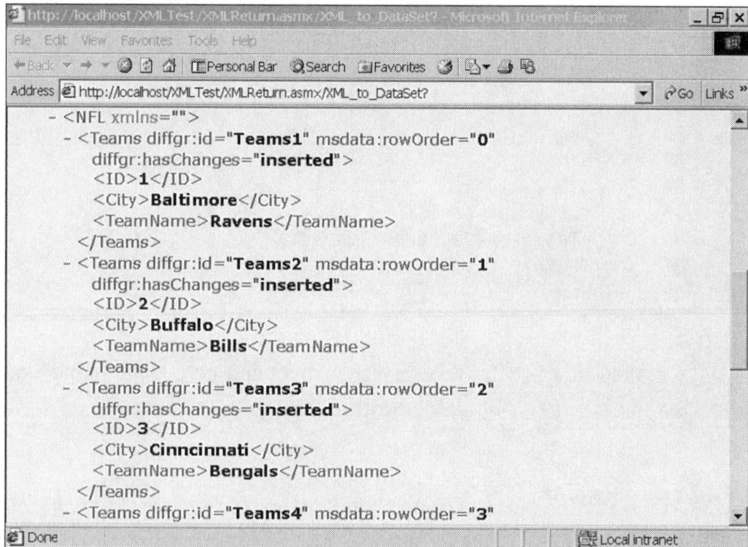

FIGURE 14.3
The `DataSet` *return of* `NFL.Xml`.

Navigating through the XML document once it is in the `XmlTextReader` object is simple. In Listing 14.5, the XML document is navigated through and its `TeamName` elements are added to an array. As in the previous example, the document is read into the `XmlTextReader` object (line 3). This time, however, the XML document is parsed directly in the `XmlTextReader` object.

In line 9, The `MoveToContent` method of `XmlTextReader` is used to navigate to each element tag. Line 10 checks to make sure that the current element is named "`TeamName`." If it is, the `ReadElementString` is used to extract the text, in this case the name of an NFL team, from the element. This text is then added to an array.

LISTING 14.5 Return an Array Built from XML Elements

```
1:   <WebMethod()> Public Function XML_to_Array() As String()
2:      Dim myArray() As String
3:      Dim myReader As New XmlTextReader("C:\Book\NFL.xml")
4:      Dim i As Integer
5:
6:
7:      While Not myReader.EOF
8:
9:        If (myReader.MoveToContent = XmlNodeType.Element) _
10:                  And (myReader.Name = "TeamName") Then
11:         ReDim Preserve myArray(i)
12:         myArray(i) = myReader.ReadElementString
13:         i = i + 1
14:       Else
15:         myReader.Read()
16:       End If
17:
18:     End While
19:
20:     Return myArray
21:
22:  End Function
```

The `ReDim` statement is an extremely slow and resource-intensive process. Care should be used in deciding whether or not it has a place in your applications.

The returned array is shown in Figure 14.4. As expected, it contains only the contents of the `TeamName` element for each team in the XML document.

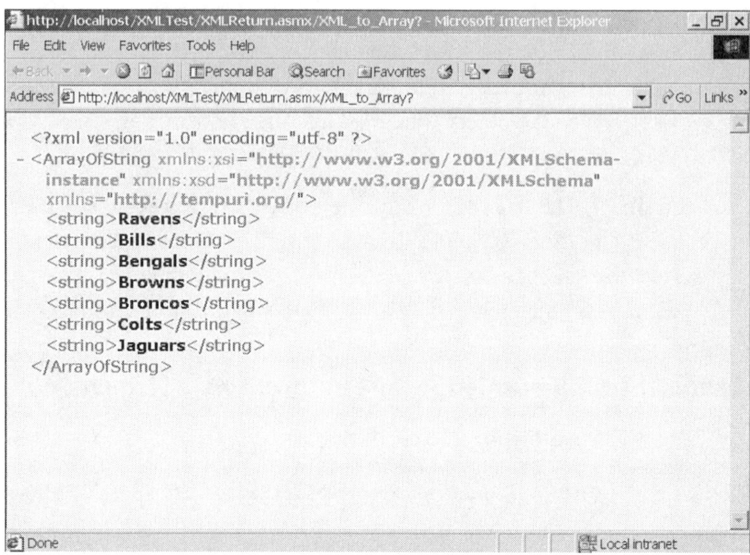

FIGURE 14.4
An array of XmlNode elements built from `NFL.Xml`.

Modeling XML Data with the XmlNode Class

The XmlNode class is another top-level class provided by the `System.XML` namespace. This class is implemented in a vast number of XML data handling objects, including those in Table 14.4. Many of the classes shown are themselves implemented in additional classes. For example, `XmlElement` implements the `XmlLinkedNode` class.

TABLE 14.4 Derived Classes of the `XMLNode` Object

Class	*Description*
`XmlAttribute`	Represents an XML Attribute
`XmlDocument`	Represents an XML Document
`XmlEntity`	Represents an XML Entity Declaration
`XmlLinkedNode`	Represents an XML immediately preceding or following this node
`XmlNotation`	Represents an XML Notation Declaration

The most common properties of the XmlNode class, and those that are commonly used in most of the derived classes shown in Table 14.4, can be seen in Table 14.5. Again, it should be noted that each of the derived classes adds its own properties and method, making a full listing of the functionality available to developers beyond the scope of this book.

TABLE 14.5 Properties of the `XmlNode` Object

Method	*Description*
`ChildNodes`	Gets all the children of the current node
`FirstChild`	Gets the first child of the current node
`HasChildNodes`	Returns `True` if the current node has children
`InnerText`	Gets or Sets the `Value` of the Node
`InnerXML`	Gets or Sets the markup of the node
`Item`	Gets the child element specified
`LastChild`	Gets the current node's last child
`Name`	Gets the node's fully qualified name
`NextSibling`	Gets the next node
`NodeType`	Gets the current node's type
`ParentNode`	Gets the current node's parent
`PreviousSibling`	Gets the previous node
`Value`	Gets or Sets the current node's value

Table 14.6 lists the common methods of the XmlNode class. Many important methods are added to the individual classes that implement the XmlNode class. For example, the `XmlDocument` object includes a number of methods, such as `CreateElement` and `CreateAttribute`, which are used to create other objects (`XmlElement` and `XmlAttribute` objects in this case) for use in working with their data.

TABLE 14.6 Methods of the `XmlNode` Class

Method	*Description*
`AppendChild`	Appends a new child node to the end of the current node's children
`CloneNode`	Returns a duplicate of the node
`CreateNavigator`	Returns an `XpathNavigator` Class
`InsertAfter`	Inserts an XmlNode after the node specified
`InsertBefore`	Inserts an XmlNode before the node specified
`RemoveAll`	Removes all attributes and children of the current node
`RemoveChild`	Removes the specified child node

In order to illustrate the usage of one of the methods of a class derived from XmlNode, let's look at the `XmlDocument` object and the `CreateAttribute` method. To use

CreateAttribute methods, you first declare an instance of XmlAttribute. You then set that attribute equal to the return of CreateAttribute method. This attribute can then be added to the original XmlDocument object through the use of the SetAttribute method.

Below, an attribute called "speed" is created and then set to "30 knots" using the Value property of the XmlNode object. The attribute is then added to the XmlDocument, myDoc, by calling the SetAttribute method of the DocumentElement object that is part of the myDoc XmlDocument object.

```
Dim myDoc as New XmlDocument()
MyDoc.Load("C:\Book\MyCar.xml")
Dim myAtt as XMLAttribute
myAtt = myDoc.CreateAttribute("speed")
myAtt.Value = "30 knots"
myDoc.DocumentElement.SetAttributeNode(mtAtt)
```

Return XmlNode Objects from an XML Web Service

As you have seen throughout this book, XML Web services are able to return an extensive array of data types ranging from simple types, such as integers and strings, to complex types, such as datasets and objects. Thus, it should come as no surprise that XML Web services can also return XmlNode objects. Doing this is very similar to returning any other data type. Simply declare the function to return type XmlNode, create the XmlNode object, perform any tasks on it that you wish, and return it.

In Listing 14.6, an array of XmlNode objects is returned. Again, this works in same manner as returning a standard array did in Hour 10. In this example, an XmlNode object, myNode; an XmlDocument object, myDoc; and an XmlNodeList are all created. The XmlNodeList is basically a collection of XmlNode objects that can be iterated through.

In line 8, the Load method of the XmlDocument object is used in order to retrieve the XML from the NFL.Xml file. Once this is loaded, the GetElementsByTagName method is called to retrieve all of the elements in the XML data that are of type "TeamName." These elements are returned as an XmlNodeList object.

Once you have the XmlNodeList object, you can iterate through the collection of nodes, as seen in line 11, and build a collection of XmlNode objects.

LISTING 14.6 Returning an Array of `XmlNode` Objects

```
<WebMethod()> Public Function XML_Return() As XmlNode()
  Dim myNode() As XmlNode
  Dim node As XmlNode
  Dim myList As XmlNodeList
  Dim myDoc As New XmlDocument()
  Dim i As Integer

  myDoc.Load("C:\Book\NFL.xml")
  myList = myDoc.GetElementsByTagName("TeamName")

  For Each node In myList
    ReDim Preserve myNode(i)
    myNode(i) = node
    i = i + 1
  Next

  Return myNode
End Function
```

The array of XmlNode objects based on the `NFL.Xml` file can be seen in Figure 14.5. If you had wished, you could have iterated through and grabbed the "`Teams`" elements instead of "`TeamName`." This way, each of the XmlNode objects would have contained the elements "`ID`," "`City`," and "`TeamName`."

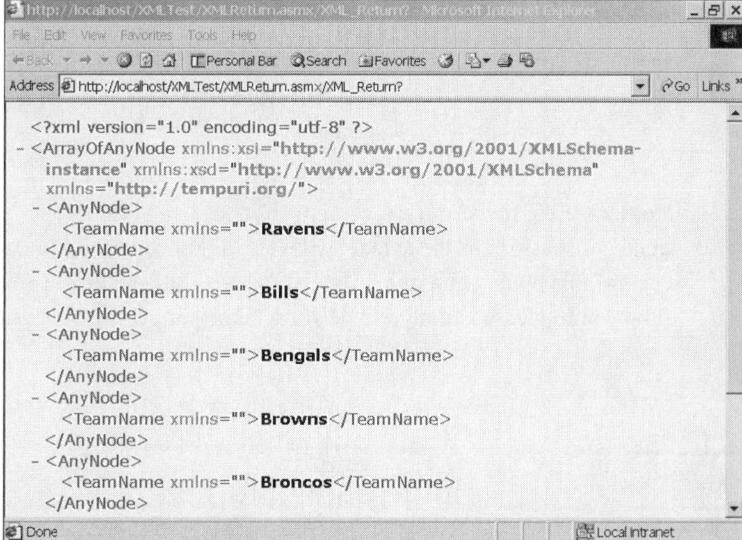

FIGURE 14.5
An array of XmlNodes based on `NFL.Xml`.

Transforming XML Data with the XslTransform Class

In many cases, it is extremely useful to be able to completely alter the structure of an XML document. For example, in our NFL.Xml example from above, the Team city and the Team name are kept separate. In some instances, it might be useful to provide this data together as one element, such as "Buffalo Bills." This can be accomplished using the XslTransform object.

The XslTransform object is contained in the System.Xml.Xsl namespace, so if you are working through these examples, you must add the following line to your code:

```
Imports System.Xml.Xsl
```

The properties and methods of the XslTransform object are shown in Tables 14.7 and 14.8, respectively. As you may have noticed, there are not a lot of properties or methods to this class. Its only real purpose is to perform transformations on XML data.

TABLE 14.7 Properties of the XslTransform Class

Method	*Description*
XmlResolver	Sets the XmlResolver object that is used to resolve any external resources

TABLE 14.8 Methods of the XslTransform Class

Method	*Description*
Load	Loads the XSL style sheet
Transform	Uses the loaded XSL style sheet to transform the given XML document

In order for the transform to accomplish its task, an XSL style sheet must be used. A detailed discussion of the actual syntax of the transform document is a bit beyond the scope of this book, but a quick look at the NFL.Xsl document shown in Listing 14.7 will allow you to pick up enough to perform some simple transforms of your own.

LISTING 14.7 `NFL.XSL` Style Sheet

```
1:  <?xml version="1.0"?>
2:  <xsl:stylesheet version="1.0"
3:       xmlns:xsl="http://www.w3.org/1999/XSL/Transform">
4:
5:  <xsl:output method="xml"/>
6:
7:  <xsl:template match="/">
8:   <NFL>
9:     <xsl:apply-templates/>
10:  </NFL>
11: </xsl:template>
12:
13: <xsl:template match="Teams">
14:   <Team>
15:     <ID>
16:       <xsl:apply-templates select="ID/text()" />
17:     </ID>
18:     <Name>
19:       <xsl:apply-templates select="City/text()" />
20:       -
21:       <xsl:apply-templates select="TeamName/text()" />
22:     </Name>
23:   </Team>
24: </xsl:template>
25:
26: </xsl:stylesheet>
```

This rather simplistic XSL style sheet creates a new XML document with "`<NFL>`" as the root element. Inside of the root element, the transformation will match each "`<Teams>`" element and replace it with a "`<Team>`" element. Inside of each "`<Team>`" element, will be "`<ID>`" and "`<Name>`" elements.

The last aspect worth mentioning is the use of the `select` statement in lines 16,19, and 21. These statements retrieve the text from the original element listed and add it to the new document.

In order to use the XSL document, create a new method called `XML_Transform`, and set it to return a `DataSet`. Alternately, you could return an XmlNode object.

The first thing that you must do is load the `NFL.XML` document. This is done in line 8 of Listing 14.8 through the use of the `XmlDocument` object, `myDoc`. After loading the XML document, you must load the XSL document into the `XslTransform` object, `myTrans`.

In line 10, we create an `XmlNavigator` object to use as the XML reader for our `XmlTransform` object. This object is a high speed, forward-only XML reader that can be found in the `System.Xml.Xpath` namespace. That means that you have to add the import statement for this namespace into your service as well.

```
Imports System.Xml.Xpath
```

Now the `Transform` method of the `XmlTransformation` object is ready to be called. Pass in the `XpathNavigator`, `myNav`, and the method will return a new `XmlReader` object with the new XML Document. The `XmlReader` object is simply read into a `DataSet` object and the object is returned to the service's clients.

LISTING 14.8 Transforming an XML Document

```
1:    <WebMethod()> Public Function XML_Transform() As DataSet
2:      Dim myTrans As New XslTransform()
3:      Dim myDoc As New XmlDocument()
4:      Dim myReader As XmlReader
5:      Dim myNav As XPathNavigator
6:      Dim myDataSet As New DataSet()
7:
8:      myDoc.Load("C:\Book\NFL.xml")
9:      myTrans.Load("C:\Book\NFL.xsl")
10:     myNav = myDoc.CreateNavigator
11:
12:     myReader = myTrans.Transform(myNav, Nothing)
13:
14:     myDataSet.ReadXml(myReader)
15:
16:     Return myDataSet
17:   End Function
```

Your new XML can now be viewed in Figure 14.6, complete with the change from "`Teams`" to "`Team`" and including the concatenated "`City`" and "`TeamName`" elements as "`Name`."

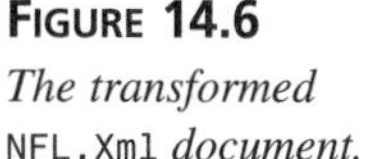

FIGURE 14.6
The transformed `NFL.Xml` *document.*

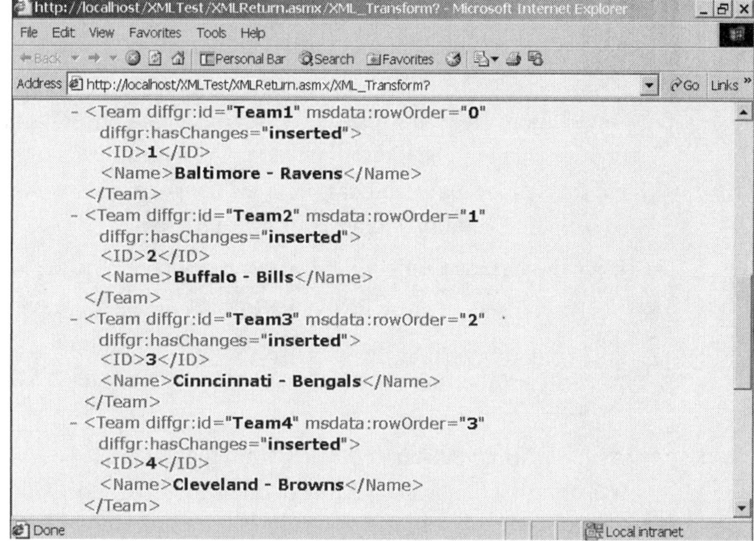

Summary

In this hour, you learned how to retrieve and manipulate XML data in your XML Web services. You also looked at some of the Objects and Namespaces provided by .NET to deal with XML data. Later in the hour, you saw how to return XML-specific data from your services. To end the Hour, you examined the `XslTransform` object and saw how to use it to quickly change the entire structure of an XML document.

Q&A

Q What is the point of allowing the DataSet object to write out XML and XSL documents?

A Well, one reason is the ability to save the `DataSet` object in a format that other programs could use. If you used ADO in previous versions, you may have come across functionality that allowed you to save your record sets to disk and then, when needed, reopen them. `WriteXml` and `WriteXmlSchema` provide that same functionality and more. Now, other code can parse the data as straight XML or open it into DataSet objects.

Q What is the point of returning XMLNode objects when the `DataSet` object is in XML anyway?

A What is the point of not simply providing one large Integer type to handle all numbers instead of providing many, such as float and long? Sometimes, it is possible to reduce the size of the data you are sending across the Internet by using straight

XML returns. Other times, if your data is manipulating large amounts of XML and not really handling any relational data, it just seems more natural to remain with the XML object model.

An additional reason is that the needs of your application may already require you or your client applications to be using the `System.XML` namespace and objects but not the `System.Data` and `DataSet`. If this is the case, why add the extra overhead of including additional objects in your program?

Q Does the `DataSet` object deal with attributes?

A Yes, if you add an attribute to an XML document, say a "`population`" attribute to the "`City`" element of the `NFL.Xml` document and run the `XML_to_DataSet` method, you will see the "`population`" attribute present in the XML markup of your `DataSet`.

As far as using attributes directly from the `DataSet`, your best bet is to perform a transform on the original XML in order to get it into a simple, all element shape before loading it into the `DataSet`. This is preferred to leaving the attributes to be inferred as columns in a table, the default method, as this may produce tables with a structure that is difficult to navigate.

Workshop

The Workshop is designed to help you review what you've learned in this hour and to point you ahead to the material that will be covered in future hours.

Quiz

1. What method of the `DataSet` object allows XML data to be read in from files or `XmlReader` objects?

   A `GetXml()`

2. Name two classes that implement the `XmlReader` class?

   A `XmlTextReader`, `XmlNodeReader`, or `XmlValidatingReader`

3. What method of the `XmlDocument` method would you most likely use if you wished to retrieve an `XmlNodelist` object of all of the nodes with the element "`<Puppies>`" as its root?

   A `GetElementsByTagName("Puppies")`

   `SelectNodes` is also acceptable.

4. What type of document must be loaded into the `XmlTransform` in order to perform the transform on an XML Document?

   A An XSL or XSLT document

5. What method of `XmlReader` objects returns `True` when you have read to the end of the document?

   A EOF

Exercises

Create your own XML document and write a series of XML Web service methods to deal with it. Try altering the functions above, as well. For example, alter Listing 14.8 to return an `XmlNodeList`, or even a single XmlNode.

A. The example below alters the `XML_Transform` method so that it returns an array of XmlNode objects based on the `Name` Node. This means that we will have an array of XmlNodes that do not contain any child nodes.

```
<WebMethod()>
Public Function XML_TransformNode() As XmlNode()

        Dim myTrans As New XslTransform()
        Dim myDoc As New XmlDocument()
        Dim myDoc2 As New XmlDocument()
        Dim myReader As XmlReader
        Dim myNav As XPathNavigator
        Dim myList As XmlNodeList
        Dim myNode() As XmlNode
        Dim node As XmlNode
        Dim i As Integer

        myDoc.Load("C:\Book\NFL.xml")
        myTrans.Load("C:\Book\NFL.xslt")
        myNav = myDoc.CreateNavigator

        myReader = myTrans.Transform(myNav, Nothing)
        myDoc2.Load(myReader)
        myList = myDoc2.GetElementsByTagName("Name")

        For Each node In myList
            ReDim Preserve myNode(i)
            myNode(i) = node
            i = i + 1
        Next

        Return myNode
End Function
```

Part IV

Web Services In-depth

Hour

HOUR 15

Using ASP.NET Intrinsics

In this hour, you will look at how to use the objects that are built into ASP.NET to add further functionality to your XML Web services. Throughout the hour, you will see how to add global data to your application as well as how to maintain state for individual users. You will also learn how to retrieve information about both your server environment and the clients that are making requests.

In this hour we will discuss the following:

- `Session` object
- `Application` object
- `Server` object
- `HttpContext` object
- `Cache` object

Session Object

The Session object provides the mechanisms through which individual clients, or, more specifically, instances of an XML Web service's proxy objects within those clients, maintain state. The Session object also provides a way of gathering information about individual clients, which is useful for delivering customized functionality.

The most common use of the Session object is the handling of Session variables. Session variables allow data to be stored and modified throughout the life of the object being referenced in the client application.

In order for a session to be tracked by your XML Web service, you need to add a property setting to your WebMethod attribute tag. This property lets your service know that it should begin saving session information. The syntax for this is

```
<WebMethod(EnableSession:=True)>
```

In C#, this would be

```
[WebMethod (EnableSession=True)]
```

The Session Object, also known as HttpSessionState, contains a collection of name/value pairs that is used for storing data. To add an item to the collection, you simply assign a key value to the object and pass in a value. The code below shows an example of using the session object to store some data, a string variable named sText, into the session object's item's collection. "Text" is being passed in as the data's key.

```
<WebMethod(EnableSession:=True)> _
Public Sub SetSessionTest(ByVal sText As String)
    Session("Text") = sText
End Sub
```

The data can then be retrieved by simply passing the key value back into the Session object as follows:

```
<WebMethod(EnableSession:=True)> _
Public Function GetSessionText() As String

    Return Session("Text")

End Function
```

Running a service with these two methods in it will demonstrate how sessions function. Run the service and navigate to the SetSessionTest page, shown in Figure 15.1, and enter some text. When you click the invoke button, the service will store this data in the Session collection of this particular client's Session object.

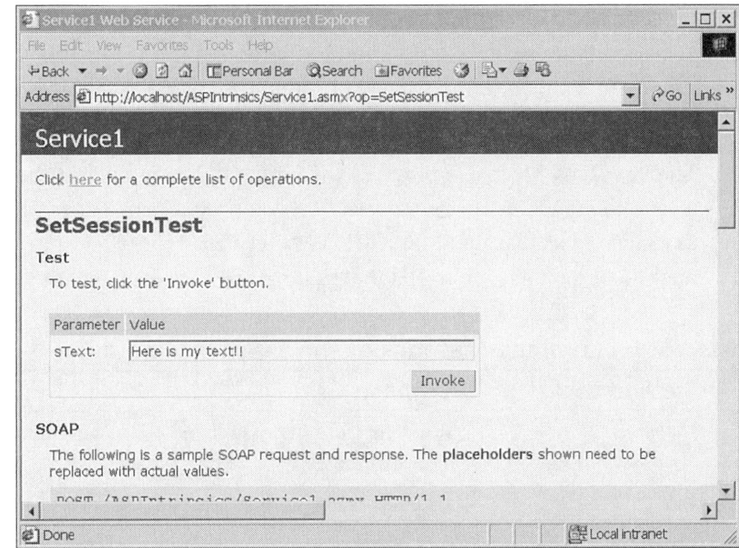

FIGURE 15.1
Setting your `Session` *level variable.*

If you invoke the `GetSessionTest` method now, you will see your text returned to you, as in Figure 15.2.

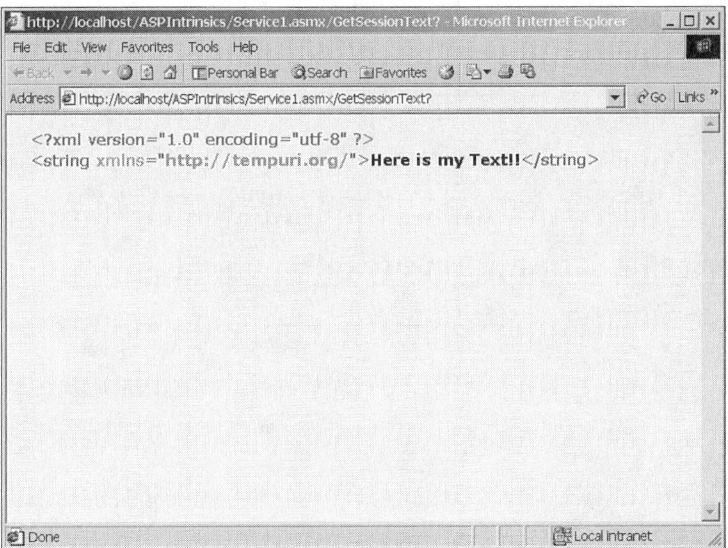

FIGURE 15.2
The variable stays set throughout the session.

If you wish to verify that additional clients will operate in a separate session, simply open addition instances of Internet Explorer and run the methods in those as well. You should notice that every instance of Internet Explorer is generating a different return value for the `GetSessionTest` function.

The `Session` object also provides functionality beyond just storing a collection of session data, although that will be the function you probably use most often when dealing with `Session` objects inside of an XML Web service. Table 15.1 shows some of the other method of the `Session` object that you may invoke in your services.

TABLE 15.1 Common Methods of the `Session` Object

Method	*Description*
`Abandon`	Cancels the Current Session and eliminates all the `HttpSessionState`'s collection's variables
`Add`	Adds a new value to the `HttpSessionState`'s collection
`Clear`	Clears all variables from the `HttpSessionState`'s collection
`CopyTo`	Copies the contents of the `HttpSessionState`'s collection into an array
`Remove`	Removes an item from the `HttpSessionState`'s collection determined by its string key
`RemoveAll`	Removes all items from the `HttpSessionState`'s collection
`RemoveAt`	Removes an item from the `HttpSessionState`'s collection with the specified integer index

In addition to the methods shown in Table 15.1, Table 15.2 lists some of the properties of the `Session` object that can be called from within your service.

TABLE 15.2 Common Properties of the `Session` Object

Property	*Description*
`Contents`	Gets a reference to the `HttpSessionState`
`Count`	Gets the `HttpSessionState`'s collection's item count
`IsCookieLess`	Gets a Boolean indicating whether cookies are being used to manage a `Session`
`IsNewSession`	Gets a Boolean indicating whether the `Session` is new; will return `True` only if a `Session` variable has been created
`IsReadOnly`	Gets a Boolean determining if the `HttpSessionState` is read only
`IsSynchronized`	Gets a Boolean determining if access to the cookie collects values is read only
`Item`	Gets or Sets an item in the `HttpSessionState`'s collection value by key name

continues

TABLE 15.2 Continued

Property	*Description*
`Keys`	Gets a collection of the `HttpSessionState` collection's keys
`LCID`	Gets or Sets the local identifier
`Mode`	Gets the `HttpSessionState`'s mode
`SessionID`	Gets the `HttpSessionState`'s unique ID
`StaticObjects`	Gets a collection of objects that were declared in the `Global.asax`
`TimeOut`	Gets or Sets the duration that a `HttpSessionState` should remain active between calls

One of the more useful methods of the `Session` object is the `Abandon` method. This method destroys the session, and the next call to a method that uses sessions from the client that generated the original session will be treated as a brand new session. The following code shows the `Abandon` method in use:

```
<WebMethod(EnableSession:=True)> _
Public Sub DestroySessionTest()
    Session.Abandon()
End Sub
```

To test if a `Session` is new, you can make use of the `IsNewSession` method, shown next, which returns `True` until the collection contains a key/value pair.

```
<WebMethod(EnableSession:=True)> _
Public Function SessionTest() As Boolean
    Return Session.IsNewSession
End Function
```

Running the service and invoking the `SessionTest` method returns `False`, as seen in Figure 15.3, after you have used the `SetSessionTest` to create a new item in the `Session`'s collection.

FIGURE 15.3
`SessionTest` *Returns* `False` *after* `Session` *level variables have been created.*

After calling the `DestroySessionTest` method, you can verify that the session has been abandoned by invoking the `SessionTest` method again. You are now in a new session.

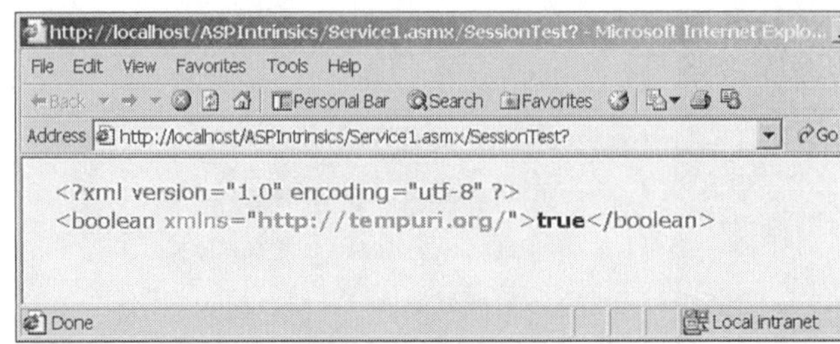

FIGURE 15.4
`IsNewSession` *returns* `True` *after a session has been abandoned.*

As an example of how a `Session` object can be used to return some custom data, look at this example that uses the `LCID`, or local identifier, property of the `Session` object to return currency type depending on the country code of the user.

First, you need to create an enumeration to be used in selecting a country code. The following would be appropriate:

```
Public Enum CountryType
    Albanian = 1052
    Estonian = 1061
    Finnish = 1035
End Enum
```

The code in Figure 15.1 accepts an argument, `Country`, of type `CountryType` and uses that to set the LCID property in line 7. Once that property has been set, functions, such as `FormatCurrency` in line 9, will behave according to the standards of the users region.

LISTING 15.1 Returning Currency from the User Nation with the `LCID` Property

```
1:   <WebMethod(EnableSession:=True)> _
2:   Public Function ReturnCurr(ByVal Country As CountryType, _
3:      ByVal iNum As Integer) As String
4:
5:      Dim retNumb As String
6:
7:      Session.LCID = Country
8:
9:      retNumb = FormatCurrency(iNum)
10:
11:     Return retNumb
12:
13:  End Function
```

If you invoke the method and type in one of the three country names from the `CountryType` enumeration, the method will return the currency to you in the denomination corresponding to the country of origin. See Figure 15.5 for an example.

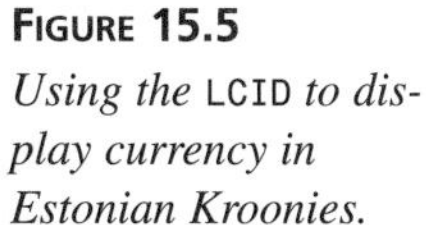

FIGURE 15.5
Using the `LCID` *to display currency in Estonian Kroonies.*

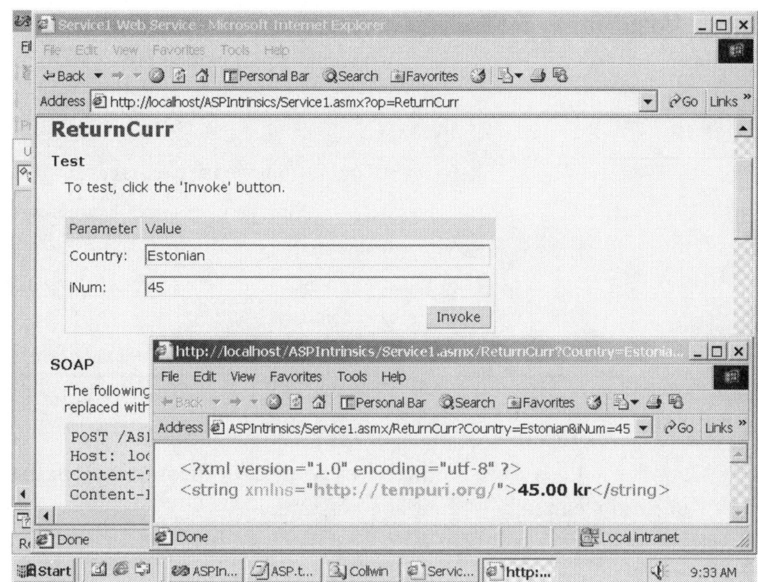

Application Object

Unlike the `Session` object, the `Application` object, or `HttpApplicationState`, contains information that is pertinent to all clients using the application. The methods and collections of the `Application` object will behave the same way for all client applications that call them. This means that name/value pairs added to the application object's collection, which is accessed in the same manner as the `Session` object's, can be seen by all clients, regardless of whether the session has been enabled or not.

Some of the more commonly used methods of the Application object can be seen in Table 15.3. As you can see, they deal mainly with placing items and their keys into a collection.

TABLE 15.3 Common Methods of the `Application` Object

Method	*Description*
`Add`	Adds a new object to the `HttpApplicationState` as a name/value pair
`Clear`	Clears the `HttpApplicationState`'s collection of all name/value pairs
`Get`	Uses a string name to get an object from the `HttpApplicationState`'s collection
`GetKey`	Uses an integer index to get an object from the `HttpApplicationState`'s collection

continues

TABLE 15.3 Continued

Lock	Locks an individual object in the HttpApplicationState's collection
Remove	Removes an item from the HttpApplicationState's collection determined by its string key
RemoveAll	Removes all items from the HttpApplicationState's collection
RemoveAt	Removes an item from the HttpApplicationState's collection with the specified integer index
Set	Uses the string name of an item to update its value in the HttpApplicationState's collection
UnLock	Unlocks an individual object in the HttpApplicationState's collection

The main properties of the Application object can be seen in Table 15.4. You should be familiar with these properties already as all of them existed in the Session object and function identically to their counterparts.

TABLE 15.4 Common Properties of the Application Object

Property	*Description*
AllKeys	Gets a string array of the HttpApplicationState's key names
Contents	Gets a reference to the HttpApplicationState object
Count	Gets a count of objects in the HttpApplicationState
Item	Gets an object from the HttpApplicationState's collection based on key or index
Keys	Gets a collection of all of the HttpApplicationState's keys

The following method accepts a string argument and stores it in the Application's collection under the key name "Text." The Lock and UnLock methods are used to lock access to the collection and prevent possible errors during additions or edits to the collection's objects. Methods trying to access the Application object during a lock will typically wait for access to be re-enabled via the UnLock method or will time out if that is too long in coming.

```
<WebMethod()> _
Public Sub SetApplicationTest(ByVal sText As String)

   Application.Lock
   Application("Text") = sText
   Application.UnLock

End Sub
```

After an item has been added to the collection, it can be retrieved in the same manner as items from the Session object. The method below returns the "Text" item that you added in the previous method.

```
<WebMethod()> _
Public Function GetApplicationTest() As String
    Return Application("Text")
End Function
```

Finally, utilizing the `Application` object's clear method, you can test to verify that all of the items can be cleared from the collection.

```
<WebMethod()> _
Public Sub ApplicationTest()
    Application.Clear()
End Sub
```

Run the service and add some text to the application object by invoking the `SetApplicationTest` method, as seen in Figure 15.6.

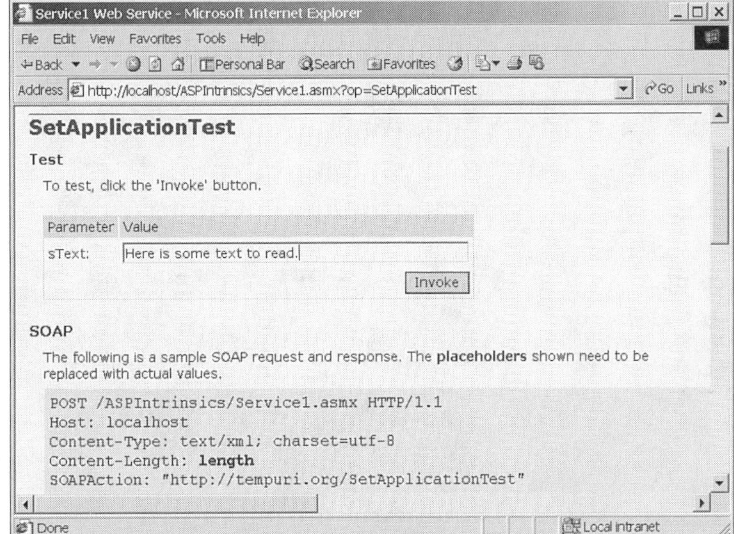

FIGURE 15.6
Setting your `Application` *level variable.*

Now, open some additional Internet Explorer windows and navigate to the `GetApplicationTest` method. This is to verify that the information saved in the `Application` is available to all sessions, as seen in Figure 15.7.

When you invoke the method in each of the instances of Internet Explorer, you should receive the same text response from every call, as seen in Figure 15.8.

Finally, if you invoke `ApplicationTest`, which clears the collection, and then return to `GetApplicationTest` and invoke that, you will receive a null string, as illustrated in Figure 15.9.

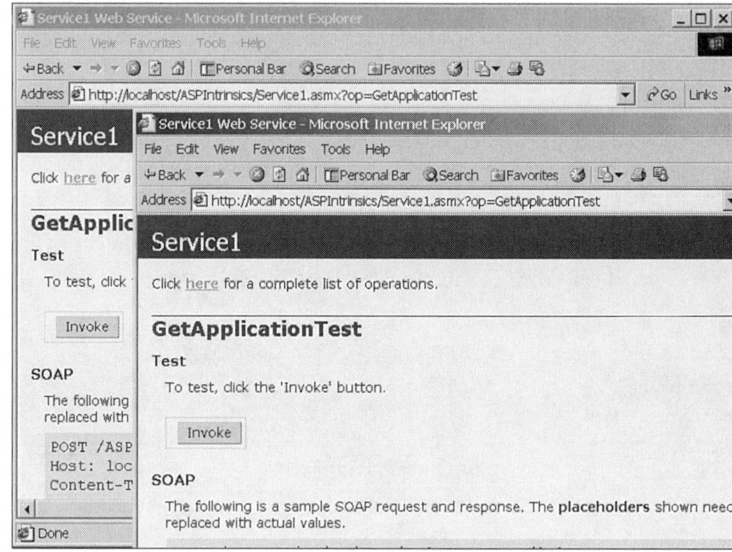

FIGURE 15.7
Opening multiple sessions.

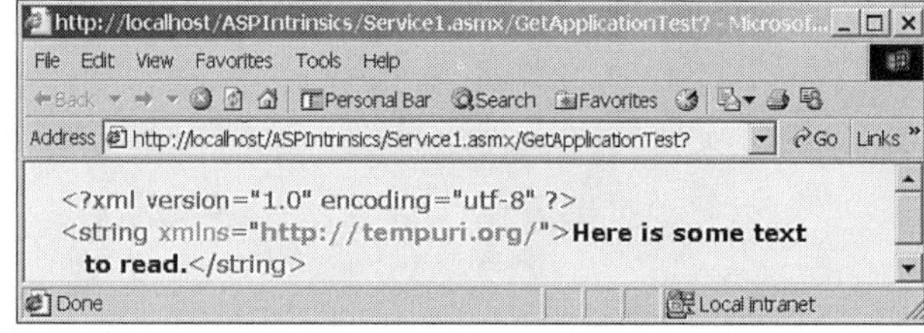

FIGURE 15.8
Every session sees the same results.

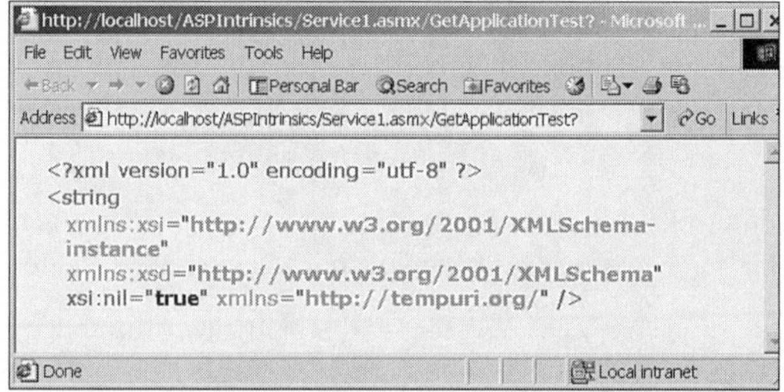

FIGURE 15.9
All of the Application variables have been cleared.

Server Object

The Server object, or HttpServerUtily, provides functionality that I utilized when processing Internet requests. Most of the functionality of this object is used more often in standard ASP.NET, but some may be useful when developing an application that needs to react to different types of requests or users.

The most commonly used method of the Server object can be seen in Table 15.5.

TABLE 15.5 Common Properties of the Server Object

Property	*Description*
MachineName	Gets the server's machine name
ScriptTimeout	Gets or Sets the time in seconds until request's timeout

The Server object's methods, many of which deal with encoding and decoding strings for working with the actual HTTP requests, something that is abstracted away from you when creating XML Web services, are shown in Table 15.6.

TABLE 15.6 Common Methods of the Server Object

Method	*Description*
ClearError	Clears the last exception
Execute	Executes a request to another page
GetLastError	Returns the last exception
HtmlDecode	Removes the encoding aspect of a string that was formatted for display in a browser
HtmlEncode	Encodes a string to allow it to be properly displayed in a browser
MapPath	Converts a virtual file path to a physical path
Transfer	Cancels execution on the current ASP file and begins the execution of another
UrlDecode	Decodes an HTTP encoded string
UrlEncode	Encodes a string for HTTP transmission
UrlPathEncode	Returns the URL encoded path portion of an URL

The following example shows how the Server object can be used to retrieve information about specific requests, client applications, and the Server environment itself. In this case, the method returns the name of the Server that is processing the request.

```
<WebMethod()> _
Public Function TestServer() As String

    Return Server.MachineName()

End Function
```

Figure 15.10 shows the machine name, as a string type, returned from the previous method.

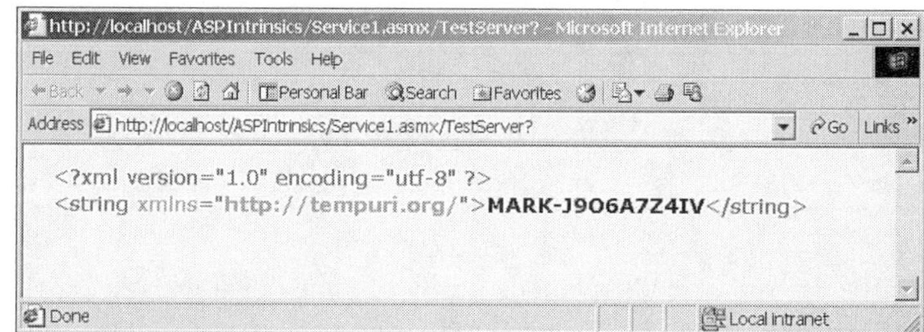

FIGURE 15.10
Returning the Server's machine name.

HttpContext Object

The `HttpContext` object is actually the top-level object of the others that you have encountered so far in this hour. What this means is that `HttpContext` actually contains all of these other objects. It should be noted however, that access to the `HttpContext` object itself is not provided in the `System.Web.Services` namespace but is instead provided in the `System.Web` namespace.

The `HttpContext` object provides only one public property, `Current`, which is used to get the `HttpContext` object for the current HTTP request. This is done as follows:

```
MyContext = httpContext.Current
```

`HttpContext` also provides one public method, `GetAppConfig`, that is used to return configuration information for the current application.

Once an `HttpContext` object has been retrieved using the `Current` property, that object exposes the properties shown in Table 15.7.

TABLE 15.7 Common Properties of the `HttpContext` Object

Property	*Description*
`AllErrors`	Gets an array of errors occurring during an HTTP request
`Application`	Gets the current request's `HttpApplicationState` object
`ApplicationInstance`	Gets or Sets the current request's `HttpApplicationState`

continues

TABLE 15.7 Continued

Property	*Description*
`Cache`	Gets the current request's `Cache` object
`Error`	Gets the current request's first HTTP error, if one has occurred
`Handler`	Gets or Sets the current request's `IHttpHandler` object
`IsCustomErrorEnabled`	Is `True` if custom errors are enabled for the request
`IsDebuggingEnabled`	Is `True` if the current request is in debug mode
`Request`	Gets the current request's `HttpRequest` object
`Response`	Gets the current request's `HttpResponse` object
`Server`	Gets the current request's `HttpServerUtility` object
`Session`	Gets the current request's `System.Web.SessionState`
`Timestamp`	Gets the current request's initial timestamp
`Trace`	Gets the current request's `TraceContext` object
`User`	Gets or Sets the current request's security information

As you can see from Table 15.7, many of the properties of the `HttpContext` object simply provide a reference to other objects that allow for greater control over every detail of the `HttpRequest` being serviced. Again, most of these objects and their properties provide information that is often more useful in a straight ASP.NET application, but they are still provided in XML Web services in the event that you should need them.

The example below shows the `Request` object being used in order to retrieve the host address of the client application that is making the method call. This information could be useful when securing a Web service.

```
Imports System.Web

    <WebMethod()> Public Function TestRequest() As String
        Dim myContext As HttpContext
        myContext = HttpContext.Current

        Return myContext.Request.UserHostAddress
    End Function
```

The host address of the calling application can be seen in Figure 15.11.

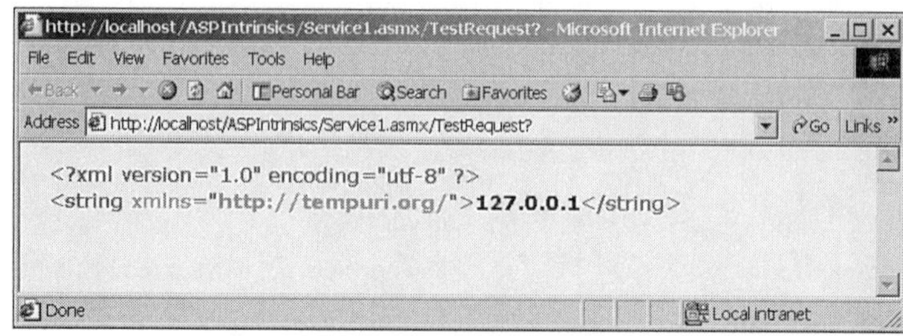

FIGURE 15.11
Returning the Internet protocol address of the client application.

Cache Object

The `Cache` object, as the name implies, is used to cache data in much the same way as the `Application` object. In fact, a look at the properties of the `Cache` object, Table 15.8, shows an `Item` property that accepts a key value, opening up a collection of name/value pairings that is identical to that seen in both the `Application` and `Session` objects.

TABLE 15.8 Common Properties of the `Cache` Object

Property	*Description*
`Count`	Get the number of item currently stored within the cache
`Item`	Gets or Sets the value of an item specified by its key

Where the `Cache` object differs from the `Application` object is in the overall control that it gives you over the behavior of the data being stored. Both provide global access to the data that is stored, but only the `Cache` object provides a built-in mechanism for clearing items out of memory based on timing or dependency relationships. The `Cache` object allows items to be added to the collection with a series of constraints that determine exactly how long they should be stored, in what order they should be cleared, and what other items or files they depend on in order to stay current. The methods in Table 15.9, particularly the `Add` method, help to provide this functionality.

TABLE 15.9 Common Methods of the `Cache` Object

Method	*Description*
`Add`	Adds an item to the cache; allows for the setting of expiration and priority parameters
`Get`	Uses a key to return an item from the cache
`Insert`	Inserts an item into the cache as a name/value pair with the provided key
`Remove`	Removes an item from the cache with the corresponding key

At its core, the Cache object behaves exactly like the application object. In fact, the following code could be used to replace the earlier SetApplicationTest method:

```
<WebMethod()> Public Sub SetCache(ByVal Stuff As String)
    Dim myContext As HttpContext

    myContext = HttpContext.Current()

    myContext.Cache("Text") = Stuff

End Sub
```

The following method could then be used to retrieve this cached information in place of GetApplicationTest.

```
<WebMethod()> Public Function GetCache() As String
    Dim myContext As HttpContext

    myContext = HttpContext.Current()

    Return myContext.Cache("Text")

End Function
```

This use of the Cache object is a bit redundant, however, because the Application already provides such functionality. As you explore the Add method of the Cache object, you will begin to understand its full usefulness.

The Add method of the Cache object, shown next, takes the name/value pairings and adds dependencies, expiration dates, and item priorities.

```
Public Function Add( _
   ByVal key As String, _
   ByVal value As Object, _
   ByVal dependencies As CacheDependency, _
   ByVal absoluteExpiration As DateTime, _
   ByVal slidingExpiration As TimeSpan, _
   ByVal priority As CacheItemPriority, _
   ByVal priorityDecay As CacheItemPriorityDecay, _
   ByVal onRemoveCallback As CacheItemRemovedCallback _
) As Object
```

In the method call, key and value are the name/value pair used in the cache collection. New to this is the dependencies argument. Dependencies refer to files or cached items upon which this cached item is dependent. If the object in question changes, then the cache item is deleted. A CacheDependency accepts a string argument representing the file path or cache key of the item upon which a dependency is being defined. This takes the following format:

```
New CacheDependency("C:\Book\NFL.xml")
```

`AbsoluteExpiration` and `slidingExpiration` provide the timing for which cached items are dropped and the server reclaims their memory. `AbsoluteExpiratetion` is a `DateTime` object that specifies exactly when an item must be dropped, whereas the `slidingExpiration` provides a `TimeSpan` object that specifies the amount of time, between requests, that an item should be kept in memory.

`priority` and `priorityDecay` provide additional control over how and when an item may be removed from the cache. `Priority` is used to assign a ranking to items, so that when the server needs to reclaim memory, items of higher importance are kept at the expense of lesser rank items. Priorities include `High`, `AboveNormal`, `Normal`, `BelowNormal`, `Low`, and `NotRemovable`. Assigning priority takes the following form:

```
CacheItemPriority.High
```

Where `priority` gives a ranking, `priorityDecay` is used to determine if that ranking should ever change. By setting an object's priority to decay at a fast rate, you can allow for an item of high importance to remain in memory at the expense of all other cached items when the item is first added to the cache, but then you can have its importance decay away until it is dropped. Some of the decay speeds include `Fast`, `Medium`, `Slow`, and `Never`. This takes the following format:

```
CacheItemPriorityDecay.Slow
```

Lastly, the `onRemoveCallback` argument allows for the cache to provide a delegate function that will be called if the item is removed from the cache.

Summary

In this hour, you learned how to use the built-in objects provided by ASP.NET to give your XML Web services greater flexibility and control over how client requests are handled. You learned how to use these objects to maintain state both globally, for all clients, and individually, for single instances of your service being referenced from within a single client application. You also learned how to cache data to improve your service's performance.

Q&A

Q Why use `Session` and `Application` variables when I can just use global variables and collections?

A There are several reasons for utilizing each of the objects. The `Session` object is useful because, unlike a global variable or collection that would be identical for and potentially seen by every client, the `Session` object provides a new instance for every client application that accesses it. The `Application` object is a bit subtler in its benefits. Globally declared variables can be used in XML Web services and indeed are used in some of the examples in this book, but the `Application` is a convenient collection that already exists globally and allows you to add, remove, or alter items in any method within your service without the extra overhead of adding additional global collections.

Q What is the benefit of using the `Cache` object if the only thing that it adds is more ways to have my data disappear?

A The cache object provides some very powerful features. First of all, if you have cache data that has been pulled from a file, such as an XML document, you can create a dependency and have the items removed from the cache if the document is altered. From there you have two options. The first always checks for the existence of the data, and if it isn't present, reloads it from the source. The second object uses the callback feature to provide a method that automatically reinstates the item. Also, the main purpose of the cache item is performance. You set your item in the cache so that if the data are being requested often, they stay in memory and are not requeried as often. If the items are not used frequently, they are dropped and valuable memory is reclaimed.

Q Is there any difference between the `Session` and `Application` objects that are exposed by the `HttpContext` object and those directly accessible from within the `System.Web.Services` namespace?

A No. The `System.Web.Services` namespace gives you direct access to these objects, which are actually part of the `HttpContext` object, because they are frequently used objects. If you were to add a name/value pair directly to the `Application` object and then check the `HttpContext`'s `Application` object and test for the same pair, you would see that you are working with the exact same instance of the `Application` object.

Workshop

The Workshop is designed to help you review what you've learned in this hour and to point you ahead to the material that will be covered in future hours.

Quiz

1. **What object would you use to store information being used by multiple methods of your service that is pertinent only to a single client application?**

   A `Session`

2. **How do you retrieve the data stored in an `Application` object under the name `"SomeText"`?**

   A `myData = Application("SomeText")` or `myData = Application.Item("SomeText")`

3. **What method do you call if you need to start a client's session over again?**

   A `Session.Abandon`

4. **What would you need to pass into the priority argument of the `Cache` object's `Add` method in order to set a priority that is below normal?**

   A `CacheItemPriority.BelowNormal`

5. **What property of the `HttpContext` object gets a reference to an object that handles security information for a particular client request?**

   A `HttpContext.User`

Exercises

Try building a service that utilizes `Application` and `Session` objects to handle global data. A rather silly, but wholly applicable, example might be an application that allows a user three guesses at a word inputed by another user.

That service might look something like this:

```
Public Class Game
    Public Answer as String
    Public Hint1 as String
    Public Hint2 as String
    Public Hint3 as String
End Class

<WebMethod()> Public Sub SetGame( _
    ByVal Answer as String, _
    ByVal Public Hint1 as String, _
    ByVal Public Hint2 as String, _
    ByVal Public Hint3 as String _
)

   Dim GameInfo As New Game()
   GameInfo.Answer = Answer
   GameInfo.Hint1 = Hint1
   GameInfo.Hint2 = Hint2
   GameInfo.Hint3 = Hint3

     Application("Game") = GameInfo
End Sub

<WebMethod()> _
```

```
Public Function GetHint(ByVal Number As Integer) As String
     Dim GameInfo As New Game()
     Dim sHint As String

     GameInfo = Application("Game")

     Select Case Number
         Case 1
             sHint = GameInfo.Hint1
         Case 2
             sHint = GameInfo.Hint2
         Case 3
             sHint = GameInfo.Hint3
         Case Else
             sHint = "Please choose a number between 1 and 3"
     End Select

     Return sHint

End Function

<WebMethod(EnableSession:=True)> _
Public Function GiveAnswer(ByVal Answer As String) As String
     Dim GameInfo As New Game()
     Dim sResponse As String

     GameInfo = Application("Game")

     If Session("Answers") Is Nothing Then
         Session("Answers") = 0
     End If

     If UCase(GameInfo.Answer) = UCase(Answer) Then
         sResponse = "Correct. You win!!!!"
     Else
         Session("Answers") = CInt(Session("Answers")) + 1
         sResponse = "Wrong Answer. You have " & _
          CStr(3 - CInt(Session("Answers"))) & " chances left."
     End If


     If Session("Answers") > 2 Then
         sResponse = "Too Many Incorrect Answers. You Lose"
     End If

     Return sResponse
End Function
```

HOUR 16

The XML Web Services Namespace/Web Method

In this hour, you will see how the `WebMethod` attribute can be used to provide advanced features to your XML Web services, such as transactions and method overloading. You will also see how this attribute can be used to increase performance through the use of results caching and buffering. Finally, you will look at the `WebService` attribute and see how it can be used to give your services their own namespaces and descriptions.

Throughout this chapter, we will discuss the following:

- Buffering output
- Caching requests
- Changing namespaces
- Method overloading
- Transactions

WebMethod Attribute

In Hour 7, you saw how the `WebMethod` attribute could be added to a function declaration in order to create an XML Web service method. Now you will see how the properties of the `WebMethod` attribute can be used to give you greater control over the behavior of your methods and even allow you to add some fairly advanced functionality.

As of this writing, the `WebMethod` provides six properties that give you access to functionality, including transactions, response buffering, and method overloading. The general syntax for setting the `WebMethod` attribute's properties is as follows:

```
<WebMethod(Property:=Value)>
```

In C#, a `WebMethod` attribute's properties are declared as follows:

```
[WebMethod(Property=Value)]
```

If you need to set multiple properties, you simply separate them by a comma as follows:

```
<WebMethod(Prop1:=Val1, Prop2:=Val2)>
```

Using the Description Property to Describe a Method

As you saw in Hour 7, it is possible to add descriptive text to your XML Web services methods for prospective users to read. This text can be extremely useful, not only to document the method and help developers in using it, but also, if you are publishing your service to the public, as a way to further sell your service to interested parties. If you can properly document your service through the use of these descriptive tags, you call further attention to your service and make the decision to consume your service, as opposed to that of your competition, that much easier.

To add a description to an XML Web service method, simply add the `Description` tag to your `WebMethod` attribute and set it equal to a string as shown below. The string will become your description text.

```
<WebMethod(Description:="This Function returns the current date…")>
    Public Function TodaysDate() As Date
```

This descriptive text will be displayed in both the WSDL file and on the XML Web service's automatically generated help page. Figure 16.1 shows the description in the service's Internet Explorer displayed page.

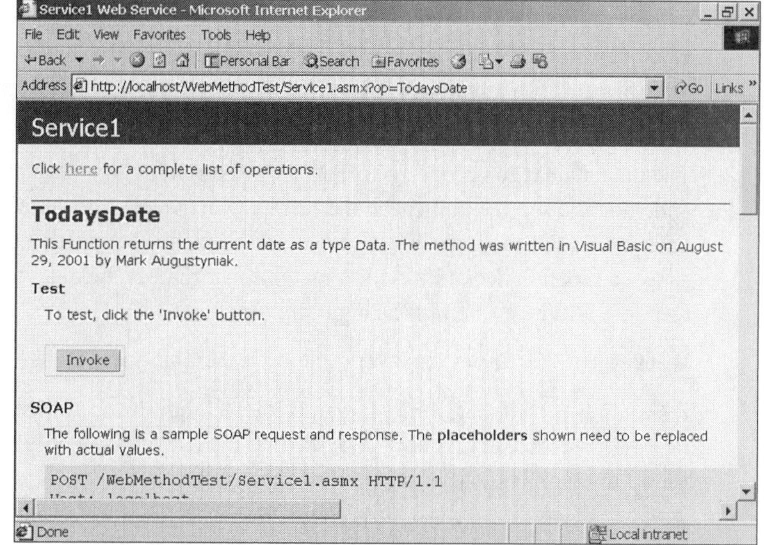

Figure 16.1
Using the `Description` *property of* `WebMethod` *to describe an XML Web service method.*

XML Web Service Sessions with `EnableSession`

In Hour 13, when you explore XML Web service events and the `Global.asa` file, you will learn more about sessions. For now, just know that `EnableSession` allows the service to utilize session level variables and events as a way of maintaining program state. This means that as long as a client application maintains a reference to an object, special session level variables may be used to store information across all methods of the service as well as multiple calls to the same method.

`EnableSession` accepts a Boolean, with `True` being used to enable sessions. If a method is not going to use a session level variable, then it should be left to the default, false, as this may have some impact on overall performance. Below is the syntax for declaring a method with sessioning enabled.

```
<WebMethod(EnableSession:=True)>
Public Function DataReturn() As DateSet
```

Reusing Cached Data Using `CacheDuration`

Another function provided by the `WebMethod` attribute is the ability to cache return results of method calls and reuse them to fulfill other incoming requests. If caching is enabled, the XML Web service will keep a copy of the requests parameters and return value and, when a request comes in whose parameters match those of a previous request, the cached value is returned. This can be especially useful if you are creating methods that accept a narrow scope of parameters, such as an enumeration, or that provide infrequently changing data, such as a list of files available on a server.

The `CacheDuration` property accepts an integer value that determines the number in seconds that the service will cache the results of requests. The default value of the `CacheDuration` property is 0, which disables caching altogether. The following code line shows a function declaration for a method that returns the date, without time. The response will be cached for a single minute.

```
<WebMethod(CacheDuration:=60)> Public Function TodaysDate() As Date
```

It should be noted that, through the use of caching, the above request loses some accuracy in its response. It is now possible that the current data will be incorrectly returned for up to one minute after the data has changed.

It should also be noted that using caching in methods that have a large set of possible return values or return large amounts of data might dramatically affect performance as memory begins to fill with cached data.

Buffering Output with `BufferResponse`

When working to improve the performance of your XML Web service, it is often important to look at how data is returned to client applications. Under normal circumstances, the results from a method call are buffered until all of the data is written, at which point the entire result is sent. This is a very efficient method for handling most results, as it minimizes the number of times that the service and its clients need to communicate with each other.

In cases when an exceptionally large return must be sent, such as large database query returns, it is sometimes better to disable buffering and allow the method to transmit data in smaller portions. If, using the `BufferResponse` property, buffering is disabled, the service will begin to transmit any return data in 16KB blocks. Performance on the server may be enhanced by limiting the size of memory that is used in order to buffer very large requests.

The code that follows shows buffering being explicitly disabled using the `BufferResponse` property. The default value of `BufferResponse` is `True`.

```
<WebMethod(BufferResponse:=False)>
Public Function DataReturn() As DateSet
```

Overloading Methods with `MessageName` Property

Overloading is the ability to create multiple methods, each having the same name but differing argument lists, and allowing these procedures to be called in code as if they were one. This allows for the creation of methods that accept different data types, for example a method that accepts integer values and a similar method that provides the same functionality for doubles or shorts.

16

The rule for creating an overloaded method states that each method must differ from every other in one of the following manners:

1. The number of arguments must be different. This allows for optional arguments to be created and processed within functions.
2. The order of argument types must be different. This means that you can have `Method1(integer, integer, double)` and `Method1(integer, double, integer)` for example.
3. At least one data type must differ. This means that you can have `Method1(Integer, double)` and `Method1(integer, short)`.

In order to use method overloading in XML Web services, it is not enough to simply declare several methods with the same name, and, in fact, doing so will produce errors. You need to make use of the `MessageName` property in order to achieve this.

The `MessageName` property accepts a string value that will actually be used in the SOAP calls to the service. The proxy handles this and the developer of client software still sees the method as being overloaded.

The code in Listing 16.1 shows the `MessageName` property being used to create a method called `Add` that will answer to SOAP calls as `Add_Shorts`.

LISTING 16.1 Creating an Overloaded Method

```
<WebMethod(MessageName:="Add_Shorts")>
Public Function Add(ByVal iNum1 As Short, ByVal iNum2 As Short) As Short

    Return iNum1 + iNum2
End Function
```

This method creates a version of the `FourFuncCalc` service's `Add` method that works on shorts as opposed to integers. If you want, you can now alter the original version of the `Add` function in order to give it a message name as well. This is not necessary, as one of the `Add` methods is allowed to operate without the `MessageName` property set; however, in this case it may be good form to have a separate message name for each type being used.

```
<WebMethod(MessageName:="Add_Integers")>
Public Function Add(ByVal iNum1 As Integer, ByVal iNum2 As Integer) As Integer
```

Finally, you can create another version of the `Add` method that accepts doubles and returns a double as well.

```
<WebMethod(MessageName:="Add_Doubles")>
Public Function Add(ByVal iNum1 As Double, ByVal iNum2 As Double) As Double
```

Now, when a client application makes a call to the `Add` method, the actual method that runs will be determined by the type of data passed to it. Obviously, client applications cannot mix and match argument types unless you specifically create more `Add` methods to accept pairs of different data types.

Interestingly, when you run the service's auto-generated help page in Internet Explorer, the message names are shown instead of three separate `Add` methods. This is demonstrated in Figure 16.2.

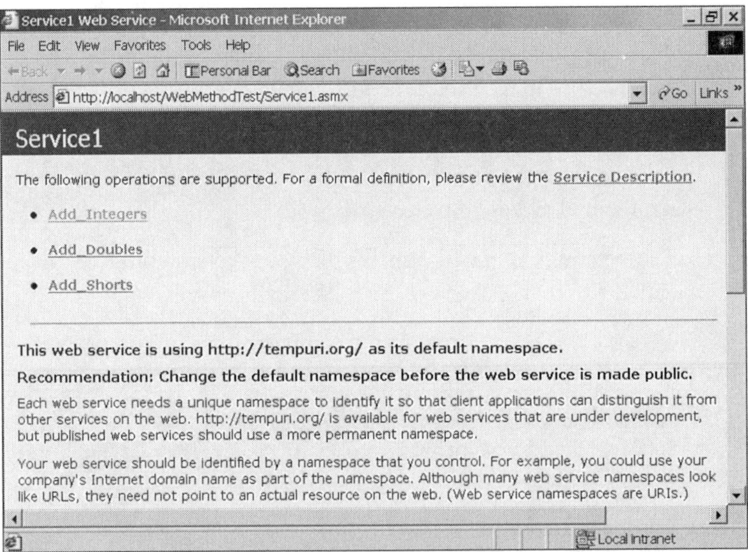

FIGURE 16.2
Overloaded methods in the .ASMX file.

Any client application with a reference to the service could call the `Add` method by using the following code, where `oCalc` is the object referencing the service and `iNum1` and `iNum2` are arguments of type integer, short, or double:

```
oCalc.Add(iNum1, iNum2)
```

To illustrate how a method can be used to accept optional parameters and perform slightly different functions, depending on what is passed to it, the following methods were created. Listing 16.2 shows a method named `Add_Child` that accepts a string as an argument and returns a string value.

LISTING 16.2 Your Base Method Accepts a String


```
<WebMethod(MessageName:="Add_Child")>
Public Function AddChild(ByVal sName As String) As String

  Return sName & " is in class."
End Function
```

The method in Listing 16.3 accepts the original string and also accepts a byte, `iAge`, as a second argument.

LISTING 16.3 Creating an Overloaded Method

```
<WebMethod(MessageName:="Add_ChildAge")>
Public Function AddChild(ByVal sName As String,_
                         ByVal iAge As Byte) As String

  Return sName & " is in class and he is " & CStr(iAge) & " years old."
End Function
```

Now, when a client application calls the `AddChild` method with a string:

```
oService.AddChild("Billy")
```

The service returns, "Billy is in class" without the use of the method name. Likewise, if the call is made using the additional integer argument, `iAge`

```
oService.AddChild("Billy", 5)
```

"Billy is in class and he is 5 years old" is returned. Again, the client did not, and in fact could not, make use of the `Add_ChildAge` method name.

Using the `Description` Property to Describe a Service

Just as you did earlier with an individual method, you can add descriptive text to the entire service. To add a description to your service, simply use the `Description` property within the `WebService` property like so:

```
<WebService(Description:="This is where your ...")>_
```

Now your text will appear at the top of the auto-generated Internet Explorer help page, as seen in Figure 16.3.

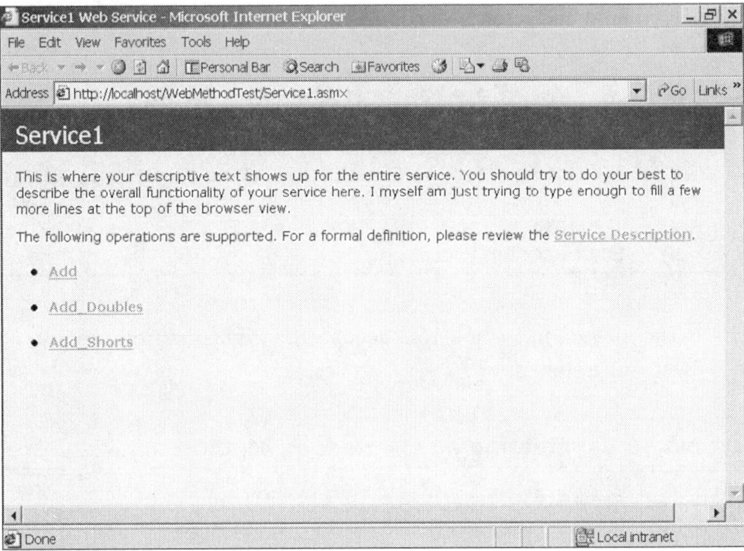

FIGURE 16.3
The description for the entire XML Web service.

In addition to showing up in the service's help page, the descriptive text shows up in the WSDL file of the service. In Figure 16.4, you can see your description, between documentation tags, within the service's definition.

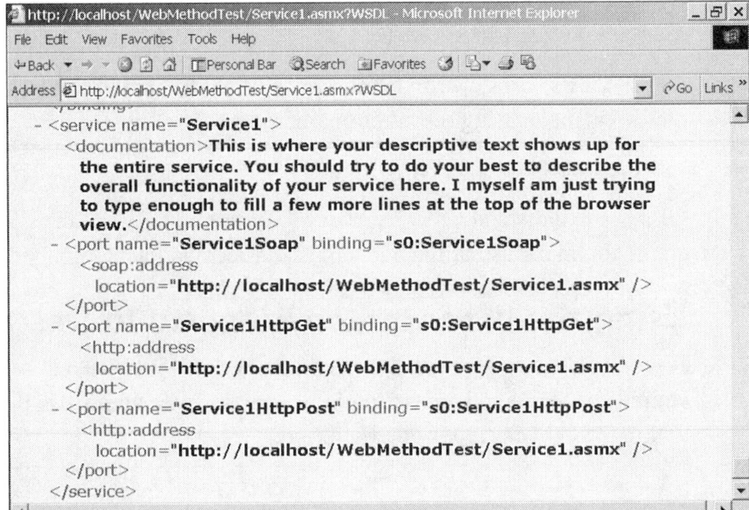

FIGURE 16.4
The Service's description in the WSDL description file.

Creating XML Web Service Transactions Utilizing the TransactionOption Property

Transactions are blocks of code that succeed or fail as a unit. This means that if an error is thrown in the last line of a transaction, every other line of the transaction fails as well. An example of this would be a group of database operations to create a new account, add funds to the account, and then delete those funds from a second account. The individual using the service would be less than happy if the addition of funds failed, but the amount was still deleted from the original account. The bank, on the other hand, would be upset if the funds were added to the new account and then the deletion of them from the second account failed. Using transactions would ensure that, if any of these operations failed, the entire set would be rolled back undone.

In the XML Web services model, a service's method must always act as the root of a transaction if it wishes to participate. What this means is that a service's method that makes a call to another XML Web service's method will not rollback the other method if an error occurs after the method has been called. Also, only objects that support transactions can be part of transactions. This means that operations on databases such as SQL Server and Oracle will work, but operations on MS Access will not.

In order to use transactions in your XML Web service methods, you must first add a reference to the `system.EnterpriseServices.dll` and include the following import statement in the namespace declarations section of your service:

```
Imports System.EnterpriseServices
```

In order to create a method that uses transactions, you need to set the `TransactionOption` property to `RequiresNew`. This will signify that a new transaction must be created for the method. The `TransactionOption` property can also be set to `Required`, but since XML Web service methods can only be the root of a transaction, and not just take part in them, this will have the exact same effect as `RequiresNew`.

If you wish to explicitly declare that a method not run a transaction, you can set the `TransactionOptiond` property to `Disabled`, which is the default setting. Setting the property to `Supported` or `NotSupported` will also have the same effect.

Listing 16.4 shows an operation that is running inside of a transaction. If any of the SQL commands should fail, the entire operation would be rolled back and nothing on the SQL Server would appear to have changed.

LISTING 16.4 Some SQL Server Operations in a Transaction

```
<WebMethod(TransactionOption:=TransactionOption.RequiresNew)> _
Public Function AddInfo(ByVal sBand As String, _
                        ByVal sTitle As String)

   Dim myDataSet As New DataSet()
   Dim conn As New SqlConnection()

   conn.ConnectionString = "Provider=Microsoft.Jet.OLEDB.4.0; _
        Data Source=C:\Book\CD.mdb;Persist Security Info=False"
    conn.Open()

   Dim sSQL As String
   SSQL = "INSERT INTO tblBands(BandName) Values('" & sBand & "')"

   Dim cmd As New SqlCommand(sSQL, conn)
   cmd.ExecuteNonQuery()

   sSQL = "INSERT INTO tblCDs(Title, BandID) _
            Values('" & sTitle & "', 888)"
   cmd.CommandText = sSQL
   cmd.ExecuteNonQuery()

End Function
```

It is possible to explicitly abort a transaction if some criteria fail by using the `ConextUtil.SetAbort` method. This method will cause the automatic rollback of the entire transaction. Listing 16.5 shows a portion of a transaction that is explicitly rolled back. The Transaction uses a COM object, oObject, but a Transaction supporting Database such as SQL Server could be used as well.

LISTING 16.5 Rolling Back a Transaction

```
<WebMethod(TransactionOption:=TransactionOption.RequiresNew)> _
Public Sub Transfer(ByVal Amount As Long, ByVal AcctNumberTo As Long, _
                    ByVal AcctNumberFrom As Long)
Dim oObject as New SomeObject

   If oObject.IsSet = True Then
     ' Rollback the transaction
     ContextUtil.SetAbort()
    Else
      oObject.Value1 = 10
      oObject.IsSet = True
   End If
  End Sub
```

The `ContextUtil` also provides the `SetComplete` method, which allows you to explicitly commit the current transaction.

Configuring Your Service with `WebService` Attributes

The `WebService` attribute allows you to add two important details to your XML Web services. The first is the ability to add some descriptive text to your service to either attract potential consumers to your service or to help developers already consuming your service, and potentially those of others. The second feature that the `WebService` attribute provides is the ability to change your service's namespace before you put it into production.

In order to use the properties of `WebService` attribute, it must first be added to the declaration of your service as follows:

```
<WebService(Property:=Value)>_
Public Class Service1
    Inherits System.Web.Services.WebService
```

This same declaration can be added to C# services as

```
[WebService(Property=Value)]
Public class Service1 : System.Web.Services.WebService
```

`NameSpace`

When an XML Web service is being developed, it is given the default XML namespace of "`http://tempori.org/`". This namespace is fine for development situations, but once the service is in production, it will need a better namespace to avoid possible confusion with other XML Web services that may have the same name.

If you find it difficult to believe that services may be created using identical names, think for a minute about how many services might be created to provide accounting services and then think how many of them might be called "`Accounting`" or "`Accountant`."

Changing the service's namespace works just like adding a description:

```
<WebService(NameSpace:="http://localHost/FourFunctionCalc")>
```

When you add the above line of code to your XML Web service, you will notice that the URL becomes live. You can now navigate to the URL that you designated for your namespace and it will appear in Visual Studio .NET, as shown in Figure 16.5.

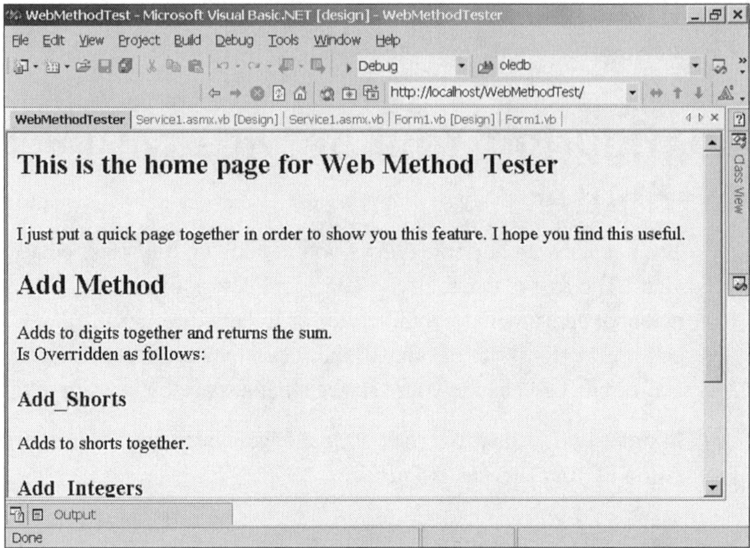

FIGURE 16.5
Using the NameSpace to navigate to documentation.

> You do not need to use an URL as your namespace—any string will do. Using an URL that you have control over just ensures that no one else will create a service with both the same name and namespace as yours. Also, it gives consumers a place to go to find documentation if you choose to provide it.

Summary

In this hour, you saw how to use the `WebMethod` attribute to control caching and buffering within your XML Web services. Further more, you learned how to add transactions to your services in order to create more robust services. You also saw how to overload methods in your services and how client applications and their proxies handled these overloaded methods. Finally, you saw how to use the `WebService` attribute to provide additional information about your service.

Q&A

Q What is the significance of changing the namespace of an XML Web service?

A Namespaces prevent two or more XML Web services that may share the same name from being confused, both by developers and by their code. By giving your service a namespace, such as an URL that you control, you ensure that no other XML Web services can be identified exactly like yours, unless, of course, you develop services with identical names and namespaces.

Q Why have description properties for both the service and its methods? Why not just place the entire description in one place, such as a users manual?

A When developers are looking to consume a service, whether they are in-house or out on the Net, they will want some general information on what the service as a whole provides. This is where the `WebAttribute` description comes in useful. When it comes time to implement a specific method, users will want to know more about the specific functionality of the method in question. This is also where it is useful to use the `WebMethod` Description.

Q I am writing sensitive data to a database that does not support transactions, but I really need that functionality. What can I do?

A You have two options in handling these data operations. The first is to upgrade to a database platform that handles your needs. If this is not possible, then you are faced with building your own support. In methods where you make these critical calls, keep track of the data that you are writing, and, if an error should occur, have the error handling code explicitly undo all of your changes. This could become a very large undertaking in a complex system.

Q If I am creating an XML Web service that will be very busy, won't it be in my best interest to always turn Buffering off, even in the case of methods that return very small sets of data, such as integers?

A First of all, small data return sets, such as integers, would fall below the 16KB size that even nonbuffered data still writes to memory. This means that you won't get any benefit from turning buffering off. Secondly, turning buffering off for a moderately sized DataSet may keep the use of memory down but will increase the number of times that your service needs to communicate across Internet connections in order to send multiple chunks of data over to the client.

Q Why go to the trouble of overloading a method if you have to give each one a separate message name and the proxy class that clients use actually refers to it by that name?

A The purpose of overloading your methods is so that a group of methods that actually provide the same basic functionality can be grouped together and presented to the client application developer in a way that is both convenient and makes sense. It is all about making your services usable to others.

Workshop

The Workshop is designed to help you review what you've learned in this hour and to point you ahead to the material that will be covered in future hours.

Quiz

1. How would you change the namespace of a service to "`http\\myServer\myService\`" and add the service description, "`This is my service`"?

   A `<WebService(Description:="This is my Service", _`
   `NameSpace="http\\myServer\myService")>`

2. What property of the `WebMethod` attribute facilitates method overloading?

   A `MessageName`

3. The `CacheDuration` property accepts what data type?

   A Integer.

4. How do you explicitly cancel a transaction?

   A `ContextUtil.SetAbort().`

5. (True or False) It is a good idea to cache a function that accepts two doubles as its arguments?

   A False; XML Web services will cache every unique pairing of arguments, thus creating the possibility that in high traffic your service might cache thousands or even millions of argument pairs and their results.

Exercises

Rewrite the `FourFunctionCalc` to include any features, such as a new namespace, buffering, descriptions, and so on, that you feel are appropriate to add. Remember, your service may be used by many clients at once, so caching the results of an add method may not be a very wise idea.

A. The following code changes the default namespace to "`http:\localhost\FourFunctCalc\`" and adds some description text to the service. In addition, all four methods are now overloaded to deal with shorts and doubles as well as integers. Finally, every method now has a description tag.

```
Imports System.Web.Services

<WebService(Description:="This service provides basic calculator functionality",
_
 NameSpace:="http://localHost/FourFunctionCalc")> _
    Public Class Service1
    Inherits System.Web.Services.WebService

#Region " Web Services Designer Generated Code "

    Public Sub New()
```

```
        MyBase.New()

        'This call is required by the Web Services Designer.
        InitializeComponent()

        'Add your own initialization code after the InitializeComponent() call

    End Sub

    'Required by the Web Services Designer
    Private components As System.ComponentModel.Container

    'NOTE: The following procedure is required by the Web Services Designer
    'It can be modified using the Web Services Designer.
    'Do not modify it using the code editor.
    <System.Diagnostics.DebuggerStepThrough()> Private Sub InitializeComponent()
        components = New System.ComponentModel.Container()
    End Sub

    Protected Overloads Overrides Sub Dispose(ByVal disposing As Boolean)
        'CODEGEN: This procedure is required by the Web Services Designer
        'Do not modify it using the code editor.
    End Sub

#End Region

#Region "CalC Functions"
    <WebMethod(Description:="This function adds two integers", _
               MessageName:="Add_Integers")> _
    Public Function Add(ByVal iNum1 As Integer, ByVal iNum2 As Integer) As
Integer
        Return iNum1 + iNum2
    End Function

    <WebMethod(Description:="This function adds two Shorts", _
               MessageName:="Add_Shorts")> _
    Public Function Add(ByVal iNum1 As Short, ByVal iNum2 As Short) As Short
        Return iNum1 + iNum2
    End Function

    <WebMethod(Description:="This function adds two Doubles", _
               MessageName:="Add_Doubles")> _
    Public Function Add(ByVal iNum1 As Double, ByVal iNum2 As Double) As Double
        Return iNum1 + iNum2
    End Function

    <WebMethod(Description:="This function returns the difference between 2
integers", _
               MessageName:="Sub_Integers")> _
    Public Function Subtract(ByVal iNum1 As Integer, ByVal iNum2 As Integer) As
Integer
```

```
        Return iNum1 - iNum2
    End Function

    <WebMethod(Description:="This function returns the difference between 2
Shorts", _
              MessageName:="Sub_Shorts")> _
    Public Function Subtract(ByVal iNum1 As Short, ByVal iNum2 As Short) As
Short
        Return iNum1 - iNum2
    End Function

    <WebMethod(Description:="This function returns the difference between 2
Doubles", _
              MessageName:="Sub_Doubles")> _
    Public Function Subtract(ByVal iNum1 As Double, ByVal iNum2 As Double) As
Double
        Return iNum1 - iNum2
    End Function

    <WebMethod(Description:="This function multiplies two integers", _
              MessageName:="Mult_Integers")> _
    Public Function Multiply(ByVal iNum1 As Integer, ByVal iNum2 As Integer) As
Integer
        Return iNum1 * iNum2
    End Function

    <WebMethod(Description:="This function multiplies two Shorts", _
              MessageName:="Mult_Shorts")> _
    Public Function Multiply(ByVal iNum1 As Short, ByVal iNum2 As Short) As
Short
        Return iNum1 * iNum2
    End Function

    <WebMethod(Description:="This function multiplies two Doubles", _
              MessageName:="Mult_Doubles")> _
    Public Function Multiply(ByVal iNum1 As Double, ByVal iNum2 As Double) As
Double
        Return iNum1 * iNum2
    End Function

    <WebMethod(Description:="This function divides one integer into another",
MessageName:="Div_Integers")> _
    Public Function Divide(ByVal iNum1 As Integer, ByVal iNum2 As Integer) As
Integer
        Return iNum1 / iNum2
    End Function

    <WebMethod(Description:="This function divides one Short into another", _
              MessageName:="Div_Shorts")> _
     Public Function Divide(ByVal iNum1 As Short, ByVal iNum2 As Short) As Short
        Return iNum1 / iNum2
```

```
    End Function

    <WebMethod(Description:="This function divides one Double into another", _
              MessageName:="Div_Doubles")> _
      Public Function Divide(ByVal iNum1 As Double, ByVal iNum2 As Double) As
Double
        Return iNum1 / iNum2
    End Function
#End Region

End Class
```

HOUR 17

XML Web Service Events (Global.ASA)

In this hour, you will learn to handle the various events that are fired throughout the lifespan of your XML Web service. You will also deal with the issue of data persistence and how it is handled through the life span of a single client application versus that of multiple users sharing a common resource.

Throughout this hour we will discuss the following:

- The Global.ASAX
- Application level events
- Session level events
- Variable scope in XML Web service applications

What Does the Global.ASAX DO?

By now, you have noticed the Global class in every XML Web service that you have created and you are probably wondering what it is used for. Well, this class gets compiled into the Global.ASAX and, as those of you who have previous experience using ASP already know, the Global.ASAX is where you handle all of the events that occur across our XML Web service application.

XML Web services exposes eight events for us to use. Like ASP, these events fall into two distinct categories, application level events and session level events.

Uses of the Global.ASAX

The Global.ASAX provides a means for allowing XML Web services to respond to events as they occur within a session, a single client application's experience with a service, or application wide, affecting all clients that are using the service. The Global.ASAX events provide the mechanism for loading global data, such as lists a list of sports scores that will be provided to clients of a box score XML Web Service. The Global.ASAX also provides the means for gathering data about an individual client, such as an account number, and using it throughout the client's interaction with the service. This could be used to build shopping cart applications, banking applications, or a host of other client driven applications.

Of the events shown in this hour, only `Application_BeginRequest`, `Application_EndRequest`, and `Application_Error` are provided for you by the Visual Studio.NET interface. For all of the other events, you will have to type in the sub declaration and `End Sub` lines for yourself.

Application Events

To understand application events, one must understand that a single XML Web service may be simultaneously handling requests from several, even several thousand, client applications at any one time. Indeed, it is possible that a single client application may create multiple references to an XML Web service and maintain them concurrently.

With this in mind, application level events exist to allow you to initialize your service for the entire user community. It is here that you can set variables and run procedures that will affect all of your client applications.

`Application_Start()`

When the very first client application creates a reference to your service and triggers its constructor, the `Application_Start()` event is fired. This event fires only once in the lifetime of the service and will not fire again, no matter how many client applications may reference and deference your service, until the server has shut the service down and the first new client comes along and starts the process over again.

When IIS actually shuts your XML Web Service down is a bit tricky. When the last client calling your service has removed its reference to your service, IIS's reference count decrements to zero and the service shuts down. IIS also references clients that "timeout." This means that IIS has decided that the client has taken too long between calls and is no longer active.

The `Application_Start()` event is a great place to initialize data that will be used by multiple routines throughout your project. Often, files or databases are opened here and information is read into application variables. In traditional Web applications, variables are created for counters and initialized to either zero or the count before the service last shut down.

Because no session is associated with the application level events, you are limited to using the ASP application and Server objects that you learned about in Hour 12.

If you reference session variables in the application level events, your code will compile, but runtime errors will occur.

To illustrate how the Global.ASAX works, create a new XML Web service and name it GlobalTest. You will modify this service throughout this hour.

Listing 17.1 shows the code that you will add to `Application_Start()` in order to demonstrate what can be done with the Global.ASAX file. This code simply creates a pair of application level variables identical to those that you saw in Hour 12 and sets them to 0. These counters, `ClientCount` and `HitCount`, will be used to count the number of users who access our application as well as the number of times requests are made to our service.

Listing 17.1 Initializing Variables in the `Application_Start()` Event

```
Sub Application_Start(ByVal Sender As Object, ByVal e As EventArgs)

    Application("ClientCount") = 0
    Application("HitCount") = 0

End Sub
```

`Application_BeginRequest()` and `Application_EndRequest()`

These events fire every time any client application makes a call to any service in your XML Web services project. This pair of events will even fire when a reference to your service is initially created in the client code.

Use the `Application_BeginRequest()` event to run code that must be triggered every time a call is made to your application. For example, if you were tracking to see how much traffic your XML Web service is generating, you could increment an application variable every time the event is fired. On the other hand, if you need to keep track of how many times specific clients use your service, you could write a routine that checks the id of the client and increments a session variable.

`Application_EndRequest()` is fired after the actual call to your method has run. It is a good place to reset application level variables that may have been changed.

Add the following line of code to the `Application_BeginRequest()` of your Global class:

```
Application("HitCount") = CInt(Application("HitCount")) + 1
```

This line increments the `HitCount` variable that you created in our `Application_Start()` event.

Now, add the procedure shown in Listing 17.2 to your Service class. This code exposes our counter and allows us to watch our service's application level events in motion.

Listing 17.2 Exposing the Counter in Our GlobalTest XML Web Service

```
<WebMethod()> Public Function AccessCount() As Integer
    Return CInt(Application("HitCount"))
End Function
```

Save the program and run it. When Internet Explorer opens, scroll down the Web Method Reference for our `AccessCount` method and click the invoke button. Notice that the answer returned is 2. This is because the `Application_BeginRequest()` event was fired when the service first opened and again when you invoked the `AccessCount` button. Click the Invoke button a few more times, as in Figure 17.1, and verify that the counter behaves as you expect.

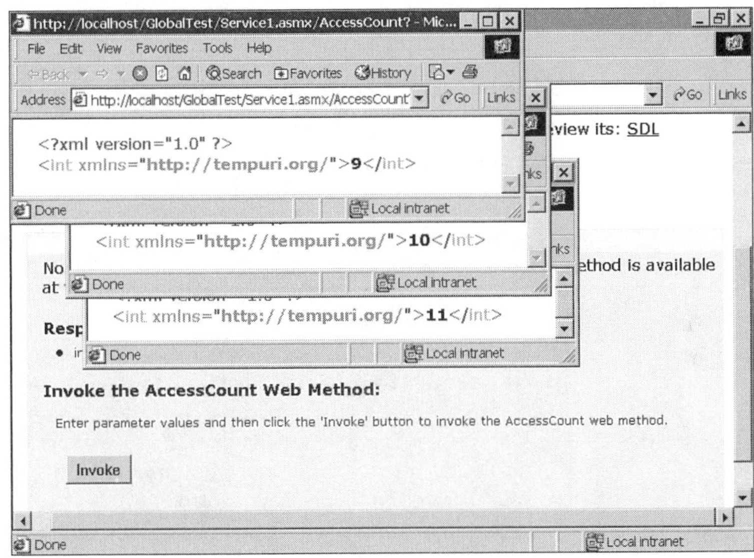

FIGURE 17.1
Invoking our `AccessCount` *method increments the counter.*

`Application_End()`

The `Application_End()` event is fired when the Web server shuts your service down. This event is often used to write application level variables to files or databases before the service is shut down. Listing 17.3 shows the code to write your `HitCount` to a file. This data would then be read in during `Application_Start()` in order to reinitialize the data.

LISTING 17.3 Using `Application_End()` to Persist Data

```
Sub Application_End(ByVal Sender As Object, ByVal e As EventArgs)
   Dim oSW As StreamWriter = file.CreateText("c:\Counter.txt")

   oSW.WriteLine(Application("HitCount"))
   oSW.Close()
End Sub
```

Now, you must add the following line to the declarations section of `Global.vb` in order for the new `StreamWriter` object to be included in our code:

```
Imports System.IO
```

When the service shuts down, you now have a log of the number of users that hit your service. A simple alteration to the `Application_Start()` event (see Listing 17.4) will allow your service to continue to track hits across multiple start-ups.

LISTING 17.4 Our New `Application_Start()`

```
Sub Application_Start(ByVal Sender As Object, ByVal e As EventArgs)
   Dim oSW As StreamReader = file.OpenText("c:\Counter.txt")

   Application("HitCount") = oSW.ReadLine
   oSW.Close()

   Application("ClientCount") = 0
End Sub
```

Please note, I have not included code to check for the existence of `Counter.txt` when the application first starts. The file is created in `Application_End()`. In order to avoid errors, either write some code to set the `HitCounter` to 0 if the file is not present or manually create the file on your C drive and simply leave it blank.

Application_Error

One additional event that is provided by the Global.ASAX is the `Application_Error()` event. This event is fired every time an error is encounter when running the XML Web Service. This error is very useful when creating ASP applications, allowing you to redirect users to other pages or provide custom error messages. In XML Web Services however, it can be used to write trace events to the trace log or provide handling for custom error objects. You will look at how to accomplish these tasks in Hours 20 and 21.

Session Events

In order to understand what session events are, you first have to understand what a session is. Sessions are defined by individual references to your service. When a client application makes its first call to your XML Web service, it starts a session, and that session lasts until the client drops reference to the service.

Every client application that uses your service will run in a separate session and fire off its own session events. In fact, a single client may instantiate several different objects based on your XML Web service, each running their very own session.

Enabling Sessions

Sessions are turned off by default in XML Web services. In order to activate them, you have to add a property to the `WebMethod` attribute when declaring a method. In Visual basic, the new method call is

```
<WebMethod(EnableSession:=True)> Public Function FunctionName() as Type
```

In C#, you would you make your call with the following syntax:

```
[WebMethod (EnableSession=True)]

Public Type FunctionName()
```

You can enable sessions in some of the method calls on your service and leave others set to false. This will enable you to determine when your session level events will fire or even if they will fire.

> If you enable sessions in one method call, but your service contains other methods without sessions enabled, client applications may use your service without ever generating a session.

`Session_Start()`

The `Session_Start()` event is fired the first time that a client application makes a call to a method with `EnableSession` set to true. This event is used to set session level variables that will be used by method calls throughout the lifetime of this instance of the service.

To demonstrate sessions, let's go back to our GlobalTest project and cut the code from the `Application_BeginRequest()` event and paste it into `Session_Start()`. Your code should now look like Listing 17.5.

Listing 17.5 The `Session_Start()` Code

```
Sub Session_Start(ByVal Sender As Object, ByVal e As EventArgs)
  Application("HitCount") = CInt(Application("HitCount")) + 1
End Sub
```

Now, run the service. Like before, you have the `AccessCount()` method, only this time, no matter how many times you invoke it, it will return only the number 1. This is because Internet Explorer represents a single client accessing our service in a single session.

Try opening a second instance of Explorer and navigating to the URL of our service, the same URL showing in the current IE window. When you invoke the `AccessCount()` method from this window, you now receive a count of 2. You now have two clients accessing your service in different sessions, as illustrated in Figure 17.2.

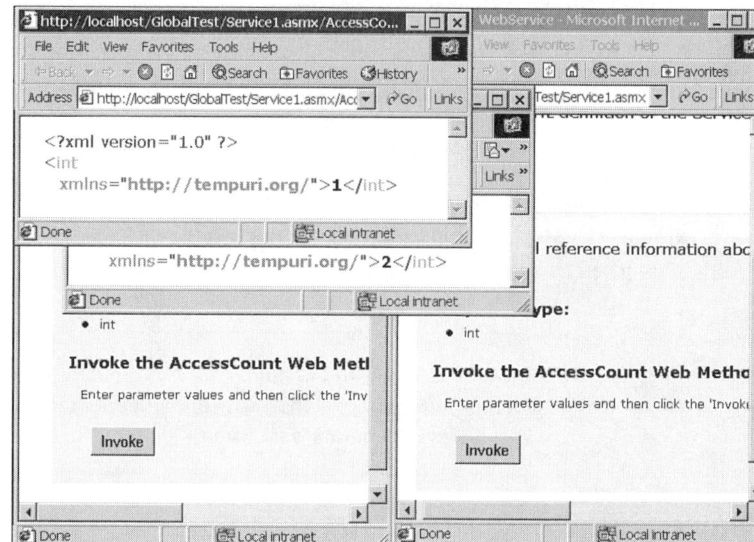

FIGURE 17.2
Multiple sessions of our GlobalTest XML Web service.

Multiple Sessions from a Single Client

As I mentioned previously, multiple sessions can be called from a single client application. This is very different from traditional ASP applications, where a session lasts for the lifespan of the client. Care must be taken to design both your service and your clients with this in mind. Data persistence across multiple sessions must be done using local storage on the client side (variables, files, databases, and so on), and methods for initializing session variables must be built on the XML Web service side.

In order to see some of the different scenarios resulting from the creation of multiple sessions, you will create a new test application to consume our GlobalTest XML Web service. Create a new Windows application and call it TwoServices.

In you project, add two button controls and two text boxes as shown in Figure 17.3.

Now, add a reference to the GlobalTest XML Web service (see Hour 8 for details on how this is done). And add the declarations in Listing 17.6 to your code:

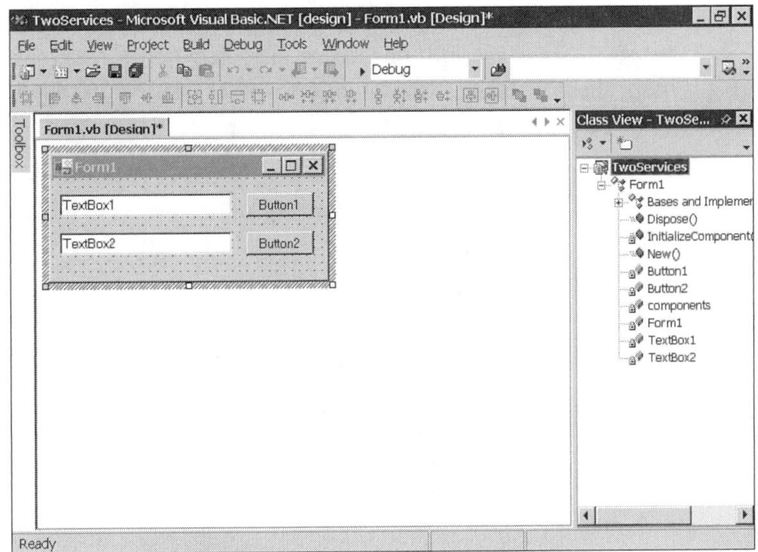

FIGURE 17.3
`Form1` *of the TwoServices application.*

LISTING 17.6 Declaring Our References to GlobalTest

```
Dim oServ1 as new localhost.Service1
Dim oServ2 as New localhost.Service1
```

Now that you have created references to the service, let's put them to use. Create click events for both buttons, as shown in Listing 17.7

LISTING 17.7 Button Click Events for TwoServcies

```
Public Sub Button1_Click(ByVal sender As Object, _
 ByVal e As System.EventArgs) Handles Button1.Click

 Textbox1.Text = oServ1.AccessCount.ToString
End Sub

Public Sub Button2_Click(ByVal sender As Object, _
 ByVal e As System.EventArgs) Handles Button2.Click

 Textbox2.Text = oServ2.AccessCount.ToString
End Sub
```

When you run the service, two separate references are created to the GlobalTest XML Web service. When you click on `button1`, a new session is started and the session number is placed in `Textbox1`. Further clicks to `button1` will not increment the session counter at all.

By clicking on `button2`, you start a new session and send its session number to `Textbox2`. Notice that it is one higher than the number in `Textbox1` (See Figure 17.3). Future clicks to either of the buttons, without restarting the application, will continue to return the new, higher number, as no new sessions are created.

Now, let's go a step further with our session example. Delete the reference that you created in Listing 17.6 and alter our `Button_Click` events to include the creation of a new reference to the XML Web service (see Listing 17.8). These new methods will create new sessions every time a button is clicked.

LISTING 17.8 Our New `Button_Click` Events Create New Sessions Every Time They Fire

```
Public Sub Button1_Click(ByVal sender As Object,_
       ByVal e As System.EventArgs) Handles Button1.Click
    Dim oServ1 As New localhost.Service1()

    textbox1.Text = oServ1.AccessCount.ToString
    oServ1 = Nothing
End Sub

Public Sub Button2_Click(ByVal sender As Object,_
       ByVal e As System.EventArgs) Handles Button2.Click
     Dim oserv2 As New localhost.Service1()

     textbox2.Text = oServ2.AccessCount.ToString
     oServ2 = Nothing
 End Sub
```

If you run the TwoServices application now, you will notice that every time you click either button, the session ID continues to increment. You are now creating and closing a session with every `Button_Click` event.

`Session_End()`

The last event that you will deal with is the `Session_End()` event. As the name implies, this event is fired whenever a session ends. Sessions end when a client application drops a reference to them or when the dispose method is explicitly called.

To take a look at the `Session_End` event, let's reopen our GlobalTest project and add the flowing line to our `Session_Start()` Event:

```
Application("ClientCount") = cInt(Application("ClientCount")) + 1
```

This line of code now increments `ClientCount` every time a session starts. You will now add some code to the `Session_End()` event to decrement this value when a session ends. This will now make `ClientCount` a count of the number of open sessions. Listing 17.9 shows the new `Session_End()`:

LISTING 17.9 `Session_End` Decrements `ClientCount` When a Session Ends

```
Sub Session_End(ByVal Sender As Object, ByVal e As EventArgs)
    Application("ClientCount") = CInt(Application("ClientCount")) - 1
End Sub
```

Finally, add the method shown in Listing 17.10 to `Service1` to expose our active session count to client application.

LISTING 17.10 `Session_End` Decrements `ClientCount` When a Session Ends

```
Public Function <WebMethod(EnableSession:=True)> _
              SessionCount() As Integer

       Return CInt(Application("ClientCount"))
 End Function
```

You now have a method that reports the number of active sessions for your service.

When you are testing this method, you may notice a lag between shutting down a client reference to the service and the actual running of `Session_End()` routine. This is because IIS is retaining the session until a session timeout occurs.

Summary

In this hour, you learned how to use the Global.ASAX in order to access XML Web service events. You delved into the differences between application and session level events and some methods for taking advantage of them. This hour also included an example of creating multiple sessions from a single client and how this differs from traditional ASP applications.

Q&A

Q I want to open a database and read in a number of e-mail addresses that will be shared with all users of my XML Web service. How do I do this?

A In your `Application_Start()` event, read in your data and store it in an application level scripting dictionary object or an array declared in a module. You can now share this across sessions. Remember, if you allow your users to make changes to the data, you will have to write the data back to your database in an `Application_End()` event.

Q Why do XML Web services use a Global.ASAX file like ASP anyway?

A Because, as has been discussed earlier, when your project is compiled and ready for real-world use, it is an ASP.Net application. The only thing separating it from standard ASP code is that an XML Web service includes the framework to expose its methods to other applications. Because ASP was designed to use the Global.ASAX file in order to handle application and session-wide events and because XML Web services are just specialized ASP applications, they too use the Global.ASAX file.

Q I have been testing the session events and can never seem to get the `Session_End()` to fire when my client ends a session. Why is this?

A Well, IIS really controls when sessions end and, if you don't tell it otherwise, it will usually hold a session open for up to 20 minutes. If you need to ensure that sessions end more quickly, try using the `timeout` property of the session object to set the length that your session will remain open and inactive or add the session's `abandon` method to your service's `dispose` method. Both of these features of the `session` object were discussed in Hour 12.

Q Can I consume different XML Web services in a single client?

A Yes, just as you built a client that made several references to the same service, you can make references to several different services and use them throughout your client application. These services can reside on one machine or several and can even be a mix of internal and external services.

Workshop

The Workshop is designed to help you review what you've learned in this hour and to point you ahead to the material that will be covered in future hours.

Quiz

1. You run your service, but your session events never seem to fire. What are you missing?

   A You have forgotten to set `EnableSession = true` in your `<WebMethod>` declaration.

2. You are keeping records of how many times each of your service's methods are used. These values are stored in application variables. When do you need to write them to a file?

   A You would write them to a file during the `Application_End()` event.

3. You are keeping track of the number of times your service is used per hour. Where would you place the code to record the time of each hit?

   A In `Application_BeginRequest()`.

4. You retrieve data for individual client applications when they begin using your service. During the time that they are hitting the service, they make changes to the data. Where do you write code to save these changes?

   A In the `Session_End()` event.

Exercises

Try writing a simple service that exposes a name and e-mail address to client applications. For the sake of simplicity, we will hard-code the names and e-mails, six of each, into the service. The name and corresponding e-mail address should be given out one at a time, in order, to each client that connects to the services. This process should start over with the first name after the sixth has been assigned.

This service could be used in a help desk application to assign a service representative that would be assigned to the client throughout its usage of the system.

If you want to explore this problem further, read the names in from a database and allow any number of records to exist in the table.

A. To create your name and e-mail returning program, open a new XML Web services project and name it ReturnNames. Add a module to the project and place the following code into that module:

```
Module Module1

    Public Class Person
        Public Name As String
        Public Email As String
    End Class
```

```
    Public oPerson(5) As Person

    Public Sub InitializeString()

        oPerson(0) = New Person()
        oPerson(0).Name = "Rowan"
        oPerson(0).Email = "RC@MyHouse.com"
        oPerson(1) = New Person()
        oPerson(1).Name = "Morrigan"
        oPerson(1).Email = "MC@MyHouse.com"
        oPerson(2) = New Person()
        oPerson(2).Name = "Naya"
        oPerson(2).Email = "NC@MyHouse.com"
        oPerson(3) = New Person()
        oPerson(3).Name = "Missi"
        oPerson(3).Email = "MC@MyHouse.com"
        oPerson(4) = New Person()
        oPerson(4).Name = "Lorindol"
        oPerson(4).Email = "LC@MyHouse.com"
        oPerson(5) = New Person()
        oPerson(5).Name = "Danielle"
        oPerson(5).Email = "DW@MyHouse.com"

    End Sub
End Module
```

This code creates a class called `person`, which will be used to hold a name and e-mail address. We then create an array of `Person` objects called `oPerson` and use the *Initialize* subroutine to call it.

Next, add the following code to your `Application_Start()` and `Session_Start()` events in the Global file:

```
Sub Application_Start(ByVal Sender As Object, ByVal e As EventArgs)
     Application("Count") = 0

     'Initialize Names
     InitializeString()
End Sub

Sub Session_Start(ByVal Sender As Object, ByVal e As EventArgs)
     Dim i As Integer

     i = CInt(Application("Count")) Mod 6

     Session("Name") = oPerson(i).name
     Session("Email") = oPerson(i).email

     Application("Count") = CInt(Application("Count")) + 1

 End Sub
```

Your `Application_Start()` event now creates an application level variable called `count` and sets it equal to 0. It also calls the `Initialize()` routine to set up your array of `person` objects.

Your `Session_Start()` event now sets session level variables for `name` and `email`. Notice how we use a counter, `i`, to hold the return of the `Mod` operation performed on our counter. Because this number will always be between 0 and 5, we can use it to count through our array of `person` objects.

Lastly, we add the following returns to `Service1` in order to return the `name` and `email` values:

```
Public Function <WebMethod(EnableSession:=True)> Name() As String
     Return Session("Name")
 End Function

 Public Function <WebMethod(EnableSession:=True)> Email() As String
     Return Session("Email")
 End Function
```

HOUR 18

Security and the SOAP Toolkit

Eventually, you'll want to secure your XML Web service so that unauthorized users aren't able to take advantage of your hard work. Security is an issue on both the client and server sides; the server must be secure, and the client must be able to access said secure service.

There are quite a few ways to secure XML Web services, and in this hour we'll take a look at the most common ones. You'll also recap some important security concepts here.

In this hour, we will discuss the following:

- How security applies to XML Web services
- What the SOAP Toolkit is and what it provides
- How to authenticate users in Internet Information Server (IIS)
- How to secure your XML Web service using IIS
- How to use the SOAP Toolkit to access secure XML Web services

What Is Security?

Security has many different contexts, so what do we mean by a secure XML Web service? A secure XML Web service is one that can be accessed only by the appropriate people. You don't want, for example, a spy accessing your top-secret database service.

Security is very important for XML Web services. Suppose Microsoft created a Microsoft Word XML Web service. Without security, anyone could come along and use that service without having to pay for it—not a good thing for Microsoft.

The good news is that XML Web services can be secured just like any other Web page or application, making things easy on you, the developer.

SOAP Is Not Secure

You learned briefly in Hour 4, "Remote Procedure Calls with SOAP," that SOAP is not by itself secure. There is no set of rules in the SOAP specification that allows for any type of security or encryption.

If you send a SOAP message to an XML Web service, a clever hacker could intercept that message and see what you sent because it is just plain text. Likewise, if the service returns data, the message could be intercepted and its contents stolen.

Because of this, SOAP relies on other systems to provide security, namely IIS.

> There are people at work trying to propose a set of modifications to the SOAP specification that would allow for built-in security mechanisms. However, there is no formal proposal yet, and any such proposal would take quite a while to be implemented. In other words, don't hold your breath waiting for SOAP to become secure.

An Overview of the SOAP Toolkit

The SOAP Toolkit (currently version 2.0, `http://msdn.microsoft.com/soap`) provides several objects that make creating and interpreting SOAP messages very easy. These include `SOAPClient` and `SOAPServer` objects that can act as the sending and receiving mechanisms, respectively, of an XML Web service. You'll be using these two objects later this hour.

The purpose of the toolkit is to enable developers to quickly consume XML Web services using SOAP. Thus, it provides all the necessary functions and objects for dealing with XML, WSDL, SOAP and SOAP headers, posting to a Web site, receiving data, and so on. If you have an XML Web service, you can use the SOAP Toolkit's objects as the service client.

The SOAP Toolkit also introduces a new type of XML document, the XML Web Services Meta Language (WSML) file. It is similar to a WSDL file but maps service functions to existing COM objects. It is also a proprietary specification, for use only with Microsoft's technologies, so we won't bother with it too much here.

The SOAP Toolkit isn't required to implement security for your XML Web services but, along with IIS, provides a strong mechanism for doing so. For the examples in this hour, you'll need to install the toolkit.

Security Basics

Before we get started securing our services, let's take a step back and examine how security works with IIS and Windows.

There are three parts of security in IIS: authentication, authorization, and impersonation. Authentication is the process of verifying a user—making sure people are who they say they are. Authorization is used to determine what resources users have access to. Impersonation is the ability for IIS to "impersonate" its users, thereby limiting its own capabilities. We'll cover only the first part in this chapter, as that is often the only security measure you will implement for an XML Web service. (For more information on security and XML Web services, check out *Sam's Teach Yourself ASP.NET in 21 Days*.)

Authentication

When someone knocks on your door, you'll usually want to find out who it is before opening the door. There are various ways to find out the person's identity, each with its own level of security.

For example, you could simply ask, "Who is it?" Most of the time, you'd be able to trust the person's response, especially if the response is "It's your mother." If you had some reason to believe the person is not your mother, you could look through your peephole or window to check. If you're afraid that the caller may have disguised herself as your mother, you could go one step further and ask for identification, such as a driver's license or even a birth certificate (a bit drastic, we know, but it sometimes helps to be paranoid).

Security in IIS and Windows works very similarly. By default, IIS lets anyone into the Web site—it leaves the door open to anonymous users. Many times this is fine—after all, the purpose of most Web sites is to allow anonymous visitors to come and check it out.

If you want additional security for your Web site, you can enable authentication, which instructs IIS to require credentials before allowing a visitor in. With .NET, there are three types of authentication.

With any type of authentication you'll learn about here, it is important to note that the visitor is stopped before they ever reach the requested resource.

Forms and Passport Authentication

Forms authentication is part of ASP.NET and probably one of the most common types of authentication, as well. You've probably seen it used all over the Internet. With this method, the visitors are directed to a login page where they supply their credentials (typically a username and password), and if they are valid, the visitors are allowed access to the site. If not, they are denied and offered the opportunity to try again. Figure 18.1 shows a flowchart with this scenario.

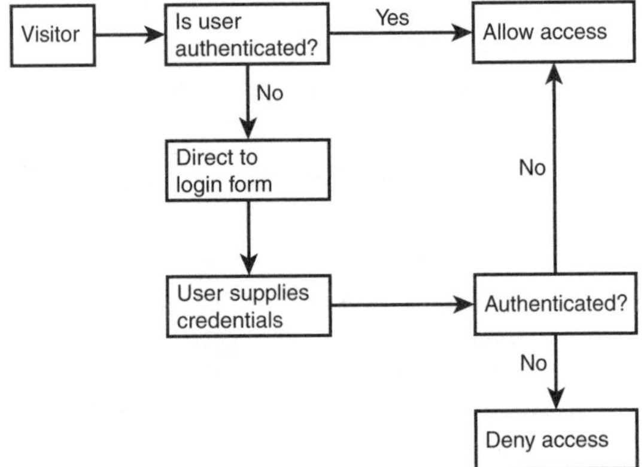

FIGURE 18.1
The process of authenticating a user.

Passport authentication is a service (not an XML Web service) that is provided by Microsoft. Essentially, it is the same as Forms authentication, but the visitor is redirected to a login page on Microsoft's site, instead of one on your site. Passport is a security mechanism used throughout many Microsoft sites, so once you log on to Passport on one site, you are automatically logged in to any other passport sites. Check out `www.passport.com` for more information.

There are, however, some drawbacks to Passport authentication. First, the Passport service does not officially support XML Web services, so there is no interface for your XML Web service to interact with Passport directly. Second, to enable Passport on your site, you'll have to register with Microsoft and pay a fee—beyond the scope of this book.

Windows Authentication

Finally, there is Windows authentication. With this type, when IIS sees an incoming visitor, it turns control over to the operating system (OS) for authentication. Windows then validates the user's identity against a list of known users for that OS. In Windows 2000, this list can be seen by clicking on Start, Settings, Control Panel, Users and Passwords. An example list is shown in Figure 18.2.

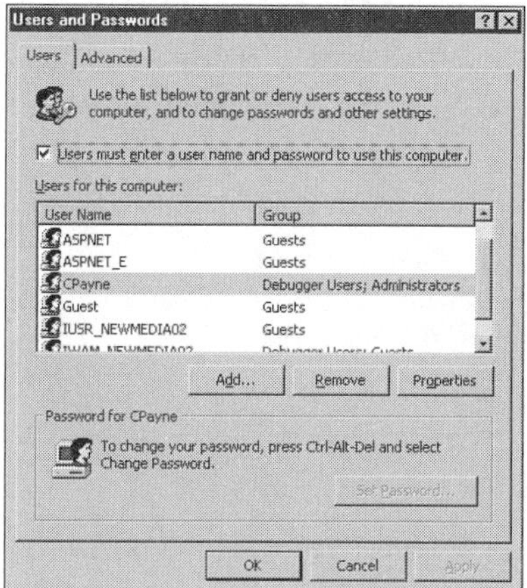

FIGURE 18.2
A list of users in Windows.

There are three subtypes of Windows authentication: basic, digest, and Integrated Windows (or NTLM). Basic and digest mode are very similar. When a visitor comes to a Web site with basic or digest authentication enabled, they are prompted with a box, shown in Figure 18.3. The supplied information is then validated against the OS's users.

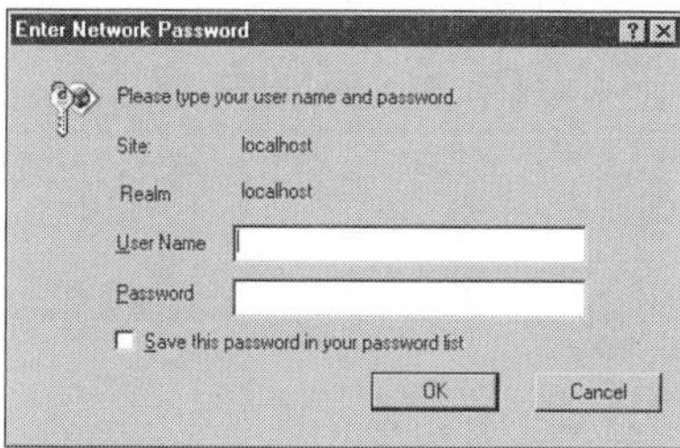

FIGURE 18.3
Basic and digest authentication modes ask for credentials.

The difference between these two modes is that the supplied credentials are not encrypted with basic mode, whereas they are for digest. Also, basic mode is part of the HTTP specification, which means any platform can implement it. So, with digest mode, you get more security but less interoperability.

NTLM, like digest mode, is specific to Microsoft's operating systems. With this mode, no dialog box is shown when a user visits a secure Web site. Instead, the visitor's copy of Windows automatically communicates with the server's copy, sending the current user's identity for authentication. The user will be allowed or denied access without any intervention. NTLM is the most secure of the three modes.

Securing the Server through IIS

Before you can secure an XML Web service, you're going to need one to secure. Let's create a simple service, shown in Listing 18.1—a modification of the calculator services you've already created.

LISTING 18.1 A Simple Calculator XML Web Service

```
<%@ WebService Language="VB" Class="Calculator" %>

Imports System.Web.Services

public Class Calculator : Inherits WebService
   <WebMethod()> Public Function Add(intA As Integer, _
      intB As Integer) As Integer
       Return(intA + intB)
   End Function
    <WebMethod()> Public Function Multiply(intA As Integer, _
       intB As Integer) As Integer
        Return(intA * intB)
    End Function
    <WebMethod()> Public Function Subtract(intA As Integer, _
       intB As Integer) As Integer
        Return(intA - intB)
    End Function
    <WebMethod()> Public Function Divide(intA As Integer, _
       intB As Integer) As Integer
        Return(intA / intB)
    End Function
 End Class
```

Create a new directory in your root Web folder, `secure`, and create this file as `calculator.asmx` inside it.

To enable authentication, you'll need to open IIS. Go to Start, Settings, Control Panel, Administrative Tools, Internet Services Manager. You'll see something similar to Figure 18.4 (click on the pluses to expand the sections).

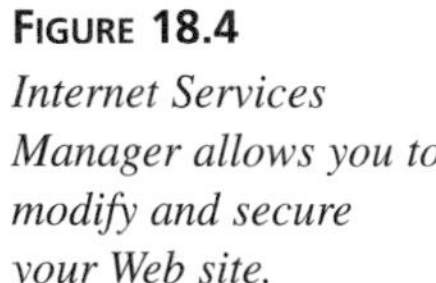

FIGURE 18.4
Internet Services Manager allows you to modify and secure your Web site.

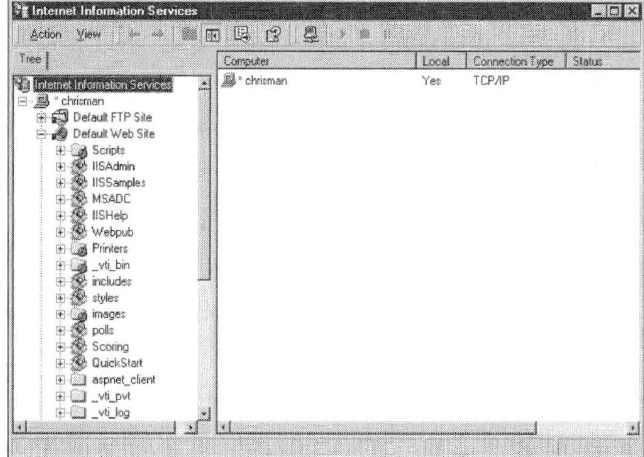

Under `Default Web Site`, you should see the new `secure` directory you created a moment ago. Right click the folder in the left hand pane and select properties. You have several options in the window that pops up, but for now, all we're interested in is the Directory Security tab. Under this tab you'll see `Anonymous access and authentication control`, with an edit button. Click edit, and you'll see Figure 18.5.

FIGURE 18.5
The authentication control panel.

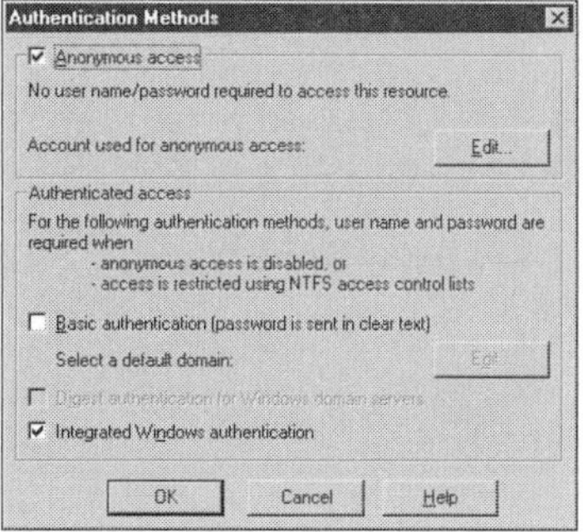

Anonymous access is selected by default. Unselect it so that visitors must be authenticated before they can view the files in the `secure` directory. Also, at the bottom of the dialog, Integrated Windows authentication may be checked by default. If this is the case, and you are accessing your services from the same machine that they are running on, you will have to uncheck this option as well in order to run this test. Next, select basic authentication, and deselect Integrated Windows authentication. A warning message should pop up indicating the security risk of basic authentication (that is, that credentials are sent via plain text). Just click OK because you're already familiar with this. Click OK twice more to apply the settings to `secure`.

Now for the true test. Try viewing the `calculator.asmx` XML Web service in your browser (`http://localhost/secure/calculator.asmx`). A dialog box should pop up asking for credentials. Enter your Windows username and password for entrance. Next we'll examine how to use the SOAP Toolkit to gain access in another way.

Accessing Secure Services

Your service is now secure. Any visitor or XML Web service that comes along and tries to access the service must supply proper credentials to use the functionality. Let's use the SOAP Toolkit to figure out how exactly to go about it.

As mentioned earlier this hour (see "An Overview of the SOAP Toolkit"), the toolkit is bundled with an object called `SOAPClient`. This object can act as an XML Web service client, sending SOAP messages and receiving XML data. It encapsulates all of the functionality we need to parse XML, read SOAP headers, and so on. And probably most important (for this lesson anyway) is its ability to provide secure access to services. Let's take a look at some code.

LISTING 18.2 Using SOAPClient to Access a Secure XML Web Service

```
<%@ Page Language="VB" %>

<script runat="server">
   Sub Page_Load(Src As Object, e As EventArgs)
      dim objSOAP

      objSOAP = Server.Createobject("MSSOAP.SoapClient")

      objSOAP.mssoapinit("http://localhost/secure/calculator.asmx?WSDL")

      lblMessage.Text = objSOAP.Add(8,9)

      objSOAP = nothing
   End Sub
</script>

<html><body>
   The answer is: <asp:Label id="lblMessage" runat="server"/>
</body></html>
```

You should be familiar with the basics of ASP.NET by now, so this page should be easy to follow. Let's take a closer look.

On line 1 you have the `Page` directive, which simply sets up the language we'll be using on the rest of the page, Visual Basic.NET. The rest of the ASP.NET code is enclosed in the `script` tags on lines 3 and 15.

The only method in this page, `Page_Load`, is called when the page loads. This is where we want to call the secure XML Web service. Line 5 declares the variable we'll use for the `SOAPClient` object, and line 7 instantiates it. (Note that the SOAP Toolkit is not managed code—that is, it was built with the .NET Framework—so we have to use `Server.CreateObject` to instantiate it.)

On line 9 we call the `mssoapinit` function, which takes as a parameter the URL (or file location) of the WSDL service description. Here we pass it the calculator service's URL. Line 11 calls the `Add` method of the service, passing in two numbers, and displays the results in the label on line 18.

Save this file as `client.aspx` in your root Web directory and view it from your browser with `http://localhost/client.aspx`. You should see something similar to Figure 18.6.

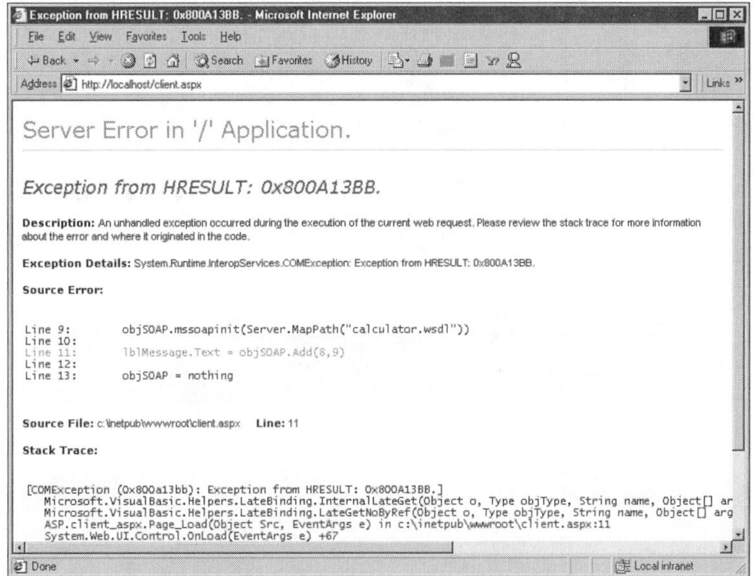

FIGURE 18.6

The service is secured, so any attempt to access it will result in an error.

> If you see instead an error on line 9, you may have an issue with encoding. See "Encoding Issues" later in this chapter.

What happened? Remember that your XML Web service is now secure. Your attempt to connect to it failed because you didn't supply proper credentials. Luckily, with the SOAP Toolkit, that's easy to fix. Add the following two lines after line 9 and before line 11 in Listing 18.2:

```
objSOAP.ConnectorProperty("AuthUser") = "clpayne"
objSOAP.ConnectorProperty("AuthPassword") = "helloworld"
```

The `SOAPClient` object has a `ConnectorProperty` collection, which provides additional information to send to the service. `ConnectorProperty` allows you to specify an authentication username and password with the `AuthUser` and `AuthPassword` properties, as shown in the code snippet. When these values are set, the `SOAPClient` object now sends this information to the service (or more specifically, to IIS) to be authenticated.

Save `client.aspx` and try viewing it from the browser again. You should see Figure 18.7. Don't forget to substitute the values `clpayne` and `helloworld` with your username and password (if you supply incorrect credentials, you'll see Figure 18.6 again).

> As noted earlier in this hour, you may encounter problems in the previous example involving encoding. If this is the case, see "Encoding Issues" later in this chapter.

FIGURE 18.7
The service now allows the authenticated user access.

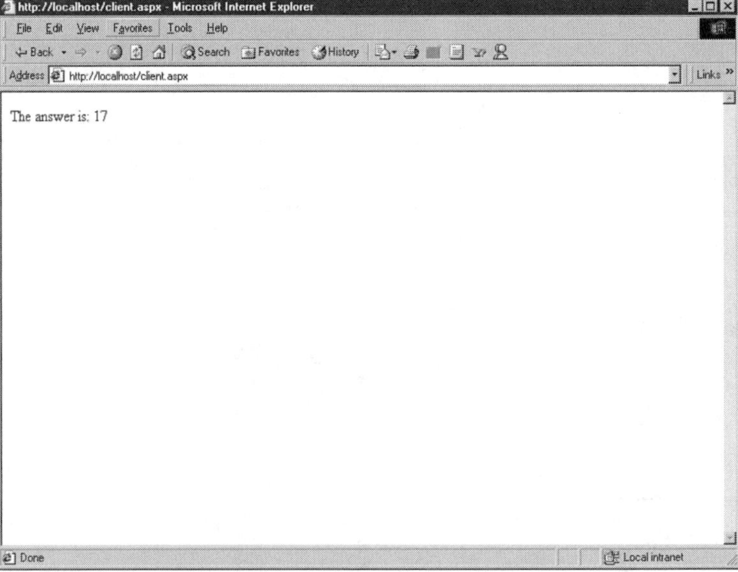

Using the SOAP Toolkit, you can now access secure XML Web services! The only additional thing you have to do is supply values for the `AuthUser` and `AuthPassword` properties of the `ConnectorProperty` collection.

Encoding Issues

When you viewed `client.aspx` through your browser, you may have seen Figure 18.8 instead of 18.6. If this is the case, you are having problems with the way the XML Web service description was encoded.

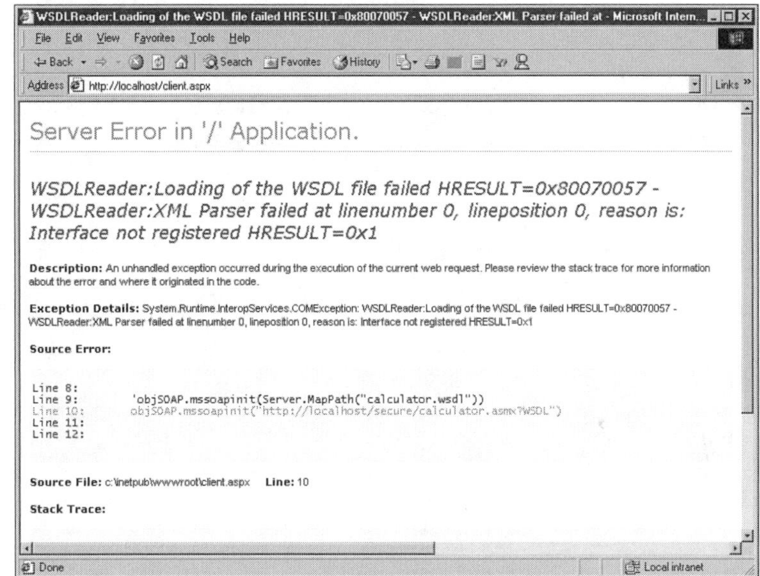

FIGURE 18.8
This error means the file encoding is incorrect.

When you view the service description with the URL `http://localhost/secure/calculator.asmx?WSDL`, ASP.NET shows you the XML output. The first line of this XML looks something like

```
<?xml version='1.0' encoding='UTF-8' ?>
```

The encoding here is specified as UTF-8, and when your client accesses this description, it expects UTF-8 data. However, when viewing the URL `http://localhost/secure/calculator.asmx?WSDL`, your browser may not actually output UTF-8, even though the XML thinks it does. Your browser is not smart enough to look at the first XML line and format the output accordingly.

The `SOAPClient` object is very picky, and if the XML Web service description says UTF-8, it must have UTF-8 or you'll receive the error shown in Figure 18.8. The solution, then, is to tell the `SOAPClient` not to expect UTF-8, and this is done by modifying the service description itself.

View `http://localhost/secure/calculator.asmx?WSDL` once again, and this time right-click and select View Source. In the file that pops up, delete the first line (see Figure 18.9), and save it in the same directory as `client.aspx`: `c:\inetpub\wwwroot\calculator.wsdl`.

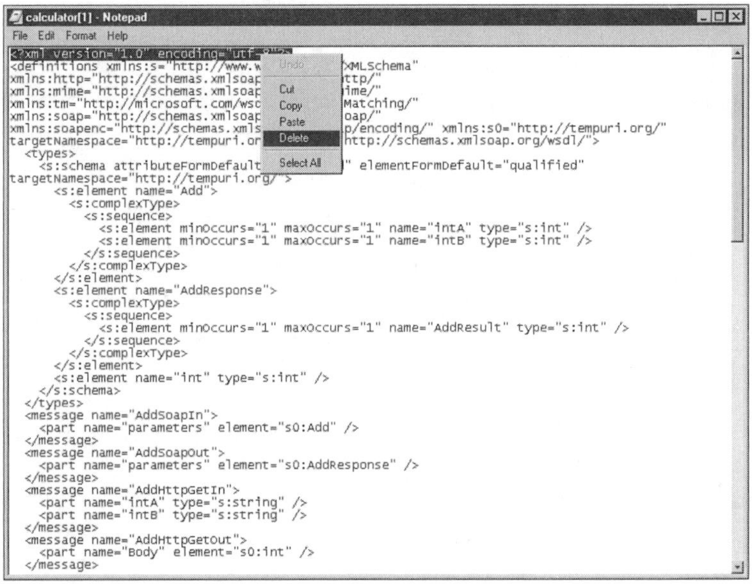

FIGURE 18.9
Delete the offending XML line from the service description.

Next, you'll have to modify `client.aspx` slightly to use this modified description instead of the URL. Change line 9 of Listing 18.2 to read as follows:

```
objSOAP.mssoapinit(Server.MapPath("calculator.wsdl"))
```

The first part of this statement is the same—calling the `mssoapinit` function. Now instead of passing it the URL of the service, you pass in the file name of the modified WSDL file you created in the previous step.

You cannot, however, pass the filename in by itself because the `SOAPClient` won't know where exactly to look for it. The `Server.MapPath` function, given a filename, returns the full path of the file. For example, this statement would return `c:\inetpub\wwwroot\calculator.wsdl`, assuming that's where you saved the file.

Leaving everything else the same, you should now be able to access the XML Web service and see the correct output, shown in Figure 18.7.

The SOAP Toolkit has loads of other useful tools, so be sure to check out the documentation that came with the toolkit.

Summary

Security is a very complex topic and must be taken into consideration when designing any application. This past hour you learned what is means to secure an XML Web service and how to go about doing so.

A secure XML Web service means one that cannot be accessed by unauthorized users. SOAP provides no security mechanisms, so without other means of protection, any visitor could use any XML Web service.

Security in IIS is handled via several different steps and methods. Authentication is the process of verifying a user's identity, authorization is making sure a user has access to specified resources, and impersonation allows IIS to restrict its own privileges to provide additional security.

Authentication is implemented in three different forms: Forms, Passport, and Windows modes. Forms and Passport modes redirect unauthenticated users to login forms for them to provide credentials. With Windows mode, IIS passes the authentication chores to the OS.

Integrated Windows mode is in turn implemented in three additional forms. Basic is the simplest and least secure. A client user supplies credentials via a pop-up box, and the data is transmitted as plain text across the network to the server. Digest mode works similarly, but the credentials are encrypted. Finally, Integrated Windows (or NTLM) mode allows the client and server machine to communicate directly without user intervention. The two machines compare user identities, and access is allowed or denied appropriately.

You used the SOAP Toolkit to easily build an XML Web service client. Using the `SOAPClient` object and the `ConnectorProperty` collection, you are able to supply authentication usernames and passwords to access secure XML Web services.

In the next hour, you'll learn about using XML Web services asynchronously. This allows your clients to continue doing other tasks while waiting for an XML Web service to return results.

Q&A

Q Will the SOAPClient authentication method work with Digest and Integrated Windows authentication modes?

A It will work with Digest mode. However, due to the way credential information is sent in Integrated Windows mode, trying to supply `AuthUser` and `AuthPassword` values when the service is secured in this way will result in errors. With Integrated Windows mode, the only option is to log into the computer calling the client as a valid user of the service.

Q I can't select digest authentication. What gives?

A Digest authentication mode is new to Windows 2000 and, as such, requires IIS 5.0 to run. It also requires that your domain controller is running Windows 2000—check with your network administrator or the Windows 2000 help files.

Q What is the difference between using SOAP headers for security and the method described here?

A With SOAP headers, you can pass username and password information from a client to the service. Recall from Chapter 4 that the `mustUnderstand` attribute requires the service to evaluate the headers, providing a very good means for implementing authentication.

Each method has its own benefits. Using the methods described in this hour, you have to write very little code and can rely on IIS and Windows to authenticate users for you. Using SOAP headers, you'll have to write much more code, but you have more flexibility in authenticating users; you can validate them against a database, a text file, or any other method you choose.

Additionally, using IIS authentication, the user is prevented from ever reaching the XML Web service until he or she is authenticated. Using SOAP headers, the user must be able to access the service in order to send the headers; in other words, visitors are able to take one more step inside your application before being stopped. The method you choose will be largely influenced by your application and the method you feel most comfortable with. The SOAP Toolkit can handle both.

Q What about SSL? Can I use that to secure my services?

A Absolutely. The Secure Sockets Layer is another protocol that can be used to access Web sites and services. The `ConnectorProperty` of the `SOAPClient` collection provides two properties—`UseSSL` and `SSLClientCertificateName`—that are expressly designed to use SSL. See the SOAP Toolkit documentation for more information.

(Note that SSL is a slower protocol than HTTP, so using it may slow down your application.)

Q I've been hearing lately of a lot of security holes in IIS 5.0. Will this be a problem for my XML Web service?

A That's a tough question to answer. Since XML Web services are part of .NET, it is an entirely new paradigm—many existing holes and hacks don't exist in .NET. However, there may be other holes that no one is aware of yet. There is quite a stir in the development community about the security of XML Web services, with many differing opinions.

In short, existing methods may be used to hack IIS, but XML Web services aren't vulnerable to these attacks.

Workshop

The Workshop is designed to help you review what you've learned in this hour and to point you ahead to the material that will be covered in future hours.

Quiz

1. What are the three steps of security?

   A Authentication, authorization, and impersonation.

2. (True or False) IIS always requires users to be authenticated.

   A False. By default, anonymous users are allowed entry.

3. Which is most secure: Basic, Digest, or Integrated Windows modes?

   A Integrated Windows mode.

4. (True or False) The SOAP specification addresses security issues.

   A False, though there are rumors of advances being made.

5. How can XML encoding cause problems? How do you get around it?

   A XML often specifies an encoding type (typically UTF-8) in the first line of an XML file. The encoding specified by this line must match the actual encoding of the file, or you will receive an error.

   To remedy the problem, simply remove the offending first line in the WSDL description and save the modified file.

Exercises

1. Build an XML Web service that returns the reverse of a string passed into it. For example, passing in `"Web Services"` would return `"secivreS beW"`. Secure this service with Basic authentication.

A The code for the service is as follows:

```
<%@ WebService Language="VB" Class="StringReverser" %>

Imports System.Web.Services
Imports Microsoft.VisualBasic

public Class StringReverser : Inherits WebService
   <WebMethod()> Public Function Reverse(strValue as String) _
      As String
      dim i as Integer, strReversed as String

       For i = 1 to strValue.Length
          strReversed = strReversed & Mid(strValue, _
             strValue.Length - i + 1, 1)
       Next i

       Return(strReversed)
    End Function

 End Class
```

Save this file as `StringReverser.asmx` and place it in the `secure` directory. Disable anonymous access and Integrated Windows authentication for this directory via the Internet Services Manager, and enable Basic authentication.

2. Create the client using the SOAP Toolkit to access the service created in Exercise 1.

A The code for the client is as follows:

```
<%@ Page Language="VB" Debug=true%>

<script runat="server">
   Sub Page_Load(Src As Object, e As EventArgs)
      dim objSOAP

      objSOAP = Server.Createobject("MSSOAP.SoapClient")

      objSOAP.mssoapinit("http://localhost/secure/
      StringReverser.asmx?WSDL")

       objSOAP.ConnectorProperty("AuthUser") = "uname"
       objSOAP.ConnectorProperty("AuthPassword") = "pword"

       lblMessage.Text = objSOAP.Reverse("Web Services Rule!")

       objSOAP = nothing
    End Sub
 </script>

 <html><body>
    The answer is: <asp:Label id="lblMessage" runat="server"/>
 </body></html>
```

If you are having encoding issues, view the source of the WSDL description of the service from Exercise 1, delete the first line with the encoding, and save it as `StringReverser.wsdl` in the same location as your client file. Then, change line 9 to read:

```
9:        objSOAP.mssoapinit(Server.MapPath("StringReverser.wsdl"))
```

HOUR 19

Asynchronous Operations

In this hour, you will examine the various methods for calling an XML Web service's methods asynchronously. Throughout this hour, you will study the `Begin` and `End` methods that are generated for your service and how they are used to allow client applications to call your service and wait for it to respond while still carrying out other operations.

In this hour, we will discuss the following:

- Asynchronous operations
- `Callback` functions
- The `WaitHandle` class
- The `IAsyncResult` interface

Asynchronous Operations in XML Web Services

Up to this point in the book, any client applications that you have seen have made calls to XML Web services synchronously. What this means is that when a call to a service was made, processing on the client side stopped and waited for the service to return a value before the client would resume running its own code.

In most cases, this manner of processing is perfectly acceptable, but what happens when the XML Web service method being called requires a considerable amount of time to process a request? In these cases, the client application sits idle and does nothing. Situations such as this require the ability to call a method and move on to the processing of other tasks. This is called asynchronous calling.

The code to implement the asynchronous calling of an XML Web service's methods is actually created automatically whenever you add a Web reference to your client applications or use the `WSDL.exe` to create a proxy class. At this point, you have probably already seen the methods to facilitate asynchronous calling when you were building the clients in previous hours. For every method exposed by the service, the proxy also generates two additional methods whose names begin with the prefixes `Begin` and `End`. If you added a Web reference to a service containing a method called `myMethod`, the proxy class would also contain `BeginmyMethod` and `EndmyMethod`.

The `Begin` method is used to make the asynchronous call to the service. This method accepts all of the parameters as the synchronous version of the method but also adds two additional methods, `callback` and `asyncState`, which you will learn more about later in this hour. The `Begin` method returns an object of type `WebClientAsyncResult`, which implements the `IAsyncResult` interface. This object is used in determining when to call the `End` method, whose return type is that of the synchronous method.

A Web Service to Call Asynchronously

In order to test the ability of a client application to call a service asynchronously, you will need a service to call. Create a new ASP.NET XML Web service called `ReturnTitleHolder`.

Add the following class to your service. This class will be used as the return type of the rather simple service that you are creating.

```
Public Class TitleHolder
     Public Name As String
     Public Belt As String
End Class
```

Now you can add the method shown in Listing 19.1 to your code. This method accepts an integer value and, based on that number, sets the `TitleHolder` object, `oBelt`, properties to contain a WWF Title Holder and the name of said title. This rather whimsical bit of information is then returned by the method.

LISTING 19.1 An XML Web Service to Return Wrestling Title Holders

```
<WebMethod()> _
Public Function Champ(ByVal Number As Integer) As TitleHolder
   Dim iNum As Integer
   Dim oBelt As New TitleHolder()

   iNum = Number Mod 5

   Select Case iNum
     Case 0
        oBelt.Name = "Steve Austin"
        oBelt.Belt = "WWF World Heavyweight"
     Case 1
        oBelt.Name = "EDGE"
        oBelt.Belt = "WWF Intercontinental"
     Case 2
        oBelt.Name = "Dudley Boys"
        oBelt.Belt = "WWF Tag Team"
     Case 3
        oBelt.Name = "The Rock"
        oBelt.Belt = "WCW World Heavyweight"
     Case 4
        oBelt.Name = "Tajiri"
        oBelt.Belt = "WCW U.S. Heavyweight"
   End Select

   Return oBelt
End Function
```


Building a Client Application That Utilizes Asynchronous Calls

Now that you have created an XML Web service to call, it is time to build a client application that will consume it. For this example, a simple Visual Basic Windows application, named `AsyncMethod`, will suffice.

The first thing that you will need to do is add a Web reference to `ReturnTitleHolder`. After you have done that, you will need to add three labels, three textboxes, and two command buttons to `Form1` of your new application, as shown in Figure 19.1.

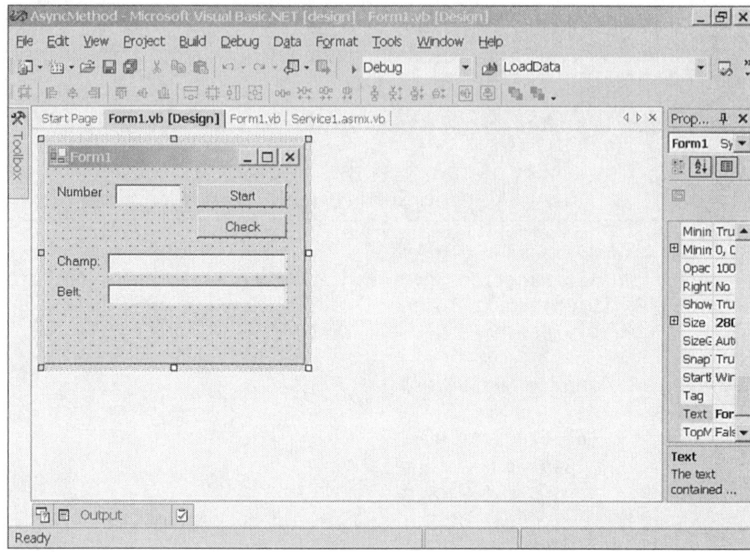

FIGURE 19.1
`Async` *method test form.*

Table 19.1 shows the property settings for the controls that you just added to `Form1`.

TABLE 19.1 Control Property Setting for `Form1` of `AsyncMethod`

Control	*Property*	*Setting*
`Label1`	Text	`Number:`
`Label2`	Text	`Champ:`
`Label3`	Text	`Belt:`
`TextBox1`	Name	`txtNum`
`TextBox2`	Name	`txtChamp`
`TextBox3`	Name	`txtBelt`
`Button1`	Name	`btnStart`
	Text	`Start`
`Button2`	Name	`btnCheck`
	`Text`	`Check`

`IAsyncResult` Interface

`IAsyncResult` is an interface that is implemented by the return objects of asynchronous operations. It, or more correctly the object implementing it, is used to determine if processing has completed during an asynchronous operation. The properties of the `IAsyncResult` interface are shown in Table 19.2.

TABLE 19.2 Properties of the `IAsyncResult` Interface

Method	*Description*
`AsyncState`	Gets the object that was passed into the `BeginmyMethod` method call's final argument, also known as `asyncState`.
`AsyncWaitHandle`	Gets the `WaitHandle` Object that can be used to determine how method calls, especially in situations where multiple calls are being made, are handled. Through the `WaitHandle`, processing can wait for one or all of the methods to return before resuming.
`CompletedSynchronously`	Is `True` if the method call, `BeginmyMethod`, completed synchronously.
`IsCompleted`	Returns True after the method call has completed. This is usually used as the signal that it is safe to call the `EndmyMethod` method.

In order to demonstrate the working of `IAsyncResult`, add the following declarations to the general declarations section of `Form1`.

```
Dim oTitleHolder As New localhost.Service1()
Dim aReturn As IAsyncResult
Dim oChamp As New localhost.TitleHolder()
```

Now, you can add the code in Listing 19.2 to the Click event of Command Button `btnStart`. Line 4 of the code calls the `BeginChamp` method—the asynchronous way to call the `Champ` method—and accepts the `IasyncReturn` implementing return object as `aReturn`. Since we are not utilizing `callback` functions, the `callback` and `asyncState` arguments are set to `Nothing`. In C#, you would set these values to `Null`.

LISTING 19.2 Calling the `Champ` Method Asynchronously

```
1:    Private Sub btnStart_Click(ByVal sender As System.Object, _
2:            ByVal e As System.EventArgs) Handles btnStart.Click
3:
4:        aReturn = oTitleHolder.BeginChamp(CInt(txtNum.Text),_
5:                    Nothing, Nothing)
6:
7:    End Sub
```

With the method called, you now need ways to determine when processing is complete and to retrieve the result of the operation. This is done by checking to see if the `IsCompleted` property of `Iasyncresult` returns `True` or not.

Add the code in Listing 19.3 to the Click event of `btnCheck`. This code causes the `IsCompleted` property to be checked and, upon receiving `True`, a call to be made to `EndChamp`. When this call is made, line 5, the Textboxes `txtChamp` and `txtBelt`, are populated with the results of the call.

LISTING 19.3 Polling `IAsyncResult` to Determine If the `Champ` Method Has Completed Processing

```
1:   Private Sub btnCheck_Click(ByVal sender As System.Object, _
2:         ByVal e As System.EventArgs) Handles btnCheck.Click
3:
4:     If aReturn.IsCompleted Then
5:       oChamp = oTitleHolder.EndChamp(aReturn)
6:       txtChamp.Text = oChamp.Name
7:       txtBelt.Text = oChamp.Belt
8:     Else
9:       MsgBox("Keep Trying")
10:    End If
11:
12:  End Sub
```

When you run this new client application, type an integer into `txtNum` and click the Start button and the Check button in quick succession. During this first call, the Server should still be processing the request and you should receive the message in Figure 19.2.

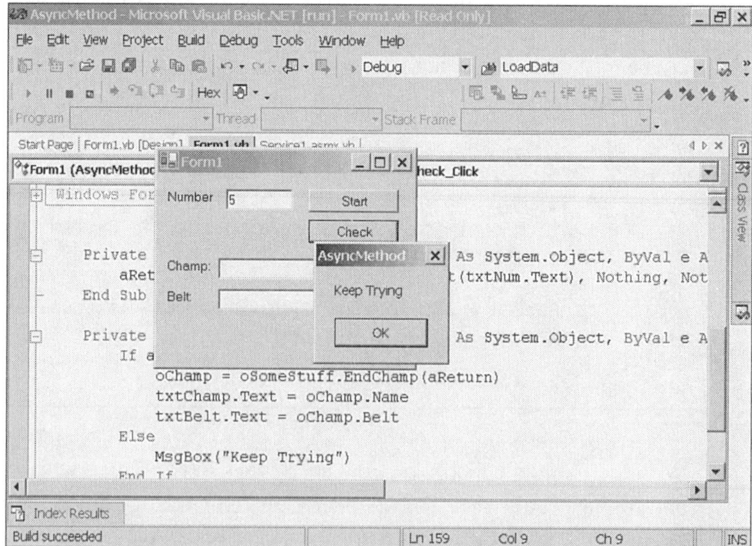

FIGURE 19.2
The `Champ` *method is still running.*

Eventually, the service should be ready to return, and the `EndChamp` method should be called. At this time, you should receive information similar to that in Figure 19.3.

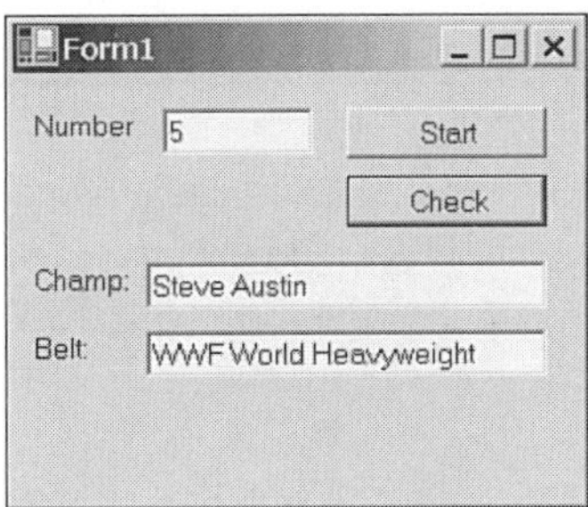

FIGURE 19.3
The `Champ` *method returns.*

This method of calling a service can be very useful if you know that an XML Web service method will require some time to process and you wish to run a few simple tasks. One way to accomplish this would be to make your call and then enter a `while` loop that checks for the return and continues to process other tasks until a value is returned.

`callback` Functions

A `callback` function is a function residing in the client application that is called when the `Begin` method is finished processing. Typically, the `callback` function contains the call to the `End` method. The `callback` method is set up by passing its address into an object of type `AsyncCallback` and then passing this object to the `Begin` method. The syntax for doing this is as follows:

```
Dim cb as New AsyncCallBack(AddressOf CallBackFunction)
Service.BeginMethod(arg1, arg2, .., cb, Service)
```

In C#, this would be

```
AsyncCallback cb = new AsyncCallback(CallBackFunction)
Service.BeginMethod(arg1, arg2, .., cb, Service)
```

Alter the Click event of `btnStart` so that it contains the code in Listing 19.4. This code sets the `ChampCallBack` function, shown in Listing 19.5, as the `callback` function used in the call to `BeginChamp` in line 6.

LISTING 19.4 Using a `Callback` Function in an Asynchronous Method Call

```
1:   Private Sub btnStart_Click(ByVal sender As System.Object, _
2:           ByVal e As System.EventArgs) Handles btnStart.Click
3:
4:      Dim cbOutput As New AsyncCallback(AddressOf ChampCallback)
5:
```

continues

LISTING 19.4 Continued

```
    oTitleHolder.BeginChamp(CInt(txtNum.Text), cbOutput, oTitleHolder)

End Sub
```

When `BeginChamp` is done processing, a call is automatically made to the `ChampCallback` function. In line 3 of the function, a call is made to `EndChamp` and the return value is retrieved. This value is then used to populate the form with the WWF Title Holder and his appropriate belt.

LISTING 19.5 `Callback` Function for Handling the Return of the `Champ` Method

```
1:  Private Sub ChampCallback(ByVal aResult As IAsyncResult)
2:
3:    oChamp = oTitleHolder.EndChamp(aResult)
4:    txtChamp.Text = oChamp.Name
5:    txtBelt.Text = oChamp.Belt
6:
7:  End Sub
```

WaitHandle

The `WaitHandle` object is used to allow client applications to make asynchronous calls to an XML Web service and then wait for them to return. The `WaitHandle` allows the calling application to resume processing after either one or all of the called methods have completed processing.

The static members of the `WaitHandle` object are shown in Table 19.3. These are the methods that you may use without declaring an object of type `WaitHandle`; for example:

```
WaitHandle.WaitAny(arrayofWaitHandles)
```

TABLE 19.3 Static Methods of `WaitHandle`

Method	*Description*
`WaitAll`	Halts processing until all method callsreturn
`WaitAny`	Halts processing until any method calls return

Both methods accept an array of `WaitHandle` objects, one for each method that is being processed, and an optional parameter, either an integer or a timespan object, that determines how long the `WaitHandle` should wait before timing out.

At this point, add a new form, `Form2`, to your project and set it as the startup form. To this form you will add nine textboxes and one control button, as shown in Figure 19.4.

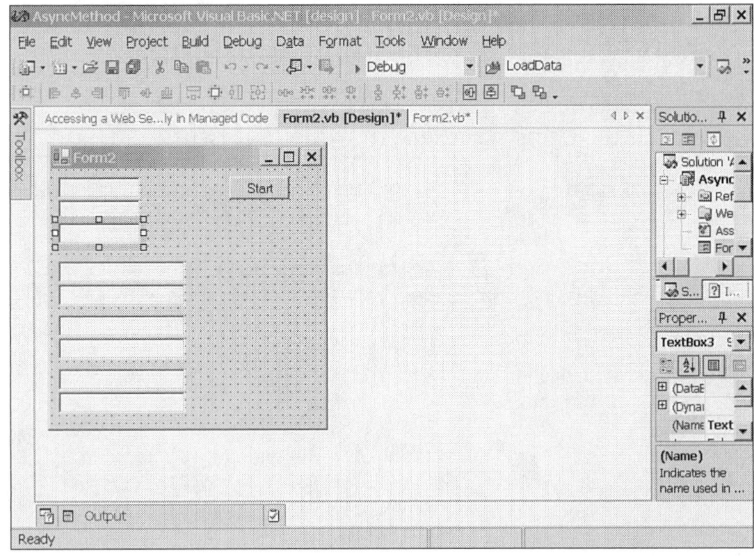

FIGURE 19.4
New form for testing asynchronous method calls.

Set the control properties to those shown in Table 19.4.

TABLE 19.4 Control Property Setting for `Form2` of `AsyncMethod`

Control	*Property*	*Setting*
`TextBox1`	Name	`txtNum1`
`TextBox2`	Name	`txtNum2`
`TextBox3`	Name	`txtNum3`
`TextBox4`	Name	`txtChamp1`
`TextBox5`	Name	`txtBelt1`
`TextBox6`	Name	`txtChamp2`
`TextBox7`	Name	`txtBelt2`
`TextBox8`	Name	`txtChamp3`
`TextBox9`	Name	`txtBelt3`
`Button1`	Name	`btnStart`
	Text	`Start`

Add the `btnStart` Click event, shown in Listing 19.6, to your code. This code makes three separate calls to the `BeginChamp` method, in lines 11 through 13, and then creates an array of `WaitHandle` objects, lines 15 through 18, with which to monitor them. This array is passed into the `WaitAll` method of the `WaitHandle` object, line 21, and processing halts there until all of the called methods return.

LISTING 19.6 Using `WaitHandle` to Call Asynchronous XML Web Service Methods

```
1:  Private Sub btnStart_Click(ByVal sender As System.Object,
2:          ByVal e As System.EventArgs) Handles btnStart.Click
3:
4:     Dim oTitleHolder As New localhost.Service1()
5:     Dim oChamp As New localhost.TitleHolder()
6:
7:     Dim aResult1 As IAsyncResult
8:     Dim aResult2 As IAsyncResult
9:     Dim aResult3 As IAsyncResult
10:
11:    aResult1 = oTitleHolder.BeginChamp(CInt(txtNum1.Text), Nothing, Nothing)
12:    aResult2 = oTitleHolder.BeginChamp(CInt(txtNum2.Text), Nothing, Nothing)
13:    aResult3 = oTitleHolder.BeginChamp(CInt(txtNum3.Text), Nothing, Nothing)
14:
15:    Dim whResults(2) As WaitHandle
16:    whResults(0) = aResult1.AsyncWaitHandle
17:    whResults(1) = aResult2.AsyncWaitHandle
18:    whResults(2) = aResult3.AsyncWaitHandle
19:
20:
21:    WaitHandle.WaitAll(whResults)
22:
23:    If aResult1.IsCompleted Then
24:      oChamp = oTitleHolder.EndChamp(aResult1)
25:      txtChamp1.Text = oChamp.Name
26:      txtBelt1.Text = oChamp.Belt
27:    End If
28:
29:    If aResult2.IsCompleted Then
30:      oChamp = oTitleHolder.EndChamp(aResult2)
31:      txtChamp2.Text = oChamp.Name
32:      txtBelt2.Text = oChamp.Belt
33:    End If
34:
35:    If aResult3.IsCompleted Then
36:      oChamp = oTitleHolder.EndChamp(aResult3)
37:      txtChamp3.Text = oChamp.Name
38:      txtBelt3.Text = oChamp.Belt
39:    End If
40:
41: End Sub
```

When you run the application this time, click the start button of `Form2`. The server will make three calls to the `BeginChamp` method and then, once all three have completed processing, `Form2` will be updated to contain all three Title Holders, as seen in Figure 19.5.

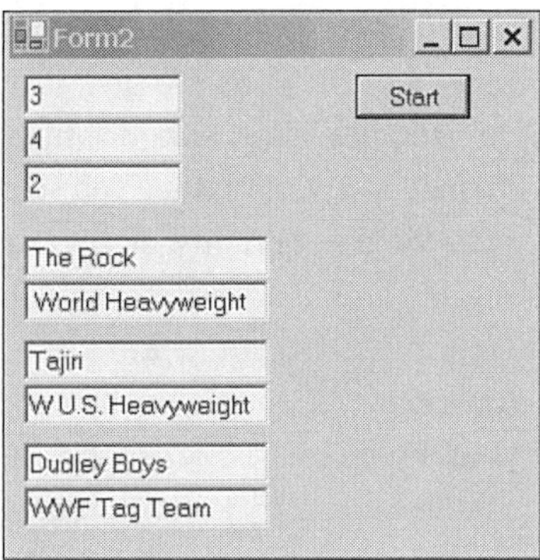

FIGURE 19.5
All returns for `Async`.

Now, change the `WaitAll` method of the `WaitHandle` object, line 21 of Listing 19.6, to a `WaitAny` method. This will cause processing to resume once any of the three methods has completed. Run the server again, and you should see results like those in Figure 19.6.

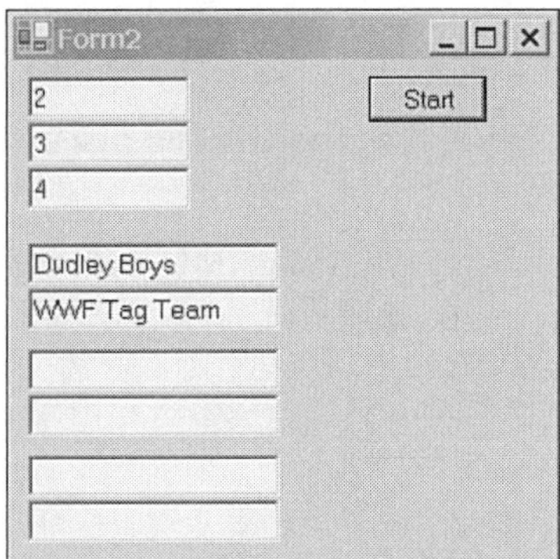

FIGURE 19.6
Returning the update `DataSet` *with* `DataTable` *bands.*

Summary

In this hour, you saw how to use the `Begin` and `End` versions of an XML Web service's methods in order to make asynchronous calls. You also learned how to use the `IAsyncResult` interface, implemented by the objects returned from `Begin` methods, in order to determine when a service's method had completed processing and was ready to deliver a return. You also examined how `callback` functions are used to process return values automatically, without the need for polling. Finally, you looked at how the `WaitHandle` object is used to provide synchronous handling of asynchronous calls.

Q&A

Q What is the purpose of making asynchronous calls if you are going to use the `WaitHandle` to stop processing and wait for a return?

A There are several reasons to use the `WaitHandle` and asynchronous calls instead of just using the synchronous version of the calls. To give just a couple of examples, out of many, where this might be appropriate, suppose that you are building a client application and performance is a great issue. You find a couple of different XML Web services that provide the functionality that you need and you use all of them in your application. Now, if you make your calls and use the `WaitAny` method, you need only to wait for the fastest one to return. This gives you speed as well as a failsafe against a down service. Another use of the `WaitHandle` is to call several methods at once, if your application relies on having all of their results before doing anything else, and use `WaitAny` to halt processing. This usually provides slightly better performance than making each call and then waiting for the return before making the next call.

Q How do `callback` functions help my application's performance?

A The use of `callback` functions allows your application to make a call to an XML Web service and then move on to other processing. When the original call is finished, a call to your `callback` function occurs, and that code is run. The main benefit of this is that your client application spends less time sitting idle.

Q I have always heard the term *threads* used when discussing asynchronous calling. What does that mean?

A When you make an asynchronous call to an XML Web service method, you are creating a new thread. A thread is simply a segment of code that executes simultaneously to your application.

Workshop

The Workshop is designed to help you review what you've learned in this hour and to point you ahead to the material that will be covered in future hours.

Quiz

1. What two methods would be called in an application that needed to execute an asynchronous call to an XML Web service method named `BoxScore`?

   A `BeginBoxScore` and `EndBoxScore`

2. What method of the `WaitHandle` object allows an application to resume processing when the first of any asynchronously called method finishes processing?

   A `WaitAny`

3. What is the return type of `BeginmyMethod`, created to handle asynchronous calls to a method called `myMethod`?

   A `IAsyncResult`

4. What property of `IAsyncResult` is used to determine if it is okay to call an `End` method?

   A `IsCompleted`

5. How would you call a method, `BeginStockQuote`, and pass it a `callback` function named `ProcessQuote`? `BeginQuote` accepts one argument, a string type named `sStock`. The object reference to the services proxy is called `oQuotes`.

   A
   ```
   Dim cb as New AsyncCallBack(AddressOf ProcessQuote)

   Service.BeginStockQuote(sStock, cb, oQuotes)
   ```

Exercises

Practice writing applications that make use of asynchronous calls to the XML Web services that you created earlier. As a starting point, try writing a simple application that accepts two integers and calls all four methods of the `FourFunctionCalc` XML Web service.

A The following code accepts two integers, entered into two textboxes on a form, and returns the results of the four methods of the `FourFunctionCalc`.

```
Dim oCalc As New localhost1.Service1()

Private Sub btnStart_Click(ByVal sender As System.Object, _
        ByVal e As System.EventArgs) Handles Button1.Click

   Dim cb1 As New AsyncCallback(AddressOf fAddHandler)
   oCalc.BeginAdd(CInt(TxtNum1.Text), CInt(TxtNum2.Text), cb1, oCalc)

   Dim cb2 As New AsyncCallback(AddressOf fSubHandler)
   oCalc.BeginSubtract(CInt(TxtNum1.Text), CInt(TxtNum2.Text), cb2, oCalc)

   Dim cb3 As New AsyncCallback(AddressOf fDivHandler)
   oCalc.BeginDivide(CInt(TxtNum1.Text), CInt(TxtNum2.Text), cb3, oCalc)

   Dim cb4 As New AsyncCallback(AddressOf fMultHandler)
   oCalc.BeginMultiply(CInt(TxtNum1.Text), CInt(TxtNum2.Text), cb4, oCalc)

End Sub

Private Sub fAddHandler(ByVal aResult As IAsyncResult)
   TextBox3.Text = oCalc.EndAdd(aResult)
End Sub
```

```
Private Sub fSubHandler(ByVal aResult As IAsyncResult)
   TxtSub.Text = oCalc.EndSubtract(aResult)
End Sub

Private Sub fDivHandler(ByVal aResult As IAsyncResult)
   TxtDiv.Text = oCalc.EndDivide(aResult)
End Sub

Private Sub fMultHandler(ByVal aResult As IAsyncResult)
   TxtMult.Text = oCalc.EndMultiply(aResult)
End Sub
```

HOUR 20

Debugging Your XML Web Services

In this hour, you will learn how to use some of the objects provided by Visual Studio. NET in order to debug your XML Web service applications. In particular, you will explore the `Debug` and `Trace` objects as ways of tracking what is happening inside your code. You will also learn to use tools, such as the Event Log, to track when events are occurring within your service.

Throughout this hour, we will discuss the following:

- The Debug object
- The Trace object
- Listeners
- The Event Log

Tracking XML Web Service Errors

As the XML Web services that you build become larger and more complex, it becomes crucial that you possess methods for tracking what happens within your code both in development and when it is in use. Visual Studio . NET and the .NET framework in general provide you with many ways to accomplish these very activities. Within Visual Studio .NET, you will find tools that allow you to log data as an application is running so that you can look back and see when and where values are changing; keep track of when application events fire, even when the service is being used in a production setting; and much more.

Automatic Tracing in XML Web Services

XML Web services are able to take advantage of the automatic tracing logs that are built into the ASP.NET framework upon which XML Web services were created. This automatic tracing allows XML Web service developers to trace requests to the service and the state of server variables and other information through the use of the Internet Explorer interface that you have used to test your services since Hour 7.

In order to enable the XML Web service to begin keeping a trace file, you need to alter the `Web.config` file. To do this, you need to use the Solution Explorer of Visual Studio.NET. To access the Solution Explorer, choose Solution Explorer from the View menu or press Ctrl+Alt+L. Once you have done this, bring the `Web.Config` file up in the code window.

Once inside the `Web.config` file, you will want to look for the entry pertaining to Trace. Figure 20.1 shows you the Trace entry in the configuration file.

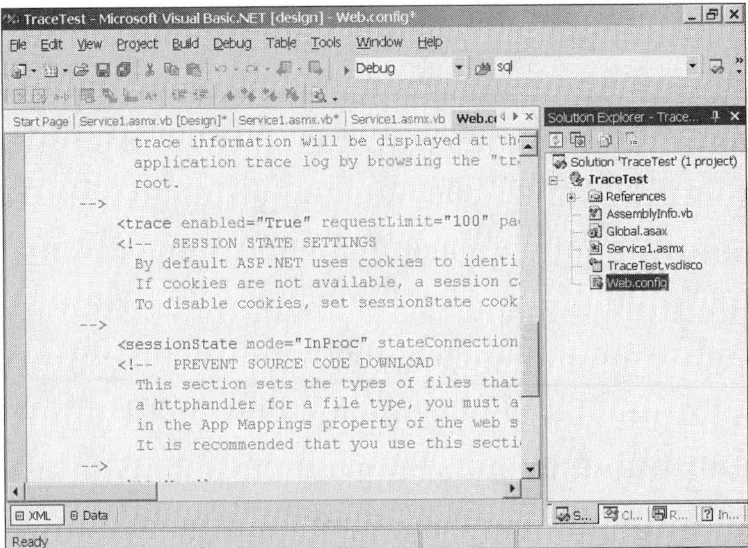

FIGURE 20.1
Editing the `Web.Config` *file.*

The Trace entry, shown next, provides you with the ability to customize several options of the XML Web service runtime environment. The first is the ability to turn the application level tracing on and off; this will have no effect on the Trace object features that you will explore later in this hour.

```
<trace enabled="false" requestLimit="10" pageOutput="false"_
traceMode="SortByTime" localOnly="true" />
```

First, change `enabled="false"` to `enabled="true"` and run the program. After Internet Explorer opens, invoke the HelloWorld method a few times in order to get some calls entered into the trace log. Now, in Internet Explorer, use the URL that is used to connect to your service, substituting `Service1.asmx` with `Trace.axd`, where Service1 is the name of your service. This will bring up the application trace file shown in Figure 20.2.

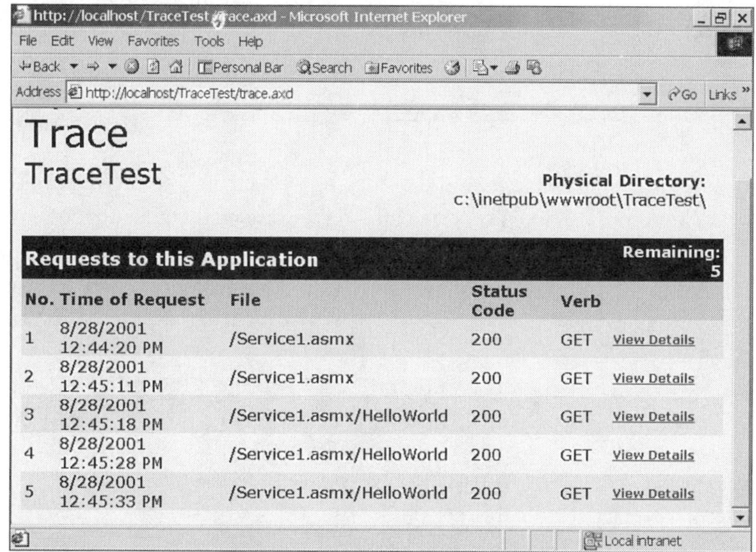

FIGURE 20.2
The Trace report after calling some XML Web service methods.

Notice, up near the top right of the trace file in Figure 20.2, the line `"Remaining: 5."` This line lets you know that the trace log will store five more requests before it starts deleting the earliest requests. This number is controlled by the `requestLimit` parameter of the trace tag in `Web.config` file.

Clicking *View Details* will bring up the details for the specific XML Web service request made by a client, as shown in Figure 20.3. This information includes the state of server variables, time of request, and much more. This can be very useful if you just need to look in and check on specific usage in a low volume XML Web service or if you suspect that something unusual is occurring on the server where the service is running.

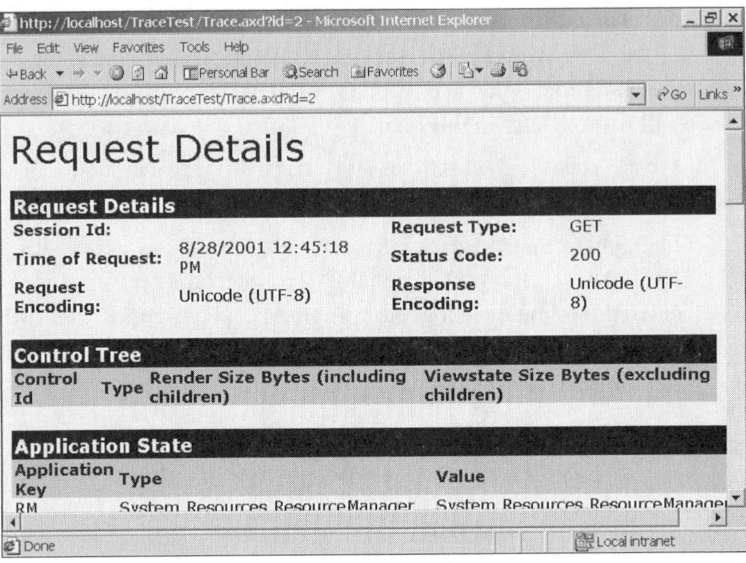

FIGURE 20.3
Request details for a specific call to TraceTest.

It is also possible to add the trace reports directly to the bottom of the page that is generated for individual service calls via the use of the `pageOutput` property, also found in the `Web.Config` file. If `pageOutPut` is set to true, the trace report is added directly to the bottom of your page, as shown in Figure 20.4. Note that the URL for this request is still a `.asax` extension.

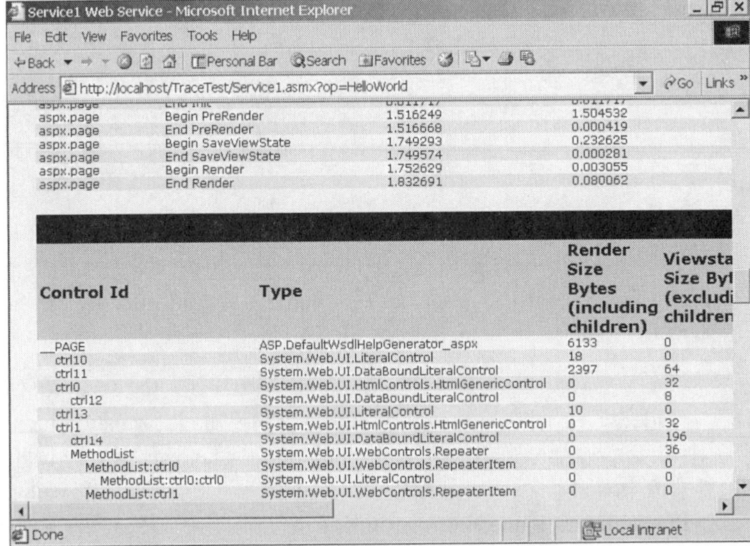

FIGURE 20.4
The Trace report displayed at the bottom of your `WebService.ASAX` *page.*

This last feature is far more useful in standard ASP.NET programs than it is in an XML Web service, as the XML return data from the service's method does not include any trace information.

Tracking Your Application with the `Debug` Object

One of the primary methods for debugging an application has been the use of the Debug object. This still holds true in Visual Studio. NET, only now the Debug object offers a richer set of methods and can work with other objects, called listeners, to provide you with a means to pipe Debug messages to text files and other sources.

The most common use of the Debug object is to write information to the Output window of Visual Studio. This can be done as follows:

```
Debug.Write("Here is some text")
```

This command will output the following to the Output window:

```
Here is some text
```

A further call

```
Debug.Write(" and some more!")
```

will change the output to

```
Here is some text and some more!
```

Notice that the second call to write added its output to the same line as the first. If you need to advance to the next line when using Debug, you use the `WriteLine` method, which is identical to the `Write` method with the added benefit of including a line terminator at the end of the string.

Table 20.1 shows the properties commonly used when dealing with the Debug object. The `AutoFlush` property and the Listeners collection deal specifically with using Debug in conjunction with listeners and will be dealt with a little later in this hour.

20

TABLE 20.1 Common Properties of the `Debug` Object

Property	*Description*
`AutoFlush`	Indicates that output should automatically be written from the Listener objects to the target media
`IndentLevel`	Level of indentation on output
`IndentSize`	Number of spaces of indentation
`Listeners`	Listeners Collection

The most commonly used methods of the `Debug` object can be seen in Table 20.2. These include various methods to write information to the output windows, or to listeners, and a few, such as `Indent`, that control the formatting of output.

TABLE 20.2 Common Methods of the `Debug` Object

Method	*Description*
`Assert`	Display a message if a supplied conditional is false
`Close`	Flushes the output buffer and closes all listeners
`Fail`	Returns an error message
`Flush`	Writes any buffered messages to all open listeners
`Indent`	Increments the indent level by one
`Unindent`	Decrements the indent level by one
`Write`	Writes supplied information to all open listeners
`WriteIf`	Writes supplied information to all open listeners if Boolean conditional returns `True`
`WriteLine`	Same as `Write`, but includes a line terminator at the end of output
`WriteLineIf`	Same as `WriteIf`, but includes a line terminator at the end of output

The methods `WriteIf` and `WriteLineIf` take the conditional as well as the message text and write output only if the conditional is true.

```
Debug.WriteIf(fConditional, sMessage)
```

If the `Indent` method is called, the output will be indented forward the number of spaces indicated by the `IndentSize` property, the default is five spaces. The `Unindent` method can be called to move further output back the same number of spaces.

Runtime Tracking with `Trace` Object

A quick look at the `Trace` object shows it to function nearly identical to the `Debug` object. In fact, you can use Tables 20.1 and 20.2 to learn about the properties and methods commonly used with the `Trace` object.

Where the `Trace` object differs from `Debug`, and where its true power lies, is in how it differs from `Debug` when an application is compiled. `Debug` statements are automatically left out of an application during compilation. This allows you to include debug statements throughout your code without having to worry about stripping them all out at some later point in time. Trace objects, on the other hand, stay in your code and continue to write messages. This is especially handy if Listeners are being used to gather these messages up and redirect them to various output sources such as text files.

Using Listeners to Write Trace Returns

Listeners, such as `TextWriteTraceListener` and `EventLogTraceListener`, are objects that allow the `Trace` and `Debug` objects to write output to various output sources. These sources include console windows, text files, and the Windows Event Log.

To use Listeners, you simply create any new listeners of the type that you need and add them to the `Listeners` collection of your `Trace` or `Debug` object as in lines 2 and 3 of Listing 20.1. After the `Listeners` have been added, any use of the `Trace` or `Debug` objects' `Write` methods will cause the message text to be outputed to all of the listeners.

The general syntax for creating a new `TextWriterTraceListener` is as follows:

```
Dim myListener as New TextWriterTraceListener(oType, [sName])
```

In the above, `sName` is an optional name for the new instance and `oType` can be either a Stream object, a TextWriter object, or a file name. In order to write to the console, for example, you would use the stream `Console.Out`. Listing 20.1 makes use of Stream objects in order to output to a text file. The Stream object is a member of the System.IO namespace and must be included by adding the following line into the namespaces area of your code:

```
Imports System.IO
```

LISTING 20.1 Writing to Multiple Listeners

```
1:   Dim myFile As Stream = File.Create("c:\TestFile.txt")
2:   Dim myListener As New TextWriterTraceListener(myFile)
3:   Trace.Listeners.Add(myListener)
4:
5:   Dim myFile2 As Stream = File.Create("c:\TestFile2.txt")
6:   Dim myListener2 As New TextWriterTraceListener(myFile2)
7:   Trace.Listeners.Add(myListener2)
8:
9:   Trace.WriteLine("This is Test Output")
10:
11:  myListener2.WriteLine("I am in TestFile2")
12:
13:  Trace.WriteLine("More Output to both")
14:
15:  Trace.WriteLine("I'll add my two cents")
16:
17:  myListener.Flush()
18:  myListener.Close()
19:
20:  myListener2.Flush()
21:  myListener2.Close()
```

The code in Listing 20.1 makes use of two separate Listeners in order to show how both the collection and the individual Listeners can be used to write output. In lines 9, 13, and 15 the `Trace` object writes various lines of output and the listeners collection writes them to `TestFile.txt` and `TestFile2.txt`. The output written to `TestFile.txt` is shown below.

```
This is Test Output
More Output to both
I'll add my two cents
```

In line 11, the `WriteLine` method of one of the Listeners, `myListener2`, is used directly to write output to `TestFile2.txt`, without sending the message to `myListener1` as well. You can see the additional line `"I am in TestFile2"` in the output to `TestFile2` below.

```
This is Test Output
I am in TestFile2
More Output to both
I'll add my two cents
```

The `TextWriterTraceListener` provides several of the same properties provided by the `Debug` and `Trace` objects for dealing with indentation. It also provides properties for setting and retrieving information about the Listener itself. Table 20.3 lists the most commonly called properties of the `TextWriterTraceListener`.

TABLE 20.3 Common Properties of the `TextWriterTraceListener` Object

Method	*Description*
`IndentLevel`	Level of indentation on output
`IndentSize`	Number of spaces of indentation
`Name`	Name for the `Trace` Listener
`Writer`	Text writer that receives output

The more commonly used methods of the `TextWriterTraceListener` are shown in Table 20.4. The `close` object can be used to close a particular write so that it stops outputting. Care should be taken to make sure that the listener isn't added to the Listeners collection and then written to specifically and closed in a function or subroutine that will be called again. If this happens, your calls to the `TextWriterTraceListener` will produce errors.

TABLE 20.4 Common Methods of the `TextWriterTraceListener` Object

Method	*Description*
`Close`	Closes the writer
`Fail`	Sends error message to listener
`Flush`	Flushes the output buffer
`Write`	Writes supplied information to all open listeners
`WriteLine`	Same as `Write`, but includes a line terminator at the end of output

Writing Events to the Event Log

One very useful feature in tracking the performance and usage of an XML Web service in either testing or production is the ability to write events to the Windows Event Log. The Event Log, for those of you unfamiliar with Windows Servers, is a database of event information that system administers can browse through the use of the Event Viewer. The Event Viewer can be found under Administrative Tools from the Windows Main Menu.

Tracking meaningful events, such as failed authentication attempts, accessing of certain critical data, or the occurrence of fatal errors, can greatly help in the maintenance and security of an XML Web service.

In order to write to the Event Log, you need to make use of the `EventLog` object within your code. `EventLog` can be found in the `System.Diagnostics` namespace. One of the main functions of the `EventLog` object are `CreateEventSource`, which can be used to create a new Log, such as one dedicated to a particular XML Web service, or to register your application with an existing log. Its general syntax is

```
EventLog.CreateEventSource(sSource, sLogName, [sMachineName])
```

`sSource` represents the name the Name of the application, `sLogName` is the name of the Log being written, and `sMachineName` is the optional name of the computer to which the event should be logged.

20

Also, important to the use of the `EventLog` object is the `WriteEntry` method. The write entry method is used throughout your code to write events to the log. With the `WriteEntry` method, you can write to any of the Windows standard logs, such as Application Log, Security Log, and System Log, or create your own as you previously saw. The most common usage of the `WriteEntry` method is

```
EventLog.WriteEntry(sSource, sMessage, oType)
```

In this code, `sSource` is a string by which the application is registered on the specific computer, `sMessage` is some string message that you are writing to the log, and `oType` is the type of entry using `EventLogEntryType`. `EventLogEntryType` is an enumeration containing types, including Error, Information, and Warning.

The most common methods of the `EventLog` object can be seen in Table 20.5. Generally speaking, you will probably delete logs and log entries from the Event Viewer and not from code.

TABLE 20.5 Common Methods of the `EventLog` Object

Method	*Description*
`CreateEventSource`	Allows an application to write to a log and creates a new Log on the system if the listed one does not exist
`Delete`	Deletes a Log
`DeleteEventSource`	Deletes a log from the event log
`Exists`	Returns True is the specified log exists
`GetEventLogs`	Returns an array of event logs
`SourceExists`	Checks the event logs for a log
`WriteEntry`	Writes an entry to the log

The properties listed in Table 20.6 are the most commonly used instance properties of the `EventLog`. Calling them instance properties means that a new instance of an `EventLog` object must be called in order for these properties to be called, as follows:

```
Dim myLog As New EventLog()
myLog.Log = "FourFunctionCalc"
```

`LogDisplayName`, in particular, is useful if you wish to provide users with some information on where to look in the Event Viewer to check on your application.

TABLE 20.6 Common Instance Properties of the `EventLog` Object

Property	*Description*
`Entries`	Contents of the current log
`Log`	Name of the log being used
`LogDisplayName`	The display name for the log
`MachineName`	The name of the computer on which the log resides
`Source`	The name of the event log

Listing 20.2 shows some code that was used to access a log called `TraceTest`; it creates the log the very first time that it is called and writes an event to the log.

LISTING 20.2 Writing to the `EventLog`

```
Dim sSource As String = "WebServiceEvents"
Dim sLogName As String = "TraceTest"

If Not EventLog.SourceExists(sSource) Then
  EventLog.CreateEventSource(sSource, sLogName)
End If

Dim Log As New EventLog()

Log.Source = sSource
Log.WriteEntry("Some Web Event Happened", EventLogEntryType.Information)
```

Compare the code in Listing 20.2 to the log pictured in Figure 20.5. Notice how the source used in the `CreateEventSource` method, `sSource`, is displayed as the source of the event. This is useful if you wish to have several XML Web services, or even several portions of the same service, use a common log but display their events under different names.

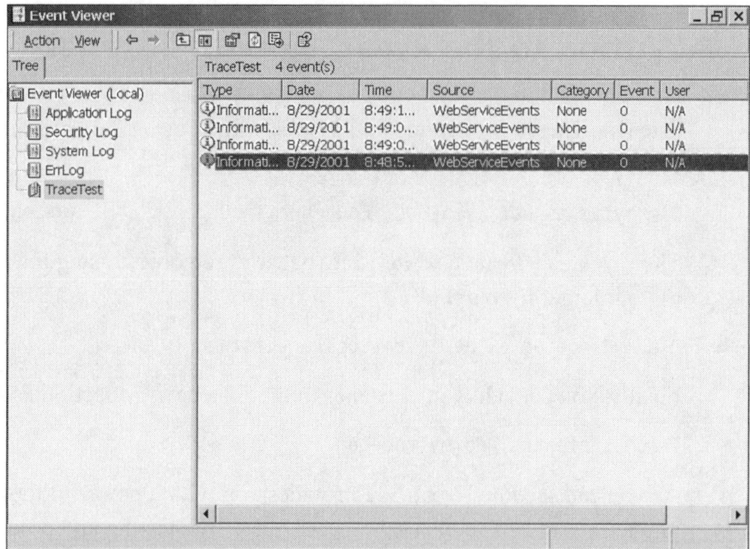

FIGURE 20.5
Viewing TraceTest in the Event Viewer.

Double clicking on an event will bring up the Event Properties window, shown in Figure 20.6, for that event. This is where the message text that you entered will be displayed.

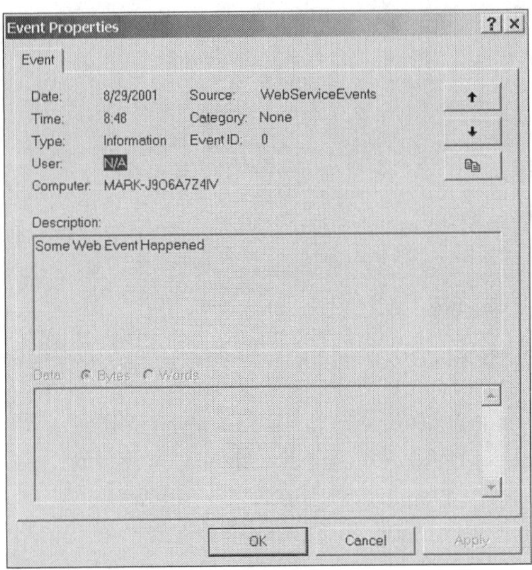

FIGURE 20.6
The Event Properties Window.

Writing to the `EventLog` with Listeners

As mentioned in the section on Listeners, it is also possible to write to the `EventLog` using listeners. This is done in much the same way as using the `TextWriterTraceListener`. First, you create a new `EventLog` object, such as

```
Dim myLog as New EventLog("FourFunctionCalc", ".", "NewLog")
```

Then, you can create an `EventLogTraceWriter` object using the `EventLog` object, `myLog`, as your target for output.

```
Dim myTraceLog as new EventLogTraceListener(myLog)
```

Finally, you can add your Listener to the Listeners Collection as follows:

```
Trace.Listeners.Add(myTraceLog)
```

As you can see, the Event Log provides you with a powerful tool to use when tracking rare events and errors that may occur during the testing and production runs of your XML Web service. Caution should be used in choosing exactly what and when to write to the Event Log however, as a crowded log quickly becomes unmanageable and tracking individual events becomes nearly impossible.

Summary

In this hour, you learned how to trap and control debugging information from XML Web services in current development through the use of the debug command. You also learned how to output this same information to a variety of sources from a fully compiled application via the use of the Trace object. Finally, you saw how to track important events in the life of your application by writing them to the Event Log.

Q&A

Q Why is it advantageous to use the `EventLog` when you could easily just write everything to text files?

A Well, the `EventLog` provides an already built and accepted standard for recording information about events. Also, the Event Viewer provides a much easier method for looking through this information then even the best-organized group of text files can provide.

Q Why would you use listeners with `Debug` objects if you can see their messages in the Output window of Visual Studio.NET?

A Although the Output window is a very acceptable means for capturing debug information while working on a single function or even a small application, it is less than perfect when dealing with large-scale development efforts. If you have lots of data that needs to be checked, possibly by nonprogrammers, it is useful to be able to write it all to a text file and work from there.

Q Why leave `Trace` objects in an application that is running in production?

A **`Trace`** statements may provide useful information to a production system by providing data such as logging user activity, tracking errors, and so on. If, when checking through Trace logged information that output from error handlers, you determine that your application fails to connect to a data source just as often as it succeeds, you know that the application needs retooling.

Q What purpose do the conditional write methods of `Debug` and `Trace` serve when I can simply use IF Then and other flow control objects?

A The conditional write methods, such as `WriteIf`, allow you to better control when messages are written by the debugger without having to resort to the addition of external flow control code, which in the case of the Debug object would be left behind to support nothing when the objects were stripped by the compiler during compilation.

Workshop

The Workshop is designed to help you review what you've learned in this hour and to point you ahead to the material that will be covered in future hours.

Quiz

1. What file do you need to edit in order to enable Application level tracing of your XML Web service via Internet Explorer?

   A `Web.config`

2. What types of objects can be passed in and used as the output target of the `TextWriterTraceListener` Object?

   A Stream object, `TextWriter` object, and a string "file name".

3. What method of the `Trace` and `Debug` objects enables Listeners to automatically write their output to targeted media instead of buffering it?

   A `AutoFlush`.

4. Which property of the `EventLog` object determines which Event Log is written to?

   A Source.

5. What happens to `Debug` statements that are left in an application at compile time?

   A They are ignored by the compiler.

Exercises

Add some code to the `Add` method of the `FourFunctionCalc` XML Web Service that you created in Hour 7 that writes to the Event Log every time a user passes in data that causes an error to occur. Also, add some code that writes to a text file every time a user causes an error in the `Subtract` method.

Change the return value of those functions to type Integer to make crashing them much easier.

A The following is one way to create the `Add` method and write a log entry when code fails. The Log will be titled `FourFunctionCalc`.

```
<WebMethod(Description:="This function adds to integers")>_
 Public Function Divide(ByVal iNum1 As Integer, ByVal iNum2 As Integer) As
Integer

   Dim iRet As Integer

    Try
       iRet = iNum1 / iNum2
    Catch
       iRet = 0
       Dim sSource As String = "DivideMethod"
       Dim sLogName As String = "FourFunctionCalc"

       If Not EventLog.SourceExists(sSource) Then
          EventLog.CreateEventSource(sSource, sLogName)
       End If

       Dim Log As New EventLog()
       Dim sMessage As String

       sMessage = "A division error occurred when "
       sMessage = sMessage & "iNum1 = " & iNum1 & " and "
       sMessage = sMessage & "iNum2 = " & iNum2 & "!!!"
       Log.Source = sSource

       Log.WriteEntry(sMessage, EventLogEntryType.Error)

     End Try

     Return iRet
   End Function
```

HOUR 21

Error Handling in XML Web Services

In this hour you will learn the basic methods of error handling and how to put them to use inside of XML Web services. You will learn how to use the Try . . . Catch . . . Finally block in your code as well as how to throw exceptions. Also, you will study the Exception object and see how to inherit it in order to create your own custom error types.

Throughout this hour we will discuss the following:

- Try . . . Catch . . . Finally
- The Exception class
- Custom errors
- Throwing errors

Error Handling

At some point in time even the most well thought out code will generate some sort of error. It is simply impossible to take every possible occurrence into account, and even if you could, the time involved in coding to handle these events would be significant, as would the increased overhead on your applications. With this in mind, a wise developer includes error-handling code for any functionality that could possibly generate an error. This error-handling functionality ensures that applications that hit an error do not simply crash but rather recover and either continue running or exit gracefully.

In an XML Web service, it is often the case that errors encountered in your code will either be the result of incorrect data submitted by the client application or the failure to retrieve data from some secondary source, such as a database or text file. In either case, it is unlikely that your service will be able to return a meaningful result when these errors occur. It is therefore the job of your error handler to return some useful error information that either lets the client application know that it has passed bad data or that your service is unable to process a request due to internal errors. By doing this, you can ensure that client applications are properly written to handle errors and can react appropriately.

Using Try . . . Catch . . . Finally to Handle Errors

Visual Studion .NET updates Visual Basic's error handling (and introduces it, in the case of C#) to include the notion of a structured error handler. This structured error handler takes the form of the Try . . . Catch . . . Finally block.

The basic premise of the Try . . . Catch . . . Finally block is that code that may generate errors, such as calls to objects, data sources, or other XML Web services, is placed into the Try portion of the block (Line 2 of Listing 21.1) and run from inside.

If any errors occur, referred to as errors being *thrown,* while the code in the Try block is being executed, then execution immediately exits the Try block and moves on to be "caught" by the Catch block, line 3, which handles the error.

Then, if the optional Finally block is included (line 5), any code included in the block is automatically run regardless of what happens in the Try and Catch blocks.

LISTING 21.1 Try . . . Catch . . . Finally Block inside Visual Basic

```
1: Try
2:   Try some operations
3: Catch
4:   Handle any errors
5: Finally
6:   This code always runs
```

The Try . . . Catch . . . Finally block works in C# in exactly the same way as it does in Visual Basic. The only real exception, as shown in Listing 21.2, is the inclusion of brackets around the code in each block.

LISTING 21.2 Try . . . Catch . . . Finally Block inside of C#

```
Try
 {
  Try some operations;
 }
Catch
 {
  Handle any errors;
 }
Finally
 {
  This code always runs;
 }
```

Now, let's look at a very basic example of the Try and Catch blocks at work. Listing 21.3 shows a new version of the `Divided` method from the `FourFunctionCalc` XML Web service. We have added a Try block around the actual division operation to handle errors, such as division by zero, that might occur in our code. For now, we simply change the return value of such errors to zero. This works as far as keeping our code running and avoiding any crashes, but it isn't really mathematically correct, as division by zero (or, for that matter, division by some decimal that may cause an overflow of the integer type) does not equal zero. We will make do with this for now.

LISTING 21.3 Using Try . . . Catch to Prevent a Divide by Zero Error

```
<WebMethod()> Public Function Divided(ByVal iNum1 As Integer, _
                             ByVal iNum2 As Integer) As Integer
    Dim iRet As Integer

   Try
     iRet = iNum1 / iNum2
   Catch
     iRet = 0
   End Try

   Return iRet
End Function
```

If you run the above code and pass in zero as the second argument, you can confirm (place a *break* statement at line 5 and step through the code) that the error caused in line 6 is caught in line 8 and the value 0 is returned.

> Do not put `Return` statements in your Try . . . Catch . . . Finally blocks. Any attempts to run code statements that break the Try . . . Catch . . . Finally statement, such as exiting the subroutine, will cause additional errors to be thrown.

Nesting Try . . . Catch . . . Finally Statements

It is possible to create much more complicated structuring of the exception handler by nesting additional Try . . . Catch . . . Finally blocks within any blocks of a previous exception handler.

The example in Listing 21.4 shows some code that will help you follow what happens in nested Try . . . Catch . . . Finally blocks. If, when running this sample, you enter two relatively small, non-zero integers, the first try will succeed, as will the second, and `iRet` will be set to 222 and returned.

Entering a zero for the second argument will cause the first Try block to fail and bypass the second altogether. At this point, the size of the first argument becomes an issue. If `iNum1` is sufficiently large enough to cause an overflow error in the multiplication in line 18, then the Catch will set `iRet` equal to 333 and that will be the return value; otherwise, the try will succeed and the second Finally block will set `iRet` equal to 444.

LISTING 21.4 Nesting Exception Handlers

```
1:     <WebMethod()> Public Function BandName(ByVal iNum1 As Integer, _
2:                                ByVal iNum2 As Integer) As Integer
3:
4:         Dim iRet As Integer
5:
6:         Try
7:
8:             iRet = iNum1 / iNum2
9:             Try
10:                iRet = iNum1 * 10000
11:             Catch
12:                iRet = 111
13:             Finally
14:                If iRet <> 111 Then iRet = 222
15:             End Try
```

continues

LISTING 21.4 Continued

```
        Catch
            Try
                iRet = iNum1 * 10000
            Catch
                iRet = 333
            Finally
                If iRet <> 333 Then iRet = 444
            End Try
        End Try

        Return iRet

    End Function
```

The Try . . . Catch . . . Finally block can actually occur multiple times from within any of the other blocks and can even be nested within previously nested blocks. Also, additional code can be placed in any of the blocks after the nested blocks, and that code will run when processing exits the nested Try . . . Catch . . . Finally code.

Handling Different Types of Errors with the Exception Object

In more complex code than the previous example, say something involving opening a database connection and retrieving information, just knowing that an error has occurred is not particularly useful. It becomes important to know just what type of error has occurred so that you can attempt to take corrective actions. This is where the Exception class comes in handy.

In order to catch and deal with Exception objects, you need to modify your `Catch` statement to look like the following:

```
Catch eError as Exception
```

With this code in place, any errors that generate an Exception object can be trapped and handled.

The Exception class is the root class for all exceptions thrown in .NET, including those that you will learn to create for yourself in just a little while. The Exception class offers properties, shown in Table 21.1, that are useful both to you, as you develop your XML Web services, and to other developers, as they attempt to consume them.

TABLE 21.1 Properties of the Exception Object

Property	*Description*
`HelpLink`	String that represents a link to the exceptions help file
`InnerException`	Provides a reference to an earlier error object that is related to this error
`Message`	String that provides the error message's text
`Source`	Name of the application or object that caused the error
`StackTrace`	Provides information on calls in the stack
`TargetSite`	Name of the method that caused the exception

The *Message* property of the Exception class can be set when a new instance of the exception is created. This message is often used in alert messages when building user interfaces. It is a good idea to always provide some meaningful message when creating your own instances of the Exception class to throw to client applications.

As was mentioned above, the Exception class is the root of all of the exception classes used in .NET. Many more specialized exception classes exist that you may catch and throw from within your code. Some of the more commonly occurring include: `OverFlowException`, `IndexOutOfRange`, `FileNotFoundException`, `ArgumentException`, `SQLException`, and `SystemException`. A listing of all of the possible exceptions and their usage would be extremely large. Search through the documentation provided with Visual Studio .NET for more information, or simply try printing the error out to the screen in your `Catch` statement like so:

```
Catch e as Exception
   Debug.Write(e.ToString)
```

Although not the most graceful solution, it is often the best way to see what types of errors are occurring in your code so that you can deal with them.

Throwing an Exception

Sometimes, either because some criteria in your code was not met or because an exception was caught but was irresolvable, an exception needs to be raised and either moved by processing to the `Catch` statement, or simply passed on to the calling code. This is done via the `Throw` statement, which works like this:

```
Throw myException
```

Often, when throwing an exception, especially when the error is one that you are generating due to some conditions in your code, it is useful to create a new exception to throw.

```
Throw New Exception("Some other exception occurred")
```

The string argument provided in the previous code is the optional `Message` property of the Exception class.

Another important property of the Exception class is the `InnerException` property. This property is used when you catch an error in your code but cannot resolve it and decide to throw a new exception. This property allows you to pass along the original error as well as your new exception as follows:

```
Catch e as Exception
   Throw New Exception("Some other exception occurred", e)
```

Handling Different Types of Exceptions

Now that you have seen some of the different types of exceptions that can be thrown and how to catch exceptions, it is time to put this information together and see how to build more structured exception-handling code. The code in Listing 21.5 shows how to catch several different types of exceptions—in this case, the `OverFlowException` shown in line 10 and the general `Exception` shown in line 14. Notice the generic `Catch` statement shown in line 16. This statement is insurance against any exceptions that might occur that do not conform to the general format of throwing an exception object.

LISTING 21.5 Catching Differing Exception Types

```
1:  <WebMethod()> Public Function MathErrors(ByVal iNum1 As Integer, _
2:       ByVal iNum2 As Integer, ByVal iNum3 As Integer) As Integer
3:
4:     Dim iRet As Integer
5:
6:     Try
7:      iRet = iNum1 / iNum2
8:      iRet = iNum2 * iNum3
9:      iRet = iNum1 * iNum3
10:    Catch e As OverFlowException
11:     iNum1 = 1
12:     iNum2 = 2
13:     iNum3 = 3
14:    Catch e As Exception
15:      Throw e
16:    Catch
17:      Throw New Exception("Some other exception occurred")
18:    Finally
19:      iRet = iNum1 + iNum2 + iNum3
20:    End Try
21:
22:    Return iRet
23: End Function
```

The code above will throw an `OverFlowException` if one of two things happen: `iNum` is zero and causes a divide error or any two of the numbers multiply together to produce a number greater than the integer type can hold. The first `Catch` statement, in line 10, will handle this error, in this case by simply resetting the variables to a low-valued integer. This is a bit frivolous, but it does demonstrate the point.

The next error handler, line 14 of Listing 21.5, handles any other errors that may occur. This is just practice, as it is usually impossible to predict all of the types of errors that may be thrown.

> It is important that `Catch` statements be placed in order, from most restrictive to least restrictive. What this means is that a generic `Catch` statement, like the one in line 16 of Listing 21.5, must come after a specific `Catch` statement, such as one to catch divide by zero errors, if the latter error is to ever be trapped.

Creating Custom Errors

It is possible, and often extremely useful, to be able to create your own custom exceptions for use throughout your XML Web services. To do this, you simply inherit from the `ApplicationException` base class, and then you can implement any of the three constructors that the `ApplicationException` class utilizes.

Listing 21.6 shows the creation of an exception called `BandNameNotFoundException`. This exception implements all three of the constructors utilized by `ApplicationException`, as seen in lines 4, 8, and 12. Implementing a class constructor consists of creating a new subroutine called `New` that accepts the same arguments as the base classes constructor. You then call the appropriate constructor using the `MyBase` keyword.

LISTING 21.6 Inheriting `ApplicationException` in Order to Create Custom Exceptions

```
1:   Public Class BandNameNotFoundException
2:     Inherits ApplicationException
3:
4:     Public Sub New()
5:        MyBase.New()
6:     End Sub
7:
8:     Public Sub New(ByVal message As String)
9:        MyBase.New(message)
10:     End Sub
11:
12:    Public Sub New(ByVal message As String, _
```

continues

LISTING 21.6 Continued

```
                ByVal innerException As Exception)

        MyBase.New(message, InnerException)
    End Sub
End Class
```

To look at the same exception being declared in C#, see Listing 21.7. Notice that C# includes an inheritance operator (`:`), shown in line 2. Also, notice that this operator is used in lieu of the `MyBase` keyword when implementing the base classes constructors.

LISTING 21.7 Inheriting `ApplicationException` in Order to Create Custom Exceptions in C#

```
1:   public class BandNameNotFoundException
2:   : ApplicationException
3:   {
4:    Public BandNameNotFoundException ()
5:      {
6:       }
7:    public BandNameNotFoundException(string message)
8:      : base(message)
9:      {
10:      }
11:   public BandNameNotFoundException (string message, ExceptioninnerException)
12:     : base(message, innerException)
13:     {
14:      }
15:}
```

Now that you have created a custom exception, it is time to use it in your code. Listing 21.8 shows portions of a method that will look up an artist's catalog based on his or her name. Line 12 shows the custom exception that you created being used to catch incidents where the band name was not found.

LISTING 21.8 Using a Custom Exception to Alert Client Applications of an Error

```
1:   <WebMethod()>
2:   Public Function FindBandName(ByVal sEntry As String) As DataSet
3:     Try
4:       If Len(sEntry) > 15 Then
5:         Throw New IndexOutOfRangeException( _
6:         "Name of Band must be less than 15 characters.")
```


continues

LISTING 21.8 Continued

```
    End If

    'check for band and if not found, throw BandNameNotFoundException
    Throw New BandNameNotFoundException("BandName " & sEntry & " not
       found")

  Catch e As BandNameNotFoundException
    'Try some other processing - maybe a secondary list
    e.helplink = "http:\MyServer\Bands.htm"
    Throw e
  Catch e As IndexOutOfRangeException
    'Try some other processing
    Throw e
  Catch e As Exception
    Throw e
  Finally
    'Cleanup code - maybe close data connections
  End Try

  Return myDataSet
End Function
```

Summary

In this hour, you saw how to utilize Try blocks in your code in order to handle code that might throw exceptions. You also learned how to catch these exceptions using the Catch block. Then you learned how to throw errors from code whenever you needed to. Later, you examined the Exception call and its methods and learned how to catch the various types of exceptions that can be thrown in .NET. Finally, you learned to create and throw custom exceptions that you create by inheriting from the Exception class.

Q&A

Q What purpose does creating custom exceptions serve in creating an XML Web service?

A Custom exceptions serve several functions, actually. The first thing that they do is to help you to create much more readable, structured code. By creating custom errors and trapping them in your code, it becomes much easier to see what is happening in a given block of code. Secondly, when these errors are raised to client code, they help the developer in building structured code that effectively deals with the particulars of your service.

Q What purpose does the Finally block actually serve?

A Because the Finally block always occurs, regardless of errors that may have caused the Try block to abort, it is a good place to run code that you absolutely need to fire off. Suppose that you have variables that need to be reset at the end of a method call or database connections that may have been opened and need closing; the Finally block is where you can do this. Be aware that closing database connections should probably have their own Try . . . Catch block within the Finally.

Q Why do you often use the Catch block last in your code?

A It is important to always use the most restrictive error trapping first in your code. For example, `Catch e as Exception` uses the base form of the `Exception` handler and will therefore Catch any Exception objects that are thrown. Following that block with `Catch e as OverFlowException` will not work, as exceptions will never pass the second exception.

Q What exceptions do I use if I come across problems while connecting with SQL Server or Oracle?

A More than likely, you will make use of some of the many custom exceptions that ship with these products. SQL Server, for instance, ships with many custom exceptions built right into it.

Workshop

The Workshop is designed to help you review what you've learned in this hour and to point you ahead to the material that will be covered in future hours.

Quiz

1. Would the following exception-handling structure work?

```
Try
   Try
Catch e as Exception
   Catch e as OverFlowException
   Finally
Finally
```

A No, .NET would not allow this and would simply treat the first `Catch` as a part of the second Try block. Furthermore, this would produce additional problems by placing the less restrictive exception handler at the front of the block.

If you were attempting to use multiple Try statements, you might write something like this:

```
Try
   Try
   Catch e as OverFlowException
   Finally
Catch e as Exception
Finally
```

Now, if the first Try succeeds, the second is attempted.

2. Declare a custom exception called `myCustomException`. Implement all of the base classes overloaded constructors.

   A `myCustomException` is shown below:

```
Public Class myCustomException
  Inherits ApplicationException

  Public Sub New()
     MyBase.New()
  End Sub

  Public Sub New(ByVal message As String)
     MyBase.New(message)
   End Sub

  Public Sub New(ByVal message As String, _
               ByVal innerException As Exception)

     MyBase.New(message, InnerException)
  End Sub
End Class
```

3. How would you trap an error of type `myCustomException` if it was thrown in a Try block?

   A `Catch e as myCustomException`

4. How would you cause a new exception of type `OverFlowException` to be returned from an XML Web service?

   A Throw new `OverFlowException`("Some error has occurred")

5. What property of the Exception class tells you the name of the method that caused an exception to occur?

   A `TargetSite`.

Exercises

Add error handling to each of the methods in the `FourFuncCalc`. Remember to throw errors back to the client application when they cannot be resolved internally.

A Your methods should look something like this:

```
<WebMethod(Description:="This function adds two integers")>
     Public Function Add(ByVal iNum1 As Integer, _
     ByVal iNum2 As Integer) As Integer

    Dim iRet As Integer

    Try
        iRet = iNum1 + iNum2
    Catch e As OverFlowException
        Throw New OverFlowException("The results of your _
            addition caused an overflow error to occur.", e)
    Catch
        Throw New Exception("An unidentified error has occurred.")
    End Try

    Return iRet
End Function

<WebMethod(Description:="This function subtracts one integer from another")>
     Public Function Subtract(ByVal iNum1 As Integer, _
     ByVal iNum2 As Integer) As Integer

    Dim iRet As Integer

    Try
        iRet = iNum1 - iNum2
    Catch e As OverFlowException
        Throw New OverFlowException("The results of your _
            subtraction caused an overflow error to occur.", e)
    Catch
        Throw New Exception("An unidentified error has occurred.")
    End Try

    Return iRet
End Function

<WebMethod(Description:="This function multiplies two integers")>
     Public Function Multiply(ByVal iNum1 As Integer, _
     ByVal iNum2 As Integer) As Integer

    Dim iRet As Integer

    Try
        iRet = iNum1 * iNum2
    Catch e As OverFlowException
        Throw New OverFlowException("The results of your _
            multiplication caused an overflow error to occur.", e)
    Catch
        Throw New Exception("An unidentified error has occurred.")
```

```
    End Try

    Return iRet
End Function

<WebMethod(Description:="This function divides two integers")>
     Public Function Divide(ByVal iNum1 As Integer, _
     ByVal iNum2 As Integer) As Integer

    Dim iRet As Integer

    Try
        iRet = iNum1 / iNum2
    Catch e As OverFlowException
        Throw New OverFlowException("The results of your _
            division caused an overflow error to occur.", e)
    Catch
        Throw New Exception("An unidentified error has occurred.")
    End Try

    Return iRet
End Function
```

HOUR 22

Publishing an XML Web Service

Now that you've got a small arsenal of XML Web services and technology under your belt, it's time to show the world what you can do. Publishing an XML Web service is the last step in developing one, so we'll take a look at how to do so in this hour. Publishing an XML Web service is actually a very easy process, so you should breeze through this hour.

In this hour, we will discuss the following:

- What you need to do to deploy your XML Web service
- How to set up an Internet Information Server (IIS) application
- How to create `.disco` files
- How to use `web.config` to configure your service

Deploying Your Service on Your Development Machine

Guess what. If you've already built and tested your XML Web service, then you've already deployed it as well. An XML Web service works much in the same way as a Web page—just put it on your server and go.

As long as people can access your server, they can access your XML Web service—that is, unless you've secured it. See Hour 18, "Security and the SOAP Toolkit."

Moving Your Service to Another Server

What if you want to move your service to another server? That's easy as well; there are only a few necessary files for deploying a service.

1. First, you'll need to copy your `.asmx` file, which is the heart of your XML Web service. As you've seen, this file declares the class you've created that inherits from the `System.Web.Services.WebService` class.
2. Second, you'll also have to copy any files in your `\bin` directory that apply to your XML Web service (see Hour 6, "Visual Studios Environment or Server Setup" for more information on this directory). All of the custom classes and assemblies you've built will be in this directory. Put these in a corresponding `\bin` directory on the server.
3. Next, you'll need to deploy any `.disco` or `.wsdl` files you've made as well. See the section "Creating a DISCO Document" later this hour for more information on `.disco` files.
4. Finally, to preserve the configuration of your service, you may also have to copy the `web.config` and `global.asax` files. After all is said and done, your deployed directory structure should look similar to Figure 22.1.

Creating an IIS Application

Although not necessary, it is a good idea to make sure the directory you copy your files to is an IIS application. What does that mean?

An application to IIS is similar to the definition of an application to the operating system. It consists of files and resources that are needed to run a program. In the case of IIS, this typically consists of `.html`, `.asp`, and `.asmx` files, images, and related documents.

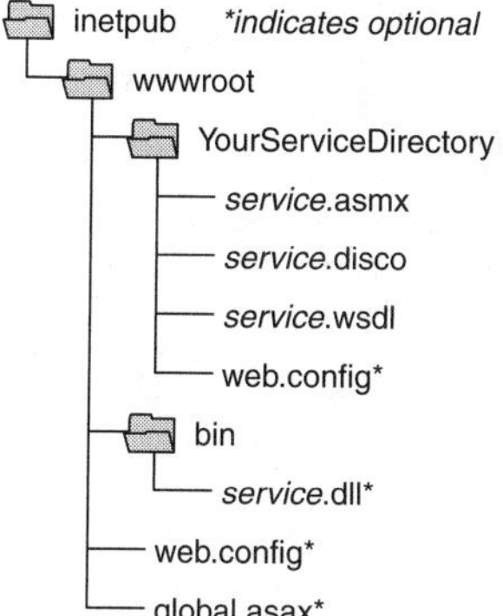

FIGURE 22.1
The complete Web service directory structure.

By default, IIS considers your root Web directory (`c:\inetpub\wwwroot`) an application. All files and folders in that directory are part of that application.

There are some drawbacks to this. The largest is that if any single file in that directory (no matter how many subdirectories deep it is) crashes or locks up, your entire application will crash or lock up. This means your entire Web site. If you've developed ASP.NET applications, you may have experienced this issue by accidentally creating an infinite loop like the following:

```
while I < 1000
   I = 10
end while
```

This loop will keep going ad infinitum, and the ASP.NET page and your Web site will freeze up until the loop is somehow terminated.

The good news is that IIS allows you to create separate applications for each directory in your site. This isolates processes so that a crash in one application won't bring down your entire site. Let's take a look at how to set this up.

Go to Start, Settings, Control Panel, Administrative Tools, Internet Services Manager (see Hour 18 for more information on working with the ISM). Right click Default Web Site, click properties, and move to the Home Directory tab. You should see Figure 22.2.

Under the Application Settings subheading, you'll see Application name, Starting point, and so on. The home directory of your Web site should already be set up as Default Application. You can click Configuration to modify advanced properties for your application, such as how each type of file behaves and whether or not debugging is enabled.

The Execute Permissions drop-down box allows you to specify what kind of files visitors can execute on your site. `Scripts`, the default selection, allows visitors to execute `.asp` files, `executables` allows them to execute `.exe` files, and `none` excludes both.

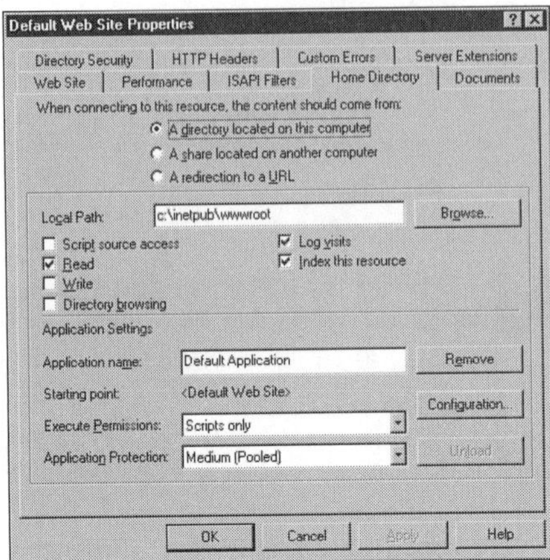

FIGURE 22.2
The ISM allows you to create IIS applications.

Finally, the Application Protection property allows you to specify how applications should behave in relation to each other. By default, they are pooled, which means they share resources. This and the `low` setting allow one crash to bring down the entire Web site, as discussed earlier. The isolated setting prevents this from happening, but can result in decreased performance for your site.

Let's create a new IIS application.

1. Navigate to the `secure` directory (we created this in Hour 18) in the ISM and select Properties from the right-click menu. The window that pops up is a bit different from Figure 22.2, but the options are the same (Figure 22.3).

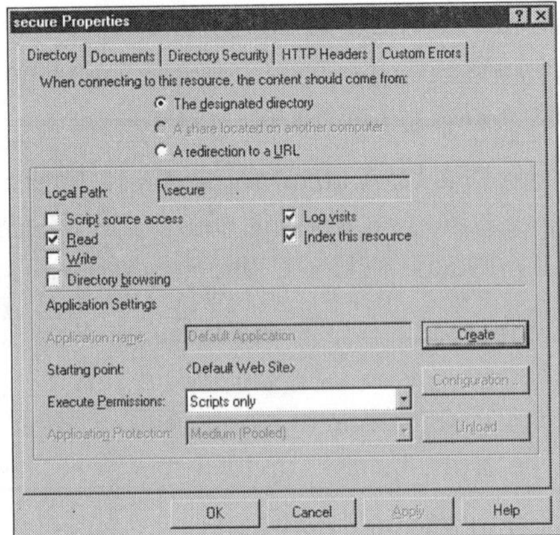

FIGURE 22.3
Creating a new IIS application.

2. In the Directory tab, click the Create button to create a new application, and set execute permissions and protection settings accordingly (we'll leave ours at default for now).
3. Hit the OK button, and you're all set! The icon next to the `secure` folder in the ISM should change to reflect that the folder is now an application, as shown in Figure 22.4.

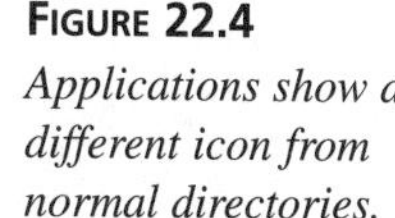

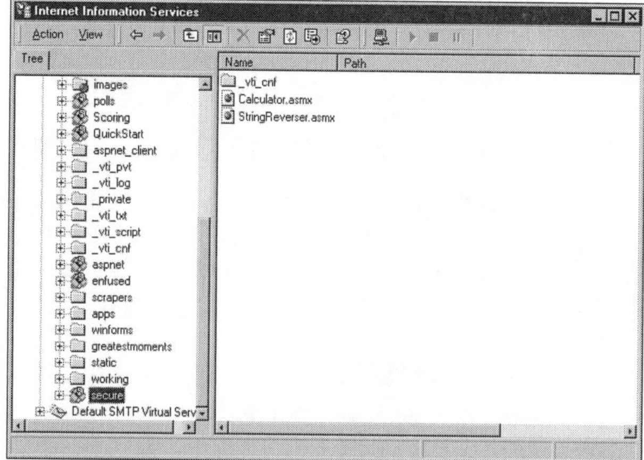

FIGURE 22.4
Applications show a different icon from normal directories.

Creating a DISCO Document

Recall from way back in Hour 5, "Finding XML Web Services with UDDI and DISCO," that `.disco` files are used by XML Web service clients to find XML Web service descriptions. Now you're going to take a look at actually building a `.disco` file.

The `.disco` file is XML-formatted, so it will be easy to create from scratch. There are two main elements you'll need in this file: `discovery` and `discoveryRef`, or `contractRef`. The first element is simply a wrapper for the file, and the second points to XML Web services on your server. `discoveryRef` points to another `.disco` file, whereas `contractRef` points to a service description. Let's take a look at a sample, shown in Listing 22.1.

LISTING 22.1 A Sample `.disco` File

```
<disco:discovery
   xmlns:scl="http://schemas.xmlsoap.org/disco/scl"
   xmlns:disco="http://schemas.xmlsoap.org/disco/">
   <scl:contractRef ref="http://localhost/secure/calculator.asmx?WSDL"/>
   <disco:discoveryRef ref="http://localhost/someother.disco"/>
</disco:discovery>
```

That's all there is to it. On line 1, you declare that this file is a discovery document. The `discovery` element is defined in the `disco` namespace, which is why you have the `disco:` prefix. The `disco` namespace is then defined. Line 1 also contains the definition for the `scl` (service contract language) namespace, which is used to provide a link to XML Web services.

Lines 4 and 5 provide the actual links. Line 4 uses the `contractRef` element to provide a link to the calculator XML Web service you built earlier. Line 5 uses `discoveryRef` to link to another `.disco` document. Clients can now use this file to find out about your XML Web service and potentially find other `.disco` files that contain more XML Web service links.

Line 5 is an optional reference and can be left off completely. If you do have need to point to an additional Disco file, be sure to change the URL to a valid address of an existing Disco file.

However, recall from Hour 4 that a potential client will need to know the exact URL of the `.disco` file to use the `disco.exe` tool—often not very feasible because a user has no way of knowing what you named your files. Let's make it easy on the client by providing a link to the `.disco` file directly from the home page.

Assuming your home page is `default.htm`, add the following line of HTML in between the `<HEAD>` and `</HEAD>` tags:

```
<link type='text/xml' rel='alternate' href='secure/service.disco'/>
```

A potential client can now use the `disco.exe` tool to examine your XML Web service with the command

```
disco http://yourhostname/
```

The `disco.exe` tool will see the link in the home page, and automatically look for the appropriate `.disco` file—saving your clients a lot of headaches. They don't even have to visit your Web site! The `disco.exe` tool does everything by itself.

The `disco.exe` tool is very sensitive about how the `.disco` files are formatted. If it is even slightly malformed, the tool will fail. Make sure your file is exactly the same as Listing 22.1 (with the exception, of course, of the names of your files). This means no line breaks inside any of the XML elements.

Remember that enabling discovery for your XML Web service is completely optional. You can keep your service to yourself by simply not creating a `.disco` file. The choice is yours.

22

Registering with UDDI

Recall from Hour 5, "Finding XML Web Services with UDDI and DISCO," that you can use `www.uddi.org` to search for XML Web services that companies have made available. Now that you have your own XML Web services, you can register yourself! Visit `www.uddi.org` and click on the Register link. You'll see Figure 22.5.

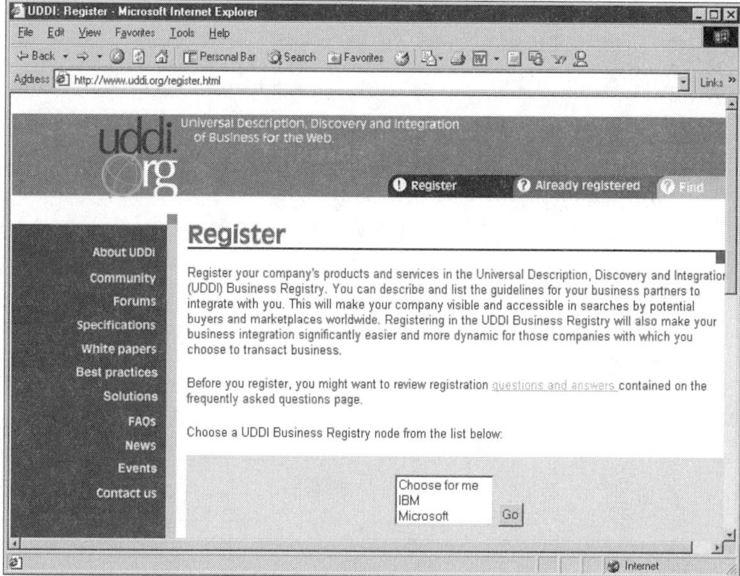

FIGURE 22.5
Registering with UDDI.org is easy and free.

There is no cost to register your service with the Registry, but you will need some technical information about your service, as well as contact information. Once the registration is processed, you (or your company) will be listed and potential clients can find you via the `www.uddi.org` search feature.

Chances are that you are not ready to register your services yet, but when you develop something that you are particularly proud of, the UDDI Business Registry is a great place to show it off.

Configuring an XML Web Service

Another thing you may wish to do is customize the types of protocols (SOAP, HttpPOST, and HttpGET) that your service will accept, or the type of output it will generate. These and other behind-the-scenes control mechanisms are available in the `web.config` file.

The `web.config` file is a very useful file for the .NET Framework. Previously, all configuration options for ASP and IIS had to be set through IIS directly. That often meant a person had to be physically located at the server. There was also no easy way to transfer settings from one computer to another—it all had to be redone every single time you deployed an application.

With .NET and `web.config`, that all changed. All the settings are now stored in one plain text file that is easily modified and transferred.

Additionally, `web.config` works with a hierarchical configuration scheme. This means that the settings in a `web.config` file will apply to all the files located in the same folder, as well as those in subfolders, unless overridden by another `web.config` file. For more information on the `web.config` file and the configuration mechanism of .NET, see the .NET Framework SDK documentation, or *Sam's Teach Yourself ASP.NET in 21 Days*.

The settings stored in `web.config` are known as runtime settings. They control the way ASP.NET and XML Web services operate when called. This is different from the settings you store directly inside your service, such as variables or functions.

Use the `web.config` file for settings that affect the inner workings of XML Web services as a whole.

`web.config`, as you may have guessed by now, is another XML file (XML is very popular in .NET). Let's take a look at an example, shown in Listing 22.2.

LISTING 22.2 `web.config` Provides Configuration Settings in XML

```
<configuration>
   <system.web>
      <webServices>
         'settings go here
      </webServices>
   </system.web>
</configuration>
```

The base element in your web.config file must always be <configuration>. Under that you have several options. On line 2 you see <system.web>, which controls settings for Web applications, such as ASP.NET and XML Web services. You could use <system.net> here to configure .NET runtime settings. For now, let's just concentrate on using <system.web>.

Note the way words are capitalized in the web.config file—the first one is not capitalized, whereas all subsequent words are. For example, webServices. This is known as camel-casing and is required in the web.config file. Don't forget your capitalization!

Configuration Option for <webServices>

Under <system.web> you have many options, such as <customErrors>, which allows you to send users of ASP.NET pages to custom error pages; <sessionState>, which controls session behavior; and so on. The element we're interested in is shown on line 3: <webServices>. Table 22.1 shows the elements available for configuration under <webServices>.

TABLE 22.1 XML Web Service Configuration Sections

Section	*Description*
<discoverySearchPatternTypes>	The object that instructs your application on how a discovery procedure should search for files
<mimeImporterTypes>	Objects used to recognize and import MIME types (usually as attachments)
<mimeInfoTypes>	Objects used to provide information about valid MIME types
<mimeReflectorTypes>	The objects that allow you to perform reflection on MIME types
<parameterReaderTypes>	The objects that will read parameters passed into your service (typically via a form post or querystring variables)
<protocolImporterTypes>	The objects that import data from specified protocols
<protocolInfoTypes>	The objects that define the protocol types
<protocolReflectorTypes>	The objects that allow you to perform reflection of the protocols at runtime
<protocolTypes>	The protocols usable for your Web services (that is, SOAP, HttpGET, HttpPOST)

continues

TABLE 22.1 Continued

`<referenceResolverTypes>`	The objects that resolve URLs and file locations for the service
`<returnWriterTypes>`	The object that returns the XML data from your service
`<sdlHelpGenerator>`	The `.aspx` file that spits out the default page when viewing a `.asmx` file
`<soapExtensionImporterTypes>`	If you are using SOAP extensions, this section will allow to you configure how they are imported by your service
`<soapExtensionReflectorTypes>`	The objects that allow you to perform reflection on your SOAP extensions
`<soapExtensionTypes>`	The types of SOAP extensions available

Listing 22.3 shows the settings for the most common of these configuration sections and their values.

LISTING 22.3 Common XML Web Service Configuration Values

```
<configuration>
   <system.web>
      <webServices>
         <discoverySearchPatternTypes>
            <add type="System.Web.Services.
                Discovery.ServiceSearchPattern"/>
         </discoverySearchPatternTypes>
         <mimeImporterTypes>
            <add type="System.Web.Services.
                Description.XmlMimeInfoImporter"/>
             <add type="System.Web.Services.
                Description.FormInfoImporter"/>
          </mimeImporterTypes>
          <mimeInfoTypes>
             <add type="System.Web.Services.Description.HtmlFormInfo"/>
             <add type="System.Web.Services.Description.XmlMimeInfo"/>
             <add type="System.Web.Services.Description.AnyMimeInfo"/>
          </mimeInfoTypes>
          <mimeReflectorTypes>
           <add type="System.Web.Services.
                Description.XmlMimeInfoReflector"/>
             <add type="System.Web.Services.
                Description.FormInfoReflector"/>
          </mimeReflectorTypes>
          <parameterReaderTypes>
             <add type="System.Web.Services.
                Protocols.HtmlFormParameterReader"/>
```

continues

Listing 22.3 Continued

```
             <add type="System.Web.Services.
                Protocols.UrlParameterReader"/>
        </parameterReaderTypes>
          <protocolImporterTypes>
             <add type="System.Web.Services.
                Description.SoapProtocolInfoImporter"/>
             <add type="System.Web.Services.
                Description.HttpPostProtocolInfoImporter"/>
             <add type="System.Web.Services.
                Description.HttpGetProtocolInfoImporter"/>
          </protocolImporterTypes>
          <protocolInfoTypes>
             <add type="System.Web.Services.
                Description.SoapProtocolInfo"/>
             <add type="System.Web.Services.
                Description.HttpGetProtocolInfo"/>
             <add type="System.Web.Services.
                Description.HttpPostProtocolInfo"/>
          </protocolInfoTypes>
          <protocolReflectorTypes>
             <add type="System.Web.Services.
                Description.SoapProtocolInfoReflector"/>
             <add type="System.Web.Services.
                Description.HttpPostProtocolInfoReflector"/>
             <add type="System.Web.Services.
                Description.HttpGetProtocolInfoReflector"/>
          </protocolReflectorTypes>
          <protocolTypes>
             <add type="System.Web.Services.
                Protocols.SoapServerProtocol"/>
             <add type="System.Web.Services.
                Protocols.HttpServerProtocol"/>
             <add type="System.Web.Services.
                Protocols.DiscoveryServerProtocol"/>
          </protocolTypes>
          <returnWriterTypes>
             <add type="System.Web.Services.Protocols.XmlReturnWriter"/>
          </returnWriterTypes>
          <referenceResolverTypes>
             <add type="System.Web.Services.
                Discovery.DiscoveryResolver"/>
             <add type="System.Web.Services.Discovery.ServiceResolver"/>
             <add type="System.Web.Services.Discovery.SchemaResolver"/>
          </referenceResolverTypes>
          <sdlHelpGenerator href="DefaultSdlHelpGenerator.aspx"/>
      </webServices>
   <system.web>
</configuration>
```

Most of the configuration settings point to objects in the .NET Framework (the exception being the `<sdlHelpGenerator>` on line 72). Often, you'll have no reason to change these settings, but they are there if you need to.

If, for example, you wanted to allow clients to use only HTTP protocols to access your service, simply change lines 55–62 to read as follows:

```
55:          <protocolTypes>
56:             <add type="System.Web.Services.
57:                Protocols.HttpServerProtocol"/>
58:          </protocolTypes>
```

Summary

In this hour, you've learned that deploying XML Web services is very simple. The only thing you have to do is copy the files of the service to the appropriate directory, and your service will be available on the Web.

You learned how to create an IIS application and about its benefits—specifically the ability to isolate your application from others, thereby preventing system-wide crashes. This can be done through the Internet Services Manager.

`.disco` files are simple XML documents that provide pointers to your XML Web service description or other `.disco` files. Creating a `.disco` file enables the discovery process, which allows potential clients to search for your service using the `disco.exe` tool.

`web.config` is the XML configuration file for the .NET Framework, allowing you to easily customize all aspects of your application. Its `<webServices>` element contains settings that you can alter to affect the way your XML Web service interacts with the .NET Framework.

After just 22 short hours, you've learned quite a bit about XML and XML Web services, from what a service document is to how to operate asynchronously. Now it's time to apply your knowledge and build a fully functional service from scratch. The next two hours will take you through this process, on both the server side and client side. Start your preparations!

Q&A

Q Is there a free host that allows me to deploy my XML Web service?

A `www.Brinkster.com` offers a free Web hosting service that supports ASP.NET and XML Web services. You can easily register there, test your services out, and allow others to see your work. Brinkster also offers pay services that provide you with more features.

22

Q I don't see any `web.config` files on my computer. Where are the default settings stored?

A Default settings for your computer are stored in a file called `machine.config`, usually located in the `c:\Winnt\Microsoft.NET\Framework\`*`version`*`\CONFIG` folder. This file contains all the default settings for ASP.NET, XML Web services, and the .NET Framework, and it is a great way to dig into the heart of .NET.

Q Can I use `web.config` to secure my service?

A Absolutely. The `<authentication>` and `<authorization>` elements will allow you to do so. But beware; when you secure your XML Web service in this way, the SOAP Toolkit (see Hour 18) will not be able to access your service properly. See the .NET Framework SDK documentation for more information.

Workshop

The Workshop is designed to help you review what you've learned in this hour and to point you ahead to the material that will be covered in future hours.

Quiz

1. What are the possible types of files that need to be copied to deploy an XML Web service?

   A `.asmx`, `.disco`, `.wsdl`, `web.config`, `global.asax`, `.dll` files

2. What URLs define the `disco` and `scl` namespaces in a `.disco` file?

   A `http://schemas.xmlsoap.org/disco/scl` and `http://schemas.xmlsoap.org/disco/`

3. What is the template for the `web.config` file?

   A

```
<configuration>
   <system.web>
      <webServices />
   </system.web>
</configuration>
```

4. (True or False) The `contractRef` element is used to point to an XML Web service description.

   A True

5. If you wanted to provide a link to a `.disco` file from your home page, what syntax would you use?

   A

   ```
   <link type='text/xml' rel='alternate' href='filename.disco'/>
   ```

6. Is the following element camel-cased?

   ```
   "<webServicesSOAPDescriptionLanguage>"
   ```

   A No, the proper format is

   ```
   "<webServicesSoapDescriptionLanguage>"
   ```

   In other words, only the "S" in "SOAP" should be capitalized.

Exercises

1. Fix the following `.disco` document. (Use `disco.exe` to test it out and make sure it works.)

   ```
   <disco:discovery
        xmlns:scl="http://schemas.xmlsoap.com/disco/scl"
        xmlns:disco="http://schemas.xmlsoap.com/disco/">
      <scl:discoveryRef href="http://localhost/secure/
        calculator.asmx?WSDL">
      <discoveryRef href="http://localhost/secure/service.disco">
   </discovery>
   ```

   A The corrected version is

   ```
   <disco:discovery
       xmlns:scl="http://schemas.xmlsoap.org/disco/scl"
       xmlns:disco="http://schemas.xmlsoap.org/disco/">
      <scl:contractRef ref="http://localhost/secure/
       calculator.asmx?WSDL"/>
      <disco:discoveryRef ref="http://localhost/
       secure/service.disco"/>
   </disco:discovery>
   ```

2. Fix the following `web.config` file:

   ```
   <configuration>
      <web.System>
         <Webservices>
            <ReturnWriterTypes>
               <add type="System.Web.Services.Protocols.
         XmlReturnWriter">
            </ReturnWriterTypes>
         </Webservices>
      </web.System>
   </configuration>
   ```

A The corrected version is

```
<configuration>
   <system.web>
      <webServices>
         <returnWriterTypes>
            <add type="System.Web.Services.Protocols.
      XmlReturnWriter"/>
         </returnWriterTypes>
      </webServices>
   </system.web>
</configuration>
```

PART V

The Quote Server (Using What You Have Learned)

Hour

HOUR 23

Building the Quote Server XML Web Service

In this hour, you will build a fully functional XML Web service. Throughout this hour, you will put to use all of the techniques that you have learned over the course of the last 22 hours. By the end of this hour, you will have built an XML Web service application that returns random quotes, lists of quotes, and other quote-related features for use in client applications of every conceivable type.

In this hour, we will discuss the following:

- Data handling
- Global events
- `WebMethod` and `WebService` methods
- XML

QuoteServer—A Fully Functional XML Web Service

The purpose of the QuoteServer XML Web service is to deliver various, famous quotes to client applications. The service will deliver these quotes in several manners:

- as a `Quote` object containing a randomly chosen quote and author
- as a listing of all of the quotes in the system delivered as a `DataSet`
- as a daily quote that is regenerated every midnight

The service also provides two other lesser methods that are variations of the methods mentioned above. The first is a method that will return a number, chosen by the user, of random quotes as a `DataSet`. The final method will return a `Quote` object containing a randomly generated quote. What separates this method from the first method discussed is the addition of the session objects, which will cause the service to return the same `Quote` object for the duration of the client objects session.

Loading QuoteServer with Relational Data

The first thing that you will need to create this service is a database. This project utilizes an Access database, but you could just as easily use SQL Server or some other relational database. The database itself is called `Quotes.mdb` and contains one table, `tblQuote`, which is defined in Table 23.1.

TABLE 23.1 Table `tblQuotes`

Column Name	*Data Type*	*Constraints*
`ID`	Long Integer	AutoIncrement
`Quote`	Memo	
`Author`	Text	Size 50
`Date`	Date/Time	

With the database created, open up a new ASP.NET Web service project and call it `QuoteServer`. The first thing that you will need to create in your service is the object that will contain the quotes that you send back to clients. Add a new class module to your code, Add Class from the Project menu, and call it `Quote`. This class will hold the quote and author's name string as shown below:

```
Public Class Quote
    Public QuoteText As String
    Public Name As String
End Class
```

Choosing Namespaces for Data Handling

The next items that you need to concern yourself with are the functions that will load the initial data into the service in order to supply your methods with the data that they need. Opening the data source within the individual methods would be too resource intensive, so you will need to create a module. To add the method, select Add New Item from the Project menu and then select Module from the Add New Item dialog. Name this module `modGlobalDB`.

Add the following `Import` statement to the top of your module, just above the module declaration itself. You may notice some XML-specific namespaces listed in the group below. These will be used later in this hour, but we will also include them here.

```
Imports System.Data
Imports System.Data.OleDb
Imports System.Xml
Imports System.Xml.Xsl
Imports System.Xml.Xpath
```

Now, create a public, globally accessible `DataSet` to hold the quote information from the `Quote` database:

```
Public dsQuoteDataSet As DataSet
```

This declaration should go just below the module declaration and outside of any other routines that you will add.

Building a Data Loading Subroutine

Now you need to add the code to actually import the data and load the `DataSet`. Add the code in Listing 23.1 to your `modGlobalDB` module within the Module declaration.

This function opens the `Quote` database, selects all of the records from `tblQuotes`, and fills in the `dsQuoteDataSet` object with them. This creates a table called `"Quotes"` with the `dsQuoteDataSet` object.

LISTING 23.1 `LoadData` Method of the `modGlobalDB` Module

```
Public Sub LoadData()
  dsQuoteDataSet = New DataSet()

  Dim conn As New OleDbConnection()

  conn.ConnectionString = "Provider=Microsoft.Jet.OLEDB.4.0; _
    Data Source=C:\Book\Quotes.mdb;Persist Security Info=False"
 conn.Open()

```

continues

LISTING 23.1 Continued

```
    Dim sSQL As String = "SELECT Quote, Author, ID FROM tblQuotes"
    Dim myAdapter As New OleDbDataAdapter(sSQL, conn)

    myAdapter.Fill(dsQuoteDataSet, "Quotes")
    conn.Close()

End Sub
```

Due to space considerations, the error-handling code in all of the functions and subroutines in this hour has been omitted.

Using Global Events to Load Application Data

The last thing that you need to do to ensure that the `LoadData` subroutine is called before any of your service's methods are run is to place a call to the `LoadData` subroutine in the `Global.ASAX` file. Open the Global class from the Class Viewer and navigate to the class's `New` method; remember from earlier that this method resides in the region labeled "Component Designer Generated Code," and you will probably have to expand this region in order to get at `New`. Add a call to `LoadData` as the very last line within the `New()` method. Now, every time the service is started, the `LoadData` event will fire before the first method request can be processed.

Returning Historical Quotes

Now that your XML Web service project is successfully pulling data in from the `Quote` database, it is time to add some methods to your service. When the QuoteServer project is finished it will contain two distinct XML Web services, but for now we will focus solely on the first service, which provides an array of functionality relating to famous and not so famous quotes from various historical figures.

Adding a Service to QuoteServer

The first order of business is to give `Service1` a more user-friendly name. From the Solution Explorer, change the name of the `Service1.asmx` file by right clicking it and selecting Rename. Call the file `myQuote.asmx`. Also, in the class itself, change the class declaration to read:

```
Public Class myQuote Inherits System.Web.Services.WebService
```

To this service, you need to add the following import statements:

```
Imports System.Web.Services
Imports System.Data
Imports System.Data.OleDb
```

These will allow your service to work with the `DataSet` object from `modGlobalDB`.

Returning a Random Quote

The `RandomQuote` method (Listing 23.2) uses the `Count` method in the `Rows` collection, line 10, to obtain the number of quotes in `DataSet dsQuoteDataSet`. This number is then used to generate a random number, line 11, between 0 and one less than the record count. This number corresponds directly to the index of the DataTable's rows.

With the row index in hand, a `Quote` object, `oQuote`, which was created in line 4, can be loaded with the text and author's name held in the corresponding row, lines 13 and 14. Object `oQuote` is then returned.

LISTING 23.2 Random Quote Generator

```
1:   <WebMethod(Description:="Provides a new random quote_
2:                    everytime that it is called.")> _
3:   Public Function RandomQuote() As Quote
4:     Dim oQuote As New Quote()
5:     Dim iCount As Integer
6:     Dim i As Integer
7:     Dim myTable As New DataTable()
8:
9:     myTable = dsQuoteDataSet.Tables("Quotes")
10:    iCount = myTable.Rows.Count
11:    i = Int(iCount * Rnd())
12:
13:    oQuote.Name = myTable.Rows(i)("Author")
14:    oQuote.QuoteText = myTable.Rows(i)("Quote")
15:
16:    Return oQuote
17:
18:  End Function
```

Run the service now to test your code. Calling the `RandomQuote` method returns an object of type `Quote`, exactly as shown in Figure 23.1.

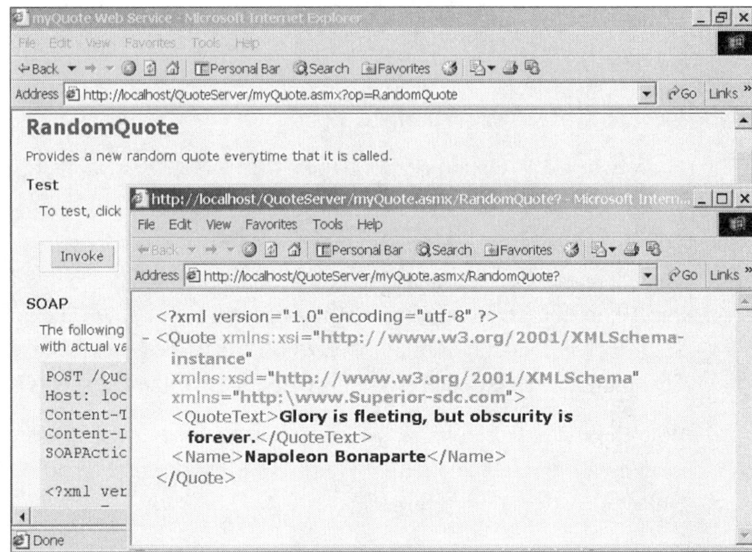

FIGURE 23.1
A quote from the random quote generator.

Returning the Entire List of Quotes

The second method that you will be adding to your service will return a `DataSet` object containing the entire listing of quotes. This service could have been created to return an array of `Quote` objects, but, as the number of quotes may increase with time, a `DataSet` seemed more appropriate.

Creating the new method is actually rather simple since you already have required data in a `DataSet` object. Add the new method, shown in Listing 23.3, to your code. This method simply returns the global `DataSet` object, `dsQuoteDataSet`.

LISTING 23.3 Returning All Quotes

```
<WebMethod(MessageName:="AllQuotes", _
   Description:="Returns the full list of quotes")> _
Public Function QuoteList() As DataSet

    Return dsQuoteDataSet
End Function
```

One important thing to note about this new method is the use of the `MessageName` property of the `WebMethod` attribute. This is done so that we can overload the `QuoteList` method, given the MessageName “`AllQuotes`,” when we create the method to return a user-selected number of quotes later on.

When you run the new `QuoteList` method, it will appear as "`AllQuotes`" in the Internet Explorer–generated help page. This is shown in Figure 23.2.

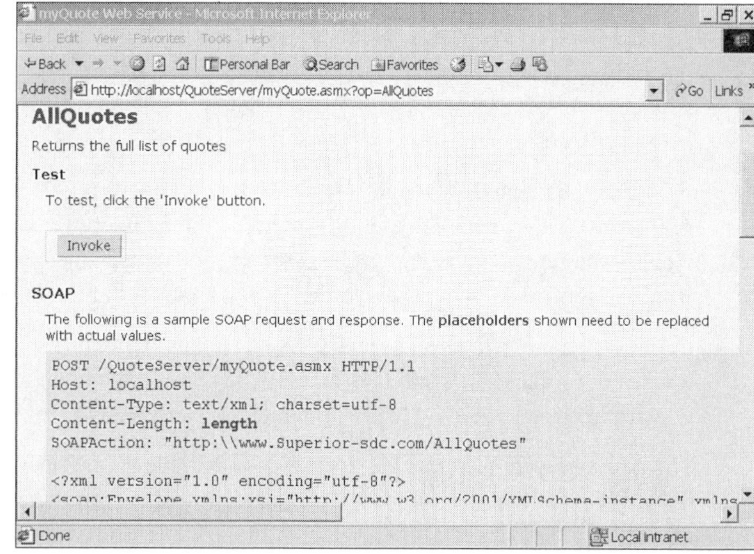

FIGURE 23.2
The `AllQuotes` *method.*

Running this method will return a `DataSet` (see Figure 23.3) containing all of the quotes in the `Quotes` database.

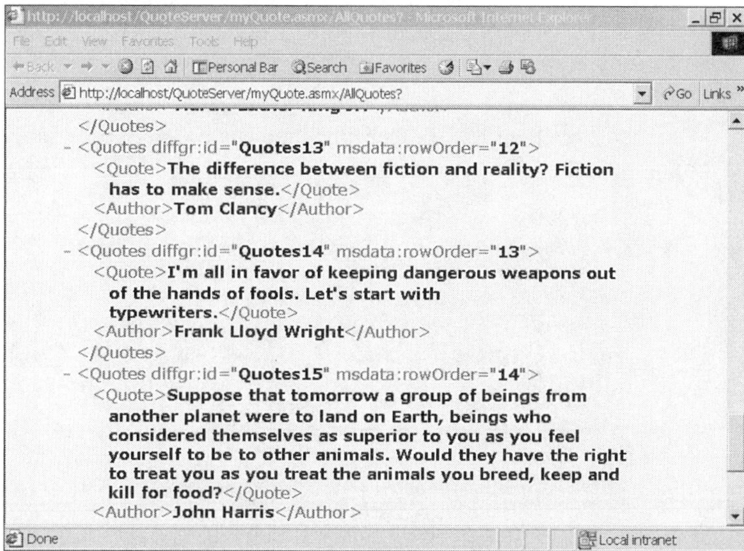

FIGURE 23.3
Returning all quotes with `AllQuotes` *method.*

Return *N* Random Quotes

As was stated earlier, the `QuoteList` method gets overloaded to accommodate the possibility that client developers may wish to select a number of quotes from the database rather than receive the entire contents. To accomplish this task, you need to add two functions to your project. The first is the overloaded `QuoteList` method and the second is a function that will generate an array of random numbers that will be used to call up individual quotes.

First, add the method shown in Listing 23.4 to your service. This method accepts an integer, `QuoteNumber`, which is used to determine the number of quotes returned. The return type for the function was kept as DataSet, even though a small array of `Quote` objects would have worked perfectly, in order to retain the feel of the other `QuoteList` method.

In line 8, the method tests to see if `QuoteNumber` is between 1 and 10, and if it is not, an error is thrown and the method is exited. The restriction on the number being entered was arbitrary and you may feel free to alter, or even remove, that constraint.

The next step you need to take, line 14, is to retrieve the number of quotes in the `dsQuoteDataSet`. If the number of quotes requested is more than or equal to the number of quotes in the `Dataset`, line 16, the entire `DataSet` is copied to the return `Dataset`, `myDataSet`, using the `Copy` method of the `DataSet` object, line 17, and `tmyDataSet` is returned.

If `QuoteNumber` falls between 1 and 10, processing enters a loop, line 29, which executes once for every quote requested. Each run of the loop calls the `AddNum()` method, which adds a new randomly generated integer to the array `iNum`. A new row is created and loaded with the values of the row `dsQuoteDataSet`'s "`Quotes`" table whose index corresponds to the number generated by `AddNum`. This row is then added to the returning `DataSet`, see lines 32–36. Once the loop has finished processing, the new `DataSet` is returned.

LISTING 23.4 `NumberReturn` Returns One to Ten Random Quotes

```
1:    <WebMethod(MessageName:="NumberQuotes", _
2:     Description:="Returns between 1 and 10 randomly selected quotes")> _
3:    Public Function QuoteList(ByVal QuoteNumber As Integer) As DataSet
4:      Dim iCount As Integer
5:      Dim myDataSet As New DataSet()
6:      Dim myTable As New DataTable()
7:
8:      If (0 >= QuoteNumber) Or (QuoteNumber > 10) Then
9:        Throw New IndexOutOfRangeException( _
10:          "QuoteList Requires an Integer Value between 1 and 10")
```

continues

LISTING 23.4 Continued

```
  End If

  myTable = dsQuoteDataSet.Tables("Quotes")
  iCount = myTable.Rows.Count

  If iCount <= QuoteNumber Then
    myDataSet = dsQuoteDataSet.Copy
  Else
    myDataSet = dsQuoteDataSet.Clone

    Dim i As Integer
    Dim j As Integer
    Dim iNum(QuoteNumber - 1) As Integer
    Dim myRow As DataRow
    Dim myTable2 As New DataTable()

    myTable2 = myDataSet.Tables("Quotes")

    For i = 0 To QuoteNumber - 1
      AddNum(iCount, i, iNum)

      myRow = myTable2.NewRow

      myRow("Author") = myTable.Rows(iNum(i))("Author")
      myRow("Quote") = myTable.Rows(iNum(i))("Quote")
      myTable2.Rows.Add(myRow)
    Next
  End If

  Return myDataSet
End Function

Private Sub AddNum(ByVal iCount As Integer, ByVal i As Integer, ByRef
   iNum() As Integer)
  Dim iTemp    As Integer
  Dim j        As Integer

  iTemp = Int(iCount * Rnd())

  If i = 0 Then
     iNum(i) = iTemp
  Else
     Dim fExists As Boolean

     For j = 0 To i - 1
        If iTemp = iNum(j) Then
           fExists = True
           Exit For
```

continues

LISTING 23.4 Continued

```
58:         End If
59:       Next
60:
61:       If fExists = False Then
62:          iNum(i) = iTemp
63:       Else
64:          AddNum(iCount, i, iNum)
65:       End If
66:    End If
67: End Sub
```

The code for AddNum, lines 43 through 68 of Listing 23.4, provides a workable, though admittedly inelegant, method for generating an array of random numbers to be used in the NumberReturn version of QuoteList. My original design required the use of a collections object and was a bit harder to follow than what is shown.

As it currently stands, AddNum generates a random number and tests it against those numbers that have already been called. If the number is unique it is returned, if not, AddNum makes a recursive call to itself to generate a new number. This method should be added to the modGlobalDB module.

The method accepts the number of Quotes being requested, iCount, to use as a seed for its random number generator, an array, iNum, containing any numbers that were previously created by calls to AddNum, and i, which contains the current number being requested. Finding the upper bounds of the array would work just as well. A random number, iTemp, is generated and compared with any previous results stored in iNum. If the number doesn't already exist, it is added to iNum and the method exits. If, on the other hand, the number does exist, a recursive call is made to AddNum to return a new number. These calls will continue until a new number is generated. This method is highly inefficient when the number of requested quotes is large.

As with the last QuoteList method, when you run your code, the method will be listed by its MessageName, NumberQuote. The method will require a number between 1 and 10, as shown in Figure 23.4.

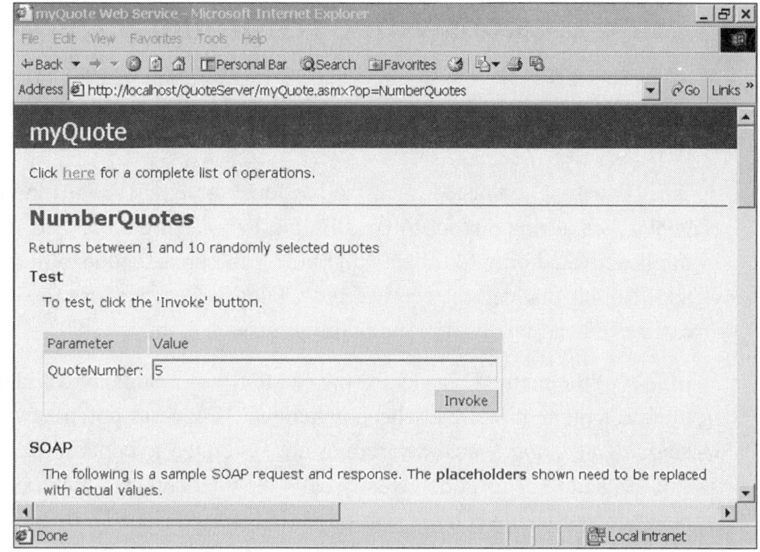

FIGURE 23.4
Selecting the number of quotes to return.

After selecting an acceptable number of quotes and clicking the "`Invoke`" button, you should be greeted with a small `DataSet` containing pearls of wisdom, such as the ones in Figure 23.5 by Kierkegaard, Edison, and Clancy.

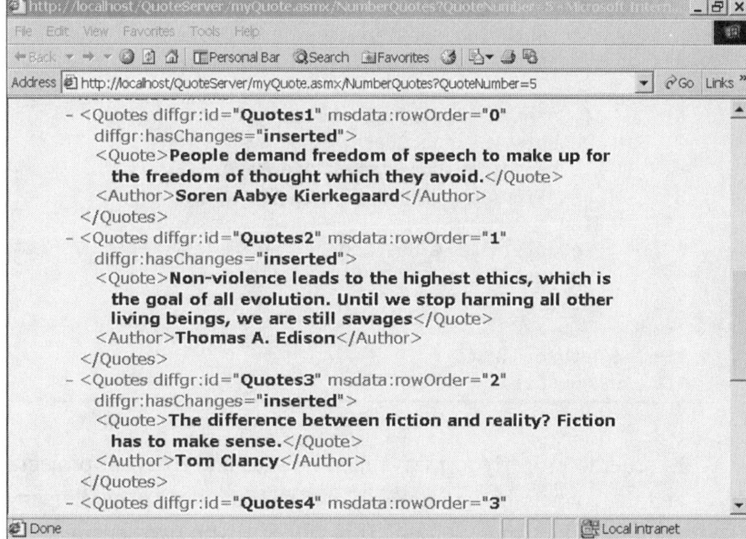

FIGURE 23.5
Returning five random quotes.

Using Sessions When Returning a Quote

The `SessionQuote` method, which you will now add to your `myQuote` service, uses ASP.NET Sessions in order to return the exact same `Quote` object every time that a client requests the method within a valid session. Place the code in Listing 23.5 in your service.

Since this function needs to utilize sessions, the `EnableSession` method of the `WebMethod` attribute is set to `True` in line 1 of Listing 23.5. This will ensure that sessioning is activated only for clients that utilize the `SessionQuote` method. Any other client applications that call the service, but do not use `EnableSession`, will not include the extra overhead involved in maintaining session state.

Line 6 of the method checks for the existence of a `Session` variable in order to determine if a quote has already been generated. If one has not, a new `Quote` object is generated, `oQuote`, and `Session` variables are generated to contain the quote and its author (lines 8 and 9). This code actually calls the `RandomQuote` method in order to retrieve a new `Quote` object when the session is first started (line 7). If the session already existed, the `Quote` object is set with the values contained in the `Session` variables (see lines 11 and 12). The `Quote` object is then returned and the method exits.

LISTING 23.5 Returns the Same Quote for the Life of the Client Reference

```
1:  <WebMethod(EnableSession:=True, _
2:  Description:="Returns the same quote throughout the life of the object")> _
3:  Public Function SessionQuote() As Quote
4:    Dim oQuote As New Quote()
5:
6:    If Session("Quote") Is Nothing Then
7:      oQuote = RandomQuote()
8:      Session("Author") = oQuote.Name
9:      Session("Quote") = oQuote.QuoteText
10:   Else
11:     oQuote.Name = Session("Author")
12:     oQuote.QuoteText = Session("Quote")
13:   End If
14:
15:   Return oQuote
16: End Function
```

In order to properly test this function, save and run your project as you normally would, and then, when the Internet Explorer window is displayed, open a second IE window and copy the URL from the first. This will give you two separate sessions from which to run the QuoteServer XML Web service (see Figure 23.6).

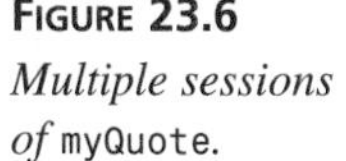

FIGURE 23.6
Multiple sessions of `myQuote`.

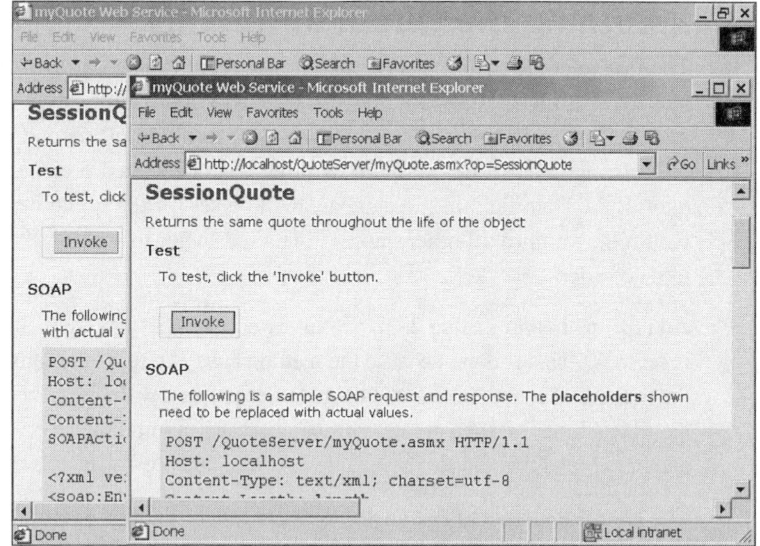

From each of the two windows, press the "Invoke button" several times and verify that each window continually returns the exact quote as shown in Figure 23.7. There is a slight chance, dependent on the number of quotes that you have entered in the `Quote` database, that both of your sessions are returning the same quote. If this happens, open a new instance of IE and try again.

FIGURE 23.7
Returning quotes for multiple `myQuote` *sessions.*

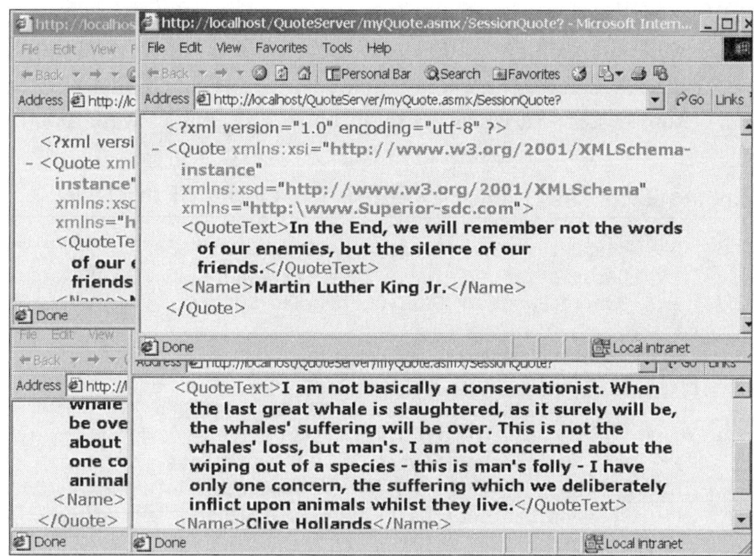

Returning the Quote of the Day

The final method that you will add to this service is the `DailyQuote` method. This method will return the same quote to all client applications over a 24 hour period. At midnight of each day, with a margin of error of about 60 seconds due to the invoking of the caching, a new random quote will be generated. As a precaution against repeating quotes, the Date field in the database will be set for the quote being used to ensure that it isn't redrawn until all other quotes are called. After this point, the quotes are just drawn in date order.

Add the method in Listing 23.6 to your service. In line 1 of the method, the `CacheDuration` is set to 60. This is done because the method always returns the same result set, regardless of the number of requests, over the course of an entire day. Indeed, the `CacheDuration` may have been set to an even greater number, keeping in mind that every second cached represents another second that the server may be returning the previous day's quote.

The rest of the code in this method works much like that seen in `EnableSession`. In line 7 of the method, a check is made to determine if the `Application` variable "`Quote`" is already in existence. If it is not, a call is made to `GetQuote`, a method in the `modGlobalDB` module that returns the quote of the day. More on `GetQuote` in a moment. The results of `GetQuote` are used to initialize the `myQuote Quote` object, which is returned to the client. The results of `GetQuote` are also used, in addition to the date, to set the three `Application` variables in lines 9–11.

If the `Application` level variables did already exist, a check is made in line 13 to determine if they are for the current date, as it is possible that a busy service may stay active well past midnight. If the date matches, the `Application` level variables are used to set `oQuote`, and it is returned. If not, `GetQuote` is called, line 17, and both `oQuote` and the `Application` variables are set just as if no variables were found at all.

LISTING 23.6 `DailyQuote` Returns the Quote of the Day

```
1:   <WebMethod(CacheDuration:=60, _
2:   Description:="Returns the Daily Quote. Quote changes at 12AM EST.")> _
3:   Public Function DailyQuote() As Quote
4:
5:     Dim myQuote As New Quote()
6:
7:     If Application("Quote") Is Nothing Then
8:       myQuote = GetQuote()
9:       Application("Author") = myQuote.Name
10:      Application("Quote") = myQuote.QuoteText
11:      Application("Date") = Format(Today, "mm/dd/yy")
12:    Else
```

continues

LISTING 23.6 Continued

```
      If Application("Date") = Format(Today, "mm/dd/yy") Then
        myQuote.Name = Application("Author")
        myQuote.QuoteText = Application("Quote")
      Else
        myQuote = GetQuote()
        Application("Author") = myQuote.Name
        Application("Quote") = myQuote.QuoteText
        Application("Date") = Format(Today, "mm/dd/yy")
      End If
    End If

    Return myQuote
  End Function
```

The `GetQuote` function, not shown, simply queries the database for the earliest date, or the first quote without a date if such exists, and returns it. The method then sets the quote's date to the current date.

Run the service and click the "`Invoke`" button of the `DailyQuote` method and you will receive a quote, such as this insightful remark (Figure 23.8) made by IBM's Thomas Watson.

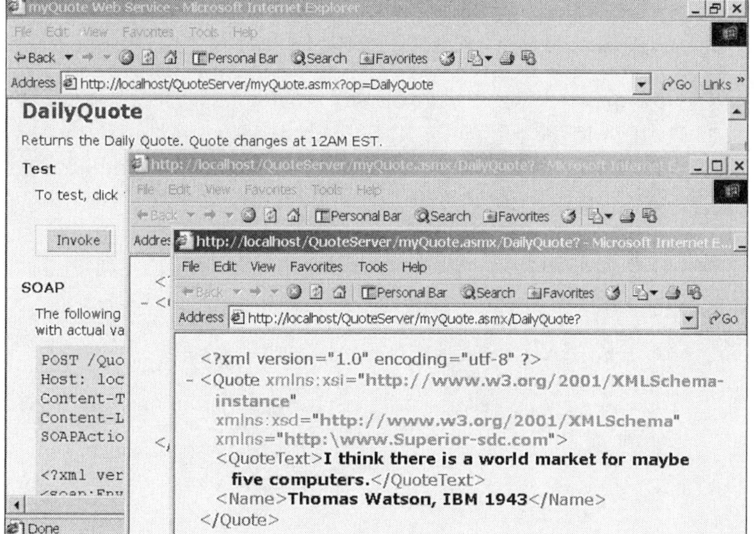

FIGURE 23.8
Returning the quote of the day for Monday.

Now, change the system date on your computer, right click the time in the lower right hand side of your computer, and click the "`Invoke`" button a second time. You should now see a new quote, such as the one from Frank Lloyd Wright shown in Figure 23.9.

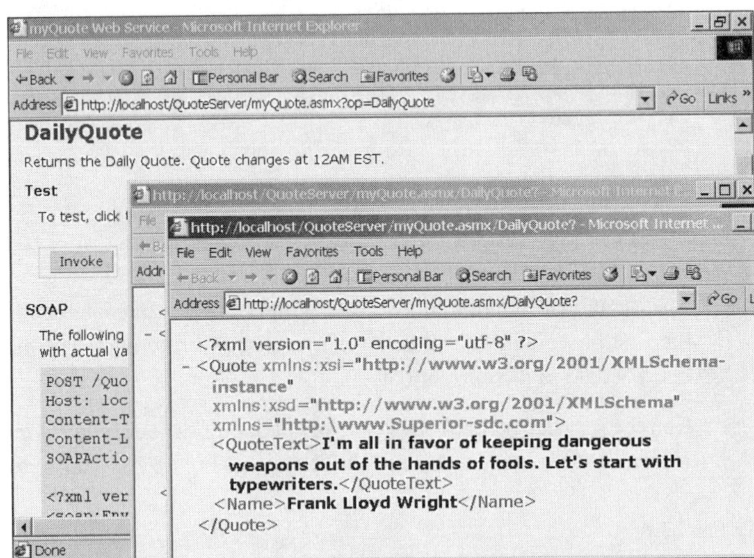

FIGURE 23.9
Returning the quote of the day for Tuesday.

Now that your service's methods are complete, it is time to complete the service itself. Add the following XML Web service attribute to the declaration of your service. This will set its namespace and description in order to better describe and define your service.

```
<WebService(NameSpace:="http:\\www.Superior-sdc.com", _
Description:="This XML Web service provides features such as a _
quote of the day, random quotes, and quote lists.")> _
Public Class myQuote
    Inherits System.Web.Services.WebService
```

You can view the results of these changes by running your service or by looking at Figure 23.10.

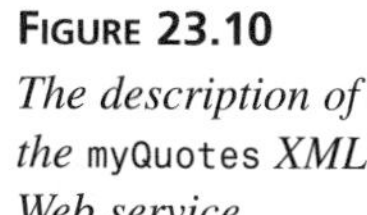

FIGURE 23.10
The description of the `myQuotes` *XML Web service.*

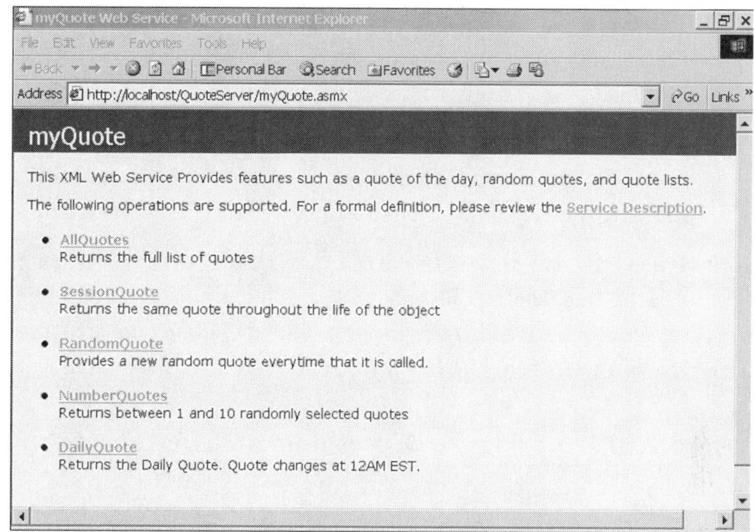

Revising QuoteServer—Adding New Functionality

At this point in the development of the QuoteServer XML Web service, your service is complete, fully functional, and ready for use. Now, let's say a request comes in from several potential consumers of your service to add support for topic-specific quotes. Let's also assume that the quotes are being provided to you in XML documents and that it is beneficial for you to leave them in that format. Maybe an application exists that allows users to update these files periodically, for example.

Add a new XML Web service to your project (Add New Item from the Project menu) and call it `PopQuotes`. This will create a separate XML Web service running in the same application space and consuming the same resources as `myQuotes`.

Now, you will need to add a dataset to hold your XML data. Add the following line, declaring a `DataSet` object named `dsPopQuoteDataSet`, to the `modGlobalDB` module. You can place it directly below the declaration for `dsQuoteDataSet`.

```
Public dsPopQuoteDataSet As DataSet
```

Loading XML Data into QuoteServer

In the `modGlobalDB` module you will need to add a subroutine that opens and loads the XML files, `Sports.xml` and `Music.xml`, into the `dsPopQuotesDataSet` object. The code in Listing 23.7 will accomplish just this.

This method reads the `Music.xml` file into a FileStream object, `myfStream`, in line 4. The file stream is then used to read the document into an XmlTextReader, `myXMLReader`, that is in turn read into a `DataSet` object in line 14.

The second XML document, `Sports.xml`, is read directly into an XmlDocument object, `myDoc`, in line 15 and then transformed into a more useful format using the `Sports.xsl` file. The file is then read into a second `DataSet` object in line 21.

Using the `Copy` method of the `DataSet`'s `DataTable` object, the two tables are added directly to `dsPopQuoteDataSet`. Several other methods for adding these XML data sources may have also been appropriate, including concatenating the two documents and transforming them into the XML representation of a two-table `DataSet`.

LISTING 23.7 Loading the Quotes from XML Documents

```
1:   Private Sub LoadXML()
2:     dsPopQuoteDataSet = New DataSet()
3:
4:     Dim myfStream As New System.IO.FileStream( _
5:         "C:\Book\Music.xml", System.IO.FileMode.Open)
6:     Dim myXmlReader As New XmlTextReader(myfStream)
7:     Dim myXmlReader2 As XmlReader
8:     Dim myDataSet As New DataSet()
9:     Dim myDataSet2 As New DataSet()
10:    Dim myTrans As New XslTransform()
11:    Dim myDoc As New XmlDocument()
12:    Dim myNav As XPathNavigator
13:
14:    myDataSet.ReadXml(myXmlReader)
15:    myDoc.Load("C:\Book\Sports.xml")
16:    myTrans.Load("C:\Book\Sports.xsl")
17:    myNav = myDoc.CreateNavigator
18:
19:    myXmlReader2 = myTrans.Transform(myNav, Nothing)
20:
21:    myDataSet2.ReadXml(myXmlReader2)
22:
23:    dsPopQuoteDataSet.Tables.Add(myDataSet.Tables(0).Copy)
24:    dsPopQuoteDataSet.Tables.Add(myDataSet2.Tables(0).Copy)
25:
26:    myXmlReader.Close()
27:    myXmlReader2.Close()
28:
29:  End Sub
```

For this function to actually accomplish its goal, a call to it needs to be added to the `Global.ASAX`. Place the call to `LoadXML` directly beneath the call to `LoadData` in the `New` method of the `Global.ASAX`.

A portion of the Music.xml document can be viewed in Listing 23.8. The ellipses in line 13 represent the section of additional "Quote" nodes that were removed.

LISTING 23.8 The Music.XML File

```
1:   <?xml version="1.0" standalone="yes"?>
2:     <Music>
3:       <Quote>
4:         <Text>There's room at the top, they are telling you still.
5:              But First you must learn to smile as you kill.</Text>
6:         <Author>John Lennon</Author>
7:       </Quote>
8:       <Quote>
9:         <Text>We hope your rules and your wisdom choke you.</Text>
10:          <Author>Radiohead</Author>
11:        </Quote>
12:
13:        ....
14:
15:     </Music>
```

Before attempting to use any hand-generated XML documents in your programs, it is a good idea to validate the document being used. If you are not already using an XML validating parser, you can simply open the document up in Internet Explorer to ensure that the structure is what you were expecting.

Listing 23.9 shows a segment of the Sports.xml document. As in the previous document, line 11 should be replaced with additional "Quote" nodes. It should also be noted that the format of Sports.xml is slightly different from that of Music.xml and will need to be altered or "transformed" in order to create a recordset that is similar to the one created by reading Music.xml into the dsPopQuotesDataSet object.

LISTING 23.9 The Sports.Xml File

```
1:   <?xml version="1.0" standalone="yes"?>
2:     <Sports>
3:       <Quote>
4:         <Name>Yogi Berra</Name>
5:           <Saying>You can't think and hit at the same time.</Saying>
6:       </Quote>
7:       <Quote>
8:         <Name>Yogi Berra</Name>
```

continues

LISTING 23.9 Continued

```
        <Saying>Nobody goes there it's too crowded.</Saying>
      </Quote>
   ....
  </Sports>
```

Finally, the `Sports.Xsl` file shown in Listing 23.10 performs the needed transform on the `Sports.xml` file.

LISTING 23.10 The `Sports.Xsl` File

```
<?xml version="1.0"?>
<xsl:stylesheet version="1.0"
  xmlns:xsl="http://www.w3.org/1999/XSL/Transform">

<xsl:output method="xml"/>

<xsl:template match="/">
  <Sports>
    <xsl:apply-templates/>
  </Sports>
</xsl:template>

<xsl:template match="Quote">
  <SportQuote>
    <Text>
      <xsl:apply-templates select="Saying/text()" />
    </Text>
    <Author>
      <xsl:apply-templates select="Name/text()" />
    </Author>
  </SportQuote>
</xsl:template>

</xsl:stylesheet>
```

Returning All Quotes of a Given Type

The first method that you will be adding to the new service is a variation of `myQuote`'s `AllQuotes` method. This method will allow client applications to retrieve a list containing all of the quotes from either music or sports.

In order to allow the developers of your service's consumers to choose a valid category, you will need to create an enumeration to be used as the argument for the `QuoteList` type. The following code will create an enumeration to handle requests for Sports or Music.

```
Public Enum QuoteType
    Music = 0
    Sports = 1
End Enum
```

The actual `QuoteList` method is actually extremely simple. The method accepts a `QuoteType` enumeration, `Style`, and uses it to determine which of the tables from the `dsPopQuoteDataSet` DataSet should be returned. The table is then copied (line 7); added to the return DataSet, `myDataSet`; and returned. This is shown in Listing 23.11.

LISTING 23.11 Returning All the Quotes from either the Music or Sports Category

```
1:    <WebMethod(MessageName:="AllQuotes", _
2:    Description:="Returns the full list of quotes")> _
3:    Public Function QuoteList(ByVal Style As QuoteType) As DataSet
4:      Dim myDataSet As New DataSet()
5:      Dim myTable As New DataTable()
6:
7:      myTable = dsPopQuoteDataSet.Tables(Style).Copy
8:      myDataSet.Tables.Add(myTable)
9:
10:     Return myDataSet
11:   End Function
```

Run the service, shown in Figure 23.11, carefully type in either **`Music`** or **`Sports`**, and click the "`Invoke`" method.

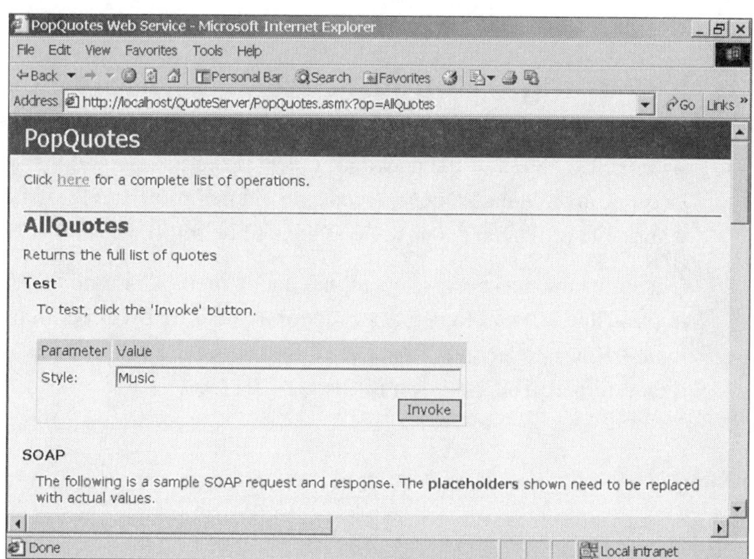

FIGURE 23.11
Selecting a quote category.

> Remember that the enumerator is case sensitive and will not treat MUSIC the same as Music.

The `DataSet` returns the entire contents of one of the quote categories, as shown in Figure 23.12.

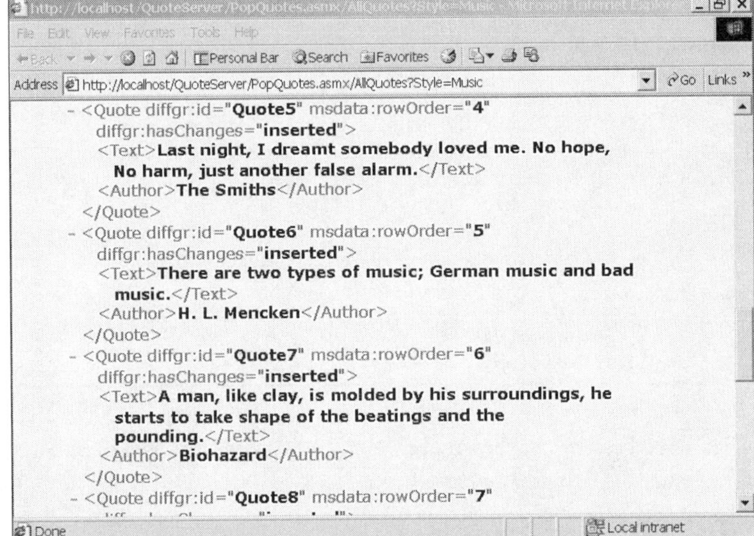

FIGURE 23.12
Returning all music quotes.

Returning a Random Quote of a Given Type

`RandomQuote` works exactly the same as the `RandomQuote` method of the `myQuote` service, with the exception of the added argument. Like the method that you just saw, `ReturnQuote`, `RandomQuote` accepts an enumeration, `Style`, which is used to determine what table of the `dsPopQuoteDataSet` is to be returned, see line 9.

Once the table has been selected, the `Count` method is used to determine the number of quotes (line 10) and to create a random number that will be used as the index of the table's Rows collection. This row is used to set the value in the `oQuote` object, which is then returned. This is shown in Listing 23.12.

LISTING 23.12 Returning a Random Quote from the Music or Sports Category

```
<WebMethod(Description:="Provides a new random _
    quote everytime that it is called.")> _
Public Function RandomQuote(ByVal Style As QuoteType) As Quote
  Dim oQuote As New Quote()
  Dim iCount As Integer
  Dim i As Integer
  Dim myTable As New DataTable()

  myTable = dsPopQuoteDataSet.Tables(Style)
  iCount = myTable.Rows.Count
  i = Int(iCount * Rnd())

  oQuote.Name = myTable.Rows(i)("Author")
  oQuote.QuoteText = myTable.Rows(i)("Text")
  Return oQuote

End Function
```

As always, save and run the service. Now, when you type in **`Sports`** and invoke the `RandomQuote` method of `PopQuote`, you stand a very good chance of seeing one of Yogi Berra's many interesting quotes, such as the one in Figure 23.13.

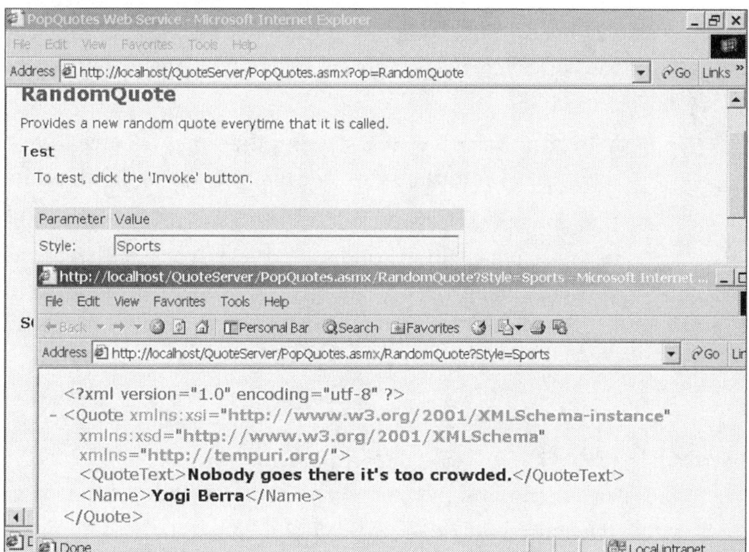

FIGURE 23.13
A random sports quote.

Summary

In this hour, you created an entire XML Web service–based suite of quote-related tools. Throughout this hour, you saw how to integrate all of the techniques that you learned over the course of the last 22 hours into a fully functioning XML Web service that could be exposed to real-world users. This service, although more frivolous than many, still provides functionality that many developers may find valuable.

Q&A

Q Why not place the functionality of the `PopQuote` service into the same XML Web service as `myQuote`?

A The functionality appears to be geared to a different user community and, although related enough in functionality to warrant being placed in the same project, the functionality offered by `PopQuote` is really quite different.

Q Is the `QuoteServer` project technically two separate XML Web services?

A Technically it is. To the developers using the service, a separate Web Reference must be created for each XML Web service created in your project. They are related in several key ways, however. Both share the same application space, which is to say, they share the same `Application` level variables, resources, and so on. The second major connection lies in the Disco file that is generated for the service. A Disco file will be created by Visual Studio .NET that includes all of the services in a given project.

Q Why, if the services are sharing the same resources, aren't the XML documents read into the same `DataSet` object as the relation data was?

A If additional tables were added to the `dsQuoteDataSet`, changes would have had to have been made to the original service to ensure that the additional tables were not delivered along with operations where a full DataSet was used as the return object. This would not have been a bad thing necessarily, but in a situation where the service was busy it could cause additional performance hits.

Workshop

The Workshop is designed to help you review what you've learned in this hour and to point you ahead to the material that will be covered in future hours.

Quiz

1. How is an additional XML Web service added to an XML Web service project?

   A Add New Item on the Project Menu.

2. (True or False) Public functions in a module can be used by all services in a project.

   A True.

3. (True or False) Methods in an XML Web service can call methods from the same service.

   A True.

4. What object needs to be used in order to handle XML data whose format prevents them from being read into a `DataSet` object?

   A `XmlTransform`

5. (True or False) It is possible to have methods with the same name in different services within the same project. Note: overloading is not being used.

   A True.

Exercises

Add two additional features to `PopQuotes` XML Web service. One should return between one and ten randomly selected quotes from either the music or sports world. The second should return a single quote of user choice of sports or music, for the lifetime of the client application's session.

A The following code adds two new functions to the `PopQuotes` XML Web service. The first, `NumberQuotes`, returns between 1 and 10 quotes from either the music or sports world. The second, `SessionQuote`, returns the exact same quote for the life of the session. This quote can be from either the sports or music world.

```
<WebMethod(MessageName:="NumberQuotes", _
Description:="Returns between 1 and 10 randomly selected quotes")> _
Public Function QuoteList(ByVal QuoteNumber As Integer, _
                      ByVal Style As QuoteType) As DataSet
    Dim iCount As Integer
    Dim myDataSet As New DataSet()
    Dim myTable As New DataTable()

    If (0 >= QuoteNumber) Or (QuoteNumber > 10) Then
        Throw New IndexOutOfRangeException( _
        "QuoteList Requires an Integer Value between 1 and 10")
    End If

    myTable = dsPopQuoteDataSet.Tables(Style)
```

```
        iCount = myTable.Rows.Count

        If iCount <= QuoteNumber Then
            myDataSet = dsPopQuoteDataSet.Copy
        Else
            myDataSet = dsPopQuoteDataSet.Clone

            Dim i As Integer
            Dim j As Integer
            Dim iNum(QuoteNumber - 1) As Integer
            Dim myRow As DataRow
            Dim myTable2 As New DataTable()

            myTable2 = myDataSet.Tables(Style)

            For i = 0 To QuoteNumber - 1
                AddNum(iCount, i, iNum)

                myRow = myTable2.NewRow

                myRow("Author") = myTable.Rows(iNum(i))("Author")
                myRow("Text") = myTable.Rows(iNum(i))("Text")
                myTable2.Rows.Add(myRow)
            Next
        End If

        Return myDataSet
    End Function

    <WebMethod(EnableSession:=True, _
     Description:="Returns the same quote throughout the life of the object")> _
     Public Function SessionQuote(ByVal Style As QuoteType) As Quote
        Dim oQuote As New Quote()

        If Session("Quote") Is Nothing Then
            oQuote = RandomQuote(Style)
            Session("Author") = oQuote.Name
            Session("Quote") = oQuote.QuoteText
        Else
            oQuote.Name = Session("Author")
            oQuote.QuoteText = Session("Quote")
        End If

        Return oQuote
    End Function
```

HOUR 24

Quote Server Clients

In this hour, you will take a look at a variety of client applications that may make use of the Quote Server XML Web service. During this hour, you will see desktop programs as well as ASP applications all making use of the various methods provided by the `QuoteServer` application. By the end of this hour, you should be fully motivated to go out and build your own services and the clients to consume them.

In this hour, we will discuss the following:

- ASP clients
- Desktop clients
- Visual Basic clients
- C# clients

ASP Clients for the `QuoteServer` XML Web Service

The first client application that you will be looking at, an ASP project, is a bit different from those that you have seen throughout the book, but it makes use of all of the techniques that you have seen so far and should not be very difficult to follow.

Create a new ASP.NET Web application and give it the name `QuoteLister`. To this project, you are going to need to add three Web forms, two more than are already in the project. Call them `Page1`, `Page2`, and `Page3`. You will also need to add a Web Reference to the `myQuote` XML Web service.

Once you have created the new Web Form ASPX pages, you can add the code in Listing 24.1 to each of them. The code shown was added directly into the HTML of the ASPX page's designer and not into the underlying class. If you have not done this before, it is very simple.

1. Select `Page1` from the class view and then click Designer from the View menu. You now have access to the HTML itself and can add your new HTML in here, shown in Figure 24.1. Alternately, you could use the designer and toolbox controls.
2. Be sure to change the links and text in lines 20 and 22 to point to the other two pages. For example, Listing 24.1 shows the code for `Page1.aspx`, thus the links point to `Page2.aspx` and `Page3.aspx`.
3. Click on the View Code button of the Solutions Explorer and enter the `Page_Load` event code shown in Listing 24.2. Do this for each of the `.aspx` pages that you created.

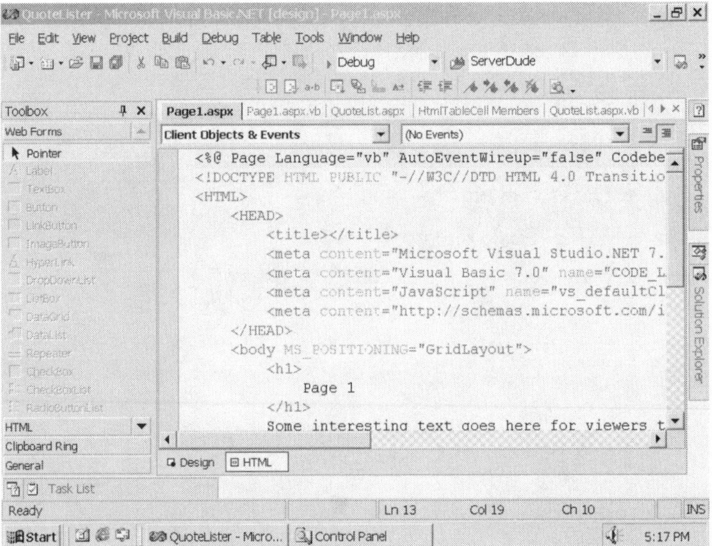

FIGURE 24.1
Working with HTML in the Visual Studio .NET Designer.

LISTING 24.1 HTML for Page1, an ASP Client

```
<%@ Page Language="vb" AutoEventWireup="false"
    Codebehind="Page1.aspx.vb" Inherits="QuoteLister.Page1"%>
<!DOCTYPE HTML PUBLIC "-//W3C//DTD HTML 4.0 Transitional//EN">
<HTML>
<HEAD>
   <title></title>
   <meta content="Microsoft Visual Studio.NET 7.0" name="GENERATOR">
   <meta content="Visual Basic 7.0" name="CODE_LANGUAGE">
   <meta content="JavaScript" name="vs_defaultClientScript">
    <meta content="http://schemas.microsoft.com/intellisense/ie5"
         name="vs_targetSchema">
 </HEAD>
 <body MS_POSITIONING="GridLayout">
    <h1>
       Page 1
    </h1>
    Some interesting text goes here for viewers to read
    <br>
    <br>
    <A href="page2.aspx">Page 2</A>
    <br>
    <A href="page3.aspx">Page 3</A>
    <br>
    <A >QuoteList</A>
    <br>
    <hr>
     
    <asp:PlaceHolder id="PlaceHolder1" runat="server">
    </asp:PlaceHolder>
 </body>
</HTML>
```

LISTING 24.2 HTML for Page1, an ASP Client

```
Private Sub Page_Load(ByVal sender As System.Object, _
  ByVal e As System.EventArgs) Handles MyBase.Load
     Dim myTable As New HtmlTable()
     Dim myRow1 As New HtmlTableRow()
     Dim myRow2 As New HtmlTableRow()
     Dim myCell11 As New HtmlTableCell()
     Dim myCell21 As New HtmlTableCell()
     Dim myCell22 As New HtmlTableCell()
     Dim sTable As String

      myTable.Border = 0
```

continues

LISTING 24.2 Continued

```
14:        Dim oQuotes As New localhost.myQuote()
15:        Dim myQuote As New localhost.Quote()
16:
17:        myQuote = oQuotes.SessionQuote()
18:
19:        myCell11.ColSpan = 2
20:        myCell11.InnerHtml = myQuote.QuoteText
21:        myRow1.Cells.Add(myCell11)
22:        myTable.Rows.Add(myRow1)
23:
24:        myCell21.InnerHtml = " "
25:        myRow2.Cells.Add(myCell21)
26:
27:        myCell22.InnerHtml = myQuote.Name
28:        myRow2.Cells.Add(myCell22)
29:
30:        myTable.Rows.Add(myRow2)
31:
32:        PlaceHolder1.Controls.Add(myTable)
33:
34:    End Sub
```

What's happening within this code? Let's take a look.

- Lines 14 through 29 of Listing 24.1 were added to the ASPX file's HTML, replacing a few lines that were already there.
- Lines 14 through 27 simply set up some content; a real application would contain much more useful information than this and would provide links to the other pages.
- Lines 28 and 29 provide the `PlaceHolder` control, which allows your ASP code to dynamically add controls to the file at runtime.
- Listing 24.2 actually calls the service and sets myQuote equal to the returned value, line 17.
- Line 19 through 30 of Listing 24.2 build an HTML table to display your result in.
- Finally, line 32 adds the table to the `PlaceHolder` object.

If you wished to keep this quote visible at the bottom of the browser at all times, frames could have been used within the HTML to break the window up into two distinct areas with the quote visible in the bottom pane.

When you run this project, Internet Explorer should open up and greet you with a quote similar to the one at the bottom of the page shown in Figure 24.2.

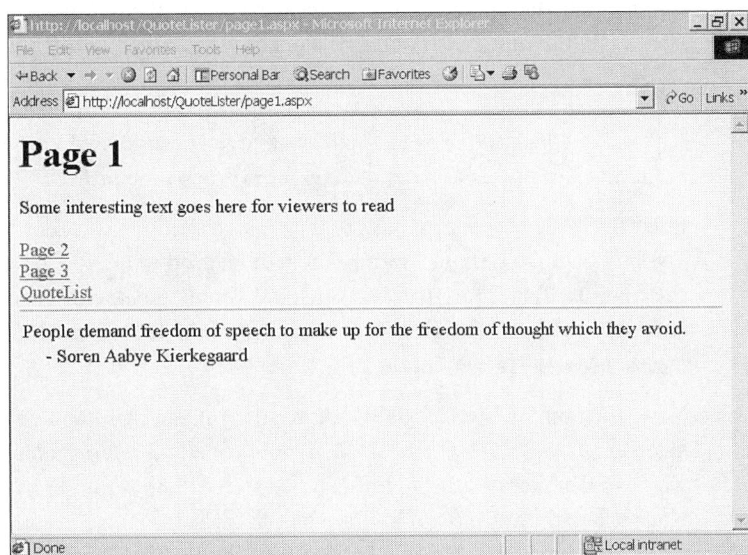

FIGURE 24.2
Returning `SessionQuotes` *at the bottom of an ASP page.*

Following the link to one of the other two pages should provide the same quote; remember that you are calling `SessionQuote` in the code at the bottom of the page. This is shown in Figure 24.3.

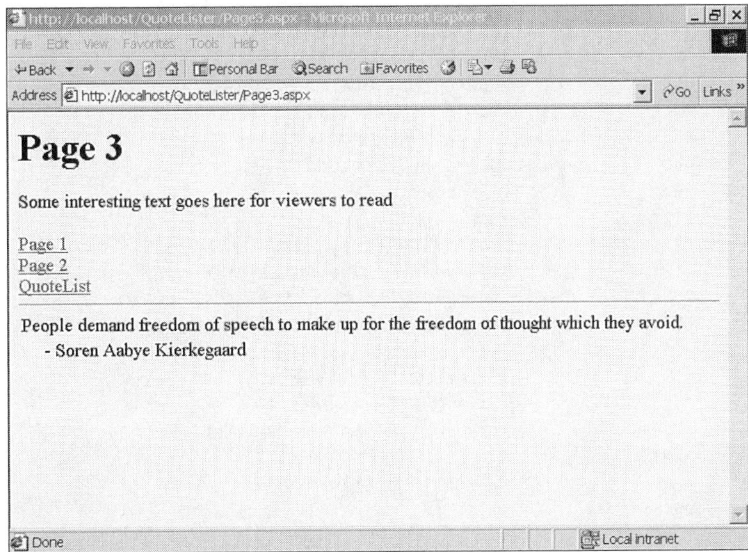

FIGURE 24.3
Confirming `SessionQuotes` *at the bottom of another ASP page.*

Returning the `QuoteList` with ASP

In order to add some more functionality to your ASP client, add yet another Web form. Call this one `QuoteList.aspx`. If you wish to add the link to this page to the previous pages, add the following code to the anchor tag in line 24 of Listing 24.1:

```
href="QuoteList.aspx"
```

If you don't want to wire the application together in this way, you can also just go to the Solutions Explorer and make the `QuoteList.aspx` the project's startup object.

Enter the designer for `QuoteList.aspx` and drag a `PlaceHolder` control from the Toolbox onto the designer form. This will be used to allow your code a place to dynamically build a Table. Alternately, you could simply create this entire page through ASP code, but since other content may be added to the HTML section, it is probably a better idea to use the `PlaceHolder`.

Now, click on the View Code button for `QuoteList.aspx` and enter Listing 24.3 into the `Page_Load` event. The call to the `QuoteList` method returns a `DataSet` object, line 8, which is then iterated through. Each iteration is then stored in `HTMLTableCell` object to place it into the various rows of a table, lines 11 through 38, and then processing moves on to the next record. Finally, line 40 adds the new `HtmlTable` object to the `PlaceHolder` object for display on your page.

Listing 24.3 `QuoteLister`, an ASP Page That Lists All Quotes

```
1:    Private Sub Page_Load(ByVal sender As System.Object, _
2:      ByVal e As System.EventArgs) Handles MyBase.Load
3:        Dim myQuote As New localhost.myQuote()
4:        Dim myDataSet As New DataSet()
5:        Dim myRow As DataRow
6:        Dim myTable As New HtmlTable()
7:
8:        myDataSet = myQuote.QuoteList
9:        myTable.Border = 0
10:
11:        For Each myRow In myDataSet.Tables(0).Rows
12:            Dim myRow1 As New HtmlTableRow()
13:            Dim myRow2 As New HtmlTableRow()
14:            Dim myRow3 As New HtmlTableRow()
15:            Dim myCell11 As New HtmlTableCell()
16:            Dim myCell21 As New HtmlTableCell()
17:            Dim myCell22 As New HtmlTableCell()
18:            Dim myCell31 As New HtmlTableCell()
19:
20:            myCell11.ColSpan = 2
21:            myCell11.InnerHtml = myRow("Quote")
```

continues

LISTING 24.3 Continued

```
                myRow1.Cells.Add(myCell11)
                myTable.Rows.Add(myRow1)

                myCell21.InnerHtml = " "
                myRow2.Cells.Add(myCell21)

                myCell22.InnerHtml = myRow("Author")
                myRow2.Cells.Add(myCell22)

                myTable.Rows.Add(myRow2)

                myCell31.InnerHtml = "<HR>"
                myRow3.Cells.Add(myCell31)

                myTable.Rows.Add(myRow3)

            Next

            PlaceHolder1.Controls.Add(myTable)
        End Sub
```


Running the application and navigating to the `QuoteList` page should give you the entire contents of the `QuoteList`'s database, as shown in Figure 24.4.

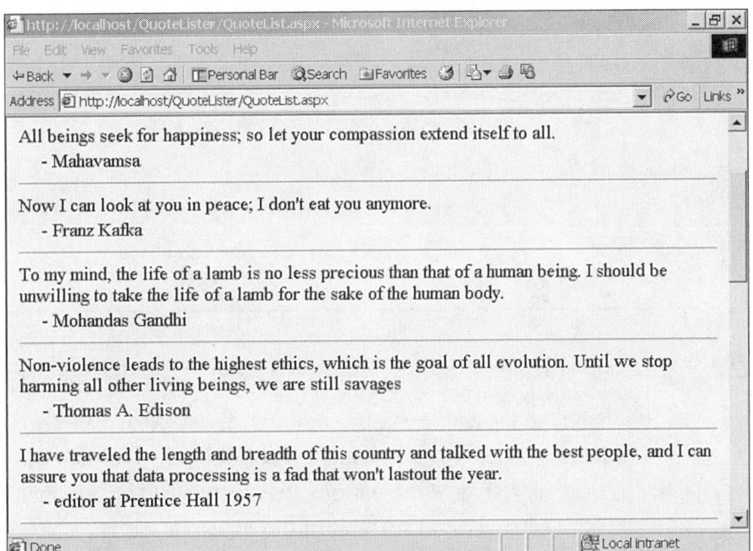

FIGURE 24.4
Returning a list of quotes.

Windows Clients for the `QuoteServer` XML Web Service

For your next client application, you will be building a Windows desktop application with Visual Basic. Select Windows application from the New Project dialog and give the project any name that you wish. Next, add the controls listed in Table 24.1 to the form and set their properties as shown there.

TABLE 24.1 `Form1`'s Controls

Control	*Property*	*Value*
Form	Text	`Main Form`
Label	Text	`Feature 1`
Label	Text	`Feature 1`
TextBox	Text	
TextBox	Text	
Button	Name	`Button1`
	Text	`Quote`
Button	Name	`Button2`
	Text	`Okay`
Button	Name	`Button3`
	Text	`Cancel`
MenuItem	Name	`MenuItem1`
	Text	`&File`
MenuItem	Name	`MenuItem2`
	Text	`&Help`
MenuItem	Name	`MenuItem3`
	Text	`&Inspiration`

When you are done with this, your form should look like the one shown in Figure 24.5.

At this point, add a Web reference to the `myQuote` XML Web service and then add the code in Listing 24.4 to your form. This code contains the `GetQuote` function, which actually calls the service, and the button click event that triggers the call. Line 6 of the function calls the `RandomQuote` method of the `myQuote` service and accepts the quote return. This is then displayed to the user in a message box, line 8.

FIGURE 24.5
`Form1.`

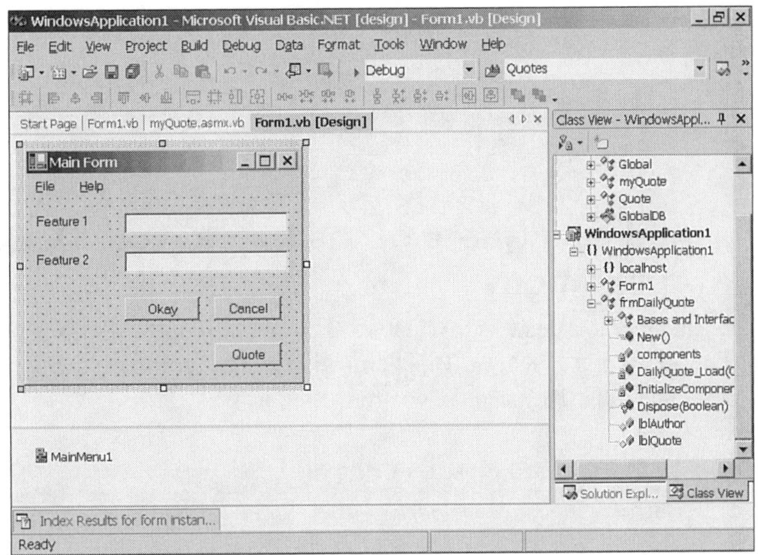

LISTING 24.4 Calling a Random Quote

```
Private Sub GetQuote()
    Dim oQuote As New localhost.myQuote()
    Dim myQuote As New localhost.Quote()
    Dim sMessage As String

    myQuote = oQuote.RandomQuote
    sMessage = myQuote.QuoteText
    MsgBox(sMessage, MsgBoxStyle.Information, myQuote.Name)
End Sub

 Private Sub Button1_Click(ByVal sender As System.Object,
             ByVal e As System.EventArgs) Handles Button1.Click
    GetQuote()
 End Sub
```

Save and run your application to confirm that a quote is returned, as in Figure 24.6.

FIGURE 24.6
Random quotes in your Windows Desktop Applications.

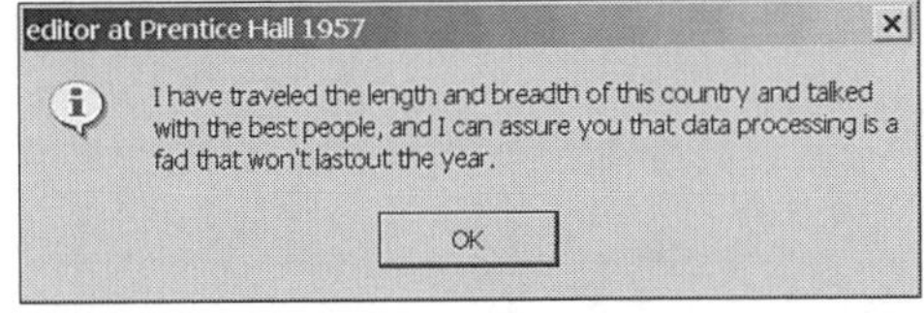

Try clicking the button a few more times to get a different quote.

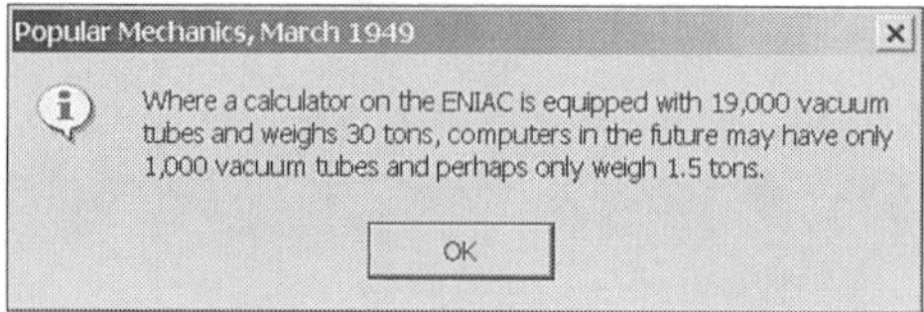
Popular Mechanics, March 1949

Where a calculator on the ENIAC is equipped with 19,000 vacuum tubes and weighs 30 tons, computers in the future may have only 1,000 vacuum tubes and perhaps only weigh 1.5 tons.

OK

FIGURE 24.7
A new quote.

Adding a Quote of the Day to Your Desktop Applications

In order to extend your Windows application, simply add a new Form to your project and call it `frmDailyQuote`. This Form will be called from one of the menu items on your previous form. Then add the controls listed in Table 24.2.

TABLE 24.2 `frmDailyQuote`'s Controls

Control	*Property*	*Value*
Form	Name	`frmDailyQuote`
	Text	`DailyQuote`
Label	Name	`lblQuote`
Label	Name	`lblAuthor`

Your form should now look like the form shown in Figure 24.8.

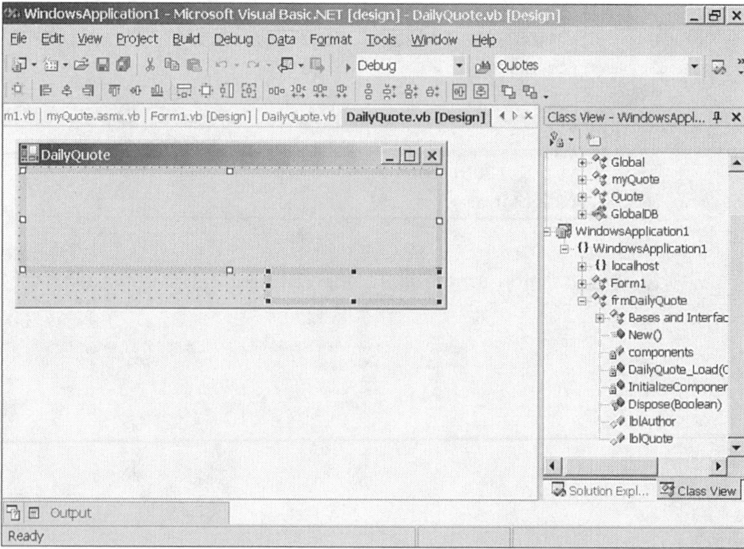

FIGURE 24.8
`frmDailyQuotes`.

Add the code in Listing 24.5 to the `Load` event of `frmDailyQuote`. This code calls the `DailyQuote` method and loads the text into the form's labels.

LISTING 24.5 Calling the Quote of the Day

```
Private Sub frmDailyQuote_Load(ByVal sender As System.Object,
            ByVal e As System.EventArgs) Handles MyBase.Load

    Dim oQuote As New localhost.myQuote()
    Dim myQuote As New localhost.Quote()

    myQuote = oQuote.DailyQuote()

    lblQuote.Text = myQuote.QuoteText
    lblAuthor.Text = myQuote.Name

End Sub
```


Finally, in order to actually call this `frmDailyQuote` from your original form, go back and add the following code to `Form1`'s `MenuItem3` click event. This code simply displays `frmDailyQuote` whenever the user clicks on the `Inspiration` menu item in the Help menu of `Form1`.

LISTING 24.6 Calling the Quote of the Day

```
Private Sub MenuItem3_Click(ByVal sender As System.Object,
          ByVal e As System.EventArgs) Handles MenuItem3.Click

    Dim fForm As New frmDailyQuote()
    fForm.Show()

End Sub
```

Run the application and click the Inspiration button. Your day should be lifted by a pearl of wisdom, such as the Frank Lloyd Wright quote shown in Figure 24.9.

Even though this is a rather simple example and not a major boon to the average business application, it never-the-less shows how XML Web services can be integrated into a desktop application.

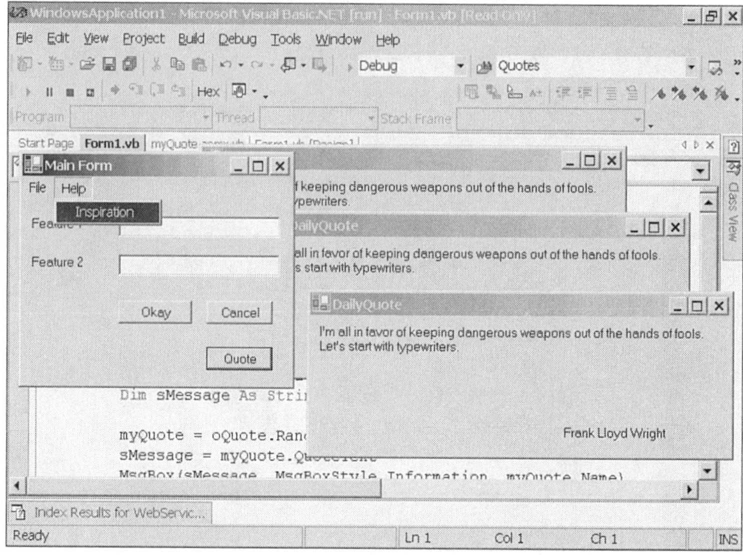

FIGURE 24.9
Frank Lloyd Wright's Quote of the Day.

Calling an XML Web Service from an XML Web Service

For a final example of the uses of the `QuoteServer` service, you will build a new XML Web service that calls the `QuoteServer`, converts the quote and author name to a string of the form "`AuthorName once said, QuoteText`", and returns this from the new service.

To start, create a new ASP.NET XML Web service application and call it `AsharpCClient`. To this service, add a Web reference to the `myQuote` XML Web service.

The new client will contain only one method, `Greetings`. Add `Greetings`, Listing 24.7, to the service. The method is very straightforward. Line 10 calls the `myQuote` service and retrieves a Quote object. The Quote object's `Name` and `QuoteText` properties are then set to build the return string, `sQuote`, as shown in Line 12.

LISTING 24.7 Repackaging the Random Quote in a New Web Service

```
1:   [WebMethod]
2:   public string Greetings()
3:    {
4:
5:      string sQuote;
6:      localhost.myQuote oQuote = new localhost.myQuote();
7:      localhost.Quote myQuote = new localhost.Quote();
8:
```

continues

LISTING 24.7 Continued

```

    myQuote = oQuote.RandomQuote();

    sQuote = myQuote.Name + " once said, '" + myQuote.QuoteText  + "'";
    return sQuote;
  }
```

When you run this service, as shown in Figure 24.10, you are provided with a completely repackaged version of the `RandomQuote` method.

FIGURE 24.10
The repackaged Random Quote.

Summary

In this hour, you saw a cross section of different application types that you can use to take advantage of a single XML Web service. Whether you are writing your applications in Visual Basic, C#, or some other language, and whether these apps are desktop, client server, ASP, or even other services themselves, the XML Web service architecture provides you with a very flexible development tool. Hopefully, your interest is sparked, as this book provides only the starting point to what can be accomplished with XML Web services and Visual Studio .NET.

Q&A

Q What is the benefit of building an XML Web service using other XML Web services?

A By leveraging the services of one XML Web service within a new XML Web service, you gain all of the benefits of object-oriented design. You encapsulate it functionally, reuse it in multiple applications, and, in the case of specialized functionality, you leverage the skills of other developers who may know more about a particular area than you do.

Q Is it possible to place an XML Web service within an ASP.NET application project?

A Yes, it is possible to create an ASP.NET application and then add an XML Web service to the application. This is done by using the Add Item option from the File menu.

Q Would anyone actually pay to use a service like the `QuoteServer`?

A Probably. If you tailored the quotes correctly and featured inspirational, religious, or other quotes, you could probably find developers who would add this functionality to their applications.

Workshop

The Workshop is designed to help you review what you've learned in this hour.

Quiz

1. What is the limit to how many levels of XML Web services consuming other XML Web services you can have?

   A There is no limit, although speed may suffer greatly from all of the network traffic involved.

2. Can XML Web services be consumed by clients other than those written in ASP.NET?

   A Yes, there is almost no limit to the number of architectures that can leverage XML Web services.

3. Is there a limit to the number of XML Web services that a single client application can call?

   A No, there is no restriction on the number of XML Web services that can be called from a single client.

Exercises

Build client applications that take advantage of some of the other methods of the Quote Server XML Web service.

A. The following calls the `PopQuotes` method and prints out a list of music-related quotes. For variety's sake, I placed the code directly into the ASP page. Only do this if you are sure that no one else will be altering the HTML in your pages and you yourself aren't planning any major reworking either.

```
<%@ import Namespace="System.Data" %>
<%@ Page Language="vb" AutoEventWireup="false"
```

```
Codebehind="WebForm2.aspx.vb" Inherits="QuoteLister.WebForm2"%>
<!DOCTYPE HTML PUBLIC "-//W3C//DTD HTML 4.0 Transitional//EN">
<html>
  <head>
    <title></title>
    <meta name="GENERATOR" content="Microsoft Visual Studio.NET 7.0">
    <meta name="CODE_LANGUAGE" content="Visual Basic 7.0">
    <meta name="vs_defaultClientScript" content="JavaScript">
    <meta name="vs_targetSchema"
       content="http://schemas.microsoft.com/intellisense/ie5">
  </head>
  <body MS_POSITIONING="GridLayout">
    <Form name="Quotes" action="Webform2.aspx" method="post">
      <input name="Number" type="text"> <input type="submit">
    </Form>
    <Table border="0">
      <%

      If isNumeric(Request.Form("Number"))
      Dim oQuotes As New localhost.PopQuotes()
      Dim myDataSet As New DataSet()
      Dim myRow As DataRow
      Dim iNum As Integer
      Dim uType As localhost.QuoteType

      iNum = Request.Form("Number")
      myDataSet = oQuotes.QuoteList(iNum, localhost.QuoteType.Music)

      For Each myRow In myDataSet.Tables(0).Rows
        Response.Write("<tr><td colspan=2>")
        Response.Write(myRow(0))
        Response.Write("</t/tr><tr><td> </td><td>- ")
        Response.Write(myRow(1))
        Response.Write("</td></tr>")
        Response.Write("<tr><td colspan=2><hr></td></tr>")
      Next
    End If
      %>
    </Table>
  </body>
</html>
```

24

INDEX

A

B

E

I

L-M

N

O-P

Q

R

S

T

U

V

W

X